At the Temple Gates

At the
Temple Gates

*The Religion of Freelance Experts
in the Roman Empire*

———◦《◎》◦———

HEIDI WENDT

OXFORD
UNIVERSITY PRESS

OXFORD
UNIVERSITY PRESS

Oxford University Press is a department of the University of Oxford. It furthers
the University's objective of excellence in research, scholarship, and education
by publishing worldwide. Oxford is a registered trade mark of Oxford University
Press in the UK and certain other countries.

Published in the United States of America by Oxford University Press
198 Madison Avenue, New York, NY 10016, United States of America.

Library of Congress Cataloging-in-Publication Data
Names: Wendt, Heidi, 1982– author.
Title: At the temple gates : the religion of freelance experts in the
Roman empire / Heidi Wendt.
Description: New York : Oxford University Press, 2016. | Includes
bibliographical references and index.
Identifiers: LCCN 2016010005 (print) | LCCN 2016023427 (ebook) |
ISBN 9780190267148 (cloth : alk. paper) | ISBN 9780190267155 (updf) |
ISBN 9780190627591 (epub)
Subjects: LCSH: Rome—Religion.
Classification: LCC BL803 .W46 2016 (print) | LCC BL803 (ebook) | DDC 200.937—dc23
LC record available at https://lccn.loc.gov/2016010005

1 3 5 7 9 8 6 4 2

Printed by Sheridan Books, Inc., United States of America

For my parents,
Nancy and Robin Wendt

Contents

Acknowledgments

TO BORROW A strategy from the religious experts I study, this book owes an incalculable debt to many figures of truly epic proportions. Instead of Pythagoras, Orpheus, or the Sibyl, however, I am privileged to claim as part of my own wisdom genealogy a number of esteemed mentors, both formal advisors and others who have contributed informally, but no less meaningfully, to my intellectual progress and academic work.

From Ross Shepard Kraemer, who, in her words, "got me into this mess in the first place," I received years of not only doctoral supervision but also undergraduate instruction at Brown University, and so much more. John Bodel's patient dedication to my interdisciplinary training in Classics also spanned two turns at Brown, while Nicola Denzey Lewis, who first introduced me to Rome, was a wonderful teacher first at Harvard Divinity School and then also at Brown. Stan Stowers's role in my graduate supervision was tireless and mind-altering, and I am so grateful for his many contributions to this project at every stage of its development. I was also fortunate to receive invaluable feedback and sage counsel at many points along the way from Cliff Ando, Bill Arnal, Ron Cameron, David Frankfurter, Fritz Graf, Caroline Johnson Hodge, Sarah Iles Johnston, Merrill Miller, Eric Orlin, and Greg Snyder.

I spent a lovely and fruitful year at the American Academy in Rome while writing the dissertation on which this book is based, and another month there as I revised the latter with the generous support of a grant from Wright State University's College of Liberal Arts. My colleagues at Wright State, especially Ava Chamberlain and Valerie Stoker, offered constant advice and encouragement during the publication process. So too did my dear (and extremely smart) friends Todd Berzon, Laura Dingeldein, Maia Kotrosits, Daniel Picus, Ryan Schellenberg, and Goran Tkalec, each of whom read chapters and shared their respective expertise. Christine Greer, Alissa MacMillan, and Suzanne Rivecca deserve special mention as three others

I treasure and without whom my world would be far less rich or interesting. By the same token, I am infinitely appreciative of my parents, Nancy and Robin Wendt, for a lifetime of love and advocacy. And while their presence is more recent, Romona and Rob Drewitt have proven no less generous with their confidence and affection. Finally, as with all things, this project has been supremely enriched from beginning to end by Aaron Glaim, my liveliest interlocutor, most honest critic, and closest friend, as well as my husband.

At the Temple Gates

Introduction

FREELANCE EXPERTS IN THE STUDY OF RELIGION

> ... yet they must make a living. These people assemble at street corners, in alleys, and at temple gates, swindling youths and sailors and that sort of crowd by stringing together puns and a lot of babble and the lowbrow discourses of the marketplace.[1]
>
> DIO CHRYSOSTOM, *Or.* 32.9.6–10

THE INHABITANTS OF the Roman world could scarcely move from place to place without falling prey to a pesky purveyor of some sought-after skill or teaching. Or so Dio Chrysostom would have his readers believe. As he lambasts pretenders to Cynic philosophy, who earn their livings thrusting hackneyed philosophical precepts on unwitting passersby, Chrysostom wastes no opportunity to differentiate swindlers of *this* sort from others who adopt the philosopher's mantle punctiliously, without pretension, guile, or ulterior motive. And yet the former everywhere gain audiences among people unprepared to discern a true specialist, in this case a true philosopher, from the adept dissemblers whom they are likely to encounter in the jostling urban spaces of the empire.

Dio Chrysostom is not the only Roman-period writer to grumble about this problem. According to Lucian, there was no surer way to gain standing and celebrity in antiquity than through this sort of entrepreneurial activity. The picture that emerges from his writings is of a second-century world infected by a pandemic of imposters in religious and philosophical expertise, with some works even reading like primers for unmasking not only

---

1. ... ἀλλὰ χρείων τροφῆς. οὗτοι δὲ ἔν τε τριόδοις καὶ στενωποῖς καὶ πυλῶσιν ἱερῶν ἀγείρουσι καὶ ἀπατῶσι παιδάρια καὶ ναύτας καὶ τοιοῦτον ὄχλον, σκώμματα καὶ πολλὴν σπερμολογίαν συνείροντες καὶ τὰς ἀγοραίους ταύτας ἀποκρίσεις.

the chicaneries of the experts themselves but also the credulity of any who would put stock in them. As the characters in his *Lover of Lies* avow the existence of ghosts, the efficacy of mysterious cures, and unusual divine interventions in human affairs, readers descry in turn the facilitators of such marvelous happenings: a Babylonian *magos* who rids a man of poisonous snake venom with incantations, charms, and purifications; a Syrian exorcist who adjures *daimones* (δαίμονες) in their native tongues; Arignotus, a Pythagorean who, aided by mysterious Egyptian books, exhumes a body from the house in Corinth that is haunted by its ghost (again, a δαίμων); and Pancrates, a scribe who learned from Isis in underground Egyptian sanctuaries, frolics with crocodiles, and enchants brooms or pestles to serve him.[2] Lucian's skepticism is plain: being bitten by the lies of such figures is like being bitten by a rabid dog; not only does the victim go mad and fear water, he bites others, filling their souls with spirits.[3]

Lucian's story of Alexander of Abonoteichus, the founder of an oracle that achieved widespread fame in the second century, provides further insight into how an aspiring specialist might set up shop.[4] In his early years, Alexander apprenticed with a man who hailed from the circle of Apollonius of Tyana and masqueraded publicly as a doctor (ἰατρός), though, Lucian divulges, he was really a "sorcerer" (γόης) who trafficked in enchantments, incantations, love charms, conjuring, and predictions about estate successions.[5] Afterward Alexander wandered the countryside of Bithynia plying his services to wealthy women.[6] Recognizing foreknowledge as the most profitable religious commodity, he contrived to establish his own prophetic shrine for Asclepius in the new manifestation of Glycon.[7] Lucian charts the development

---

2. Lucian, *Philops.* 11–15; 16; 30–31; 33–36.

3. Lucian, *Philops.* 40.

4. For discussion of the text, see Christopher P. Jones, *Culture and Society in Lucian of Samosata* (Cambridge: Harvard University Press, 1986), 133–48.

5. Lucian, *Alex.* 5. Since γόης, like *magus*, was a term that carried a range of meanings, both technical and perjorative (e.g., sorcerer or charlatan), I often leave it untranslated unless the intended sense is fairly clear. For a useful discussion of the evolution of the *goēs*—as a mythic figure and actual practitioner—in ancient Greece, see Sarah Iles Johnston, *Restless Dead: Encounters between the Living and the Dead in Ancient Greece* (Berkeley: University of California Press, 1999), 102–23.

6. Lucian, *Alex.* 6.11–12.

7. Lucian, *Alex.* 8.4–10. For an excellent discussion of Alexander's oracle, see Andreas Bendlin, "On the Uses and Disadvantages of Divination: Oracles and Their Literary Representations in the Time of the Second Sophistic," in *The Religious History of the Roman*

of the oracle in some detail, noting the signs and wonders that Alexander affected to confirm his religious credentials: fits of inspired madness, speaking in tongues, and prophesying in cooperation with the god's proxy, a live python.[8] When news of Glycon reached Rome, people traveled or sent envoys to consult him, none more eagerly than powerful men of the highest rank; Alexander even gained a patron in a pious Roman magistrate, whose enthusiasm for the new god inflamed the city.[9] With Italy in his palm he was emboldened to establish mysteries predicated on a myth of his own arrangement, intimating during the initiation rite that his was the soul of Pythagoras.[10] Lucian's disdain for Alexander is matched only by his loathing of Peregrinus of Parion, a philosopher-*cum*-religious expert, also with a following at Rome, who pivoted between several specialist guises and areas of expertise.

Lucian may have a particular score to settle with the likes of Alexander and Peregrinus, but he is hardly alone in complaining about these purveyors of assorted cultural and religious offerings that were popular in his day. If one looks for it, the evidence for this sort of activity expands exponentially and with corroboration from every genre of classical literature. The imaginative first-century novel of Petronius—a dedicated parody of itinerant pedagogues—introduces any number of characters who profess or dabble in idiosyncratic forms of religion: Quartilla and the orgiastic mysteries of Priapus over which she presides, Trimalchio's *mathematicus* Serapa, and the "priestess" Oenothea enlisted to cure Eumolpus's chronic impotence, among others.[11] Whether their ambition is unbridled licentiousness or pure profit, each selects from a vast menu of religious options to assemble rites that are both personally beneficial and enticing

---

Empire: Pagans, Jews, and Christians, ed. John A. North and Simon R. F. Price (Oxford: Oxford University Press, 2011), 175–250, esp. 232–41.

8. Notably, perhaps, Alexander's tongues even include that of the Hebrews (*Alex.* 13). He garners additional credibility when a Sibylline-style verse oracle about a prophet who shall rise among the Romans is read in his favor (*Alex.* 11). Likewise, Apuleius's Thessalian witches deliver Sibylline weather oracles (*Metam.* 2.11.5–12.2).

9. P. Mummius Sisenna Rutilianus, who completed his *cursus honorum* during the reign of Marcus Aurelius (c. 170).

10. Lucian, *Alex.* 37–40.

11. Petronius, *Sat.* 16–26; 76.10–77.2; 131.1–7; 11.136–37. See Gareth Schmeling, "The Small World of the Holy Man: A Small Beginning in the *Satyrica*," in *Holy Men and Charlatans in the Ancient Novel*, ed. Stelios Panayotakis, Gareth Schmeling, and Michael Paschalis, ANS

to others. Depicting a similar milieu, Apuleius's novelistic protagonist Lucius hears rumors of Diophanes, an itinerant Chaldean prophet presently residing in Corinth; observes the Egyptian necromancer Zatchlas; travels with a Syrian lot divination racket after being transformed into an ass; and is restored to his human form after undergoing initiation into emulous Egyptian mysteries at Cenchreae and Rome.[12] Fewer lines are spared on religious claptrap in historical writings, but there is much to glean from their anecdotes about specialists and foreign *superstitiones*. Rarely are incidents of mischief or intrigue complete without the machinations of *magi*, astrologers, and other diviners; it is with an acrid tone that historians note the corrosive effects these actors have had on Roman values and unmistakable approval when they recount the expulsions and other punishments regularly issued against them at Rome and elsewhere in the empire.

Lest one think that writers bore only negative sentiments toward self-authorized experts, one need only to recall the lengthy *Vita* of Apollonius of Tyana, whose reputation for religious expertise and wisdom in the first century persisted still in the time of Julia Domna, who commissioned Philostratus to research and write it. Even Lucian writes favorably of specialists on occasion, although his reluctant praise is reserved for such figures as Demonax, a Cynic philosopher in Athens, and Nigrinus, his counterpart in Rome, two exceptions among the more plentiful lot of those who pretend to be philosophers.[13] Still, where experts in religion are concerned, Apollonius is largely the exception that confirms the rule: most writers are more interested in denouncing them as charlatans or inculpating them in some mishap than they are in accurately describing their teachings and practices or explaining their appeal.

---

19 (Groningen: Barkhuis & Groningen University Library, 2015), 17–29; Costas Panayotakis, "Encolpius and the Charlatans," in Panayotakis, Schmeling, and Paschalis, *Holy Men and Charlatans in the Ancient Novel*, 31–46.

12. Apuleius, *Metam.* 2.12–13; 2.28–31; 8.27–30; 11.22–24; 11.27–30. For itinerant religious experts in the first ten books, see Ulrike Egelhaaf-Gaiser, "Fickle Coloured Religion: Charlatans and Exegetes in Apuleius' *Metamorphoses*," in Panayotakis, Schmeling, and Paschalis, *Holy Men and Charlatans in the Ancient Novel*, 85–104. For the initiations, see Sarolta A. Takács, "Initiations and Mysteries in Apuleius' *Metamorphoses*," *ElectroAnt* 12 (2008): 73–87.

13. Lucian, *Nigr.* 24–25. On Lucian's characterization of philosophers in general, and his portrayal of Demonax specifically, see Jones, *Culture and Society in Lucian of Samosata*, 24–32, 78–89. On philosophy as mimesis, and on Lucian's treatment of Nigrinus, see Tim Whitmarsh, *Greek Literature in the Roman Empire: The Politics of Imitation* (Oxford: Oxford University Press, 2001), 261–63, 265–79. See also Diskin Clay, "Lucian of Samosata: Four

Whatever their angles, together these authors bear witness to the ascendency of myriad would-be experts over the course of the first two centuries of the Roman Empire. By the time Petronius wrote, and all the more so Lucian or Apuleius, the figure of the scheming charlatan was sufficiently recognizable for authors to presume great familiarity with this type in their intended readers.[14] This is not to imply that earlier writers are silent about the topic. Cato the Elder warns his estate overseer (*vilicus*) not to consult a wandering diviner of entrails (*haruspex*), an *augur*, an inspired prophet (*hariolus*), or a Chaldean, an ethnonym synonymous with astrologer.[15] Cicero quotes verses from Ennius that repudiate the Marsian *augur* (*Marsum augurem*), *haruspices*, astrologers of the circus (*de circo astrologi*), Isis diviners (*Isiaci coniectores*), and dream interpreters (*interpretes somniorum*).[16] All of these pursuits, Cicero explains, lack the rigorous methodology, program of inquiry, and theory of practice that characterize a true *scientia* or *ars*. Adumbrating a theme to which Juvenal would dedicate a full satire, a confirmed bachelor in one of Plautus's comedies defends his decision not to marry on the grounds that wives are too expensive for the money they demand each month to pay the woman who utters incantations (*praecantrix*), the one who interprets dreams (*coniectrix*), the inspired prophetess (*hariola*), and the female diviner of entrails (*haruspica*). Nor will any wife turn away empty-handed the woman who observes the heavens (*qua supercilio spicit*).[17] Even Plato complains of begging priests and seers who lurk at the thresholds of the wealthy, boasting about the power of their proprietary initiations and sacrificial methods, often in conjunction with texts that somehow support such claims.[18]

Philosophical Lives (Nigrinus, Demonax, Peregrinus, Alexander Pseudomantis)," *ANRW* II.36.5 (1992): 3406–50.

14. For a useful overview of the Latin terminology associated with charlatans, see Panayotakis, "Encolpius and the Charlatans," 34–36.

15. Cato, *Agr.* 5.4.4; cf. Columella, *Rust.* 1.8.6.1, 11.1.22.6.

16. Cicero, *Div.* 1.132. It is debated whether Cicero is truly quoting Ennius as opposed to attributing to him verses that critique figures and sentiments of his own day. For a succinct summary of the matter, see M. S. Salem, "Ennius and the 'Isiaci Coniectores,'" *JRS* 28 (1938): 56–59. The Marsi were a people of Latium famous for their incantations and other religious skills.

17. Plautus, *Mil.* 692–94. For other references to such figures in Plautus, see Matthew W. Dickie, *Magic and Magicians in the Greco-Roman World* (New York: Routledge, 2003), 162–63.

18. Plato, *Resp.* 364b–365a. Regarding the consultation of Orphic initiators for any askance happening, even a weasel crossing one's path, see Theophrastus, *Char.* 16. See also Hippocrates, *Morb. sacr.* 1.22–28, where real doctors, as the author defines them, are

Sources prior to the imperial era confirm that these religious actors were a continuous presence in ancient life, and yet writers of the first and second centuries seem to grow steadily more preoccupied with them and the practices with which they were commonly associated: divination, initiations and other foreign rites, esoteric teachings, atypical sacrifices, and healing, among others. Joining these literary references are scanter, if more revealing, texts and objects that crop up in the epigraphic and archaeological records. In material ranging from expulsion decrees to *funeraria*, we learn of cities in the empire—or specific spaces within cities—where religious experts congregated; of instruments, texts, and other items that they utilized in their crafts; of those who enlisted them and to what ends.[19] In short, information about them can be culled from nearly every body of evidence that informs our understanding of the ancient Mediterranean world, and maybe nowhere more so, I argue, than in the earliest writings of what would become Christianity.

Despite the wealth of evidence for self-authorized religious experts in the Roman period, modern historians of religion have been somewhat uncritical of the prolific attention that they received from their contemporaries. At times these figures have been viewed as amusing curiosities, more often, as marginal practitioners of "illicit" or "subversive" religion, emblems of cultural decline, or social deviants, for better or for worse. There has been less interest in providing a normalized account of their place within the complex religious ecology of the Roman Empire or the earlier Mediterranean world.[20] The situation has improved in recent years due to a number of publications that offer comprehensive and nuanced investigations of the evidence for individual kinds of experts and the social

---

contrasted with *magoi*, purifiers, and begging priests, all of whom Hippocrates considers to be charlatans with false pretensions to superior knowledge and piety.

19. Plautus pinpoints a market in Rome's Velabrum, where one would find, alongside the bakers and butchers, *haruspices* and "those who change form or provide the means for others to change form" (*Curc.* 483–84). On common venues for instruction and paideutic display in the imperial period, see Kendra Eshleman, *The Social World of Intellectuals in the Roman Empire: Sophists, Philosophers, and Christians* (Cambridge: Cambridge University Press, 2012), 25–34.

20. That is, many studies of the evidence for specialists either begin from the premise that they represent an exceptional sort of religious activity (e.g., "magic") or cordon them off from other activities and institutions. See, e.g., Robert Parker's *Polytheism and Society at Athens* (Oxford: Oxford University Press, 2005), where they are included in the chapter "Unlicensed Religion and Magic" (116–35).

contexts they inhabited.[21] While the narrow foci of these studies allow for only occasional gestures toward broader affinities between, say, astrologers and *magi*, together they reveal characteristics, interests, and strategies that were common to many varieties of specialists. My own study, which seeks to theorize all self-authorized or "freelance" experts in religion as participants in a common type or class of religious activity, is only possible because of the fruitful labors of scholars who have amassed and carefully analyzed this otherwise unwieldy source material.

I am not the first to treat varieties of religious experts as an object of study *en masse,* irrespective of differences in the content of their offerings.[22] Perceiving some relationship between these actors, Ramsay MacMullen and Morton Smith, to name two notable and early examples, documented their prevalence and appreciable impact on the empire's civic and cultural institutions nearly fifty years ago.[23] The instinct to conjoin

---

21. Select publications of relevance for the Greek and Roman periods include Elizabeth Rawson, *Intellectual Life in the Late Roman Republic* (Baltimore: Johns Hopkins University Press, 1985); David Frankfurter, "Dynamics of Ritual Expertise in Antiquity and Beyond: Towards a New Taxonomy of 'Magicians'," in *Magic and Ritual in the Ancient World,* ed. Marvin Meyer and Paul Mirecki, RGRW 141 (Leiden: Brill, 2002), 159–78; Dickie, *Magic and Magicians in the Greco-Roman World,* esp. 142–250; Marie-Laurence Haack, *Les Haruspices dans le monde romain,* Scripta Antiqua 6 (Pessac: Ausonia, 2003); William E. Klingshirn, "Inventing the *Sortilegus*: Lot Divination and Cultural Identity in Italy, Rome, and the Provinces," in *Religion in Republican Italy,* ed. Celia E. Schultz and Paul B. Harvey Jr., Yale Classical Studies 33 (New York: Cambridge University Press, 2006), 137–61; Sarah Iles Johnston, *Ancient Greek Divination* (Malden, MA: Wiley-Blackwell, 2008), 109–82; James B. Rives, "*Magus* and its Cognates in Classical Latin," in *Magical Practice in the Latin West: Papers from the International Conference Held at the University of Zaragoza 30 Sept.–1 Oct. 2005,* ed. Richard L. Gordon and Francisco Marco Simón, RGRW 168 (Leiden: Brill, 2010), 53–77; Pauline Ripat, "Expelling Misconceptions: Astrologers at Rome," *CP* 106 (2011): 115–54; Fritz Graf and Sarah Iles Johnston, *Ritual Texts for the Afterlife: Orpheus and the Bacchic Gold Tablets,* 2nd ed. (New York: Routledge, 2013); Richard L. Gordon, "Individuality, Selfhood, and Power in the Second Century: The Mystagogue as a Mediator of Religious Options," in *Religious Dimensions of the Self in the Second Century CE,* ed. Jörg Rüpke and Greg Woolf, Studien und Texte zu Antike und Christentum 76 (Tübingen: Mohr Siebeck, 2013), 146–72; Radcliffe G. Edmonds III, *Redefining Ancient Orphism: A Study in Greek Religion* (Cambridge: Cambridge University Press, 2013).

22. That is, whether one explicated prophecies from Sibylline or Judean oracles or initiated followers into the mysteries of Anubis or Christ.

23. Ramsay MacMullen, *Enemies of the Roman Order: Treason, Unrest, and Alienation in the Roman Empire* (Cambridge: Harvard University Press, 1966); Morton Smith, *Jesus the Magician: Charlatan or Son of God?* (San Francisco: Harper & Row, 1978), repr. as *Jesus the Magician: A Renowned Historian Reveals How Jesus Was Viewed by the People of His Time* (San Francisco: Hampton Roads, 2014). See also David Potter, *Prophets and Emperors: Human and Divine Authority from Augustus to Theodosius* (Cambridge: Harvard University Press, 1994); Graham Anderson, *Sage, Saint, and Sophist: Holy Men and Their Associates in the Early Roman*

them is not without precedent in the ancient world, where writers often treated self-styled priests, prophets, initiators, and their ilk collectively, as if they constituted an implicit, if unsavory, group. With the implicit category, however, many scholars have also inherited and reproduced in their own works shades of the evaluative judgments imparted by ancient critics, whose disdain for "charlatans," "magicians," and "false prophets" reverberates in the ignominious language with which MacMullen, Smith, and others describe them and their role in precipitating the decline of a bygone civilization.

At one level, charlatanry and comparable language reflects normativity where one should expect objective analysis with a premium on redescription and explanation. More important, the semantic implications of such terms are symptomatic of a deeper, more structural misunderstanding of self-authorized expertise. Simply put, it cannot be the case that Lucian's caricatures of Alexander and Peregrinus are typical of the religious actors who pervade our sources and upon whose services so many people, from all walks of life, seem to have relied. The facile explanations that Lucian and authors who shared his perspective and interests supply for their popularity—that those who embraced them were easily deceived and overly prone to *superstitio*—render this sort of religious activity inexplicable for the modern scholar of religion. All the more so since it seems to have appealed to educated social elites and the "ignorant masses" in roughly equal measure.

How do we reconcile this incongruity between the apparent prominence of the religion of freelance experts and the skeptical lenses through which we glimpse it? The points of view of its ancient critics should neither be ignored nor taken at face value. By the same token, however, we should be as reticent to concede the self-representation of the "apostle" Paul when he avows his own sincerity and disinterest at the expense of perceived rivals. It is precisely this kind of either/or scheme—either someone was a true apostle or a false one, the son of a god or a charlatan, a holy man or a magician—that hinders an accurate understanding of the recipients of these labels. The same dichotomy has obscured the relationship of Judean and Christian experts to a more comprehensive set of actors with whom they were clearly in competition and with whose practices their own

---

Empire (New York: Routledge, 1994); James A. Francis, *Subversive Virtue: Asceticism and Authority in the Second-Century Pagan World* (University Park: Pennsylvania State University Press, 1995). I comment on these earlier studies in turn.

overlapped, often to a discomfiting degree.[24] Whereas we know the latter primarily from their detractors, the former have been allowed to speak for themselves, and with voices lent additional credibility by rich (and often recuperative) historiographic legacies.

In making these observations, it is not my aim to defend any of the actors in question from accusations of charlatanry or antisocial behavior or, for that matter, to indict someone such as Paul, whose inclusion among *magi*, astrologers, mystery initiators, and diviners may seem like an attempt to cast shade on his sincerity. Rather, I am suggesting that traditional approaches to this evidence have distorted its character, with the result that the relevance of this class of activity for explaining the emergence of "Christianity" and other religious phenomena of the first and second centuries has not been appreciated fully. While I am neutral on the question of whether this or any other form of ancient religion was positive or negative, I intend to show that the religion of freelance experts was more robust than one would gather from most sources, and that inhabitants of the ancient world sought them out on a regular basis in pursuit of a range of religious interests.

Theorizing the Religion of Freelance Experts

In this study I examine the apparent expansion of the religion of freelance experts over the course of the first two centuries of the Roman Empire, roughly the last decades of the first century BCE through the first part of the second century CE. There are many indications that within this window religious specialists grew increasingly influential, more diverse with respect to the skills or methods in which they claimed expertise, and more global in the ethnic coding of their wisdom and practices. I am inclined to think that they also increased in number, but with due caution given the relative scarcity of earlier evidence. This kind of religious activity was not limited to Rome or to comparable cosmopolitan centers such as Ephesus, Corinth,

---

24. Throughout this book I consciously adopt the language of "Judean," "Judaic," "Judean writings," and "Judean religion" in favor of "Jewish," "Scripture," "LXX," or "biblical literature," and "Judaism." The former language helps us to imagine the people, practices, paraphernalia, and institutions that were *associated* with Judea from a Roman point of view, broadly defined, in terms analogous to how Roman audiences understood and characterized other foreign peoples, cultures, and forms of religion. Where I do use "Jewish" or "Judaism" it is to reproduce the language or sense of other scholars with whose work I am in conversation. For a more detailed discussion of these terms, see chapter 2.

Athens, and Alexandria. To the contrary, our sources, both those critical of freelance experts and those written by experts themselves, track their movements through the rural terrains and less eminent cities of Bithynia, Galatia, and Spain in addition to those of Italy, Greece, and the Greek East. Nevertheless, urban settings were highly conducive to its dynamics, and the same sources reveal patterns in the movements of such figures and places where they clustered, especially Rome.

With the category of "freelance expertise," an analytical rather than a native designation, I intend to capture any self-authorized purveyor of religious teachings and other practices who drew upon such abilities in pursuit of various social benefits and often more transparent forms of profit.[25] Unlike members of the Roman priestly colleges or other civic priesthoods whose religious authority accrued from institutional affiliation, social status, and political power, freelance experts earned their recognition and legitimacy through demonstrations of skill and learning.[26] Typically, they purported to offer extraordinary religious services—that is, ones that exceeded the effects of more mundane religious practice—although such pretensions of novelty and uniqueness should not be mistaken for actual exceptionality.[27] For lack of the misrecognition afforded by institutional settings, freelance experts were also highly vulnerable to connotations of interest, ambition, and profit, qualities that were readily exploitable for any who would denounce them, including other participants in the same phenomenon.[28]

---

25. I am not the first to employ the term "freelance" in reference to these actors. See, e.g., James B. Rives, *Religion in the Roman Empire* (Malden, MA: Wiley-Blackwell, 2007), 163; Iles Johnston, *Ancient Greek Divination*, 177.

26. For civic priests, see, e.g., Mary Beard, "Priesthood in the Roman Republic," in *Pagan Priests: Religion and Power in the Ancient World*, ed. Mary Beard and John A. North (Ithaca, NY: Cornell University Press, 1990), 19–48; Zsuzsana Várhelyi, *The Religion of Senators in the Roman Empire* (Cambridge: Cambridge University Press, 2010); James H. Richardson and Federico Santangelo, eds., *Priests and State in the Roman World*, PAWB 33 (Stuttgart: Steiner, 2011).

27. Cf. Rives, *Religion in the Roman Empire*, 168; Edmonds, *Redefining Ancient Orphism*, 8.

28. For the misrecognition of capital within political and economic institutions, see Pierre Bourdieu, *The Logic of Practice*, trans. Richard Nice (Stanford, CA: Stanford University Press, 1990), esp. 67–68, 114–18. For a theorization of religious institutions, see Bradford Verter, "Spiritual Capital: Theorizing Religion with Bourdieu Against Bourdieu," *Sociological Theory* 21 (2003): 150–74, esp. 160. For characteristics of religious institutions in the Roman period, see Clifford Ando, "Ontology of Religious Institutions," *HR* 50 (2010): 54–79. The marks of institutionality differed, however, in accordance with different areas of social life. For

The freelance or independent quality of these actors does not mean, however, that they were insular or divorced from different forms of religious activity; many seem to have cooperated with others like them, as well as with existing groups and institutions.

To be sure, there were many forms of expertise and people who were acknowledged as experts in the Roman world, including architects, engineers, and other professesionals who possessed specialized knowledge and skills. The ones I have in mind catered principally to "private" interests—that is, interests not financed by or undertaken on behalf of the state—and offered services that were less tangible than something such as aqueduct design: education, moral instruction or another form of self-improvement, healing, divination, a better afterlife, and so forth. So too were the potential yields of their expertise—power, influence, prestige, social mobility, and improved standing—less obvious or straightforward than the salaries earned by specialists of other varieties.[29]

While the wider field of freelance expertise included self-authorized experts in philosophy, medicine, jurisprudence, and rhetoric, among other areas, the focus of this study is experts in religion, by which I mean those who directly enlisted in their practices gods and similar beings (e.g., *daimones*, divine *pneuma* [πνεῦμα], or spirits of the dead). I also include in this category astrologers, who typically held theological understandings of celestial bodies and their relevance to human affairs.[30] I prefer the open-endedness of "freelance expertise" for uniting these religious actors in favor of categories that are based on selective characteristics that pertain to only some examples, whether that is asceticism, itinerancy, divination, ritual expertise, or another criterion in this vein. My category encompasses experts who

institutional dimensions of philosophy and education, see Eshleman, *The Social World of Intellectuals in the Roman Empire*, 25–28.

29. More along the lines of what Bourdieu and his successors refer to as "cultural" or "symbolic capital." See Pierre Bourdieu, *Outline of a Theory of Practice* (Cambridge: Cambridge University Press, 1977), esp. 159–97; idem, *The Field of Cultural Production: Essays on Art and Literature,* ed. Randal Johnson (New York: Columbia University Press, 1993). For an expansion of Bourdieu's undertheorized work on religion with attention to "spiritual capital" as a subset of symbolic capital, see Verter, "Spiritual Capital."

30. Cf. Stanley K. Stowers, "The Ontology of Religion," in *Introducing Religion: Essays in Honor of Jonathan Z. Smith,* ed. Willi Braun and Russell T. McCutcheon (London: Equinox, 2008), 434–49.

practiced asceticism, who were itinerant, who divined, and who boasted ritual expertise, but adducing the category itself from such features creates certain methodological problems: either examples that share affinities with other members of the category are excluded for lack of a relatively marginal criterion (e.g., an expert who remains in one city and thus is not itinerant), or the category becomes so elastic that it no longer matches the meaning that its nomenclature ordinarily conveys, with the result that its contents are distorted (e.g., all of the actors in question are "ritual experts," therefore their practices are all instances of ritual). Although I use "specialists" or "experts" as synonyms for the fuller phrase, the central feature of my category is, again, that the actors it encompasses operated independently of existing institutions to offer skills, teachings, and other practices that involved the direct participation of divine beings.[31]

Given the dramatically changing territory and population demographics of the early Roman Empire, as well as the networks of trade and connectivity that enabled its administration, it is to be expected that a large number of freelance experts were foreigners—from either the Roman provinces or even farther afield—who capitalized on interest in wisdom, teachings, rites, and techniques perceived to be novel or exotic among certain audiences.[32] Some alleged to represent or modeled their practices on those of a renowned cult site from abroad, travel to which was impossible for all but the wealthiest interested parties.[33] In some cases a religious expert acting in a freelance capacity in Rome or another cosmopolitan city might, in fact, have held a prestigious position within a native priesthood. Nevertheless, appealing to the authority of a remote institution often

---

31. "Imagined" is not meant to imply "imaginary," only that human participants in these practices understood divine beings to be involved in them regardless of whether other observers would affirm or deny that understanding.

32. See, e.g., Simon R.F. Price, "Religious Mobility in the Roman Empire," *JRS* 102 (2012): 1–19; Greg Woolf, "Female Mobility in the Roman West," in *Women and the Roman City in the Latin West*, ed. Emily Hemelrijk and Greg Woolf (Leiden: Brill, 2013), 351–68; Anna Collar, *Religious Networks in the Roman Empire: The Spread of New Ideas* (Cambridge: Cambridge University Press, 2013).

33. Klingshirn argues that the figure of the *sortilegus* traded on the renown and basic oracular practices of the temple of Fortuna Primigenia at Praeneste, while Graf and Iles Johnston arrive at a similar conclusion about Bacchic initiators, who seem to have drawn on the basic framework of the Eleusinian mysteries in crafting offerings that were otherwise idiosyncratic ("Inventing the *Sortilegus*," 154; *Ritual Texts for the Afterlife*, 72, 107–8). Along these lines, Tacitus tells us of a Cilician *haruspex* named Tamiras, the founder of a temple whose divinatory practices were an extension of those of the Cypriot temple of Venus (*Hist.* 2.3.1).

amounted to a form of self-authorization in places where such claims were largely unverifiable and where the recognition of the expert in question was likely more complex, and less taken for granted, than in his or her local environment. By the same token, remoteness might also embolden self-authorized actors who lacked institutional religious authority within a particular context to present themselves as official priests or occupants of other prestigious offices to audiences willing to acknowledge them as such.

These possibilities were not limited to foreign temples or priesthoods, however: there is ample evidence for Italian specialists who modeled their authority and legitimacy on the civic institutions of Roman religion. Several writers warn of wandering *augures* and *haruspices*—surely not members of Rome's esteemed augural *collegium* or haruspical *ordo*—while others recount episodes whereupon magistrates attempted to limit the private circulation of "unauthorized" oracles attributed to the Sibyl and other renowned prophets.[34] Whereas the *Augures*, curators of the *Sibylline Oracles* (*quindecimviri s.f.*), and many *haruspices* were financed and approved by the state, freelance experts who calqued these positions catered to individual matters and without the state's explicit endorsement.[35]

Nevertheless, the evidence for the religion of freelance experts in the Roman Empire emphasizes foreignness and for reasons elucidated by this historical setting. Recent publications have drawn attention to conditions—both those nourished consciously as part of the Roman imperial project and also those that arose circumstantially through voluntary and involuntary migration and the increasing heterogeneity of cities throughout the empire—that promoted basic familiarity with provincial religious practices, even if in somewhat caricatured forms. Andrew Wallace-Hadrill has also argued that the last decades of the republic witnessed an elevation of specialists, usually of foreign extraction, in various areas of Roman public life, especially civic religion. Noting the use of Alexandrian

---

34. As John A. North has argued, the relative anonymity, remove, and diffuseness of some of these positions, especially that of the *haruspex*, made it easy enough to lay claim to their associated expertise ("Diviners and Divination at Rome," in Beard and North, *Pagan Priests*, 51–71).

35. For the distinction between "public" and "private" as largely a matter of who paid, see John Bodel, "Cicero's Minera, *Penates*, and the Mother of the *Lares*: An Outline of Roman Domestic Religion," in *Household and Family Religion in Antiquity*, ed. John Bodel and Saul M. Olyan (Malden, MA: Blackwell, 2008), 248–75, esp. 249.

astronomers to intercalate the Roman calendar, as well as the popularity of astrologers and *magi* among Julio-Claudian emperors, he concludes that the heightened profile of experts in exotic wisdom and techniques within the apparatus of Roman religion and politics seems to have contributed to their broader legibility and appeal.[36]

The civic realm was not the only area of religious life into which freelance experts intervened.[37] In the domestic sphere, where a male head of household presided over offerings, prayers, and ritual meals on behalf of his *familia* or *oikos*, situations such as death or childbirth might warrant a specialist with technical skills to perform sacrifices or purifications, divination, dream interpretation, and so forth.[38] In addition to the fairly ordinary matters that occasioned the consultation of freelance experts, many writers complained of them traveling door-to-door with proprietary remedies to defects or divine offenses only made apparent during the same interactions.[39] Some households employed such figures on a sustained basis, whether because they depended on their skills or as more of a status symbol.[40]

Other points of overlap between specialists and domestic religious practice might be posited circumstantially. As the eclectic assemblages of images and objects excavated from household shrines attest, religious activities conducted in these spaces followed a fairly loose script that was flexible and accommodating of idiosyncrasy.[41] Apuleius adds an explanatory

---

36. For the rise of knowledge professionals at Rome, see Andrew Wallace-Hadrill, "'Mutatas Formas': The Augustan Transformation of Roman Knowledge," in *The Cambridge Companion to the Age of Augustus*, ed. Karl Galinsky (New York: Cambridge University Press, 2005), 55–84; idem, *Rome's Cultural Revolution* (New York: Cambridge University Press, 2008), 213–58.

37. In reality, there were not neat boundaries between different classes of religious activity, nor between "public" and "private" religious practices and interests. Since all forms of religious activity entailed practices connected with beliefs about gods and similar beings, their practitioners would have experienced them seamlessly, relying on common expectations and understandings to participate in any given form.

38. For the religion of households, see Stanley K. Stowers, "Theorizing Religion of Ancient Households and Families," in Bodel and Olyan, *Household and Family Religion in Antiquity*, 5–19. Even people renowned for interpretive abilities resorted to specialists: Marius was remembered for his exceptional skill in religious interpretation (Valerius Maximus, 1.5.5) yet never campaigned without Martha, a Syrian expert in matters of *sacra* and on whose authority he was said to have made every move (Valerius Maximus, 1.2.3; Frontinus, *Str.* 1.11.12; Plutarch, *Mar.* 17).

39. E.g., Juvenal, 6.314–614.

40. See the discussion in chapter 3 especially.

41. For discussion of this evidence see Bodel, "An Outline of Roman Domestic Religion," 250, 262–63.

dimension to the archaeological record when, defending himself against accusations of magic, he presents tokens that he has amassed from initiations into the mysteries of various gods, the significance of which, he insists, should be apparent to audience members who have undergone the same rites. This general context accounts for a controversial statuette of Mercury that has aroused suspicion about him: just as the fellow initiates whom he addresses secret their objects away at home for private supplication, this unusual image, which Apuleius keeps swaddled in a linen cloth in his stepson's *sacrarium*, is requisite for cultivating the god according to his own distinct custom (*cui ex more meo supplicassem*).[42]

While freelance experts might be inferred as the initiators or wisdom instructors lurking between the lines of these references to private initiations and customized religious practice, Suetonius is more explicit when he reports that Nero—despite having contempt for all forms of *religio*, even the Dea Syria, whom he had once followed fervently—became captive and clung tenaciously to another *superstitio*. After receiving the figurine of a maiden from an unknown commoner (*plebeius quidam et ignotus*) who promised that she would protect him from plots, Nero was persuaded of her power when a conspiracy against him immediately came to light. Hence he was convinced that the image was a powerful divinity and sacrificed to it thrice daily in order to obtain further knowledge of the future.[43] One wishes that Suetonius had more to say about the man who gave Nero the statuette and informed him of her powers, but this is not the only mention of this emperor having enlisting the services of specialists or equivalent figures.[44]

Voluntary associations, particularly ones that were explicitly cultic in focus, represent another form of religious activity that might bear some relationship to freelance expertise. Indeed, a number traced their origins to founders recognized for having transported a god's rites from abroad or having established new ones after receiving a divine revelation.[45] These

42. Apuleius, *Apol.* 53–56, 61–62.

43. Suetonius, *Ner.* 56.

44. Pliny, *Nat.* 30.14–17; Suetonius, *Ner.* 34.4.

45. Evidence of this sort constitutes a retrospective on freelance expertise, insofar as the associations themselves represent a different, if overlapping, form of religious activity. For voluntary associations generally, see Stephen G. Wilson, "Voluntary Associations: An Overview," in *Voluntary Associations in the Greco-Roman World*, ed. John S. Kloppenborg and Stephen G. Wilson (New York: Routledge, 1996), 1–15; John Scheid, "Graeco-Roman Cultic Societies," in *The Oxford Handbook of Social Relations in the Roman World*, ed. Michael Peachin (Oxford: Oxford University Press, 2011), 535–47; Philip A. Harland, *Associations, Synagogues,*

examples indicate that some private temples or associations only developed institutional features—membership criteria, offices, dedicated meeting places—through the efforts of individuals alleging to be foreign priests or to possess other qualities that bolstered their credibility as religious experts.

In other sources we observe freelance experts working actively to regularize their own followings, to form networks with one another, or to develop mutually beneficial relationships with existing religious groups and institutions. Alexander of Abonoteichus is said to have earned the approval of priests at the oracles of Mallos, Claros, and Didyma by referring his clients to them for further consultation.[46] He also employed a host of colleagues, some who gathered personal information about potential clients that might bolster his predictions and others who expounded the written prophecies that he issued as they grew increasingly obscure.[47] Paul formed individual assemblies whose members, having been transformed by divine *pneuma*, were ontologically alike and comprised a single body that spanned the cities and regions to which he traveled. In anticipation of the apostle's visits, associates acting on his behalf cultivated those who had received (or would receive) his teachings, while rivals might capitalize on his efforts to their own ends. The vulnerability of such religious groups to entrepreneurial opportunists was not lost on second-century Christian writers, many of whom warn of or seek to regulate itinerant prophets. Likewise, Lucian observes that Christians are all too prone

---

and Congregations: Claiming a Place in Ancient Mediterranean Society (Minneapolis: Fortress, 2003); idem, Dynamics of Identity in the World of the Early Christians: Associations, Judeans, and Cultural Minorities (New York: T&T Clark, 2009); Jonathan S. Perry, "Organized Societies: Collegia," in Peachin, The Oxford Handbook of Social Relations in the Roman World, 499–515; Richard S. Ascough, Philip A. Harland, and John S. Kloppenborg, eds., Associations in the Greco-Roman World: A Sourcebook (Waco, TX: Baylor University Press, 2012). For evidence of foundation by individuals, see James C. Hanges, Paul, Founder of Churches: A Study in Light of the Evidence for the Role of Founder-Figures in the Hellenistic-Roman Period, WUNT 292 (Tübingen: Mohr Siebeck, 2012); Richard S. Ascough, "Redescribing the Thessalonians 'Mission' in Light of Greco-Roman Associations," NTS 60 (2014): 62–82, esp. 69–70.

46. Lucian, Alex. 29. Apollonius of Tyana also has sympathetic relationships with famed oracles of the Greek world, namely those of Colophon, Didyma, and Pergamum, from which he received commendation (Philostratus, Vit. Apoll. 4.1). For cooperation between independent diviners and institutional oracles, see Iles Johnston, Ancient Greek Divination, 178–79; Esther Eidinow, "Oracles and Oracle-Sellers: An Ancient Market in Futures," in Religion and Competition in Antiquity, ed. David Engels and Peter Van Nuffelen, Latomus 343 (Brussels: Latomus, 2014), 55–95.

47. Lucian, Alex. 37, 49.

to crafty *goētes* such as Peregrinus, looking to take advantage of their shared resources.[48]

Demarcating Religious Experts from Other Freelance Actors

The examples introduced thus far embroider the religious landscapes of the Roman Empire with a multitude of individuals operating independently or semi-independently of existing religious groups and institutions while affecting the latter in appreciable ways. Theirs was a particularly fertile field for cultural experimentation and one whose expansive possibilities pose a number of challenges to demarcating experts in religion from similarly self-authorized specialists.

Many examples require little justification for inclusion within the category of freelance religious expertise: self-proclaimed priests, prophets, mystery initiators, *magi*, sacrificers, most astrologers, and so on. Many negative examples are also fairly straightforward. A Roman jurist might work independently, earn compensation or equivalent benefits, compete with rivals, and offer idiosyncratic juridical opinions, but he would be unlikely to incorporate religious practices significantly into his professional activities.[49] Similarly, while a philosopher might elaborate matters of theology, or weigh and even affirm the value of certain religious practices, taking up the gods and religion as an intellectual theme or writing a book about such matters is not tantamount to invoking divine beings directly. One might, however, claim to possess a divinely authored text, write under divine inspiration, divine from inspired writings, or enlist philosophical language to explain the effect of a religious rite.[50] Related skills and forms of prestige obtain for both sets of intellectual practices, yet in the latter examples learning and writings are part of what I would call a religious activity.

---

48. E.g., Didache 11–13; Lucian, *Peregr.* 13.

49. That said, Roman jurors were engaged in similar processes of competitive specialization and disciplinary formation during the same period. See Bruce W. Frier, *The Rise of the Roman Jurist: Studies in Cicero's Pro Caecina* (Princeton: Princeton University Press, 1985), 252–68.

50. For an excellent overview of such practices from the Classical period through Late Antiquity, see Peter T. Struck, *The Birth of the Symbol: Ancient Readers at the Limits of their Texts* (Princeton: Princeton University Press, 2004). I devote further discussion to the distinction between ordinary literary criticism and allegorical reading as divination in chapter 3.

To the extent that religious activities are a matter of degree or focus as opposed to absolute criteria, there might be extensive overlap between the practices of an intellectualizing religious expert and those of another intellectual specialist for whom religious elements are absent or less pronounced. This observation is important because some of our best-attested freelance religious experts were writer-intellectuals whose offerings were either related to their learning or were the writings themselves. Moreover, those who were able to enlist intellectual practices in the context of religious activity seem to have had considerably more latitude than non-literate experts for innovation and versatility. Lucian satirizes this quality in Peregrinus, tellingly called Proteus, whose wanderings bring him to Palestine where he learns the marvelous wisdom of the Christians from their priests and scribes (ἱερεῦσιν καὶ γραμματεῦσιν) and becomes a Christian prophet (προφήτης), cult leader (θιασάρχης), and synagogue head (ξυναγωγεύς) in his own right.[51] Authoring commentaries on their sacred writings and even composing new ones, Peregrinus is revered as a lawgiver (νομοθέτης) second only to the one crucified for having introduced a new initiation into the world. After reinventing himself as a wonder-working (θαυματοποιῶν) Egyptian ascetic and then a Cynic, Peregrinus commits suicide at the Olympic Games by means of a dramatic self-immolation in the style of Indian Brahmans.[52]

For Lucian, versatility is evidence of making it up as one goes along, that the "expertise" of such a person is entirely arbitrary while his or her scurrilous motivations remain constant. But this is not the only way to read things. Suetonius notes in passing one M. Pompilius Andronicus, a Syrian *grammaticus* who, wearied by an unequal struggle against competitors in Rome, gave up his school there to author Epicurean writings from Cumae.[53] Notably, the mutations of both Peregrinus and Andronicus are

---

51. Lucian, *Peregr.* 11. For Peregrinus in general, see Francis, *Subversive Virtue*, 53–81; Ilaria L. E. Ramelli, "Lucian's Peregrinus as Holy Man and Charlatan and the Construction of the Contrast between Holy Men and Charlatans in the *Acts of Mari*," in Panayotakis, Schmeling, and Paschalis, *Holy Men and Charlatans in the Ancient Novel*, 105–20. For his relations with Christians, see Jason König, "The Cynic and Christian Lives of Lucian's *Peregrinus*," in *The Limits of Ancient Biography*, ed. Brian C. McGing and Judith Mossman (Swansea: Classical Press of Wales, 2006), 227–54; Jan N. Bremmer, "Peregrinus' Christian Career," in *Dead Sea Scrolls and Other Early Jewish Studies in Honor of Florentino Garcia Martinez*, ed. Anthony Hillhorst, Emile Puech, and Eibert Tigchelaar (Leiden: Brill, 2007), 729–47.

52. Lucian, *Peregr.* 17, 18, 25.

53. Suetonius, *Gramm.* 8.8; Rawson, *Intellectual Life in the Late Roman Republic*, 23.

inseparable from their intellectual abilities, foremost of which are teaching and the production and interpretation of writings.[54] Since the perceived quality and reputation of a freelance expert depended at least partially upon the sort of followers he or she managed to attract, it is unsurprising that many infused their religious programs with philosophical and other intellectual elements that were highly sought-after by Roman elites.[55]

In this vein, sources such as the Pauline Epistles—or, to shift our attention momentarily to Classical and Hellenistic times, the Derveni papyrus and Orphic ritual texts—furnish rare but illuminating examples of how literate religious specialists drew on intellectual resources to elaborate the significance of practices such as divination or initiation.[56] It is productive, then, to consider how beneficial textual production could be in this context. The ability to commit one's teachings to writing invited exponentially more elaborate religious programs buttressed by learned exegesis, myth-making, and narratives of human decline that might then be remedied by the expert who had thus diagnosed some resulting defect. Writings could also expand the scope of an expert's influence and maintain relationships with followers over great distances. Paul exchanged letters continuously with his assemblies (ἐκκλησίαι), a habit that enabled him to clarify, reinforce, or augment his teachings; to offer encouragement; and to contend with rivals *in abstentia*. Written correspondence was equally indispensible to an astrologer named Pammenes, who continued to draft horoscopes for his clients and even commanded a pension from one while in exile on a Cycladic island.[57]

Categorizing these experts can be tricky, since any one worth his or her salt catered to many tastes and religious interests. Likewise, one's success might depend on out-maneuvering not only others claiming the same or closely related "areas of expertise"—rival Epicurean teachers or rival philosophers more generally—but also actors whose skills and practices resembled one's own even if their principal specialty differed—someone such as

---

54. Despite Demonax's Cynic garb, Lucian remarks that he combined many forms of philosophy without adhering to any one school. Evidently, intellectual sampling was not always a negative habit. In addition, both Demonax and Peregrinus are said to have studied with the same Egyptian teacher, Agathoboulos (*Demon.* 3; *Peregr.* 17).

55. Cf. Ripat, "Astrologers at Rome," 125.

56. See chapter 3.

57. Tacitus, *Ann.* 16.14.

Paul, whose use of philosophical discourses, doctrines, and techniques has been well demonstrated but whom I consider a religious expert, not a philosopher.[58] Competitive dynamics within and across subsets of freelance expertise attached incentives to wielding multiple skills and to being able to make the case that one's program was more beneficial or exigent than any other.

It used to be the case that scholars characterized these tendencies toward innovation and ambitiousness as "eclecticism," which they understood to be a misappropriation of distinct disciplines and institutions.[59] In recent years the term *bricolage* has replaced the negative connotations of cultural phenomena—forms of philosophy, religion, and even art—of the Roman period that refuse to conform to modern expectations about what qualities define particular categories of practice, intellectual fields, and aesthetics.[60] These recuperative efforts have considerable implications for my study. On the one hand, they put pressure on the assumption that such combinations resulted from a poor grasp of their constitutive elements, when, in fact, heterogeneity was more the norm than the exception in the ancient world.[61] While certain figures—for instance, the sort with

---

58. Moreover, as Jason König has argued of third-century rivalries, there was a relationship between competition and social status that governed whom an expert would perceive as a rival: "Competitiveness and Non-Competitiveness in Philostratus' Lives of the Sophists," in *Competition in the Ancient World*, ed. Nick Fisher and Hans van Wees (Swansea: Classical Press of Wales, 2011), 279–300.

59. See, e.g., MacMullen, *Enemies of the Roman Order*, 106–9, 245.

60. For critical engagement with these issues, see Clifford Ando, *The Matter of the Gods: Religion and the Roman Empire* (Berkeley: University of California Press, 2009), 1–18; Iles Johnston, *Ancient Greek Divination*, 1–32. For *bricolage*, see Graf and Iles Johnston, *Ritual Texts for the Afterlife*, esp. 70–78, 82–94; Edmonds, *Redefining Ancient Orphism*, 6. For "eclecticism," see John M. Dillon and A.A. Long, eds., *The Question of "Eclecticism": Studies in Later Greek Philosophy* (Berkeley: University of California Press, 1988). For similar issues that have arisen in Roman art history, see Tonio Hölscher, *The Language of Images in Roman Art*, trans. Anthony Snodgrass and Annemarie Künzl-Snodgrass (New York: Cambridge University Press, 2004). For a refinement of Hölscher's model with an emphasis on representations of foreign religion in Roman art, see Jaś Elsner, "Classicism in Roman Art," in *Classical Pasts: The Classical Traditions of Greece and Rome*, ed. James Porter (Princeton: Princeton University Press, 2006), 270–97, esp. 276–92.

61. As Rawson observes, competitive dynamics between similar specialists encouraged variety, although the opportunity for originality varied depending on the form of expertise in question. The innovative potential of teachers, in her example, was usually restricted to a limited area such as terminology, the organization of subjects, disciplinary criteria, and so forth (*Intellectual Life in the Late Roman Republic*, 322). In theory there were considerable constraints on claiming philosophical expertise, but in actuality the stakes of close doctrinal

whom Roman emperors and other educated patrons associated—might be constrained by well-defined traditions or institutions they represented, others with less exacting audiences had more freedom for ingenuity. To gain legitimacy in a recognized form of expertise, it was incumbent on any would-be expert to work ostensibly out of some tradition, whether a branch of philosophy or a familiar religious idiom. By satisfying a few reference points, however, one could fulfill basic expectations about specialists in that area while reserving ample space for idiosyncrasy in one's offerings. In this regard eclecticism need not be framed negatively but might instead be seen as a creative process by which individual actors formed coherent connections between practices and representations that could be arranged otherwise.

On the other hand, the existence of the disciplines and religions whose boundaries freelance experts traversed so unscrupulously, whose content they appropriated so liberally, is largely a modern mirage. As Kendra Eshleman has argued of the second century, "philosopher," "sophist," and "Christian" were not axiomatic but differential categories "maintained at the cost of an unending labor of discursive and social distantiation from others who marked [their] boundaries." One's ability to claim such a label, Eshleman argues, "could not be established once and for all but had to be continually defended through assiduous self-presentation that in turn advanced implicit definitions of one's own field(s) and its rivals."[62] Here too we must exercise caution about reproducing the tone of ancient authors who had a vested interest in devaluing purportedly composite offerings as they advanced their own criteria for "pure" Stoic philosophy, medicine, Christianity, and so forth. Although it is conventional to speak of astrology, medicine, mystery cults, philosophy, and, for that matter, Judaism and Christianity as though they were entities with

---

adherence were tied to the location and ambitions of the philosopher in question. Cicero complains often of philosophical hacks and is especially attentive to the prolific circulation of Epicurean writings, the first philosophical texts to be translated into Latin, throughout Italy. He singles out the works of Catius, an Insubrian Gaul from northern Italy, Amafinius, and Rabirius, as especially inaccurate and crude, noting that there are now far from learned Epicureans in every village (*Fam.* 16.1, 19.2–3; *Fin.* 2.44; *Tusc.* 4.6–7). For the broad circulation of philosophical discourses and pseudepigraphic texts, see Miriam T. Griffin, "Philosophy, Politics, and Politicians at Rome," in *Philosophia Togata I: Essays on Philosophy in Roman Society*, ed. Miriam T. Griffin and Jonathan Barnes (New York: Oxford University Press: 1989), 1–37.

62. Eshleman, *The Social World of Intellectuals in the Roman Empire*, 1.

clearly defined ontological statuses in the Roman world, this should not be taken for granted during the period in question. Rather, the first and second centuries were a time when many "disciplines" and—as some have argued—"religions" were only beginning to take shape, processes impelled by the extensive discursive efforts of writer-intellectuals and the social formations they represented.[63]

On this point many of the aforementioned authors are especially instructive and help to refine my category. Consider the inclusion of astrologers among freelance religious experts, since many imagined celestial bodies to be under the control of the gods or gods themselves; thus their calculations were undergirded by a religious epistemology, according to my definition. Of course there were some astrologers—often differentiated as astronomers although the terms were used more or less interchangeably in antiquity—who argued that their art was a naturalistic discipline unencumbered by religious understandings.[64] Comparable contestations occur at the edge between the practice of medicine and forms of healing that shaded into religion. Galen, a second-century physician and medical writer, discloses that he always refrains from bragging about his cures and treatments lest other physicians and philosophers label him a *goēs* or diviner (μάντις).[65] Elsewhere he industriously disambiguates doctors from *goētes*, whose practices and skills, he admits, can exhibit inconvenient similarities. Ulpian weighs whether doctors are to be included within liberal studies (*studia liberalia*) and answers affirmatively, provided

---

63. For disciplinary formation in general, see Eshleman, *The Social World of Intellectuals in the Roman Empire,* passim. For medicine as a discipline, see Vivian Nutton, "Healers in the Medical Market Place: Toward a Social History of Graeco-Roman Medicine," in *Medicine in Society: Historical Essays,* ed. Andrew Wear (Cambridge: Cambridge University Press, 1991), 1–58; Evelyne Samma, *Les médecins dans le monde grec: Sources épigraphiques sur la naissance d'un corps medical* (Droz: Génève, 2003); Rebecca Fleming, *Medicine and the Making of Roman Women: Gender, Nature, and Authority from Celsus to Galen* (New York: Oxford University Press, 2000), 45–63. For the emergence of "religions" in the Roman imperial period, especially the third century, see Daniel Boyarin, *Borderlines: The Partition of Judaeo-Christianity,* Divinations (Philadelphia: University of Pennsylvania Press, 2004); Jason BeDuhn, "Mani and the Crystallization of the Concept 'Religion' in Third Century Iran," in *Mani at the Court of Persian Kings: Studies on the Chester Beatty Kephalaia Codex,* ed. Iain Gardner, Jason BeDuhn, and Paul Dilley, Nag Hammadi and Manichaean Studies 87 (Leiden: Brill, 2015), 247–75.

64. For the religious leanings of astrologers, see Tamsyn Barton, *Ancient Astrology* (London: Routledge, 1994), 86–113, esp. 107–9; Serafina Cuomo, *Pappus of Alexandria and the Mathematics of Late Antiquity* (Cambridge: Cambridge University Press, 2000), 9–56; Roger Beck, *A Brief History of Ancient Astrology* (Malden, MA: Wiley-Blackwell, 2007), 1–8.

65. Galen, *Praecog.* 10.15. Cf. Francis, *Subversive Virtue,* 49.

that one excludes people who perform incantations (*si incantavit*), curses (*si imprecatus est*), and exorcisms (*si ... exorcizavit*), for these are not kinds of "medicine" (*non sunt ista medicinae genera*).[66]

Nor were medicine and astronomy the only inchoate fields whose horizons were being established and defended in this way. The first-century Stoic philosopher Epictetus taught that training exercises (ἀσκήσεις) must not be performed that are contrary to nature and incredible (παραδόξων), since then we who call ourselves philosophers would be in no way different from wonder-workers (θαυματοποιοί).[67] Marcus Aurelius, himself a student of Stoicism, likewise recalled how his instructor in Greek *paideia*, Diognetus, disabused him of the tales of miracle-mongers (τερατευομένων) and *goētes* about incantations and the exorcisms of *daimones*.[68] Notwithstanding, Epictetus elsewhere delineates the Cynic sage from "charlatans" on the grounds that Zeus appoints and equips the former for his role, whereas the latter choose the Cynic lifestyle by their own volition.[69]

We inherit several opinions of would-be disciplinary authorities from this period who define themselves in opposition to people offering similar services, but whose practices fall short of standards that they advocate. For many, the critical distinction between a real expert in a given subject and an imposter can be distilled to the matter of whether someone's disposition is religious in my sense. Even apart from these discourses,

---

66. Ulpian, *Dig.* 50.13.1.2; Cuomo, *Pappus of Alexandria*, 35. Such efforts were not limited to writer-intellectuals drawing disciplinary boundaries to privilege their own authority. As Giovanni Battista Bazzana has noted, the first and second centuries witnessed the issue of imperial legislation that incentivized the practice of medicine while also defining its scope and limiting the number of people eligible to claim medical expertise and its attendant benefits. In one case, the restrictions explicitly excluded any who healed through exorcisms and incantations from consideration for a civic appointment. "Seemingly," Bazzana concludes, "the imperial rule intended to draw a clear line distinguishing the 'scientific' Greek healing methods, which can obtain official recognition, from those practices that cannot be included within the boundaries of the dominating Greco-Roman culture. ... [T]hose practitioners who achieved civic recognition became clearly distinguishable from charlatans and quacks, because of their increased responsibility in administrative and judicial affairs" ("Early Christian Missionaries as Physicians: Healing and its Cultural Value in the Greco Roman Context," *NT* 51 [2009]: 232–51, at 245).

67. Epictetus, *Diatr.* 3.7.1; cf. Francis, *Subversive Virtue*, 16.

68. Marcus Aurelius, *Med.* 1.6.

69. Epictetus, *Diatr.* 3.22.2–53; cf. Francis, *Subversive Virtue*, 68; Timothy Luckritz Marquis, *Transient Apostle: Paul, Travel, and the Rhetoric of Empire*, Synkrisis (New Haven: Yale University Press, 2013), 99–101.

the boundaries between doctor, philosopher, astronomer, and religious expert are difficult to draw. A doctor and a religious healer might share any number of methods, instruments, and remedies but differ fundamentally with respect to the diagnosis of an ailment—the patient contracted an illness, as opposed to the patient is afflicted by a *daimōn*—and to the course of treatment—medicine or surgery versus solutions such as exorcism or purification, perhaps even in addition to "medicine."[70]

It is also important to recognize the stakes that these writers had in tackling the subject of freelance expertise, especially since many stood to gain personally from discrediting its participants. An author such as Lucian provides ample fodder for looking down on hack philosophers, priests, and prophets, yet it was precisely by derogating those cultural authorities that Lucian and his interlocutors staked out command over the matters about which they wrote.[71] As he relates Alexander's chicaneries to

---

70. Beyond a religious epistemology, the sex of an expert might serve as an additional source of reproach. Varro speaks of women who consult *praecantatrices* instead of presenting their symptoms to a *medicus* (fr. 15). Porphyrion, a second-century commentator on Horace, equates this type of female expert with another familiar in his day when he explains, "*Sagae* are *praecantatrices* who employ incantations to summon ills to harm people or who employ incantations to drive out such ills" (*Hor. Carm.* 1.27.21). See also the poet's recollection of an old Sabine woman whom he had seen prophesy with an urn when he was a boy (Horace, *Sat.* 1.9.29–30). Remarks about women's participation in the religion of freelance experts often reveal more about the agenda of the person delivering them than they do about the religious activities of actual women. However, women are implicated in such activities too often, and by authors who assess their participation both positively and negatively, for all of these examples to be exclusively a matter of constructing gender. At the root of many remarks is the basic assumption that women were notable participants in this sort of religious activity, cropping up with some frequency as both purveyors and, even more often, as its most enthusiastic consumers. All the more so since, as Dickie notes, their presence is likely underrepresented when masculine nouns and pronouns are used to refer collectively to specialists and followers that might include both sexes, a point that has been made repeatedly for Paul's groups and is reflected in the NRSV translation of ἀδελφοί as "brothers and sisters." For discussion of these references, and of gender-inclusive language for experts, see Dickie, *Magic and Magicians in the Greco-Roman World*, 133 nn. 36 and 39, 193. For the interpretive problems that arise from accounts of women's religious activities, see Ross Shepard Kraemer, *Unreliable Witnesses: Religion, Gender, and History in the Greco-Roman Mediterranean* (New York: Oxford University Press, 2011). For more straightforward evidence of women as healers, see Holt Parker, "Women and Medicine," in *A Companion to Women in the Ancient World*, ed. Sharon L. James and Sheila Dillon (Malden, MA: Wiley-Blackwell, 2012), 107–24, at 122–23; Fleming, *Medicine and the Making of Roman Women*, 35–44.

71. Cf. Whitmarsh, who characterizes Lucian's writings as performative not descriptive, by which he means that they are actively engaged in creating difference and distance between Lucian himself and the figures about whom he writes (*Greek Literature and the Roman Empire*, 248, 265). For Lucian's self-positioning as a Syrian cultural authority, see Nathanael J. Andrade, *Syrian Identity in the Greco-Roman World* (Cambridge: Cambridge University Press, 2013), 261–87, 288–313.

his correspondent Celsus, Lucian refrains from listing all of the devices by which he deceived his followers because Celsus had already cited instances enough in the treatise he wrote against *magoi*.[72] Oenomaus, another writer of the first half of the second century, published a similar work intended to expose the deceptions of *goëtes* (γοήτων φώρα) that included a section on oracular inquiry.[73] Artemidorus prefaces his encyclopedic work on dream interpretation by appealing first to people who would do away with divination completely and then to those who have practiced divination erroneously, inciting others to mock and reject the discipline. Yet he writes foremost against the authors of similar treatises on dream divination:

> For there is no book on dream-interpretation which I have not acquired, expending much zeal in this regard, and I have also consorted for many years with the much-maligned diviners of the marketplace, whom the high and mighty and the eyebrow-raisers call beggars (προΐκτας) and charlatans (γόητας) and altar-lurkers (βωμολόχους), though I have rejected their slander. And in Greece, in its cities and festivals, and in Asia and in Italy and in the largest and most populous of the islands I have listened patiently to old dreams and their outcomes. For in no other way was I able to gain perspective on these matters. As a result, out of this abundance, I become able to speak about each thing such that, speaking the truth itself, I do not babble on, but furnish proofs that are clear and easily grasped by all based on straightforward examples.[74]

For Artemidorus, as for Lucian and Celsus, one's own authority depended on demonstrating exhaustive familiarity with the practices of other alleged experts, only to then denounce them.[75] In this case,

---

72. Lucian, *Alex.* 21. While it can be neither proved nor disproved, for the suggestion that this Celsus was also the author of *True Doctrine*, see Francis, *Subversive Virtue*, 135.

73. See Bendlin, "Uses and Disadvantages of Divination," 229–32. Bendlin posits Lucian's knowledge of this text and its influence on his depiction of Alexander of Abonoteichus.

74. Artemidorus, *Oneirocrit.* praef. 1.2 (trans. Daniel E. Harris-McCoy).

75. Indeed, throughout his own work Artemidorus mentions a number of writers who have produced other kinds of dream volumes, particularly ones that catalog the details of specific dreams or prescriptions and cures transmitted through them: Geminus of Tyre (three books), Demetrius of Phalerum (five books), and Artemon of Miletus (twenty-two books). For discussion, see William V. Harris, *Dreams and Experience in Classical Antiquity* (Cambridge: Harvard University Press, 2009), 113–15.

the act of writing a manual on the best practices for his craft was implicated directly in elevating the author's standing within this particular subset of expertise. It is precisely by claiming to have surveyed rival interpretive methods and producing a superior technical treatise on his own that Artemidorus positions himself and his son, to whom he imparted his knowledge, above those who offer the same or related services.

This is not to suggest that anyone who wrote about freelance experts and their practices did so to advance a position immediately within the same field. As best we can tell, Lucian and Celsus were not actual participants in this form of religious activity, although they occupied a closer location to it than writers such as Varro or Cicero, whose writings advance elite norms, or Horace and Juvenal, whose perspective was that of bemused satirists. Nor does proficiency in novel religious practices or teachings make someone a freelance expert per se. More than one Roman elite seems to have crossed from the intense study of esoteric subjects into their actual practice. The late-republican intellectual P. Nigidius Figulus authored writings on Pythagorean doctrines, astrology, and the traditions of the Persian *magi*, in addition to works on theology and other religious topics, and is said to have become a skilled practitioner in those areas, so much so that Jerome remembers him as a *Pythagoricus et magus*.[76] In the same vein, according to Josephus, the emperor Tiberius, a famed astrology enthusiast and disciple of the eminent court astrologer Thrasyllus, learned to cast horoscopes more accurately than those who voluntarily devoted their life to it.[77] His talents also seem to have translated into other forms of divination, insofar as he was able to detect and trace the origins of a harmful *daimōn* sent to him in a dream by a political adversary.[78] Nero likewise pursued instruction in exotic arts, although he preferred to learn the secret teachings of the *magi* from

---

76. Jerome, *Chron.* 183.4. For a comprehensive list of references to P. Nigidius Figulus, in his multiple guises, see James B. Rives, "Magic, Religion, and Law, The Case of the *Lex Cornelia de sicariis et veneficiis*," in *Religion and Law in Classical and Christian Rome*, ed. Clifford Ando and Jörg Rüpke, Potsdamer Altertumswissenschaftliche Beiträge 31 (Stuttgart: Steiner, 2006), 47–67, at 63 n. 59.

77. Josephus, *AJ* 18. 216–17. Josephus continues that Tiberius believed that everything connected with divination was trustworthy; and because its revelations turned out to be true, he, more than any other emperor, resorted to it in handling his affairs.

78. Tacitus, *Ann.* 6.20.

Tiridates.[79] Despite certain affinities between the practices of social elites and those of freelance religious experts, it is hard to imagine a Roman emperor or senator resorting to such activities to advance the interests that are central to my category. That is, Roman elites who developed these skills hardly depended on them for power or legitimacy, let alone their livelihoods.

Another scenario that shares many formal characteristics with the provision of religious expertise is one in which a slave utilized religious skills or presided over foreign rites within the immediate context of his or her *familia*. References to the religious heterogeneity of households are plentiful for this period. Reflecting on the ethnic diversity of slave populations, each with its foreign religious practices (*externa sacra*) and different manners of worship (*diversi ritus*), Tacitus complains that Romans now house multiple nations under their roofs.[80] Such intimate exposure to exotic religion might pique the interest of Roman family members and, with this interest, create opportunities for slaves to act as translators of their local religious customs. It was also generally the case that slaves with specialized abilities enjoyed greater privileges, and a handful of examples confirm that religious expertise was among the skills prized by masters. In Acts of the Apostles, Paul and Silas cross paths with a female belly-talker (ἐγγαστρίμυθος) who earned a great deal of money for her masters through prognostication.[81] When the apostles drive out her prophetic *daimōn* in the name of Christ, her masters drag them before authorities on the accusation that they have thrown Philippi into an uproar by advocating customs unlawful for Romans to accept or practice. It is difficult to say whether a slave offering religious expertise for the benefit of a master warrants inclusion in my category, but I am inclined to exclude such examples unless the evidence suggests otherwise. A *former* slave might, however, draw on such skills in a manner in keeping with my category of freelance expertise.

I propose all of these distinctions cautiously, since the evidence for any of the experts in question is often partial and may capture only one facet of his or her practices or social location. Chaffing against Lucian's roundly critical portrait of Peregrinus is Aulus Gellius's description of the same

---

79. Pliny, *Nat.* 30.14–7; Suetonius, *Ner.* 13.1.1, 30.2.2. The same emperor made a habit of consulting Balbillus, thought to be the son of Thrasyllus (Tacitus, *Ann.* 6.22; Suetonius, *Ner.* 36.1).

80. Tacitus, *Ann.* 14.44.3; Bodel, "An Outline of Roman Domestic Religion," 255–58.

81. Acts 16:16–40.

figure, whom he visited in his hut outside of Athens, as "a serious and disciplined man" (*virum gravem atque constantem*).[82] Paul devised an ambitious religious program whose elements included exegesis of Judean writings, philosophical discourses, initiation into divine mysteries, and afterlife rewards. As I argue, his epistles offer a rare and intimate sightline into the internal dynamics of freelance expertise, revealing both its challenges and also how a given expert might adjust his or her self-representation and teachings in order to negotiate them. Thus situated, Paul is an invaluable witness to how seamlessly intellectualizing experts might combine practices associated in modernity with distinct ancient disciplines (e.g., philosophy, rhetoric) or religions (e.g., Judaism, Christianity) to produce a mutually entailing scheme that is not fully at home in any one scholarly category but has affinities with many.[83] His writings also underscore the impossibility of judging whether such combinations were consciously strategic—that is, whether specialists drew upon certain skills, concepts, and practices with full awareness of how these might position them in particular discourses or fields—or merely reflect the understandings and intuitions that they brought to their religious activities. If we did not have Paul's own writings, however, and only a passing reference to him, he might be classified as a teacher, scribe, philosopher, or magician.[84]

Far from being discouraged by these methodical considerations, we should welcome the opportunity that they present to rethink our scholarly categories and to pay greater attention to different forms of religious activity collapsed within them.[85] Where the evidence permits, we must

---

82. Aulus Gellius, *Noct. att.* 12.11.1–7; cf. Ammianus, *Rer. gest.* 29.1.39. Likewise, epigraphic and numismatic evidence for the cult of Glycon's impressive spread—as far as Dacia and the Carpathians in the West and Antioch in the East—and duration is attested through the reign of Trebonianus Gallus (251–53). See Bendlin, "Uses and Disadvantages of Divination," 235.

83. Other examples of this sort of evidence include the authors of the Hermetic writings, the *Chaldean Oracles*, the *Greek Magical Papyri*, and, from an earlier period, the Derveni papyrus. Although there are nonliterary forms of evidence that capture the perspectives of experts—basic inscriptions and nontextual artifacts such as divining instruments—the quality and complexity of writings produced by freelance experts contribute more to our picture than other items commissioned or enlisted by participants in this class.

84. In the Acts of Paul and Thecla, for example, Paul is denigrated as a *magos* (3.9 and 5.6). We see this sort of problem clearly for other freelance experts who are attested by multiple ancient sources: a man named Sudines is called a *mathematicus* by Strabo but a *haruspex* by Frontinus (Strabo, *Geogr.* 16.1.6; Frontinus, *Str.* 1.11.15).

85. As Stanley K. Stowers has written, "religion is always a matter of more and less" ("The Ontology of Religion," 444). Here Stowers refers to other kinds of social practices with

make judgments about the practices in which we know an expert to have engaged while avoiding the trap of uncritically accepting the labels of our ancient writers. For all of the problems with our sources for the religion of freelance experts, together they a bequeath a wealth of information about the shape and character of a form of religious activity that was not only pervasive in the Roman Empire but that also enhances our understanding of the emergence and development of phenomena better attested in subsequent centuries, including Christianity. There is no doubt that many authors write about these figures from a normative and typically negative point of view, exploiting the problem of interest associated with freelance expertise by depicting their subjects as profit-mongering charlatans. Nevertheless, basic elements of their accounts are consistent with how experts represent their own practices in the rare instances where their writings survive. If we disentangle these highly interested commentaries from the basic phenomenon at issue, together they begin to flesh out a historical context wherein specialized forms of religion abounded and self-authorized experts competed intensely and with great creativity for potential followers or students. Once coordinated and adjusted for their respective biases, our multiform evidence throws into relief a pattern of characteristics that captures many points of view on this class of religious activity, including ones situated directly within it.

In considering the variety of practices that comprised specialized offerings, as well as the different kinds of social formations that specialists might produce, we should not be constrained by current scholarly categories that do not make sense of the evidence. As I suggested earlier, this class of religious activity necessarily embraces elements of magic, astrology, mystery cults, philosophy, Judaism, and Christianity, among other headings under which varieties of freelance experts have been sorted. Theorizing them instead as a common set of religious actors allows us to juxtapose and compare examples of their practices wherever, and in whatever combinations, they occur, while also inviting us to rethink the limitations of previous

---

which religious practices might be bundled and weighs in on how one determines that the latter are proportionately significant enough for an activity or program to be classified as "religious," in his sense—more so, say, than offering a brief prayer to a god at the start of a meeting that contains no other religious practices. A map of possible combinations is especially rich for the ancient Mediterranean world, where religion pervaded nearly every human activity. In instances where religious practices were only marginal components of an activity, the basic assumption that gods were relevant to the task at hand might result in a religious practice playing a minor role in another form of activity—for instance, divination to determine a course of military action.

classificatory schemes and methodologies. Rather than reverse-engineering our categories from the content or representations of the experts' programs, we should note affinities in the skills that particular actors shared, as well as religious benefits—secret information, foreknowledge, esoteric learning, healing, purification, self-improvement, escape from divine judgment, even immortality—that many offered, irrespective of whether these were articulated in an Egyptian, Persian, Judean, or Christian idiom.

Freelance Experts in the Study of Ancient Mediterranean Religion

The past decade has seen renewed efforts to theorize religion in the ancient Mediterranean world, with recent publications questioning the utility of this concept for antiquity. Having followed the discussion with great interest, I would be remiss not to engage a few of its yields as they bear on this study. Earlier I defined freelance experts in religion as self-authorized actors whose practices directly enlisted gods and similar beings to a significant degree and who formed a particular type or class of religious activity attested in the Roman Empire. This is consistent with my understanding of religion as one area of social life defined by practices that involved divine agents and imputed to them, in addition to any number of special abilities and powers, human-like characteristics that allowed people to interact with them according to an intuitive social logic. Religion did not form an exceptional or discrete domain; rather, religious practices were widely distributed in any number of overlapping social activities. And while participants in ancient religion held any number of ideas about what the gods were like, about how to interact with them, and so forth, this kind of practical knowledge did not require assent to elaborate theological propositions of the sort implied in modern notions of religious belief.

Others have written at length about how religious practices that were basic and widespread throughout the ancient Mediterranean and Near East—prayer and other speech acts, sacrifice and other offerings, divination, purifications, special communal meals, caring for the spirits of ancestors, being initiated (or initiating someone else) into a god's mysteries, and so on—could be linked with other kinds of social practices and organized into simpler or more complex activities suited to particular contexts, spaces, and institutional bodies. Defining religion as a range of practices or bundles of practices is a conscious move away from speaking of "religions" of the Roman Empire, which implies coherent and stable entities tethered to complex institutions with the following sort of characteristics: professional clerics, a system of beliefs shared by like-minded practitioners, a bounded group, an exclusive identification, specific places and times for worship, a moral code, a scriptural canon, and often considerable literary activity that reinforces all of these features.[86] The latter notion is not only anachronistic but also fundamentally misleading for the ancient world. In short, "religions" are suggestive of rival systems of belief and the features that accompany them, when there is little if any evidence for such entities in the early empire.

Brent Nongbri has argued in a recent book that religion is a distinctly modern category and one without any corollaries in antiquity.[87] Although most scholars use the term "as if it were a universal concept native to all human cultures," the idea of religion as a distinct social sphere is, Nongbri explains, a relatively recent development that has been projected onto antiquity and, in turn, naturalized as a timeless component of human history.[88] Among other objections to the use of "religion" for the Roman period, he points to the absence in Greek and Latin of words that correspond to the modern concept of religion, as he understands it, as well as the fabrication of Greek and Roman religion as objects of study by Enlightenment thinkers who sought in classical antiquity favorable alternatives to Christianity yet who nevertheless modeled these alternatives in kind.[89]

There is much to recommend Nongbri's critique, especially when taken with an earlier piece in which he identifies a scholarly habit of describing religion as "embedded" in the structures of ancient societies to signal difference between antiquity and modernity, but without managing to discard concepts of "a religion" or "religions," maybe for lack of an alternative vocabulary and theoretical model.[90] Yet Nongbri and like-minded critics tend to frame the problem in such a way that we are limited to one of

---

86. For further discussion of these features see Rives, *Religion in the Roman Empire*, 5; Stowers, "The Ontology of Religion," 445–47.

87. Brent Nongbri, *Before Religion: A History of a Modern Concept* (New Haven: Yale University Press, 2013).

88. Nongbri, *Before Religion*, 7.

89. Nongbri, *Before Religion*, 132–53; cf. Russell T. McCutcheon, *The Discipline of Religion: Structure, Meaning, Rhetoric* (London: Routledge, 2003), 255.

90. Nongbri, "Dislodging 'Embedded' Religion: A Brief Note on a Scholarly Trope," *Numen* 55 (2008): 440–60, esp. 451–53.

two options: either ancient people engaged in practices and held beliefs that fit a *modern concept of religion*, with all of its recognized baggage, or else they would have recognized nothing like this concept and we cannot speak of their religion without transforming "our ancient sources into well-polished mirrors that show us only ourselves and our own institutions."[91] Since the first option is clearly wrong, only the latter remains: at risk of thrusting our own conceptual categories upon the ancient world, we must seek a way of describing interactions with the gods in antiquity without enlisting the potentially distortive language of religion.[92]

I do not share the view that any definition of religion is too modern and too fraught with intractable difficulties to be applied to antiquity. On the one hand, there is no *one* or *the* modern concept of religion but rather a seemingly infinite number of ways that practitioners and scholars alike categorize beliefs and practices involving god(s), implicitly and explicitly, on the basis of their respective normative schemes, intellectual positionings, and local frames of reference. Any modern concept is, as Nongbri ably demonstrates, necessarily the product of precisely such historically particular discourses about religious practices, in my sense. To say that we cannot define and theorize an object in one period because its authors lack a term that matches another contingent discourse about that object, in this case "our" own, seems to conflate two things that should be distinct: discourses *about* what I and others identify as religion and the evidence *for* religion, as I have defined it analytically. It is the task of scholars of religion to disentangle the emic and often highly interested points of view captured in discursive schemes of categorization from the underlying phenomena on which they comment.[93]

Theorizing religion as a matter of variously linked social practices moves beyond historically contingent discourses about these practices, while the analytical category "religion" is potentially as large as all the ways in which human beings in all their cultures have thought about and engaged with

---

91. Nongbri, *Before Religion*, 153.

92. Nongbri, "Dislodging 'Embedded' Religion," 456.

93. See also David Frankfurter, review of *Before Religion: A History of a Modern Concept*, by Brent Nongbri, *JECS* 23 (2015): 632–34. For the position that concepts such as religion exist as social realities apart from discourses formed about them in the linguistic realm, see Kevin Schilbrack, "Religions: Are There Any?" *JAAR* 78 (2010): 112–28; Stowers, "The Ontology of Religion," 436. I say more about this issue in chapter 3, where I argue that evidence for "magic" should be recast as the religion of freelance experts.

divine beings.[94] Such a definition also captures practices and actors that many ancient writers would label as "magic" or "superstition" in order to privilege their own sensibilities about appropriate ways to interact with the gods. Emic categories can have a powerful effect on perception and doubtlessly influence the self-perception or self-representation of those to whom they pertain. Yet an ancient writer's application of discourses about "magic" to express disapproval of someone's religious practices, in my sense, does not undermine the social ontology of those practices, even if the latter person refers to him- or herself as a *magus/-a*.[95]

As to the appropriateness of using "religion" and "religious" to refer to practices involving divine beings, I see a greater disadvantage in discarding this language than in working to disabuse it of notions that are inapplicable to antiquity and, for that matter, to many modern phenomena. Since "religion" stands in for all such practices, it is flexible enough to include examples from any historical period or cultural area. I also find semantic debates about whether ancient languages had words that map exactly onto the modern English "religion" to be largely unproductive. Greeks and Romans had many descriptive terms for the practices, dispositions, institutions, and offices that structured their own relations with the gods, as they did for identifying and relativizing equivalent constellations among other peoples.[96]

On occasion I use the phrases "Roman religion," "Greek religion," "Egyptian religion," and "Judean religion," not to affirm the existence of *religions* of the sort that Nongbri, James B. Rives, and Stanley K. Stowers rightly find incongruous with the ancient world but in one of two senses: either to refer collectively to any and all religion coexisting in a particular geographical area or to refer to ideas about the religion of other peoples or cultural areas that were held by nonnative audiences. The latter sense receives ample discussion in subsequent chapters, since many specialists utilized ethnic

---

94. Stowers, "The Ontology of Religion," 242–43.

95. Cf. Bernd-Christian Otto, "Towards Historicizing 'Magic' in Antiquity," *Numen* 60 (2013): 308–47, esp. 326–27. See also Kimberly B. Stratton, "Magic Discourse in the Ancient World," in *Defining Magic: A Reader*, ed. Bernd-Christian Otto and Michael Stausberg, Critical Categories in the Study of Religion (New York: Routledge, 2014), 243–54, at 248.

96. Cf. Jörg Rüpke, *The Religion of the Romans* (Malden, MA: Polity, 2007), 3–38; Rives, *Religion in the Roman Empire*, 13–53; John A. North, "Pagans, Polytheists, and the Pendulum," in *The Spread of Christianity in the First Four Centuries: Essays in Explanation*, ed. William V. Harris, Columbia Studies in the Classical Tradition 27 (Leiden: Brill, 2005), 125–43, esp. 136.

or provincial caricatures to their advantage by claiming expertise in what I call "ethnically coded" skills, practices, and artifacts, including texts, that were strongly associated with a particular people or region. Inhabitants of the empire were broadly acquainted with such concepts of foreign religion, which, in turn, presented opportunities for complex and strategic acts of identification as some experts capitalized on and even exaggerated ethnic characteristics.

I raise these matters of definition not simply to bring my own study into line with recent disciplinary debates but because prior treatments of the evidence on which I draw yield very different conclusions depending on the models of religion that underpin them. This is especially true of studies predicated on structuralist or social-functionalist theories of religion, which tend to position freelance experts in an antagonistic relationship to communally oriented institutions and activities that ensured the continuity of civilized society or social groups (e.g., civic or polis religion, the religion of families, and kin groups).[97] If religion is ultimately an instrument of order or social cohesion, how are we to reconcile these largely independent actors who did not contribute to such aims and even, in some cases, went against them?

For lack of a demonstrable social function, freelance experts are often understood to have operated at the margins of society; hence their religious activities are necessarily antithetical to behavior or practices that enact and sustain community. This impression is both engendered and reinforced by literary tropes that highlight the self-interest and insincerity of these actors, qualities that clash with modern notions of what religion *should* entail. The same problem arises in explaining people's incentives for consulting them. Since groups, not individuals, are the meaningful units of analysis in social-functionalist accounts, religious acts undertaken to advance personal interests rather than those of a larger social unit automatically acquire a selfish, antisocial valence. Even when freelance experts are viewed in a more positive light—for instance, as social dissidents who nobly reformed civic structures or, following Peter Brown's influential model, as holy men who, in their own persons, came to usurp the social functions of institutions—their posited function is distinctly group

---

97. For critiques of social-functionalist theories of religion, see Hans H. Penner, "The Poverty of Functionalism," *HR* 11 (1971): 91–97; Schilbrack, "Religions: Are There Any?" passim; Paul Firenze, "Value and the Economics of Religious Capital" (PhD diss., Brown University, 2013), 16–47.

oriented. Whether mediating social tensions, arbitrating disputes, symbolically purging violence and unrest, or allaying anxieties, the primary role of the Christian holy man and his equivalents was to bolster the stability and vitality of communities or systems.[98]

There is often little if any basis for reading social functions into our evidence for freelance experts. Tellingly, many of these scholarly accounts have an air of romanticism: specialists are either villains or heroes who stood outside and in tension with some larger corporate body, whether society, a religious system, or, later, the Church. Some are also inattentive to historical contingencies that contributed to the general popularity of these religious actors in the imperial period and of particular kinds of experts at particular moments. Instead, the scholars in question chalk up their appeal either to some deficiency in traditional religious institutions or to inherent charisma, a special and mysterious brand of religious authority best represented in concepts of the holy man or *theios anēr* (θεῖος ἀνήρ).[99] I am not denying that specialists themselves sometimes grounded their religious programs in premises of essential difference, espoused esoteric theologies

---

98. See Peter Brown, "The Rise and Function of the Holy Man in Late Antiquity," *JRS* 61 (1971): 80–101, esp. 97–98; idem, "The Rise and Function of the Holy Man in Late Antiquity, 1971–1997," *JECS* 6 (1998): 353–76; Garth Fowden, "The Pagan Holy Man in Late Antique Society," *JHS* 102 (1982): 33–59. James A. Francis regards ascetics as cultural dissidents or deviants who reoriented religious authority away from external social institutions by refusing to conform to prevailing standards (*Subversive Virtue*, xiii). Since these figures, whom he places within the category "holy men," championed new and empowered forms of subjectivity—for Francis a good thing—he casts their perceived tension with civic religious institutions in a positive light. Nevertheless, *these* culture heroes are not to be confused with "the sort of wonderworkers and demagogues that . . . infested the street-corners and marketplaces of the second-century Empire" (19). Not dissimilarly, David Potter argues that some specialists periodically refreshed or revised traditional religious systems, thereby ensuring their vitality and currency (*Prophets and Emperors*, 4–14). Potter divides the elements of a "religious system" into passive and active elements, which reflect "the distinction between the acceptance of old knowledge and the search for new." In his view, oracles and other media of divine communication were the essential vehicles of active religious experience, while cult ritual was the essential public feature of passive experience (5).

99. E.g., Graham Anderson, who attributes the market for "holy men" in the early Roman Empire to "a moral climate in which there were ills of society to be put right and regulation of the social order required. . . . Also a part of this moral universe [was] the quest for personal security, identity, and salvation" (*Sage, Saint, and Sophist*, 8). It is not difficult to see how explanations in this vein are often conspicuously tailored toward the emergence of Christianity: the spiritual offerings of "pagan holy men" were counterparts to or prepared the way for a Christian salvation scheme. See also Francis (*Subversive Virtue*, 122–25), for affirmation that the holy man, understood as "an extraordinary *man* with a special relationship to the gods and a practical function in his society based upon his perceived authority," is a

or cosmogonies, and imbued ordinary religious practices with special significance; many seem to have done so with great success. Nor, for that matter, am I excluding the possibility that highly successful figures were socially charismatic. Rather, my critique applies to the inference of psychological or spiritual dispositions when we might look instead to more secure historical factors that help to understand and explain this sort of religious activity.[100]

It is worth restating that the pursuit of certain interests through the provision and acquisition of religious expertise are not grounds for impeachment, inasmuch as all religious practices might be said to impart some benefit, whether health, fertility, safe passage during travel, prosperity, character development, the recovery of lost property, romantic affection, or a favorable afterlife. Positing plausible interests for religious actors on the basis of the effects of their practices does not require the presumption of insincere or otherwise questionable motives, even when economic exchange is involved. Comparable transactions and perquisites accompanied most, if not all, positions of religious authority in the ancient world, though institutional contexts afforded more misrecognition of financial arrangements. However, the conspicuous economic dimension of freelance expertise was a major incentive for forming regular groups of followers that might acquire the sort of institutional characteristics that concealed or normalized such exchanges.

---

sufficient and flexible definition. I respectfully disagree with the position that the defining characteristic of these religious actors was an innate quality of divinity and that their apparent differences stem only from relations to the societies in which they were situated. In my view, the recognition, attractiveness, and self-positioning of freelance experts depended entirely on particular historical contingencies.

100. Cf. Leif E. Vaage, "Ancient Religious Rivalries and the Struggle for Success: Christians, Jews, and Others in the Early Roman Empire," in *Religious Rivalries in the Early Roman Empire and the Rise of Christianity*, ed. Leif E. Vaage (Waterloo: Wilfred Laurier University Press, 2006), 3–19. In more recent scholarship, identity has loomed large as the reason why people sought out the religion of specialists. James C. Hanges, whose examination of Hellenistic cult founders is enhanced by the insights of postcolonial theory, views experts in ethnically coded forms of religion especially as hypostasizing the constant struggle between possible identities determined by broad ethnic categories but expressed in terms of gods and humans (*Paul, Founder of Churches*, 287–88). The motivation for founding a new cult is thus to be found in the needs of immigrant communities, whose members were in the process of struggling with their identities. As with claims about the spiritual or psychological appeal of the religion of specialists, we often have too little evidence to make inferences about the self-understandings of ancient peoples but are on safer ground in talking about the ways in which they identified toward particular ends. Hanges's observation that people located

Dimensions of Freelance Expertise

My own investigation of the religion of freelance experts proceeds along the following lines. The first chapter surveys evidence for the expanding influence of these actors in the Roman Empire, with a view to historical developments that promoted their credibility and allure. A particular focus falls on legislative actions issued against specialists in Rome—namely, expulsions and proscriptions of practices with which they were commonly associated—insofar as the escalation of these measures in both frequency and severity over the course of the first imperial century attests the growth of the perceived issue they were intended to address. In lieu of a specific Greek or Latin word that referred collectively to freelance experts, I argue that consistency in the tactics employed to manage all varieties of specialists (e.g., *magi*, astrologers, and diviners) suggests an unspoken recognition of their wider affinities. I also propose that this pattern of action, in place long before Christians became the recipients of such punishments, informed how Roman magistrates and other local authorities would recognize and respond to them in later periods.

Chapter 2 considers experts in ethnically coded wisdom and practices who catered to a widespread interest in foreign religion. Although I touch on Greek, Etruscan, Persian, Chaldean, and even Indian examples, my principal case studies are experts in Judean and Egyptian skills and practices, as well as texts. Locating some Judeans within a class of religious activity populated by other foreign specialists underscores the anachronism of the model of proselytism and conversion to "Judaism" for making sense of this evidence. As a result, the assorted actors, activities, and social formations that I gather under the heading "Judean religion" appear more diverse and more comparable in their diversity to other examples of foreign religion found outside their respective native environments.[101]

Chapter 3 examines evidence for experts who enlisted intellectual skills and writings in the context of religious activity. Here my focus falls on Roman-period Pythagoreans, *magi*, and other figures known for

---

themselves in culturally available narrative repertoires is important, however, and he makes a persuasive case that the "cult founders" he considers did so with respect to a particular narrative of cult foundation.

101. This is not to suggest that the same variety did not also occur in native contexts, but my primary interest is in the reception of foreign experts by audiences to whom they appeared exotic.

combining esoteric and, in many cases, ethnically coded wisdom with philosophical discursive practices. In addition to other ways in which writing
and texts might participate in the religion of freelance experts, I am especially interested in how particular corpora of inspired writings—*Sibylline*
and *Chaldean Oracles*, Hermetica, Orphica, and other Greek poetry, the
holy writings of the Judeans, the books of Hystaspes, and so forth—either
became resources for allegorical exegesis and myth-making or served as
paradigms for the composition of new, often pseudepigraphic literature. I
then question the utility of "magic" for theorizing this evidence and propose that the evidence for "magic" be subsumed into the religion of freelance experts, with attention to differences in the skills and aptitude of the
motley actors who earned this label in the Roman period.

In chapter 4 I argue for the location of Paul within this particular class
of religious activity by demonstrating how each of the characteristics and
dynamics considered in the previous chapters are attested in his epistles.
These include but are not limited to the particular punishments that Paul
alleges to have suffered, the frequent appeals that he makes to his ethnic
status, his use of Judean writings for myth-making and literary divination,
his claim to possess divine mysteries and revealed wisdom, the religious
services he offers (initiation, purification, immortality, as well as the acquisition of skills such as prophecy, healing, the discernment of spirits,
and so on), his facility with philosophy, and even his Jerusalem collection.
I then argue that redescribing Paul as a kind of freelance expert in Judean
religion offers new interpretive options for the content of his letters.

The last chapter turns to rival Christian teachers—Marcion, Justin,
Valentinus, Ptolemy and Irenaeus, and so forth—who coincided in
second-century Rome in order to evaluate their activities, too, within the
framework of freelance expertise. Although these figures denounced
one another in harsh polemics, they also formed coterminous groups
with intimate knowledge of one another's teachings, practices, and texts.
Furthermore, there are indications of their participation in a broader literary network that included other writer-intellectuals. Their conflicts thus
tell only a partial story of seemingly rich and regular interaction not only
among Christians but also between Christians and experts of other varieties. As a result of how scholars of early Christianity have trained their
lenses—that is, primarily on evidence for Jews and Christians during the
period in question—the range of practices (e.g., exorcism, astrology, numerology, and other forms of divination) attested for certain Christian

groups has been difficult to categorize and explain. When viewed against the backdrop that I am suggesting—a methodological inversion that arrives at rather than begins from the Christian evidence—this diversity appears less extraordinary and more in keeping with patterns observable for other forms of religion that arose from this class of activity.

In this book I grapple with a larger question that might be pursued along different lines of inquiry: How did freelance experts contribute to broader religious transformations in the Roman Empire, and what is their relationship to other kinds of religion that coexisted in its territories? The impetus for such a study stems from the methodological problems that ensue when misleading but intractable expectations of essential difference are projected onto the evidence for religious actors who seem to have occupied the same social niche of the Roman world. Such expectations are clearest with respect to the default conclusion that Jews and Christians were *somehow* unique in this historical context, even in studies that demonstrate their thoroughgoing resemblances to contemporaneous figures, practices, and groups. My approach seeks to undermine the artificial boundaries that have arisen between similarly self-authorized experts–largely as the result of modern theological interests and disciplinary arrangements—by theorizing all as variations on a common type of religious actor, regardless of how their respective programs might differ. To the contrary, in the arena of freelance expertise a vast assortment of skills, practices, and ethnic idioms intersected, and with weighty consequences for the subsequent history of religion as it would later be defined.

I

The Religion of Freelance Experts in the Roman Empire

IN THE INTRODUCTION we encountered a number of freelance experts in religion, whether in caricatures of their practices, in fleeting references to their (typically unwelcome) interventions in Roman public life, or in scarcer firsthand accounts of the sort represented by the Pauline Epistles. These examples could be multiplied to a point where the present study would become more of a catalogue of the actors in question than a redescription and theorization of the form of religious activity they represent. For this reason, I do not pretend to offer a comprehensive survey of the evidence, a task that has already been undertaken for certain types of experts and forms of expertise. Rather, in this chapter I pull back from the more detailed portraits of specialists with which I began in order to advance a twofold argument: first, that the first century of the Roman Empire witnessed a steady expansion of the religion of freelance experts, and second, that this phenomenon was nourished by incidental circumstances that accompanied the empire's formation.

As I noted earlier, freelance experts did not originate in the Roman period; to the contrary, individuals possessing many of the qualities that I attributed to them turn up in narratives about the origins of Rome's oldest institutions and institutional practices. Attus Navius, a legendary diviner of the regal period famous for splitting a whetstone with a razor, was hailed as the defender of augury by Livy and Dionysius of Halicarnassus, who both recounted the tradition.[1] More than an obscure literary relic, a

---

1. Dionysius of Halicarnassus, *Ant. rom.* 3.71.1–5; Livy, 1.36.2–6. See Mary Beard, "Acca Larentia Gains a Son," in *Images of Authority: Papers Presented to Joyce Reynolds*, ed. Mary Margaret Mackenzie and Charlotte Roueché, Cambridge Philological Society, Suppl. 16

statue of the *augur* stood before the Comitium in the Roman Forum where it was in close proximity to that of Pythagoras, another expert from the distant past who continued to captivate first-century imaginations, and whose Italian school was a point of pride for many Romans.[2] So too did many writers relate stories about an unknown foreign woman who attempted to sell a set of oracular texts that foretold the entirety of Rome's history to Tarquin, the fifth king of Rome and one of its purportedly Etruscan rulers.[3] She offered first nine books, then six, then three, burning three after each of his refusals and offering the volumes that remained always for the original price. Only after consulting the *augures* did the king learn that he had rebuffed a gift from the gods and paid the mysterious woman, really the Sibyl, the full original price to acquire the remaining books, what would become the *Sibylline Oracles*. As old as the extant Latin literary record, these storied ancestors of familiar skills and established institutions were well known to Roman audiences during the republic and probably even earlier, as were their Greek (Orpheus, Teiresias), Persian (Zoroaster), and Israelite (Joseph, Moses, Solomon) counterparts within those cultural areas.

Be that as it may, by the late republic our picture of freelance expertise begins to change. Tales of fabulous diviners, prophets, and sages from the distant past give way to more reproachful commentaries on their contemporary, less dignified equivalents. In his survey of methods for soliciting knowledge and assistance from the gods, Cicero bears witness not only to a proliferation of competing divinatory practices at Rome but also, as we saw earlier, to a mess of specialists in these different methods: *haruspices, sacrificuli, vates, sortilegi, magi, augures Marsi, astrologi, harioli,* and *Chaldaei.*[4] He invokes all of these titles exactly, expecting his readers to recognize

---

(Cambridge: Cambridge Philological Society, 1989), 41–61, at 50–53; Beard, North, and Price, *Religions of Rome, Vol. 1*, 23–24. Similar traditions surrounded the Etruscan seer Tages, who, despite having the appearance of a boy, was famous for wisdom that he committed to writing (e.g., Cicero, *Div.* 2.50.4–51.1). This, according to Cicero, is the story the Etruscans preserve about the source of their haruspical knowledge.

2. Pliny, *Nat.* 34.26; Plutarch, *Num.* 8.10. See Michel Humm, "Numa and Pythagoras: The Life and Death of a Myth," in *The Roman Historical Tradition: Regal and Republican Rome,* ed. James H. Richardson and Federico Santangelo (Oxford: Oxford University Press, 2014), 35–52, at 42–45.

3. Dionysius of Halicarnassus, *Ant. rom.* 4.62; Plin. *Nat.* 8.27; Aulus Gellius, *Noct. att.* 1.19. See Herbert W. Parke, *Sibyls and Sibylline Prophecy in Classical Antiquity* (New York: Routledge, 1988), 76–78.

4. Cicero, *Div.* 1.132.1–6.

the figures in question and their corresponding practices. Some titles receive secondary ethnic or geographic qualification: whereas the *haruspex*
was traditionally tied to Etruria, Cicero notes *haruspices* of Elis, Egypt, and
Carthage. In contrast to those in Cicero's catalogue, earlier experts appear
less exotic and, in the case of Cato's aforementioned *augur* and *haruspex*,
more embedded in Roman civic institutions for the titles and authority
they claim. Writing at the turn of the second century, Juvenal inventories
an even more assorted bunch of specialists, a list that includes, as we will
see, ambassadors of gods and foreign rites or services that span nearly
every region of the empire, as well as territories beyond its limits. By his
day, the motley specialists who preyed upon women prone to *superstitio*,
the subject of his sixth satire, were as varied as the territories either under
Rome's administration or in its orbit.[5]

Cicero and Juvenal are apt bookends for a period within which the phenomenon of freelance expertise seems to have taken off to a hitherto unprecedented degree, at least in most parts of the empire. As I suggested
in the introduction, there are many indications that from the late republic
onward freelance experts began to acquire an increasingly public profile,
to claim expertise in a more diverse range of skills or methods, and to align
themselves with a more ambitious topography of ethnically coded practices. They also seem to have increased in number, although, again, any
argument about quantity must take into consideration the much richer
literary and epigraphic records of the imperial period. We are on firmer
ground in noting their heightened visibility and sheer variety at this time,
especially at Rome, where an abundance of evidence allows us to observe
them more fully than in other cities and regions.

*Legislative Evidence for the Rise
of Freelance Experts*

One sign that this sort of religious activity was on the rise occurs in the
language assigned to or utilized by religious specialists. In some cases,
titles familiar in earlier periods gain new inflections. The term *haruspex*, a

---

5. I have chosen not to translate the Latin term *superstitio*, whose English cognate "superstition" derives its meaning from Enlightenment and modernist ideas about rational religion
and which fails to capture the normative perspectival sense in which Latin authors used it.
See Dale B. Martin, *Inventing Superstition: From the Hippocratics to the Christians* (Cambridge:
Harvard University Press, 2004).

stock figure and area of expertise associated with a particular people—in this case the Etruscans—might be extended to comparable diviners associated with different regions; hence Cicero's *haruspices* of Elis, Egypt, and Carthage, as well as Armenia and Commagene, as Juvenal will later attest. Other titles or forms of expertise surface anew in this period, as William E. Klingshirn has shown for the *sortilegus*, a type of specialist that first appears in Cicero's *On Divination* and whose expertise seems to have been modeled on the practices of the Praenestine oracle.[6] Likewise, Syrian religious experts crop up in late republican literature and remain a continuous presence in the empire until the second century, when Apuleius writes about duplicitous Syrian lot diviners.[7]

Also within this window an interesting shift occurs in the ethnic coding of certain kinds of actors and the religious skills or practices with which they are linked. Surveying instances of *magus* and its cognates in Latin literature, James B. Rives determines that this language consistently connotes expertise in Persian religion or religious wisdom until the last quarter of the first century CE, when its semantic range expands to include non-Persian actors and practices. Following a similar trajectory within roughly the same timeframe, *Chaldaeus* fractures into *mathematicus* and *astrologus*. All three terms continue to refer interchangeably to astrologers, but the latter two conspicuously lack an ethnic valence.[8] As I propose in the next chapter, *Iudaeus*/Ἰουδαῖος seems to have functioned in certain contexts as an ethnonym akin to Chaldean, but intimating expertise in a regular assortment of practices for which Judeans were especially well known: exorcism, prophecy, dream interpretation, and divination or wisdom instruction from ancient and authoritative Judean writings. If there is merit to this idea, one wonders whether these practices underwent processes of ethnic dissolution comparable to the trend that Rives observes for *magus* and *Chaldaeus*, although maybe with greater expediency.[9] Given the tendencies toward innovation and

---

6. Klingshirn, "Inventing the *sortilegus*."

7. J. Bert Lott, "The Prince and the Cutting Prophet: A Commentary on Dio 55.31.2–3" (Paper presented at "Religion in Pieces," an interdisciplinary conference sponsored by the Society for Ancient Mediterranean Religions and the Joukowsky Institute for Archaeology and the Ancient World, Brown University, Providence, RI, April 29, 2012).

8. Rives, "*Magus* and its Cognates in Classical Latin," 53–77.

9. Shaye J. D. Cohen observes a shift away from the ethnic meaning of Judean toward a more general meaning of "anyone who venerates the God of the Judaeans" at the end

creativity that many specialists exhibited, I provisionally suggest that these shifting taxonomies correlate, on the one hand, with the territorial and cultural expansion of the empire, and on the other, with competitive dynamics among experts who offered progressively more comprehensive religious programs comprising multiple skills and practices, articulated in different ethnic idioms.

An even stronger indication of growth in the religion of freelance experts occurs in historical writings, which testify to an escalation in both the frequency and severity of efforts intended to counteract specialist influence, particularly over the course of the first century CE.[10] Although experts in religious knowledge and services appear often, maybe even most often, in our sources for these punishments, equivalent actions were taken against other freelance actors, especially certain philosophers.[11] The measures themselves might take the form of an expulsion, a proscription of certain practices, or the confiscation of certain objects or materials, and issue from an individual magistrate, the Senate, or the emperor. Some targeted specific kinds of experts, but the same or similar measures might also encompass their followers or activities and items with which they were regularly associated.[12]

In a rich article on astrologers at Rome, Pauline Ripat advises against conflating occasional expulsions of these actors with a pervasive

---

of the first century CE: *The Beginnings of Jewishness: Boundaries, Varieties, Uncertainties* (Berkeley: University of California Press, 1999), 96. The coincidence of this timeframe and parallel developments with respect to *magus* and *Chaldaeus*, the latter especially, lend support to the hypothesis. I return to this matter in chapter 5.

10. For the first-century trend, see Frederick H. Cramer, "Expulsion of Astrologers from Ancient Rome," *C&M* 12 (1951): 9–50.

11. For expulsions and punishments of philosophers, see Francis, *Subversive Virtue*, 7–19; John T. Fitzgerald, *Cracks in an Earthen Vessel: An Examination of Catalogues of Hardships in the Corinthian Correspondence*, SBLDS 99 (Atlanta: SBL, 1988).

12. For an overview of much of this evidence, see Eric M. Orlin, *Foreign Cults in Rome: Creating a Roman Empire* (New York: Oxford University Press, 2010), 191–214. Although my approach to these episodes has much in common with the now-classic treatment of Mary Beard, John A. North, and Simon R.F. Price (*Religions of Rome, Vol. 1*, 211–44), it nevertheless differs with respect to the perceived motivations for religious legislation (managing the expanding influence of specialists versus maintaining the symbolic purity of the empire's center) and the types of social formations posited (freelance experts and their followers versus cults or rival systems of belief). For the ability of individuals to influence civic religion through "private" religiosity, see Clifford Ando, "Evidence and Orthopraxy: A Review Article of John Scheid, *Quand faire, c'est croire: Les rites sacrificiels des Romains*," *JRS* 99 (2009): 171–81, esp. 179–80.

ambivalence about astrology. The problems with the latter interpretation are several. Most obviously, she shows that relatively few of these measures targeted a single kind of expert or category of practice; instead, they tended to cast a wider net by naming multiple figures or permutations of religious activity. There is no shortage of examples that pair two or more figures in a piece of religious legislation. Both Tacitus and Cassius Dio mention joint expulsions of astrologers and "magicians" (*mathematici* and *magi*, and ἀστρολόγοι and γόητες, respectively) that occurred under Tiberius, while, according to Ulpian, a decree was published at this time against *mathematici*, Chaldeans, *harioli*, and all who do similar things (*et ceteris qui simile inceptum fecerunt*).[13] Furthermore, more than one Roman elite endured a high-profile trial for consulting an astrologer or diviner regarding a sensitive political matter, and sometimes multiple kinds of specialists with the same query.[14]

To return to Ripat's critique, another argument in favor of taking a more nuanced approach to these measures is that they simply cannot have been intended or applied as broadly as their language might suggest. Tiberius embraced certain astrologers and astrology, as well as divination more generally, yet his reign is remembered for a hitherto unprecedented number of actions undertaken against freelance experts, including Chaldeans, other kinds of astrologers, and other diviners. Additional recipients included *magi* (Gk. *goëtes*), *haruspices*, *harioli*, cursers and specialists in other nefarious practices (*venenarii*, *malefici*), diviners of all varieties,

---

13. Tacitus, *Ann.* 2.32; Cassius Dio, 57.25.8; Ulpian, *De off. proc.* 7; Ulpian, *Mos. et Rom. legum coll.* 15.2.1–3; Ripat, "Astrologers at Rome," 118. Tacitus mentions a general expulsion of *mathematici* and *magi* from Italy then qualifies that one from this lot, L. Pituanius, was cast off the Tarpeian rock, while another, P. Marcius, was executed in the ancient fashion (*more maiorum*) outside the Esquiline gate (*Ann.* 2.32). An explication of *more maiorum* occurs in Suetonius's account of the death of Nero, when the fugitive emperor receives a letter informing him that the Senate has pronounced him a public enemy and is seeking to punish him in the custom of the ancestors and he must inquire about that manner of punishment. Nero learns that the criminal is stripped, fastened by the neck in a fork, and then beaten to death with rods (Suetonius, *Ner.* 49.2; cf. Livy, 1.26.6; Suetonius, *Claud.* 34.1; Suetonius, *Dom.* 11.2–3).

14. Namely, those of Libo Drusus, Lollia Paulina, and Pomponia Graecina, a discussion of which follows shortly. Dio notes an edict issued by Augustus limiting the subjects about which diviners (*manteis*) could be consulted, and in whose presence, that addresses the basic issue (56.25.5). Cicero highlights the epistemological illogic of posing the same question to more than one type of diviner whose techniques and interpretive possibilities vary widely (e.g., *Div.* 2.12, 26, 71).

and certain practitioners of Egyptian and Judean religion.[15] On at least two occasions he is said to have adjudicated the status of oracles circulating privately under the Sibyl's imprimatur, a problem that had previously been addressed by Augustus, although apparently to no avail since Tiberius saw fit to repeat his actions.[16] Also echoing Augustus, he issued an edict forbidding anyone to consult diviners secretly, without witnesses.[17]

The seemingly paradoxical stance that Tiberius and other social elites took on astrology, among other specialized religious practices, thus requires explanation. Ripat's thesis is that the measures in question pertained not to any and all astrologers indiscriminately but to select populations of actors within "astrology," a general and fluid area of expertise that might compromise any number of methods and figures with a notional relationship to it.[18] In other words, an expulsion might affect certain astrologers, but not the likes of Thrasyllus or Balbillus, who would have been spared due to their intellectual pedigrees, their status at court, or the status of their patrons.[19] The lack of specificity in many sources for

---

15. E.g., Suetonius, *Tib.* 36.1, 63; Cassius Dio, 56.25.5, 57.15.8. The fervor of his efforts was not lost on later historians; the *Chronicle of the Year* 354 notes the unprecedented number of executions of *venenarii* and *malefici* ordered by Tiberius, forty-five men and eighty-five women (*Chron. ann. ccliv MGH IX*, 145). Although *venenum* and *venenarius* are not always a matter of religious practice—sometimes these words connote poisons or potions and those who produced them—Rives argues that by the first century BCE this word group had come to signify more generally any prayer or ritual that consigned some person or thing to the gods of the underworld for destruction. See Rives, "Magic, Religion, and Law," esp. 56–57. For further discussion of this legislation, see Dickie, *Magic and Magicians in the Greco-Roman World*, 154; Rives, "Magic, Religion, and Law," 62–63; Ripat, "Astrologers at Rome," 136–37 n. 121.

16. Suetonius, *Aug.* 31.1; Tacitus, *Ann.* 6.12; Cassius Dio, 57.18.3–4; cf. Cassius Dio, 57.18.5a.

17. Cassius Dio, 56.25.5; Suetonius, *Tib.* 63.

18. Ripat's term for those affected by expulsions is "street astrologers," which signals their distance from astrologers who enjoyed some informal standard of accreditation. Her main criteria for disentangling street astrologers from their courtly counterparts are that they peddled derivative or crude offerings, a less intellectually rigorous version of the sort of astrology found at court, and also that they did so for money ("Astrologers at Rome," 123–24). In my view, such distinctions depend too uncritically on the biased perspectives comprising most of the ancient sources. Ripat is right, however, to isolate a specific target within the assortment of divinatory techniques, ethnic designations, schools of instruction, and ideological programs gathered under the rubric astrology.

19. Ripat, "Astrologers at Rome," 120–23. Dio supplies a telling illustration of this principle: "Tiberius . . . was forever in the company of Thrasyllus and made use of the art of divination every day, becoming so proficient in the subject himself that when was once bidden in

this legislation—that is, that their authors rarely dissect "astrologers" to reflect such status distinctions or narrower subsets of practitioners within the diffuse and nebulous entity "astrology"—does not weaken Ripat's arguments. To the contrary, the untroubled imprecision of ancient authors may be revealing in and of itself. If all of these measures were ultimately employed to address the phenomenon of freelance expertise, it might have mattered less what type of figure had created a pretext for action than that self-authorized specialists posed a general regulatory problem that was counteracted time and again by the same tactics. Even when the language of a decree, edict, or *senatus consultum* is more exact, in light of the robust character of many specialized offerings there is reason to suspect that its scope had a broader intent. Freelance experts were slippery targets in antiquity for the same reasons that they evade neat classification in contemporary scholarship.[20] This raises the possibility that concerns about these actors might be inferred in certain cases where they are not mentioned explicitly, especially ones that feature practices, social formations, and artifacts common to their activities.

A multiply attested incident said to have occurred in 19 CE underscores this point. The three authors who report it—Tacitus, Suetonius, and Josephus—variously cite foreign rites or ceremonies, Egyptian priests and Judean wisdom instructors, astrologers, and freedpersons as the catalyst for an expulsion that affected a combination of people involved in such things.[21] Although all three agree about certain elements of the story, each writer has his own take on the particulars. Tacitus begins with

---

a dream to give money to a certain man, he realized that a *daimōn* had been called up before him by deceit, and so put the man to death. *But as for all the other astrologers and goētes and such as practiced divination in any other way whatsoever,* he put to death those who were foreigners and banished all the citizens who were accused of still employing the art at this time after the previous decree by which it had been forbidden to engage in any such business in the city; but to those that obeyed immunity was granted" (57.15.7; trans. Earnest Cary, LCL, emphasis added). On occasion a foreign expert active at court might receive Roman citizenship and other honors. Flavius Josephus enjoyed such privileges, as did the Julio-Claudian court astrologers Thrasyllus and his successor (and possibly son) Balbillus.

20. See MacMullen, *Enemies of the Roman Order*, 129; Ripat, "Astrologers at Rome," 132. As Ripat remarks, for Roman magistrates and others tasked with enforcing legislation, getting a handle on the specialist phenomenon must have been "equivalent to an attempt to scoop water from a bucket with a slotted spoon" (140).

21. Tacitus, *Ann.* 2.85; Suetonius, *Tib.* 36; Josephus, *AJ* 18.81–84. For a more sustained treatment of legislation against Judeans, see Heidi Wendt, "*Iudaica Romana*: A Rereading of Judean Expulsions from Rome," *JAJ* 6 (2015): 97–127.

a senatorial debate concerning Egyptian and Judean religious practices (*de sacris Aegyptiis Iudaicisque*), the outcome of which was that four thousand men of freed status (*libertini generis*) were dispatched to Sardinia for military service while others were instructed to leave Italy unless they gave up their unsanctioned activities (*profanus ritus*).[22] It is unclear whether the people affected were Egyptians and Judeans or whether their activities were merely construed as such. Suetonius is alone in including *mathematici* in the expulsion, with the exception of ones Tiberius pardoned in exchange for a promise to abandon their practices. He also mentions a confiscation and destruction of religious *instrumentum*, a Latin term that encompassed a range of portable objects, including texts. In keeping with his broader literary agenda, Josephus's primary interest is the plight and exoneration of those Judeans caught up in the affair, barring the four deserving of blame.[23] In his account, the emperor ordered an expulsion of "Rome's Judaic population" (πᾶν τὸ Ἰουδαϊκον τῆς Ῥώμης) in response to acts of deception perpetrated by the priests of an Isis temple, who facilitated the seduction of one Roman noblewoman, and by a disreputable Judean and his accomplices, who posed as experts in Mosaic law instruction in order to swindle another.[24]

Although these differing narratives are not without historiographic problems, they take for granted a link between the activities of freelance religious experts—Judean wisdom instructors, certain Egyptian priests, and *mathematici*—religious practices that were coded Egyptian and Judean, as well as astrology, and any participants in such *superstitiones*, especially freedpersons. Similar overlap appears in the account of the Bacchanalia affair, which, notably, Livy pins on the itinerant Greek "sacrificer and seer"

---

22. Rives has shown that *profanus ritus* was a technical term for something consecrated privately, as opposed to through an official public ritual, hence my language of "unauthorized" in this specific context, which captures a civic perspective on the matter at hand: "The Control of the Sacred in Roman Law," in *Law and Religion in the Roman Republic*, ed. Olga Tellegen-Couperus, Mnemosyne Supplements 336 (Leiden: Brill, 2011), 165–80. As Rives explains, "[Res] sacrae were things that had undergone the specific ritual of consecration, carried out on public authority. In normal circumstances, only a Roman magistrate acting under the guidance of a *pontifex* could perform a consecration. . . . As our sources indicate, the *pontifices* were the ones who both defined the term *sacer* as meaning 'consecrated by a particular ritual' and controlled the knowledge necessary to perform that ritual" (169–70).

23. Although, as per usual, he wastes no opportunity to point a recriminatory finger at Egyptians.

24. For the implications of the Greek phrase, see Wendt, "A Rereading of Judean Expulsions from Rome," 112–13.

(*sacrificulus et vates*) who first introduced these rites to Italy before they began to propagate independently.[25] The *graecus* recedes from his commentary on Bacchic fervor at Rome, but the consular speech that concludes the investigation of the cult invokes a series of rejoinders to what are, presumably, apposite religious actors and phenomena: prohibitions against foreign *sacra* (*sacra externa fieri vetarent*) introduced to Rome without the Senate's approval; bans of sacrificers and seers from the forum, the circus, and the city limits (*sacrificulos vatesque foro circo urbe prohiberent*); searching out and burning prophetic books (*vaticinos libros conquirerent comburerentque*); and abolishing every manner of sacrifice except the customary Roman one (*omnem disciplinam sacrificandi praeterquam more Romano abolerent iudicabant*).[26] Livy does not tether each of these items explicitly to the phenomenon of freelance expertise, but what he leaves unsaid is revealing. His description of the *graecus* as a *sacrificulus et vates*, taken with the subsequent reiteration of this formula in a list of actions resonant of specialist activity, forms a cautionary *inclusio* about freelance experts and the problems that follow in their wake.[27]

---

25. Livy, 39.8.3–5: *Graecus ignobilis in Etruriam primum venit nulla cum arte earum, quas multas ad animorum corporumque cultum nobis eruditissima omnium gens, invexit sacrificulus et vates; nec is qui aperta religion, propalam et quaestum et disciplinam profitendo, animos errore imbueret, sed occultorum et nocturnorum antistes sacrorum.* The historian belabors the point that, unlike other foreign religious experts whose rites, if novel, were at least transparent, the *graecus* professed openly neither his occupation nor his teachings. The profile betrays his disdain for the enterprising (*quaestus*) and multifaceted expertise of the *graecus*, who is not only the overseer of occult initiations but also a *sacrificulus et vates* to round things out.

26. Livy, 39.16.8–9.

27. It is also possible, if not likely, that authors writing about earlier religious legislation interpreted these events in part through the lens of a contemporary climate rife with punitive incidents involving freelance experts. Debra L. Nousek has made a similar argument regarding a carefully constructed relationship between Livy's narrative of the Bacchanalian investigation and Cicero's of the more recent Catilinarian conspiracy: "Echoes of Cicero in Livy's Bacchanalian Narrative (39.8–19)," *CQ* 60 (2010): 156–66. Just as Livy, Valerius Maximus (1.3.3) narrates an expulsion of Chaldeans and Judeans from republican history (139 BCE) in terms consistent with what he would have observed firsthand in early imperial Rome, especially in the time of Tiberius, whose documented agitations against these categories of actors, along with certain practitioners of Egyptian religion, we have seen. Moreover, the concatenation of Chaldeans and Judeans as culprits in this case—the former for casting false horoscopes, among other ploys, and the latter for trying to introduce their *sacra* to Romans—supplies further fodder for taking "Judeans" in this and similar episodes to mean freelance experts in Judean religion. See Wendt, "A Rereading of Judean Expulsions from Rome," 106–9. The historical exactitude of such accounts matters less for our purposes than that their authors cast freelance experts as the most plausible epicenters for the introduction and spread of foreign or otherwise novel religious practices. For other dimensions of the

Two other matters of note occur in Livy's account. The first is his reference to the confiscation and destruction of prophetic writings, a fairly regular event at Rome judging from the consul's opening remark—"How . . .
often has the task been assigned to the magistrates of . . . searching out
and burning books of prophecies"—and the aforementioned events under
Augustus and Tiberius.[28] While freelance experts are not incriminated unequivocally on these occasions, there is good reason to think that they were
the primary producers and interpreters of such materials for the benefit of
private audiences. Indeed, in the pages that follow we find many figures,
representing different perspectives, who enlisted oracular writings, including Judean texts, to legitimate their own authority as well as other elements of their religious programs.[29] Elsewhere I have proposed that Judean
oracles—that is, the texts that would come to comprise the Hebrew Bible,
as well as non-canonical literature that was granted authoritative status by
particular audiences—may have been among "whatever writings of Greek
or Latin origin were in circulation anonymously or under the names of
authors of little repute" whose possession Augustus outlawed and which
ban Tiberius reinforced.[30] From Justin Martyr's claim that "death had been
decreed for any who read the books of Hystaspes, the Sibyl, or the [Judean]
prophets," it would appear that by the mid-second century some, if not all,

---

Bacchanalia affair, see R. A. Bauman, "The Suppression of the Bacchanals: Five Questions,"
Historia 39 (1990): 334–48; Sarolta A. Takács, "Politics and Religion in the Bacchanalia Affair
of 186 B.C.E." *HSCP* 100 (2000): 301–10.

28. Livy, 13.16.8.1–2.

29. One need look no further than the story of Alexander, who concocted a Sibylline-style
oracle to presage his initial claim to religious authority and another each time he developed
a new facet of his religion business (Lucian, *Alex.* 11). In the same spirit, Lucian speculates
that news of Peregrinus's death will be met with reports of cures and dream appearances,
oracles, priests, and nocturnal mysteries; after all, he reports, his most devoted disciple,
Theagenes, has already been quoting the Sibyl concerning him (*Peregr.* 28). Tongue-in-cheek
though these details may be, the practice to which they point is consistent with how Paul appeals to Judean writings, which he characterizes repeatedly as oracles from God that require
specialized interpretation. These texts are multipurpose in his religious program: they legitimate his authority; they disclose clues about Christ's mythic and eschatological significance;
and they supply ancient models (τύποι) for the practices he advocates, among other purposes. For this use of writings by specialists, see Mary Beard, "Writing and Religion: Ancient
Literacy and the Function of the Written Word in Roman Religion," in *Literacy in the Roman
World,* ed. Mary Beard, Alan K. Bowman, and Mireille Corbier, JRA Suppl. 3 (Ann Arbor,
MI: Journal of Roman Archaeology, 1991), 35–58.

30. Heidi Wendt, "'Entrusted with the Oracles of God': The Fate of the Judean Writings in
Flavian Rome," in *A Most Reliable Witness: Essays in Honor of Ross Shepard Kraemer,* ed. Susan

of these texts did indeed fall within the scope of legislation against oracular corpora, as they may have on previous occasions.[31]

The apparent need to renew similar measures, often within short spans of time, points to a growing frustration on the part of Roman magistrates about how to effectively regulate this class of religious activity, exacerbated by the ineffectiveness and paradoxical outcomes of prior actions. Prophetic writings are not the only matter for which we might posit a dialectic relationship between regulation and resurgence. Egyptian religion held a complicated status at Rome from the middle of the first century BCE through the reign of Augustus. In 28 BCE and while still Octavian, he banned Egyptian rites from inside the *pomerium*, an injunction that Agrippa extended a mile beyond the *pomerium* only seven years later.[32] These efforts were preceded by a Senate initiative in 58 BCE to remove existing altars for the Egyptian gods from the Capitol and to ban new ones from being built. According to Varro, the altars were restored shortly thereafter in response to popular disapproval of their removal.[33] Dio neglects to mention this incident but notes two subsequent attempts by the Senate (in 53) and the *haruspices* (in 48) to destroy "private" Egyptian religious spaces.[34] Even as the Senate voted repeatedly to decommission popular altars for the Egyptian gods and shrines built at private expense, however, the members of the second triumvirate allegedly decided in 43 BCE to build a temple at Rome in honor of Isis and Sarapis.[35] Moreover, as Eric M. Orlin

---

Ashbrook Harvey et al., Brown Judaic Studies 358 (Atlanta: Society of Biblical Literature, 2015), 101–9.

31. Justin, *1 Apol.* 44.12.

32. Cassius Dio, 54.6. For discussion of the evidence for the proscription of Egyptian practice, see Sarolta A. Takács, *Isis and Sarapis in the Roman World*, RGRW 124 (Leiden: Brill, 1995), esp. 65–78; Eric M. Orlin, "Octavian and Egyptian Cults: Redrawing the Boundaries of Romanness," *AJP* 129 (2008): 231–53, esp. 235–37; idem, "Foreign Cults in Republican Rome: Rethinking the Pomerial Rule," *MAAR* 47 (2002): 1–18, esp. 6–7.

33. Apud Tertullian, *Ad. Nat.* 1.10.

34. Cassius Dio, 40.47, 23.26.1; Orlin, "Octavian and Egyptian Cults," 237 and n. 11. While Orlin concludes that our sources "provide no hints for the motivations of these actions," I wonder whether considering them within a broader pattern of actions directed at specialist activity would enrich our understanding of why they might have been issued. Indeed, Takács views the aim of such measures as the restriction of *sacra* to temples in order to enforce a greater degree of control over them, which underscores the possibility that it is precisely those forms of Egyptian religion not linked with temple institutions that were seen to be problematic on these occasions (*Isis and Sarapis in the Roman World*, 77).

35. Cassius Dio, 47.16.

observes, "At the same time as he prohibited Egyptian rites within the *pomerium*, Augustus made provisions for their shrines; Dio (53.2.4) reports that 'those which had been built by private individuals he ordered their sons and descendants, if any survived, to repair, and the rest he restored himself.' . . . So long as worship of Isis and Sarapis was restricted to certain locations, Octavian not only allowed worship of these divinities, he also took positive action to support them."[36]

These undulations shed light on some of the regulatory challenges that private religious activity might pose. While many have seen these frenetic responses to *aegyptiaca* as symptomatic of Rome's complicated political relations with Egypt, one wonders whether Ripat's argument applies to the fluctuating status of Egyptian religion at the capital. In other words, might some of these incidents have stemmed from concerns not about Egyptian religion per se but about the sort of itinerant priests and Isis diviners (*Isiaci coniectores*) that we learn of from various sources?[37] Juvenal dwells at length on one such figure, an impersonator of Anubis who, going door-to-door with his linen-clad and shaven crew, persuades Roman women they have offended Osiris unwittingly by violating impurity laws on days that should be kept holy. He will intercede on their behalf to secure the god's pardon, but only at a cost.[38]

Justin's earlier remark draws attention to another trend and regulatory challenge in the evidence for these measures: punishments meted out against freelance experts were being issued more frequently and with harsher penalties within our window. While some experts might be exempt from suspicions that attended the wider class, others were not only vulnerable but might even, and somewhat counterintuitively, solicit stricture to their own benefit, as proof of their sincerity, disinterest, or the efficacy of their skills.[39] The favorable stakes of public stricture and exile are unmistakable in Lucian's chagrined observation that Peregrinus's reputation only grew when Rome's urban prefect expelled him for his frank speech and excessive freedom (διὰ τὴν παρρησίαν καὶ τὴν ἄγαν ἐλευθερίαν), earning him a place in the ranks of Musonius Rufus, Dio Chrysostom, and Epictetus,

---

36. Orlin, "Octavian and Egyptian Cults," 235–36.

37. E.g., Cicero, *Div.* 1.132.6.

38. Juvenal, *Sat.* 6.532–41.

39. Ripat, "Astrologers at Rome," 138–41.

among other philosophers censured for the same virtues.⁴⁰ Likewise, Juvenal quips that the most famous astrologer is he who has most often been in exile, who breeds trust in his skills if a handcuff encircles his wrist, for no one is credited with talent who has not been condemned.⁴¹ Later I argue that Paul and early Christian writers were aware of the advantages that punishments carried in this context and skillfully deployed the rhetoric of suffering—their own, that of Christ, and that of fellow assemblies in Christ or individual Christians—to their own competitive advantage.⁴²

To the legislation already mentioned could be added several other examples from the imperial period. Expulsions alone were issued with greatest concentration from 33 BCE to 93 CE, and, inasmuch as most targeted particular subsets of freelance experts, it would appear from the uptick that their activities were garnering increasing attention. Confirmation that the assortment of legislation mentioned earlier stemmed from an underlying concern about these religious actors occurs in the third-century juridical writings of Ulpian and Julius Paulus, who collate individual items into sweeping indictments of any and all practices associated with specialists.

Consider the following exposition of the *lex Cornelia de sicariis et veneficiis* from Paulus's *Opinions*, which contains sections of legislation that enumerate punishments for the following culprits: those who have performed, or arranged for the performance of, impious or nocturnal rites (*sacra impia nocturnave*) in order to enchant (*obcantarent*), transfix (*defigerent*), or bind (*obligarent*) someone; those who have sacrificed a man, have obtained omens from his blood (*hominem immolaverint exve eius sanguine litaverint*), or have polluted a shrine or a temple (*fanum templumve polluerint*); those guilty of the magic art (*magicae artis conscios*), who, judging from the different punishments prescribed for each, are different from actual *magi;* and those who have in their possession books of the magic art (*libri artis magicae*), which, if found, are to be confiscated and burned publicly.⁴³ In an earlier section the code recommends expulsion

---

40. Lucian, *Peregr.* 18. Exiled philosophers were often quite explicit about the advantages of banishment; some writers—e.g., Musonius Rufus, Favorinus, Plutarch—devoted entire treatises to its virtues.

41. Juvenal, *Sat.* 6.550–64; Ripat, "Astrologers at Rome," 141.

42. As I argue in "*Ea Superstitione:* Christian Martyrdom and the Religion of Freelance Experts," *JRS* 105 (2015): 183–202 and to some extent in chapter 4.

43. Paulus, *Sent.* 5.23.15–18; cf. Acts 19:18. See also Suetonius, *Tib.* 36 for the confiscation and burning of *instrumentum*, in this case Egyptian items, which could include texts.

for prophets (*vaticinatores*) who pretend that they are filled with a god (*qui se deo plenos adsimulant*), though not before they have been beaten with rods; if they persist, they are to be thrown into public prison or deported to an island.[44] Those who introduce religious practices that are new and unknown either in use or reason (*novas et usu vel ratione incognitas religiones inducunt*) are to be deported or put to death, depending on their civil status.[45] Moreover, anyone who consults *mathematici, harioli, haruspices*, or *vaticinatores* about the health of the emperor or matters of the state shall receive a capital sentence, along with the one who gives the response.[46] It is better for one to abstain not only from divination (*divinatio*) but also from the entire body of knowledge (*ipsa scientia*), including any associated books.[47]

Paulus provides a neat summary of strategies used to counteract every conceivable manifestation of freelance expertise and, in specifying each penalty, sketches a fairly comprehensive picture of what these activities might entail. As Rives notes, the passage provides excellent evidence for the use of legislation to police religious behavior, for the gradual and complex construction of a legal category of "religious deviance." In particular, he suggests that the practices it condemns are not carefully defined and were perhaps even incapable of more exact definition, leaving considerable room for negotiating the application of punishments on an almost case-by-case basis.[48] Although I largely agree with Rives's assessment, I would reframe the underlying matter as having to do not with religious deviance but with the activities of freelance religious experts, who are here treated as a united category of actors and practices irrespective of their myriad skills, teachings, and other offerings.[49]

---

44. Paulus, *Sent.* 5.21.1; cf. 2 Cor 11:25, Acts 16:22–23.

45. Paulus, *Sent.* 5.21.2.

46. Paulus, *Sent.* 5.21.3.

47. Paulus, *Sent.* 5.21.4; cf. Didache 3.4. For these much discussed precepts, see Smith, *Jesus the Magician*, 76; Francis, *Subversive Virtue*, 91; MacMullen, *Enemies of the Roman Order*, 125, 130; Rives, "Magic, Religion, and Law," 47–49, 64–67.

48. Rives, "Magic, Religion, and Law," 47–48.

49. Rives, "Magic, Religion, and Law," 67.

Challenges and Concerns Posed by Freelance Experts

As to the question of why freelance experts provoked these legislative responses, the sources furnish some insight into what might motivate Roman magistrates to take a stand against them. Astrologers, *magi*, and other diviners attracted negative attention on occasion by casting imperial horoscopes for contenders to the throne or by prognosticating about the affairs of powerful people.[50] The treasonous ambitions of Libo Drusus were allegedly stoked by Chaldeans, *magi*, and dream interpreters, while Furius Scribonianus was exiled for consulting astrologers about the demise of Claudius.[51] Women were not immune from this sort of intrigue: Munatia Plancina and Aemilia Lepida were each prosecuted in 20 CE for dealings with the Syrian woman Martina, infamous for her skill at poisoning (*infamis veneficiis*), and for adultery, poisoning, and posing inquiries to Chaldeans, respectively.[52] Lollia Paulina, Caligula's third wife, was tried for consulting the Clarian oracle of Apollo, Chaldeans, and *magi* about the marriage prospects of his successor Claudius, while Claudius's eventual wife (and niece), Agrippina Minor, kept the poisoner Locusta in her long-term employ and allegedly enlisted her services against both the emperor and his son, Britannicus.[53] Describing how astrologers "declared from their observation of the stars . . . that the year would be a glorious one for Otho," Tacitus adds as an aside that they are the worst possible tools for an imperial consort, namely, Nero's mistress Poppaea Sabina, who plotted secretly with Ptolemy Seleucus to become his wife even as the same

---

50. As evident in Tacitus's characterization of astrologers as "a tribe of men (*genus hominum*) untrustworthy for the powerful and deceitful towards the ambitious, a tribe that in our state will always be forbidden and retained" (*Hist.* 1.22 [trans. Clifford H. Moore, LCL]). The latter remark underscores further the futility of legislation against such figures.

51. Tacitus, *Ann.* 2.27.5–7; 12.52.

52. Tacitus, *Ann.* 2.74; 3.22–23. For these and similar incidents involving aristocratic Roman women, see Elizabeth Ann Pollard, "Magic Accusations Against Women in Tacitus's *Annals*," in *Daughters of Hekate: Women and Magic in the Ancient World*, ed. Kimberly B. Stratton and Dayna S. Kalleres (New York: Oxford University Press, 2014), 183–218, at 187–93. See also Anthony J. Marshall, "Women on Trial Before the Roman Senate," *EchCl* 34 (1990): 333–66.

53. Tacitus, *Ann.* 12.22.1–5; 12.66; 13.15. Locusta, who also supplied Nero with the poison that he intended to take while fleeing assassination, was put to death by Galba (Suetonius, *Ner.* 47; Cassius Dio, 64.3). See Pollard, "Magic Accusations Against Women in Tacitus's *Annals*," 197–99.

astrologer promised her lover's rival that he would become emperor.[54] Nor were specialists acting in this capacity always exotic. Josephus writes of Pharisees alleging to possess divine foreknowledge who incurred favor with Salome and Pheroras at Herod's court after guaranteeing their political future.[55]

In view of the fact that freelance experts—or, in the case of the Pharisees, other kinds of religious specialists acting in a similar capacity—were regularly sought to forecast or authenticate such ambitions, it is unsurprising that they pervade accounts of tumultuous events such as the Social and Judean Wars or the Year of Four Emperors.[56] Sometimes the political climate was such that specialists issued politically weighty pronouncements with no obvious benefit for any individual but were instead directed against the person presently in power. This was the case for Larginus Proculus, a Germanic seer said to have forecasted the demises of both Caligula and Domitian; Sulla, an astrologer who informed Caligula of his impending death; Ascletarion, an astrologer tried before Domitian for making predictions about his life; and Apollonius of Tyana, who uttered detailed prophecies about the unstable political and military events of 69.[57] It was on

---

54. Tacitus, *Hist.* 1.22. Another woman, Marcia Servilia, was accused around the same time (66 CE) of consulting astrologers on her father's behalf and paying *magi* to conduct *magicos sacros* to determine the safety of her family and the outcome of her father's trial (Tacitus, *Ann.* 16.30–3; Cassius Dio, 62.26.3). Although these stories are not without misogynistic overtones, as Pollard writes, "Focusing on topoi and describing women such as Plancina, Agrippina, Pulchra, et al., as 'characters' and 'personae' . . . denies these real women the agency and actions that inspired the historical accusations in the first place. Tacitus's rhetorical fashioning certainly influences what he emphasizes and even why the topos was profoundly effective, but his rhetoric does not explain what these agents did (or were thought by their contemporaries to have done), nor does it explain the historical circumstances within which the accusations balanced the complex, competitive nexus of the Roman aristocracy" ("Magic Accusations Against Women in Tacitus's *Annals*," 187).

55. Josephus, *AJ* 17.41–43. See Wendt, "A Rereading of Judean Expulsions from Rome," 113; Steve Mason, "Pharisees in the Narratives of Josephus," in *Josephus, Judea, and Christian Origins: Methods and Categories* (Peabody, MA: Hendrickson, 2009), 185–215. Even though experts were commonly linked with the treasonous ambitions of certain Roman elites, Ripat notes that not one of the eight well-attested mass expulsions of astrologers can be definitively tied to such activities ("Astrologers at Rome," 117–18). Her observation subtly rounds out our picture of the uneasiness of members of the Roman ruling class about freelance experts.

56. Cf. MacMullan, *Enemies of the Roman Order*, 133.

57. Cassius Dio, 59.29.4, 67.16.2; Suetonius, *Calig.* 57.2; Suetonius, *Dom.* 15.3, cf. Cassius Dio, 67.16.3; Philostratus, *Vit. Apoll.* 5.13, 8.26. See also Cicero, *Div.* 1.47.3, cf. 2.52.7 for Callanus of India foretelling the imminent death of Alexander the Great from atop his own funeral pyre.

charges of conspiring against him with Nerva and his friends, however, that Domitian brought Apollonius, too, to trial.[58]

All of these examples point to a wider phenomenon of Romans experimenting with novel, typically foreign religious offerings that is not identical with the effects of freelance experts but was undoubtedly furthered by their activities. It is within this general climate that I am inclined to locate Seneca's recollection of a time early in Tiberius's reign when *alienigena sacra* were suppressed and abstention from the flesh of certain animals became a point of debate, among other arguments against *superstitio*.[59] Moreover, it is reasonable to surmise from close *comparanda* that Pomponia Graecina, a woman arraigned on the generic charge of *superstitio*, might have been involved with freelance experts.[60]

At the extreme end of the spectrum are incidents whereupon self-authorized religious figures galvanized rebellions against Rome, in many cases, with devastating consequences. The republic witnessed slave revolts in close succession that were led by two such experts, an inspired prophet of the Dea Syria and a diviner.[61] Several other uprisings occurred with imperial expansion: in Thrace, Vologaeus, a Bessian priest of Dionysos, won a band of followers by "performing deeds under divine inspiration" that he incited against the local ruler allied with Augustus; in Gaul, the seer Veleda, spurred a revolt in the late 60s CE after foreseeing the demise of Roman troops; in Judea and its environs, various prophets instigated disturbances with claims of divine inspiration and certain wise men provoked the rebels whom Josephus blames for the Judean War with favorable interpretations of oracles in their holy writings.[62]

---

58. Philostratus, *Vit. Apoll.* 8.4.

59. Seneca, *Ep. Mor.* 108.22.

60. Tacitus, *Ann.* 13.32. See Margaret H. Williams, who evaluates the affair in order to decide whether it was an instance of Jewish proselytism; "The Expulsion of the Jews from Rome in A.D. 19," *Latomus* 48 (1989): 765–84, esp. 771; cf. Wendt, "A Rereading of Judean Expulsions from Rome," 117.

61. Most famously, a prophet of Dea Syria named Eunus prophesied an imminent inversion of the social order and commanded a force of seventy thousand slaves, whom he called his Syrians, against Rome in 135 BCE. A generation later a second revolt was led by Salvius, a man skilled in divination (Florus, 2.7.4–12; Diodorus Siculus, 34.2.5–9, 36.1–11). See Keith R. Bradley, *Slavery and Rebellion in the Roman World, 140 B.C.–70 B.C.* (Bloomington: Indiana University Press, 1989), 46–82.

62. Cassius Dio, 54.34.5–7; Tacitus, *Hist.* 4.61–65; Josephus, e.g., *BJ* 2.253–65, 2.271, 6.285–87, 6.310–13. See Rives, *Religion in the Roman Empire*, 188; Steve Mason, *Josephus and the New*

The potential and sometimes very real power of freelance experts—whether they lent credence to someone else's ambitions or became figureheads themselves—challenges purely symbolic or social-functionalist explanations of this evidence, for instance, that the threat they posed was ultimately a matter of Roman identity or values.[63] Rather the sheer frequency of measures undertaken to get a handle on the influence and reverberations of their activities suggests that they were causing real headaches—bureaucratic, political, and military—for Roman magistrates and presumably also, if not more so, for the lower-level officials responsible for policing them on the ground.[64]

At the same time, one should be cautious about overstating how great and persistent a threat these actors actually posed. The more salacious accusations that informants made about worshippers of Bacchus often overshadow the less titillating reports of them giving false testimony and forging wills and other private documents (*falsi testes, falsa signa testamentaque et indicia ex eadem officinal exibant*)—more of a bureaucratic nightmare than lèse-majesté.[65] Nor was the problem with these actors always a matter of subversive or disquieting behavior. As many have noted, Marcus Agrippa expelled *magi* and astrologers from Rome in 33 BCE as part of a city improvement initiative that also involved sewer cleaning, public building and street repair, and the provision of hygiene services, among other efforts.[66] In this case, the issue seems to be that specialists were simply undesirable, a public nuisance, even as the perspectives of social elites such as Agrippa or Suetonius surely differed from those of the people who relied on their services as a regular feature of their religious behavior.

Testament, 2nd ed. (Peabody, MA: Hendrickson, 2003), 79–80, 170–72. For further discussion of freelance experts in Judean uprisings, see chapter 2.

63. E.g., Erich S. Gruen, *Diaspora: Jews amidst Greeks and Romans* (Cambridge: Harvard University Press, 2002), 52; Beard, North, and Price, *Religions of Rome*, Vol. 1, 211–44. For the limits of the symbolic reading, see David Noy, *Foreigners at Rome: Citizens and Strangers* (London: Duckworth, 2000), 52; Wendt, "A Rereading of Judean Expulsions from Rome," 103–4.

64. For policing methods in Rome and throughout the empire, with occasional discussion of episodes involving freelance experts, see Christopher J. Fuhrmann, *Policing the Roman Empire* (New York: Oxford University Press, 2012), esp. 58–61, 140–45. Fuhrmann usefully draws attention to the lack of systematicity in policing methods, but also notes that particular cities or provinces were policed more rigorously than others (e.g., Rome and Egypt).

65. Livy, 39.8.7.3–4.

66. Cassius Dio, 49.43.1–5; cf. Ripat, "Astrologers at Rome," 117.

There also appear to have been considerable constraints on implementing legislation against these figures. Suetonius, for instance, explains that Vitellius became especially ill-disposed toward astrologers after issuing a proclamation that banned them from the city before the Kalends of October, in response to which they posted a placard assuring the public that the emperor would no longer be alive by that date.[67] In this and presumably other cases, an expulsion or proscription was more of a warning shot fired across the bow than a policy to be implemented aggressively and systematically. Indeed, an inchoate category of actors might be elucidated only through self-incrimination or the testimony of interested parties. Livy notes a reward posted by the Senate to solicit informants on Bacchic activities, an obvious incentive for informing on a matter already under investigation, while Pliny famously complains that the charge against Christians has rippled outward and more examples have appeared, "as usually happens," whenever a matter is being scrutinized.[68] Moreover, Trajan's exclusion of incriminating evidence of undisclosed authorship— namely, a publicly published but unsigned *libellus* identifying those listed as Christians—echoes a precedent set by Nerva, who outlawed anonymous accusations of *maiestas* or against any leading the Judaic life (οὔτ' Ἰουδαϊκοῦ βίου καταιτιᾶσθαί τινας συνεχώρησε) to counteract the climate of suspicion that he had inherited from Domitian.[69]

What the combined details of these sources suggest is that Roman religious legislation was often ineffective and at least partially dependent for its enforcement on some degree of voluntary participation and public cooperation. Furthermore, while it might appear from our sources that magistrates had a panoptic view of what was happening in the city and took action against specialists by their own initiative, other perspectives on the investigation and punishment of these actors indicate that complaints about them often came from the ground up. I return to this point later on, in relation to Paul's complaint about "false brothers" (ψευδαδέλφοι) brought in to spy on the apostles and Justin's prediction that Crescens, a man unworthy to be called a philosopher in his estimation, will offer

---

67. Suetonius, *Vit.* 14.4–5.

68. Livy, 39.14.6.3–4; Pliny, *Ep.* 10.96.4.2–5.1: *ut fieri solet, diffundente se crimine plures species incinderunt.*

69. Pliny, *Ep.* 10.96.5.1, 97.2; Cassius Dio, 68.1.2.

public testimony against Christians.[70] Even if magistrates did have a specific set of actors and practices in mind when they issued edicts targeting
specialist activity, because freelance experts overlapped with various social
formations and institutions in Rome's population, the ability of those in
power to determine the boundaries of the specialist phenomenon relative to other forms of religion was poor. The task of elucidating categories
under investigation was thus itself a competitive enterprise and one that
engendered opportunities for apologetic writers, entrepreneurial competitors, and informants alike.[71]

While one could easily overemphasize the seditious or otherwise dis-
ruptive potential of freelance experts to explain Roman responses to them,
the more general concern they raised seems to have been foremost regulatory in nature: they were at once highly influential but difficult to isolate
and contain, whatever circumstances had drawn attention to them. What
actions were taken to circumscribe their influence probably had less to
do with the neighborhood dream interpreter, who posed no measurable
threat to the current Roman social order, than with the handful of well-
positioned experts who might assert considerable power in situations of
instability. The mere possibility that freelance experts could pose this sort
of threat, however, makes sense of the general sensitivity about them and
the forceful, even disproportionate, reactions to their practices.

Whereas the tendency of most scholars has been to posit corporate
entities—cults, religious or ethnic communities, temples, religions, or religious systems—as the intended recipients of these measures, many of the
incidents in question seem to stem rather from concerns about individual
actors and self-authorized expertise. Some studies acknowledge structural
parallels between categories commonly affected by religious legislation,
but this sort of comparison stops short of seeing the artificial distinctions
being drawn by the categories themselves.[72] The result is that we fail to
see the forest for the trees: a fairly coherent pattern of actions—legislation
directed against freelance experts or practices and social formations that

---

70. Gal 2:4; Justin, 2 *Apol.* 8.1–2.

71. Such rivalries operated at different registers, so that literate experts might denounce
competitors in writing, while others might cast suspicion upon or inform against the activities of a competitor.

72. E.g., Leonard Victor Rutgers, "Roman Policy Toward the Jews: Expulsions from the City
of Rome During the First Century C.E.," *CA* 13 (1994): 56–75.

were highly suggestive of their activities—is overlooked in favor of narrow attention to its individual components.[73]

To the contrary, I propose that we investigate a relationship between recipients of common regulatory measures that is not specific to the content of their programs or services but acknowledges the features they shared from an administrative perspective in order that they were managed by the same means, often concomitantly. Although Ripat trains her sight on astrologers and astrology, the upshot of her argument can and should be extended to other actors and categories affected by the same kinds of measures, again, certain Egyptian priests and forms of religion, *magi* and "magic," and also, as I have argued elsewhere, some Judeans and forms of religion.[74] Equally paradoxical dispositions, or so it would seem, pertain to these entities too. Close ties between the Julio-Claudians and the Herodians, for instance, did not prevent Tiberius, Caligula, and Claudius from expelling or otherwise legislating against Judeans during their reigns. And yet Philo makes special note of how fairly Tiberius responded when certain accusations were made against Judeans at Rome, reassuring Judeans throughout the empire that the incident had not affected the city's entire Judean population, only the guilty few.[75]

With subtler parsing of aggregate scholarly categories such as Egyptian religion, Judaism, magic, and astrology, what may register at first as inconsistent attitudes toward undifferentiated entities comes into focus, at least in some instances, as a regular set of tactics employed more or less consistently against a common field of religious actors. I do not mean to imply that Roman administrators had exact procedures for authorizing religious actors and phenomena operating outside civic institutions. Yet for many experts we can observe an incidental pattern whereby some were spared stricture on occasions when others of their

---

73. See Wendt, "Christian Martyrdom and the Religion of Freelance Experts," 189.

74. To be clear, I am not making any assumptions about the actual provenances or self-identifications of these people, that is, whether they were Egyptian or Judean with respect to ancestry, origins, or locality. Rather, here and elsewhere I am interested in conceptions of foreignness that formed in relation to particular religious figures, paraphernalia, and rites, regardless of what relationship these ideas bore to the native contexts on which they were based.

75. Philo, *Leg.* 24.159–61. While it is unclear whether Philo is referring to the expulsion of 19, his remarks suggest at a minimum that such incidents did not alter the status of Judeans at Rome and that Roman authorities were capable of exercising discretion in their punishment of select individuals within this population.

kind were expelled or proscribed. With such a picture, one sees a contrast not between authorized/legitimate and unauthorized/illegitimate
actors or phenomena in any strict sense, but between different sources
of authority and legitimacy, skill and reputation, the status of patrons,
followers, or clientele, and perceptions about certain kinds of specialized offerings. Roman magistrates regularly, if in an ad hoc fashion,
took it upon themselves to determine the limits of religious activity in
certain respects, with the result that we can speak on a case-by-case basis
of something like legitimate and illegitimate religious actors, groups,
or activities, so long as these labels are understood to be relational and
in flux.

What is also clear is that the thickening presence of freelance experts
at Rome, and by extension throughout the empire, heightened competition for clients interested generally in the sort of cultural and religious
offerings they purveyed. This dynamic held important consequences
for the shape of specialist activity, since experts had incentives to devise
composite programs that catered to a range of enthusiasms and religious
interests. I say more about the contingencies that defined such tastes
momentarily. However, from a regulatory perspective the diversification
occurring among specialists, and specialists in religion especially, posed
tandem difficulties for identifying and managing them. Notwithstanding,
the consistency with which they *were* managed underscores deep analo-
gies in the activities and positions of specialists of all varieties. That is,
freelance experts were viewed as a coordinated set of actors, irrespective
of the content of their programs, teachings, and services or the ethnic
framing thereof.

The Expansion of Freelance Expertise Under the Empire

Thus far the focus of this chapter has been to demonstrate the expansion
of freelance expertise in the first century of the Roman Empire, principally
by examining a constellation of legislative measures issued, on my reading, in response to this class of religious activity. However, this evidence
offers only a partial and reactionary account of the popularity of specialists in foreign or otherwise novel religious offerings. I turn now to the
historical conditions that bolstered the credibility of these actors and also
heightened their appeal.

Several factors promoted the recognition and attraction of the religion of freelance experts in this time and place. As a consequence of those mentioned in the introduction—new sources of wealth and other resources, improved mobility, networks of trade and connectivity, new territorial and cultural horizons, and increasingly heterogeneous populations—cities throughout the empire began in the early imperial period to achieve a level of cosmopolitanism that had previously been found only in places such as Alexandria. Nowhere was this more pronounced than Rome, the refashioning of which as an imperial capital had a notable impact on characteristics ranging from the scale and grandeur of the urban environment to the volume and quality of its cultural resources.[76] Efforts to recast Rome as a city akin to Alexandria provided a stimulus to would-be cultural authorities of all stripes, especially ones skilled in intellectual practices.[77] An influx of teachers, philosophers, doctors, and other specialists occurred within our window and, though the reception of these figures was ambivalent at times, there were also specific impetus drawing them to the new capital.[78] Suetonius, to name one example, credits Caesar with conferring citizenship on "all who professed medicine at Rome, and on all teachers of the liberal arts, to make them more desirous of living in the city and to induce others to resort to it."[79]

---

76. The bibliography on the refashioning of Rome as a world city is vast. See, e.g., Whitmarsh, *Greek Literature in the Roman Empire*, 257; Catharine Edwards and Greg Woolf, eds., *Rome the Cosmopolis* (Cambridge: Cambridge University Press, 2003); Daniel S. Richter, *Cosmopolis: Imagining Community in Late Classical Athens and the Early Roman Empire* (New York: Oxford University Press, 2011). By "cultural resources" I have in mind the varieties of cultural producers that came to reside there, as well as rich art collections, public and private libraries, a thriving book industry, and, with the latter two items, a general swell in the production and consumption of writings during our period. See J. J. Pollitt, "The Impact of Greek Art on Rome," *TAPA* 108 (1978): 155–74; George W. Houston, "Tiberius and the Libraries: Public Book Collections and Buildings in the Early Roman Empire," *Libr Cult Rec* 43 (2008): 247–69; Harry Y. Gamble, "The Book Trade in the Roman Empire," in *The Early Text of the New Testament*, ed. Charles E. Hill and Michael J. Kruger (Oxford: Oxford University Press, 2012), 23–36; Jason König, Katerina Oikonomopoulou, and Greg Woolf, eds., *Ancient Libraries* (Cambridge: Cambridge University Press, 2013), esp. 279–417.

77. For the argument that Caesar, and then Augustus, consciously developed Rome with Alexandria in view, see Sarolta A. Takács, "Alexandria in Rome," *HSCP* 97 (1995): 263–76; Diana E. E. Kleiner, *Cleopatra and Rome* (Cambridge: Harvard University Press, 2005), 93–102.

78. Rawson notes mass migrations of intellectuals from Alexandria to Rome in the wake of Actium (*Intellectual Life in the Late Roman Republic*, 318).

79. Suetonius, *Jul.* 42.1.10–1 (trans. J. C. Rolfe, LCL).

As I mentioned earlier, Andrew Wallace-Hadrill has shown that the same period witnessed a gradual slackening of aristocratic control over religious knowledge and authority in favor of more reliance on the skilled counsel of freelance experts.[80] The dominance of senatorial elites during the republic had always coincided with and drawn legitimacy from their effective administration of such civic religious institutions as the major priestly colleges, civic temples, and the Roman calendar. This scheme of governance was naturalized and reinforced by the perceived will of the gods, but it had inherent elements of instability, not the least of which was competition among certain aristocrats who would attempt periodically to establish themselves autocratically. Because civic religion was set up precisely to support the interests of the aristocratic order as a whole rather than the interests of its individual members, it left a powerful niche for freelance experts to support singular political aspirations on the basis of alternative religious claims. They begin to occupy this role more and more frequently in the late republic, when they appear prominently alongside Gaius Gracchus, Marius, Sulla, and Julius Caesar, among others. A comparable impetus is evident in Caesar's reform of the Roman calendar, which had suffered, he claimed, such neglect that it was entirely out of sync.[81] To remedy that situation he wrested control over the calendar from the *pontifices,* entrusting its intercalation instead to leading philosophers and *mathematici,* most notably the Alexandrian astronomer Sosigenes.[82] Determining the divisions of Roman time was more than an archaic privilege: it was an expression of the power of the pontifical priesthood. As such, transposition of that responsibility signaled broader changes in the administration of religious life.[83]

---

80. Wallace-Hadrill is persuaded by the thesis that religion and control of priesthoods was as foundational to the social dominance of Roman nobility as patronage ("The Augustan Transformation of Roman Knowledge," 56–57). He expands these arguments in *Rome's Cultural Revolution,* esp. 213–314.

81. Wallace-Hadrill, "The Augustan Transformation of Roman Knowledge," 59. See also Dennis C. Feeney, *Caesar's Calendar: Ancient Time and the Beginnings of History* (Berkeley: University of California Press, 2007); Jörg Rüpke, *The Roman Calendar from Numa to Constantine: Time, History, and the Fasti,* trans. David M. B. Richardson (Malden, MA: Wiley-Blackwell, 2011), esp. 38–43, 109–39.

82. Pliny, *Nat.* 18.211; Plutarch, *Caes.* 59.5.

83. As Wallace-Hadrill explains, "The calendar defined when certain words could be spoken in public (*fasti*), when not (*nefasti*), when assemblies could be held (*comitiales*), and when by contrast the gods should be worshipped. It was the business of the *pontifices* to know when

Augustus, who undertook an ambitious program of cultural reform that purposefully relocated religious authority away from Rome's entrenched nobility, contributed further to the unraveling of aristocratic political dominance that had begun in the late republic.[84] The conservative aspects of his religious platform are well known and included the restoration of "traditional" institutions and selective suppressions of foreign cults.[85] Later writers credit the emperor with having resisted the "nontraditional" influences of foreign religion. In a famous speech that Dio attributes to Maecenas, the latter warns Augustus of any who would introduce foreign elements into Roman ancestral customs, *goētes*, some diviners, and experts in "magic."[86]

Despite this rhetoric of frugality in matters of religion, Augustus followed in his adoptive father's footsteps by enlisting the legitimation and services of freelance experts to his own advantage.[87] Suetonius takes care to delineate alien rites in which the emperor participated out of respect for their antiquity from the *superstitiones* he rightly avoided. Yet he has no qualms about the astrologer Theogenes—whom Octavian and Agrippa visited while in Apollonia—having predicted the young man's future reign.[88] Augustus would go on to publish his horoscope, made

Romans should act and how, to know the rhythms of life that would secure divine approval. Caesar's reform denied the *pontifices* that knowledge, and transferred the knowledge of the year to the rational calculations of the mathematician. ... Conversely, the use of 'professionals' to correct the calendar is a political use of the professional authority of experts who enjoyed widespread esteem to trounce the authority of the traditional priestly cast" ("The Augustan Transformation of Roman Knowledge," 59–60). There has been considerable scholarly debate about whether this rhetoric of deterioration reflects the actual state of civic institutions at this time or whether it was merely a convenient political platform. For our purposes it matters only that the perceived chaos of Roman religious institutions at the close of the republic set the stage for great transformations in the organization of civic religious authority.

84. Wallace-Hadrill, "The Augustan Transformation of Roman Knowledge," 58.

85. See Karl Galinsky, "Continuity and Change: Religion in the Augustan Semi-Century," in *A Companion to Roman Religion*, ed. Jörg Rüpke (Malden, MA: Blackwell, 2007), 71–82.

86. Cassius Dio, 52.36.2–4.

87. Notably, the reasons "Maecenas" provides echo some of the concerns raised in the preceding section: such men persuade people to adopt foreign practices, whence spring up conspiracies, factions, and cabals that are unprofitable to a monarchy. "Magicians," here distinguished from "authorized" diviners such as *augures*, generally speak falsehoods and often encourage revolution. So too do those who pretend to be philosophers.

88. Suetonius, *Aug.* 93, 94.12.

extensive use of his zodiac sign in imperial imagery, and even harbored an interest in physiognomy.[89]

In 9 BCE, Augustus employed another Alexandrian astronomer, Facundius, to recalculate the calendar to resolve confusion between a four- versus three-year leap cycle.[90] What the aristocratic priesthood lost in this case was a tremendous gain for the public persona of the freelance expert, whose credibility surely benefitted from the trust placed in Sosigenes and Facundius. Even when some of their more conspicuous dealings elicited negative reactions of the sort considered earlier, the power with which foreign specialists were credited on these occasions surely bolstered confidence in their abilities in equal measure to notoriety. Freelance experts might also prevail upon civic religion without solicitation. Dio recounts one such occasion in 7 CE, when Augustus was compelled to make a vow regarding the Megalensian games because "some woman had cut some letters on her arm and practiced some sort of divination." [91] The emperor knew, of course, that she was not truly possessed by any divine power but had done this thing deliberately. Nevertheless, Dio explains, since the populace was roiling over recent wars and famine, "he, too, affected to believe the common report and proceeded to do anything that would make the crowd cheerful, regarding such measures as necessary."

These examples reveal a strategic interest in the religion of freelance experts that only escalated with imperial successors and other social elites, many of whom were closely associated with such figures and even retained them in their permanent retinues.[92] In addition to Tiberius and Thrasyllus there is Nero, whose dealings with the mysterious man who gave him his protective statuette, as well as Persian *magi*, I have already mentioned. Nero's second wife, Poppaea Sabina, was also known to patronize exotic forms of

---

89. On the emperor's use of astrology in his imperial ideology, see Paul Zanker's classic work, *The Power of Images in the Age of Augustus* (Ann Arbor: University of Michigan Press, 1988).

90. Wallace-Hadrill, "The Augustan Transformation of Roman Knowledge," 59.

91. Cassius Dio, 55.31.2–3 (trans. Earnest Cary, LCL).

92. Personal religious consultants were not exclusive to the imperial period but had appeared beside Gaius Gracchus, Marius, Sulla, and Julius Caesar, *inter alios*. See Valerius Maximus, 1.2.3, 9.12; Frontinus, *Strat.* 1.11.12; Plutarch, *Mar.* 17; Plutarch *Sull.* 5; Suetonius, *Jul.* 81.2.

religion, though her interests gravitated toward Judea and the Jerusalem temple, along with astrology.[93] Vespasian hitched his own dynastic claims not only to astrology but also, and even more so, to signs interpreted by the priest Basilides at the Serapeion of Alexandria and the prophecies of Josephus, a captive Judean of priestly lineage.[94] Tacitus recalls further how, upon hearing that their general might become emperor, his men "surrounded Vespasian, encouraged him, and recalled the prophecies of seers and the movements of stars" (*responsa vates et siderum motus*).[95] Once in power he relied on the *mathematicus* Ptolemy Seleucus as an advisor and clairvoyant (*rector et praescius*). Apparently Ptolemy was in good company: Philostratus claims that Apollonius of Tyana was so regular a counselor to Vespasian that those in his circle complained the emperor was more devoted to him than pilgrims to oracles.[96]

Enthusiasm for foreign religion among Roman aristocrats was not limited to their dealings with freelance experts. The epigraphic and archaeological records of famed sanctuaries throughout the empire attest to the willingness of those who could afford it to travel far and wide to be initiated into the mysteries of Demeter and Persephone at Eleusis, the mysteries of the Great Gods on Samothrace, and the mysteries of Artemis at Ephesus.[97] Lucian mocks

---

93. This is in addition to retaining the astrologer Ptolemy Seleucus (Tacitus, *Hist.* 1.22). On the religious leanings of Poppaea Sabina, see Margaret H. Williams, "θεοσεβὴς γαρ ἤν: The Jewish Tendencies of Poppaea Sabina," *JTS* 39 (1988): 97–111; Ross Shepard Kraemer, "Giving up the Godfearers," *JAJ* 5 (2014): 61–87, esp. 69–72.

94. See the discussion in chapter 3.

95. Tacitus, *Hist.* 2.78.

96. Philostratus, *Vit. Apoll.* 33. 1. The same Seleucus, to whom Juvenal gives the epithet "always in exile" (*saepius exul, Sat.* 6.557), was a confident of Poppaea Sabina and accompanied Otho in Lusitania (Tacitus, *Hist.* 1.22; Suetonius, *Oth.* 4.1; Plutarch, *Galb.* 23.4). See also Ripat, "Astrologers at Rome," 135; Cynthia Damon, *Tacitus "Histories" Book I*, Cambridge Greek and Latin Classics (Cambridge: Cambridge University Press, 2003), 151.

97. For Roman benefactions and initiations at these sites and their general growth in the Roman period, see Kevin Clinton, "The Eleusinian Mysteries: Roman Initiates and Benefactors, Second Century B.C. to A.D. 267," *ANRW* II.18.2 (1989): 1499–539; idem, "Eleusis and the Romans: Late Republic to Marcus Aurelius," in *The Romanization of Athens*, ed. Michael C. Hoff and Susan I. Rotroff (Oxford: Oxbow, 1997), 161–82; idem, "Stages of Initiation in the Eleusinian and Samothracian Mysteries," in *Greek Mysteries: The Archaeology of Ancient Greek Secret Cults*, ed., Michael B. Cosmopoulos (London: Routledge, 2003), 50–78; Susan Guettel Cole, "The Mysteries of Samothrace During the Roman Period," *ANRW* II.18.2 (1989): 1564–98; Nora M. Dimitrova, "*Theoroi* and Initiates in Samothrace," *Hesperia Suppl* 37 (2008): iii–xvi, 1–280; Guy MacLean Rogers, *The Mysteries of Artemis of Ephesos:*

this practice in the figure of Rutilianus, who first dispatched a series of emissaries to the oracle of Glycon to inquire on his behalf and then supported Alexander at Rome, where the prophet developed his own mystery initiation and managed to persuade the aging but wealthy man to marry Alexander's own daughter.[98] Others might seek out famous religious sites in the course of travel for another purpose, such as trade or military service. Whatever the reason, these acts of remote patronage were opportune for the freelance experts who offered more affordable, portable versions of initiations, oracles, and other attractive services being sought abroad.[99]

Institutional and Demographic Transformations

If elite habits shed light on the demand for foreign experts and religious offerings, other factors account for their apparent abundance in this period. The first century of the empire witnessed considerable changes in the structures of religious authority in numerous provincial areas. Egypt and Judea saw ruptures in the organization of provincial temples, while in Italy the Praenestine temple of Fortuna Primigenia suffered severe economic penalties in the aftermath of the Social Wars.[100] Sulla's siege of Athens in 86 BCE also resulted in the destruction of the Academy and the Lyceum, similarly destabilizing the traditional loci of the major philosophical schools

---

Cult, Polis, and Change in the Graeco-Roman World, Synkrisis (New Haven: Yale University Press, 2013), 171–204. For comparable patterns of evidence from Egyptian sites, see Frederick E. Brent, "Religion Under Trajan: Plutarch's Resurrection of Osiris," in *Sage and Emperor: Plutarch, Greek Intellectuals, and Roman Power in the Time of Trajan (98–117 A.D.)*, ed. Philip A. Stadter and Luc Van der Stockt, Symbolae 29 (Leuven: Leuven University Press, 2002), 72–92; Pauline Ripat, "The Language of Oracular Inquiry in Roman Egypt," *Phoenix* 60 (2006): 304–28. For similar benefactions bestowed on the Jerusalem temple, a topic to which I return in the next chapter, see Cohen, *The Beginnings of Jewishness*, 143.

98. Lucian, *Alex.* 30–35.

99. There are occasional references to Roman emperors trying unsuccessfully to import popular practices to the capital, such as when Tiberius, who did away with oracles near the capital except that of Fortuna Primigenia at Praeneste, attempted to bring the temple's *sortes* to Rome in a sealed chest. They vanished from the container, however, not to reappear until it had been returned to the temple (Suetonius, *Tib.* 3.63.1). For a similar attempt by Claudius to transfer the Eleusinian rites from Attica to Rome, see Suetonius, *Claud.* 25.5.

100. For Praeneste, see Klingshirn, "Inventing the *Sortilegus*," passim. For Egypt, see David Frankfurter, *Religion in Roman Egypt: Assimilation and Resistance* (Princeton: Princeton University Press, 1998), 198–237; cf. Livia Capponi, "Priests in Augustan Egypt," in Richardson and Santangelo, *Priests and State in the Roman World*, 501–28. For the aftermath of the destruction of the Jerusalem temple, see Martin Goodman, "Jewish Proselytising in

and precipitating an emigration of many philosophers, and philosophical writings, to Rome.[101] As Roman administrative pressures and other forms of upheaval impinged on assorted religious and intellectual institutions, our evidence for freelance Egyptian priests, scribes, interpreters of Judean writings, lot diviners, and philosophers increases concomitantly. This is not to say that institutional integrity imposed limits on freelance expertise in deliberate or measurable ways. It stands to reason, however, that the dissolution or alteration of the former lent plausibility and new possibilities to the latter.[102]

Another illustration of this dynamic occurs with respect to Rome's collection of *Sibylline Oracles*, which were lost when Sulla burned the Capitoline temple where they were kept. Shortly thereafter the Senate began to dispatch envoys throughout the Mediterranean world with the intention of reconstituting the civic corpus. Years were spent gathering prophecies issued by Sibyls in Erythrae, Cumae, Samos, Ilium, Libya, and Sicily, verses that were then brought to Rome for evaluation by the *quindecimviri*.[103] One can imagine what an impetus this global effort to recover the "authentic" oracles was for their discovery, and also, judging from the aforementioned legislative incidents involving these texts, for their fabrication. In point of fact, new texts continued to surface well into the imperial period, when the Augustan seizure turned up genuine Sibylline verses that were culled from more than two thousand expropriated

---

the First Century," in *Judaism in the Roman World*, Ancient Judaism and Early Christianity 66 (Leiden: Brill, 2006), 91–116; idem, *Rome and Jerusalem: The Clash of Ancient Civilizations* (New York: Vintage Books, 2008), 424–87. I return to the matter of Judean experts in the next chapter.

101. Plutarch, *Sull.* 12.3. See Federico Santangelo, *Sulla, the Elites, and the Empire: A Study of Roman Policies in Italy and the Greek East*, Impact of Empire 8 (Leiden: Brill, 2007), 134–46. Sulla's actions against the schools were retaliatory insofar as first a Peripatetic philosopher and then an Epicurean had briefly gained absolute power at Athens and sided with Mithridates against Rome. It is unclear how exactly these events contributed to the waning institutional stature of the Athenian schools, but they diminished in importance henceforth, possibly owing to the dispersion of their libraries. For the consequences of this "philosophical diaspora," see, e.g., David Sedley, "The School, from Zeno to Arius Didymus," in *The Cambridge Companion to the Stoics*, ed. Brad Inwood (Cambridge: Cambridge University Press, 2003), 7–32, at 24–32.

102. In addition to the possibility that actual temple priests or members of major philosophical schools might be forced to act as freelance experts in the absence of institutional affiliation.

103. Parke, *Sibyls and Sibylline Prophecy in Classical Antiquity*, 142.

prophecies and incorporated into the civic collection.[104] Likewise, Tacitus recalls a query put to Tiberius concerning a new oracle, ostensibly Sibylline, whose admission to the official corpus a member of the *quindecimviri* had demanded.[105] The emperor responded by reminding all parties involved of the usual process for authenticating such verses but not without reinstating the precedent of Augustus, who—because of the many apocryphal works circulating under the Sibyl's name—had mandated that all privately owned prophecies be submitted to the urban praetor by a certain date, after which time their unauthorized possession became illegal. These subtle details suggest, and maybe even grant, that the emperors, the *quindecimviri*, and the Senate contributed unwittingly to the perceived authenticity of such writings by occasionally accepting some as legitimate.

While all of these circumstances contributed in different ways to the recognition and appeal of the religion of freelance experts, no factor promoted its diffusion more than demographic shifts taking place throughout the empire as the result of mass migrations—those undertaken voluntarily for purposes of trade, travel, and colonization as well as the involuntary displacement of peoples through war and conquest—and high rates of slave manumission. While the former produced unprecedentedly heterogeneous populations, the latter gave rise to observable inconsistencies in the power, wealth, and education of some foreigners and freedpersons and the limited opportunities available to them for political and public religious office.[106] Similar obstacles pertained to women, although, as Celia E. Schultz has shown, religion was one of the few avenues for wealthy women to participate in civic life, either as officiants in cults whose priesthoods were open to them or through religious benefaction.[107]

In light of these social developments, it is noteworthy that many of the purveyors and participants involved in the religion of freelance experts seem to have been foreigners (*peregrini*), freedpersons (*liberti*), and women not already included in the other categories. This is not to suggest that none

---

104. Suetonius, *Aug.* 31.1.6–7: *solos retinuit Sibyllinos, hos quoquo dilectu habito.*

105. Suetonius, *Ann.* 6.12; cf. Cassius Dio, 57.18.3–5.

106. John Patterson, *Landscapes and Cities: Rural Settlement and Civic Transformation in Early Imperial Italy* (Oxford: Oxford University Press, 2006), 236.

107. Celia E. Schultz, *Women's Religious Activity in the Roman Republic* (Chapel Hill: University of North Carolina Press, 2006), esp. 47–94. See also Joan Breton Connelly, *Portrait of a Priestess: Women and Ritual in Ancient Greece* (Princeton: Princeton University Press, 2007), 27–56, 57–84.

had civic ambitions. Throughout the imperial period there was a growing demand for formal religious participation among upwardly mobile social actors that was met by an observable effort to expand opportunities for civic religious office-holding and collegial membership.[108] Some wealthy freedmen aspired to the *Augustales*, a group attested for nearly every urban area of the empire and whose ranks occasionally included freeborn members (*ingenui*), indicating the relative respectability of such positions.[109] However, the vast majority of the evidence is for freedmen, whose participation included bestowing civic benefactions, financing urban development, and erecting statues for the emperor and his family members, often in excess of *decuriones*.[110] It is this sort of unbridled benefaction that Petronius lampoons in his depiction of the freedman Trimalchio, who is a *sevir Augustalis* and displays the *fasces* prominently in his dining room.[111] If not in the *Augustales*, freedmen might serve as *magistri* and *ministri* of the *Lares compitales*, offices that were expanded significantly by Augustus in 7 BCE.[112] Although special priesthoods for freedmen extended limited opportunities for sanctioned civic religious participation, these new offices were nevertheless beholden to the state by means of accountability structures such as the official Roman calendar, which designated specific occasions

---

108. See Patterson, *Landscapes and Cities,* 190. This more assorted set of possibilities for social mobility included many opportunities engendered by religious activity specifically.

109. See Patterson, *Landscapes and Cities,* 242–50; John D'Arms, "Memory, Money, and Status at Misenum: Three New Inscriptions from the *Collegium* of the Augustales," *JRS* 90 (2000): 126–44; Steve E. Ostrow. "'Augustales' Along the Bay of Naples: A Case for Their Early Growth," *Historia* 34 (1985): 64–101; Robert Duthoy, "Les Augustales," *ANRW* II.16.2 (1978): 1254–309. Although the origin and purposes of local *Augustales* are obscure, those of their activities that are captured in inscriptions include cultic and commemorative rites performed at imperial cult temples (*templum Augusti*), as well as public rites conducted in urban fora before statues of emperors who received cult.

110. Patterson elaborates, "The predominance of freedmen is very significant for the understanding of the role of the *Augustales* in urban society. Since freedmen were excluded from the *ordo*, service in the body of *Augustales* provided the only way in which the wealthy and ambitious freedman could engage in public life. . . . Many of those attested as *Augustales* appear to have acquired wealth through trade, manufacture, or commerce, and the creation of the *Augustales* likewise had the effect of allowing the city to draw upon the resources gained by these means. The institution thus provided a means of acquiring additional prestige for the wealthier among the city's freedmen, as well as an opportunity for the city to exploit their enthusiasm for participation in civic life" (*Landscapes and Cities,* 247).

111. Petronius, *Sat.* 30.

112. The emperor redistricted Rome into fourteen regions of 265 *vici*, each with a *collegium* and *compita* performed for the *lares* and the *genius Augusti*. See Ramsay MacMullen, *Roman Social Relations: 50 B.C. to A.D. 284* (New Haven: Yale University Press, 1974), 68–69.

for the performance of their respective roles, and by virtue of the fact that the rites in their purview were financed by the state. Like many freelance religious experts, people who sought positions in the *Augustales* and other civic associations earned prestige and honor through religious activity. And yet, connecting with the religion of the state and its attributed prestige held different possibilities and limitations than wielding specialized skills in a fairly unstructured capacity.

Despite these efforts to meet the civic-oriented interests of upwardly mobile noncitizens, there remained in the empire a vast swath of religious life that lacked defined rules and hierarchies, wherein status and authority could be articulated in various ways. Another prominent form of religious activity that flourished in this space were the numerous voluntary associations known from the imperial period, which were especially popular among freedpersons and freeborn women, as well as some slaves.[113] The *raisons-d'être* of these groups were notoriously varied, ranging from professional or ethnic affiliations to shared servitude to the cultivation of a particular deity. Explicitly cultic private groups—those whose membership was determined primarily by a shared religious orientation—tended to be the most inclusive type, often admitting members of either sex and of any social status, although their leadership criteria might be more restrictive.[114]

The implications of the myriad titles and ranks associated with such groups are often unknown, and it is unlikely that these positions corresponded to power and authority beyond their boundaries.[115] Within associations, however, members enjoyed opportunities for participation and office, bestowed benefactions, acquired honors, and even courted elite patrons—all opportunities that might be unavailable to them on an individual basis.[116] A number of organizations attracted the patronage of important persons in their respective locales, relationships that could confer financial

---

113. On the status and participation of women in such groups, see Schultz, *Women's Religious Activity in the Roman Republic*, 139–50; Ross Shepard Kraemer, *Her Share of the Blessings: Women's Religions Among Pagans, Jews, and Christians* (New York: Oxford University Press, 1992), 80–92, 106–27; Philip A. Harland, "Familial Dimensions of Group Identity (II): 'Mothers' and 'Fathers' in Associations and Synagogues of the Greek World," *JSJ* 38 (2007): 57–79; Tessa Rajak and David Noy, "*Archisynagogoi*: Official, Title and Social Status in the Greco-Jewish Synagogue," *JRS* 83 (1993): 75–93.

114. Kloppenborg, "Collegia and *Thiasoi*," 25.

115. Wilson, "Voluntary Associations," 10.

116. Kloppenborg, "Collegia and *Thiasoi*," 26–27.

support and advocacy in exchange for loyalty to the patron. Furthermore, even though freedmen themselves were ineligible to enter citizen orders, at least in the early imperial period, religious patronage constituted an important means by which a parent might begin to lay the foundation for the future civic prospects of his or her children.[117] A well-known example from Pompeii credits the restoration of the temple of Isis in 62 CE to the young son of a freedman.[118] Obviously commissioned by the boy's father, the benefaction bestowed in his name captures the deferred civic aspirations common of this social location. It may also be notable that the temple is that of an Egyptian deity. As certain rites and temples transitioned from private to public status—including the cult of Isis, which was sanctioned as *sacrum publicum* either at the end of Caligula's or in the beginning of Claudius's reign—they afforded more opportunities for office and patronage than were available within long-established religious institutions.[119]

Conclusions

All of these considerations, I submit, contributed in different ways to the heightened appeal of freelance experts who catered to broad interests in specialized religious offerings, often ones that were perceived as foreign. Though under the republic religious authority had been largely restricted to social elites, in the shifting social terrain of the early empire one might garner prestige, wealth, or influence in new ways: by holding a low-level civic religious office, by patronizing or wielding authority in a voluntary organization or private temple, or by claiming and gaining recognition for religious expertise, among other possibilities. This last possibility reinforces John Patterson's observation that the increase in number and variety of potential avenues for social mobility tracked with an increase in specialization across many domains of social practice. The emergence of a distinct class of professionals in religion appears to have been particularly salient at Rome, but the phenomenon of freelance expertise was far from limited to the capital, and its effects can be traced throughout and beyond the empire's territories.

---

117. Cf. Patterson, *Landscapes and Cities*, 237. The promotion of freedmen's sons into the *ordo* becomes common by the second century, although the trend may be distorted by a concomitant rise in epigraphic commemorations.

118. *CIL* X 846 = *ILS* 6367.

119. See Takács, "Alexandria in Rome," 274.

2

Ethnically Coded Experts and Forms of Religion

IN HIS SIXTH satire, Juvenal deplores the infelicitous pastimes of Roman women, foremost of which is *superstitio*. Speculating about what wives do when their husbands are away, he introduces a revolving door of exotic visitors who include a masked "professor of obscenities" (*professus obscenum*) with saffron robes and soot-rimmed eyes, on whose authority women marry or divorce; a eunuch of Bellona, who warns them of impending disasters defrayed only through the purifications he offers in exchange for old dresses; the man posing as Anubis, who, with a silver asp and thronged by his linen-clad troupe, issues prescriptions for purity and extracts fines from wives who have violated them unwittingly; and a trembling Judean woman who "begs into the ear" (*mendicat in aurem*), revealing her herself to be a high priestess (*magna sacerdos*) and faithful intermediary of the highest heaven (*summi fida internuntia caeli*), as well as an interpreter of the laws of Jerusalem (*interpres legum Solymarum*).[1] "She, too, fills her hand, though with less," Juvenal remarks, "since Judeans sell whatever kind of dreams you wish for the smallest coin" (*implet et illa manum, sed parcius; aere minuto qualiacumque voles Iudaei somina vendunt*). Promises of a tender lover or a bequest from a childless millionaire are the purview of *haruspices* from Armenia or Commagene, who probe the entrails of doves, chickens, puppies, and sometimes even a boy.[2] Greater confidence is

---

1. Juvenal, *Sat.* 6.346–65, 512–21, 532–41, 542–47.

2. Juvenal, *Sat.* 6.548–52. The author's passing remark that the last deplorable act is one that the *haruspex* in question might himself report to the authorities (*faciet quod deferat ipse*) is suggestive of self-incrimination and the favorable consequences of being investigated and punished that he chides elsewhere (e.g., *Sat.* 6.557–64).

placed in the Chaldeans, whose every pronouncement is thought to stem from Ammon's fountain.[3]

From these motley specialists wives solicit services ranging from co-ercion to prognostication about the deaths of burdensome relatives and everything in between. Women of humble means might have their lots cast or features read by a seer at the circus, while wealthier ones consult the Phrygian *augur* or another brought to Rome from abroad at great cost.[4] Whereas most would not dare try their own hands at such skills, Juvenal warns of the woman who, having procured an almanac of Thrasyllus, "no longer consults anyone else but these days is consulted herself."[5] Others scrutinize the horoscopes of Petosiris or slavishly cast lots to determine their daily courses of action.[6] The wife who aspires to the ranks of Caesonia and Agrippina will procure incantations (*magici cantus*) and Thessalian philters (*Thessala philtra*) to confuse her husband's mind and abuse him however she chooses.[7]

The mayhem that Juvenal depicts—of foreign priests, diviners, and initiators run amuck—answers a question posed earlier in the satire: "Whence come these wonders, you ask, what is their source?"[8] He is hardly the only writer to bewail or marvel at the proliferation of foreign religious practices at Rome, but his attribution of the assorted religious practices and

---

3. Juvenal, *Sat.* 6.553–57. That is, the oracle of Jupiter Ammon in North Africa, whose pro-file, he explains, has risen in lieu of Delphi.

4. Juvenal, *Sat.* 6.582–85. Juvenal specified a location for this expensive specialist, but a lacuna in the text prevents its identification. Two manuscripts (*Vat.* 3192 and 3286) supply *indus* after *Phryx augur*, which Susanna Morton Braund, following PΦΣ, construes as *inde* (LCL, 288). However, Indians and Indian imports appear elsewhere in the satire (e.g., 6.466), and it is not inconceivable that an Indian diviner would fit this context.

5. Juvenal, *Sat.* 6.574–75.

6. Juvenal, *Sat.* 6.581. An Egyptian astrologer of the second century BCE, whose predictions, like those attributed to Nechepso, were, despite their distinctly "Egyptian" attribution, actu-ally written in Greek. See Richard L. Gordon, "Memory and Authority in the Magical Papyri," in *Historical and Religious Memory in the Ancient World*, ed. Beate Dignas and R. R. R. Smith (Oxford: Oxford University Press, 2002), 145–80, at 162–63.

7. Juvenal, *Sat.* 6.610–26. Two empresses on whose notorious conjurings and potions im-perial successions were thought to have turned. The remark is also reminiscent of the trial in 24 CE of Fabia Numantina, who was suspected of enlisting *carmina* and *veneficium* to incite her ex-husband, Plautius Silvanus, to push his current wife out a window in a fit of insanity (Tacitus, *Ann.* 4.22). See Pollard, "Magic Accusations Against Women in Tacitus's *Annals*," 194.

8. Juvenal, 6.286: *unde haec monstra tamen vel quo de fonde requiris?*

paraphernalia he goes on to describe to freelance experts and their captive female audiences echoes an explanation now familiar from writers such as Livy and Josephus. While all three drew on common clichés about charlatans, as well as women's religion, that should be regarded with skepticism, the link between freelance experts and women or freedpersons occurs too often, in too many different kinds of sources, to be ignored.[9]

In the preceding chapters I suggested that the religion of freelance experts grew more influential in the early imperial period and also diversified apace with the empire's expanding territories and cultural geography.[10] Juvenal captures the latter development aptly insofar as the vectors that converge in his depiction of the capital's religious terrain emanate from all provinces and more distant lands that were nevertheless linked with Rome through trade networks. The kinds of figures he burlesques were evidently fixtures there, even if their offerings were perceived as anything but prosaic. For the dramatic population changes that accompanied the empire's formation and expansion, it is to be expected that residents of the capital and cities with comparable demographics became increasingly aware of the distinctive languages, customs, and institutions of an expanding array of cultural areas. Such knowledge might amount to no more than vague and imprecise ideas about foreign peoples and places, but it held important implications for the basic recognition of foreign experts and the particular skills or services they might purvey.

Ethnic Coding in the Roman Period

Much recent scholarship has drawn attention to the promotion of familiarity with provincial cultural practices, and religious practices in particular, within the Roman imperial project.[11] Eric M. Orlin has argued

---

9. See Kraemer, *Unreliable Witnesses*, 29–56.

10. For this sense of cultural geography, see Roshan Abraham, "The Geography of Culture in Philostratus' *Life of Apollonius of Tyana*," *CJ* 109 (2014): 465–80. Grant Parker uses the language of "mental maps" in reference to conceptions of exotic places that existed in the minds of Roman consumers: "Topographies of Taste: Indian Textiles and Mediterranean Contexts," *AO* 34 (2007): 19–37.

11. See in general Hubert Cancik, "Die 'Repraesentation' von 'Provinz' (nationes, gentes) in Rom. Ein Beitrag zur Besinnung von 'Reichsreligion' vom 1. Jahrhundert v. Chr. bis zum 2. Jahrhundert n. Chr.," in *Römische Reichsreligion und Provinzialreligion*, ed. Hubert Cancik and Jörg Rüpke (Tübingen: Mohr Siebeck, 1997), 129–43; Sheila Dillon and Katherine E. Welch, eds., *Representations of War in Ancient Rome* (New York: Cambridge University Press, 2006).

persuasively that a suffusion of foreign cults in Rome beginning in the late republic prompted the Romans to fashion a discrete identity centered on the superiority of their own religious customs and institutions, over and against those of the various peoples with whom they came into contact.[12] Representations of foreigners and their peculiar religious customs do not originate with the Romans, but, if Orlin is correct, they were especially poignant in the late republican and imperial periods. Importantly, such representations were also broadly accessible due to the assorted media in which they were communicated and reinforced, including ethnographic and other writings, frescoes, mosaics, reliefs, statues, coins, perfor-mances, and even public viewing galleries.[13] The cultural heterogeneity of the empire was also most evident at the capital, which came to be regarded as a microcosm of the territories under its administration.[14] From the vivid exhibitions of triumphal processions—many items of which were subse-quently put on permanent display—to the exotic materials and motifs that permeated Rome's urban fabric, the city was, by all appearances, a vibrant world fair of its geographic reach.[15]

The same conditions facilitated the recognition of foreign gods, rites, ritual paraphernalia, and religious office or authority.[16] Depictions of Egyptian religion were commonplace enough for Juvenal to suppose that not a single person is ignorant of "the monsters that crazy Egypt worships" before he lists the many animals and vegetables that receive cult there.[17] The famous Palestrina Nile mosaic depicts more favorable vignettes of

---

12. Orlin, *Foreign Cults in Rome,* 3–30.

13. See, e.g., Ann L. Kuttner, "Culture and History at Pompey's Museum," *TAPA* 129 (1999): 343–73; Trevor Murphy, *Pliny the Elder's Natural History: The Empire in the Encyclopedia* (New York: Oxford University Press, 2004), esp. 154–60; Bettina Bergmann, "The Art of Ancient Spectacle," in *The Art of Ancient Spectacle,* ed. Bettina Bergmann and Christine Kondoleon, (New Haven: Yale University Press), 9–36.

14. For an overview of these points, see Catharine Edwards and Greg Woolf, "Cosmopolis: Rome as World City," in Edwards and Woolf, *Rome the Cosmopolis,* 1–20.

15. For this effect of the triumph, see Ida Östenberg, *Staging the World: Spoils, Captives, and Representation in the Triumphal Procession,* Oxford Studies in Ancient Culture and Representation (New York: Oxford University Press, 2003); Mary Beard, *The Roman Triumph* (Cambridge: Harvard University Press, 2007), esp. 106–86.

16. For example, that Egyptian priests wore linen and sported shaven heads, or that Persian religious experts were known as *magi* and were skilled in divination and practices involving the dead.

17. Juvenal, *Sat.* 15.1–13.

religious activity unfolding realistically in a "native" context, although here too the images probably reveal more about how Italians imagined the religion of Egypt.[18] Molly Swetnam-Burland has drawn attention to the prevalence of Egyptian priests and cult instruments in Roman art, images whose popularity underscores the widespread appeal of Egyptian religion and religious experts among nonnative audiences.[19] Even where evidence of actual religious practice is concerned, however, Swetnam-Burland argues that Italian temples and monuments to the Egyptian gods were more *Egyptianizing* than Egyptian.[20] That is, examples of Egyptian religion in Rome and elsewhere outside of Egypt often comprised fairly traditional or local activities that, through the use of imported objects, exotic images, costumes, and so forth, were imbued with connotations specific to this province.

Swetnam-Burland's characterization of *aegyptiaca* shares much in common with John Scheid's of ethnically qualified *sacra, mores,* or *ritus* conducted by Roman priests or magistrates, the primary example being practices carried out "in the Greek manner" or *graeco ritu*. Scheid demonstrates that foreign valences usually amounted to no more than a slight modification of ordinary Roman religious activities that subtly harnessed qualities attributed to the frame of reference employed.[21] For example, *ritus* conducted *cincto gabino*—a way of wrapping the toga that left both arms free—more than facilitated the taking of auspices; by evoking, the

---

18. Miguel John Versluys, *Aegyptiaca Romana. Nilotic Scenes and the Roman Views of Egypt*, RGRW 144 (Leiden: Brill, 2002), 52–53; Paul J. P. Meyboom, *The Nile Mosaic of Palestrina: Early Evidence of Egyptian Religion in Italy*, RGRW 121 (Leiden: Brill, 1994).

19. Molly Swetnam-Burland, "'Egyptian' Priests in Roman Italy," in *Cultural Identity in the Ancient Mediterranean*, ed. Erich S. Gruen (Los Angeles: Getty Research Institute, 2011), 336–53, esp. 339–41.

20. See Molly Swetnam-Burland, "Egyptian Objects, Roman Contexts: A Taste for *Aegyptiaca* in Italy," in *Nile into Tiber: Egypt in the Roman World. Proceedings of the 3rd International Conference of Isis Studies, Faculty of Archaeology, Leiden University, May 11–14, 2005*, ed. Laurent Bricault, Miguel John Versluys, and Paul G. P. Meyboom, RGRW 159 (Leiden: Brill, 2007), 113–36. In the same volume, see also Miguel John Versluys, "Aegyptiaca Romana: The Widening Debate," 1–14; Grant Parker, "Obelisks Still in Exile: Monuments Made to Measure?" 209–22.

21. John Scheid, "*Graeco Ritu*: A Typically Roman Way of Honoring the Gods," *HSCP* 97 (1995): 15–31, at 19. Scheid's construal of *ritus* as a manner of conducting religious practice is especially useful for our purposes and has broader implications for religious concepts and activities associated with other cultural frameworks than the Greek example that he explores in his study.

practice invoked the prominent augural legacy of Gabii.[22] The *graeco ritu* was limited neither to Greek priests nor to temples for Greek gods at Rome but designated a mood or manner that could be applied in a range of religious contexts. Through pointed elements of style, staging, and language, it infused typically Roman rites with conceptions tied to notions of "Greekness."[23]

What these scholars have in common is interest in what I referred to earlier as the "ethnic coding" of certain skills, types of knowledge, practices, and paraphernalia—anything from costumes to sacred images or ritual implements to writings. As they and others have emphasized, the differences between religion found in the various cultural areas of the ancient Mediterranean were nonessential. Rather, religious practices throughout the empire shared a basic intelligibility tinted with regional distinctiveness: a curious rite or manner of worship, a god with a special purview or unusual characteristics, an impressive corpus of writings, or a rare and attractive religious benefit.[24] In Cicero's *On Divination*, Quintus entertains a series of naturalistic explanations for the assorted divinatory methods of foreign peoples. Egyptians and Babylonians have devoted their attention to astrology, he opines, owing to the level plains and unobstructed view of the sky in the regions they inhabit. Arabians, Phrygians, and Cilicians study the songs and flights of birds, which they have ample occasion to observe as they wander the plains with their herds of cattle.[25] The discussion narrows to individual cities recognized for superiority in a particular technique and the titles of experts trained in these skills.[26] *Magi*

---

22. Scheid, "*Graeco Ritu*," 18.

23. Jonathan M. Hall, *Hellenicity: Between Ethnicity and Culture* (Chicago: University of Chicago Press, 2002), 193. Grant Parker has advanced similar arguments for Indian wisdom, as well as more routine imports such as mushrooms or spices: "*Ex Oriente Luxuria*: Indian Commodities and Roman Experience," *JESHO* 45 (2002): 40–95; idem, *The Making of Roman India* (Cambridge: Cambridge University Press, 2008).

24. See also Rives, *Religion in the Roman Empire*, 23–32, 54–88; idem, "Religion in the Roman Provinces," in *The Oxford Handbook of Roman Epigraphy*, ed. Christer Bruun and Jonathan Edmondson (New York: Oxford University Press, 2014), 420–44; Stanley K. Stowers, "The Religion of Plant and Animal Offerings Verses the Religion of Meanings, Essences, and Textual Mysteries," in *Ancient Mediterranean Sacrifice*, ed. Jennifer Wright Knust and Zsuzsanna Várhelyi (New York: Oxford University Press, 2011), 35–56, esp. 36–41.

25. Cicero, *Div.* 1.92–94.

26. Telmessus in Caria and Elis in the Peloponnesus both boast reputations for haruspication (Cicero, *Div.* 1.91.5–7).

are the Persian equivalents to *augures*; in Syria, Chaldeans are preeminent for their knowledge of astronomy and for their quickness of mind; even among the uncivilized tribes of Gaul, druids possess intimate knowledge of physiognomy, augury, and conjecture.[27] Cicero is but one of many authors to catalogue and theorize the religion of other peoples, in this case non-Romans. Attention to distinctive features of this sort might pique exaggerated expectations of difference, but these discursive constructions mask an underlying continuity in both the logic and practice of ancient religion.

The qualities ascribed to certain regions or ethnic groups did, however, present opportunities for people alleging expertise in ethnically coded skills, toward which they were thought to be naturally disposed due to their ancestry or provenance. Not only were foreign specialists familiar to Roman audiences, but particular figures, like the regions or cultural milieus they represented, were associated with regular specialty and characteristics. As I noted earlier, James B. Rives has shown that the term *magus* and cognate language, before acquiring the sense of "magician," denoted expertise in Persian religion and implied a tradition of esoteric wisdom and exceptional skills in divination and matters pertaining to the dead.[28] Likewise, Chaldeans were so inseparable from astrological knowledge that the term was synonymous with "astrologer," even when other options (*astrologus, mathematicus*) were in common use. In a study of *haruspices*, a type of diviner associated strongly with Etruria, Marie-Laurence Haack notes that many of her examples seem to have exaggerated or affected Etruscan ethnicity in their nomenclature and dress, presumably to signal their suitability to the forms of divination (extispicy and fulguration) for which the Etruscans were famous; Juvenal hints at other experts doing the same.[29] It is for this reason, perhaps, that Plutarch feels the need to delineate "true" Isis devotees—those who, lacking all *superstitio* and pedantry bear Egyptian sacred writings within their souls as though

---

27. "Quintus" recognizes a particular druid, Divitiacus the Aeduan, who was Cicero's guest and professed knowledge of nature, what the Greeks call *physiologia*. He also made predictions by means of augury and conjecture (Cicero, *Div.* 1.90.1–6). For Roman actions against druids and practices with which they were associated, see Pliny, *Nat.* 30.4, 12; Suetonius, *Claud.* 25.5.

28. Rives, "*Magus* and Its Cognates in Classical Latin," 60–61. This presentation is consistent with Classical and Hellenistic Greek depictions of *magoi*, which increasingly emphasized the philosophical character of their wisdom originating with Zoroaster.

29. Haack, *Les haruspices dans le monde romain*, 103–4; Ripat, "Astrologers at Rome," 129–30.

within a casket—from others who merely dress in linen and shave their heads.[30] While his remark is embedded in second-century discourses about authenticity, it also alludes to the strategic self-representation of people seeking recognition in roles with predictable ethnicizing attributes. Particular dress, *instrumentum*, and behaviors were so strongly associated with foreign religion that those who appropriated them were able to signal expertise in the areas to which they pointed, albeit with varying credibility.[31]

The "Foreignness" of Freelance Experts

We inherit any number of examples of freelance experts in foreign religion, ones who appear to have operated independently of existing groups or institutions. To the aforementioned Persian, Babylonian, Syrian, and Gallic examples we can add numerous specialists in Egyptian and Judean religion whose "freelance" character is often overlooked because they are presumed to have acted on behalf of a larger corporate entity: a temple or cult in the former case, "Judaism" or a "Jewish community" in the latter. Earlier I intimated that Pauline Ripat's insights about astrology could be brought to bear productively on other scholarly categories—including magic, mystery cults, Egyptian cult, Judaism, and Christianity—whose lack of differentiation masks internal diversity while also reinforcing impressions of essential difference between the actors and phenomena they contain. In this chapter I demonstrate the analytical value of atomizing such categories in order to isolate particular actors and phenomena that cut across their boundaries. Using freelance experts in Egyptian and Judean religion as examples, I argue that these and other foreign experts shared a number of characteristics that justify theorizing them as participants in a common class of religious activity even if they differed with respect to ethnicity, particular skills and practices, and representations (claims, teachings, myths, etc.).

We have already come across several Egyptian actors who would appear to fit my definition of freelance religious expertise. The Alexandrian

---

30. Plutarch, *De Is. et Os.* 1.3.

31. This is the implication in the story of Marcus Volusius, a proscribed aedile who donned the *Isiaci habitu* to escape Rome (Valerius Maximus, 7.3.8), and that of Domitian passing undetected among a band of Egyptian priests when followers of Vitellius trapped him on the Capitoline (Appian, *BCiv* 4.47).

astrologers Sosigenes and Facundius were employed by Caesar and Augustus, respectively, to reform the Roman calendar, while Thrasyllus, the court astrologer of Tiberius, is thought to have been from either Alexandria or Mendes, a city in the eastern Nile delta. Nero had, in addition to Seneca, the Egyptian tutor Chaeremon, while the astrologer Ptolemy Seleucus is mentioned in relation to Nero's mistress, Poppaea Sabina, then to Vitellius, and finally, along with Apollonius of Tyana and Josephus, to Vespasian. A miracle that occurred during Marcus Aurelius's campaign against the Macromani is attributed to his Egyptian advisor Arnouphis (a *magos* to Dio), who by praying to various deities summoned a rainstorm at a crucial moment.[32] Pausanias tells of Amphion of Thebes, who traded in mysterious objects and surpassed even Orpheus in his command of wild animals.[33]

Joining these specific figures are Egyptian specialists who appear in accounts of fiction or questionable historicity, or who, like Juvenal's Anubis impersonator or Josephus's scheming Isis priests, are depicted generically. In the first category falls Zatchlas, an Egyptian prophet and priest (*propheta et sacerdos*) who raises and interrogates a corpse about the circumstances of his death, and maybe also the priests of Isis and Osiris who preside over Lucius's different initiations in Book Eleven of the *Metamorphoses*.[34] Kalasiris, the Egyptian prophet (προφήτης) in Heliodorus's *Ethiopian Story*, is yet another example in this vein, while the Egyptian Pancrates, like Alexander and Peregrinus, seems to straddle fiction and reality; he was an actual person but one who undoubtedly suffered considerable distortion in Lucian's fantastic rendition of his biography.[35] Though Pancrates boasted that he spent twenty-three years in the sanctuaries of Memphis and learned his skills from Isis while working as a sacred scribe, this is not the noble setting in which the author envisages him. In the same text

---

32. Cassius Dio, 71.8.4. Cf. Josephus's story about Onias, a righteous man and beloved by God, who had once ended a severe drought with his prayers for rain and was killed during the Hasmonean civil war by those who feared that he would use his powers to curse Aristobulus and his supporters (AJ 14.21).

33. Pausanias, *Descr.* 6.20.18–19.

34. Apuleius, *Metam.* 2.28–29.

35. Lucian, *Philops.* 34–35. For Kalasiris, see Ken Dowden, "Kalasiris, Apollonius of Tyana, and the Lies of Teiresias," in Panayotakis, Schmeling, and Paschalis, *Holy Men and Charlatans in the Ancient Novel*, 1–16; Alain Billaut, "Holy Man or Charlatan? The Case of Kalasiris in Heliodorus' *Aithiopika*," in Panayotakis, Schmeling, and Paschalis, *Holy Men and Charlatans in the Ancient Novel*, 121–32.

we learn of Egyptian writings being consulted for wisdom involving necromancy and exorcism, while, as we saw earlier, Juvenal knows of horoscopes attributed to at least two different Egyptian astrologers in circulation at Rome.[36] References to Egyptians as a collective set of religious specialists akin to *magi* or Chaldeans are also fairly plentiful. Philostratus claims that Apollonius of Tyana drove out Chaldeans and Egyptians who had flocked to the Hellespont after a series of earthquakes where he found them charging ten talents to perform placating rites.[37] This sense is also clear to the second-century writer Celsus, who likens Jesus to *goētes* and those Egyptians who, for a few obols, display their sacred lore in the middle of the marketplace: exorcizing *daimones*, curing diseases, invoking the souls of heroes, conjuring expensive banquets, and making inanimate objects move as though they are alive.[38]

Many of these Egyptian experts are well represented in studies of magic or astrology yet rarely factor into discussions of Egyptian *religion*. Others, by virtue of boasting a priestly title, are presumed to represent a temple even when the latter is not evident but must be inferred.[39] As was the case for itinerant *augures*, however, self-authorized actors wishing to align themselves with a recognized form of expertise might claim prestigious titles opportunistically or even optimistically. To recall Plutarch's warning, not everyone who seems to be an Egyptian priest actually was, at least not in the institutional sense that modern readers often imagine. Porphyry supplies a useful illustration when he relates that Plotinus accompanied an Egyptian "priest" to an Isis temple at Rome, where the latter intended to reveal a visible manifestation of the philosopher's indwelling *daimōn*. The

---

36. Lucian, *Philops.* 30–31; Juvenal, 6.574–55, 581.

37. Philostratus, *Vit. Apoll.* 6.41. As Dickie notes, "The Egyptians present . . . are best understood to be persons trading on the renown that Egyptian priests had as experts in the divine and in the occult" (*Magic and Magicians in the Greco-Roman World*, 159).

38. Origen, *C. Cels.* 1.68.

39. That is, a reference to Egyptian *sacrificuli*, to a *sacerdos Isidis*, or to a scribe (γραμματεύς) is understood to imply some institutional context with the likes of which the figure(s) in question may or may not have been associated: for instance, the Egyptian *sacrificuli* among whom Domitian concealed himself in order to escape from the Capitoline (Suetonius, *Dom.* 1.2). For epigraphic examples of Egyptian religious experts of ambiguous status, see Jörg Rüpke, *Fasti Sacerdotum: A Prosopography of Pagan, Jewish, and Christian Officials in the City of Rome* (Oxford: Oxford University Press, 2008), esp. 152. For Judean examples, see Martin Goodman, "Texts, Scribes, and Power in Roman Judea," in *Judaism in the Roman World*, Ancient Judaism and Early Christianity 66 (Leiden: Brill, 2006), 79–90, esp. 80–82.

temple was chosen for this feat not because the Egyptian was a member of its (or any priesthood)—he was not—but because, according to him, it was the only pure place in the city.[40] Here we glimpse a freelance expert working in cooperation with an institutional temple—even if the relationship is one-sided—without holding one of its offices.

A famous inscription from Delos recounting the arrival of Sarapis in the Hellenistic period bears more intimate witness to the complexity of such matters.[41] The text traces the god's installation on the island to Apollonius, a priest, an Egyptian from the priestly class (ἱερεύς ... ὢν Αἰγύπτιος ἐκ τῶν ἱερέων), who established Sarapis's cult implements under his own roof—a rental apartment—and began to perform sacred rites there in the customary manner.[42] It was not until the grandson of Apollonius received a dream oracle from Sarapis expressing his desire to have a sacred precinct of his own, the location of which he would indicate through a sign (σημαεῖν), that this "cult" seems to have acquired a distinct profile as such.[43] Once a proper temple was erected at the entry of the agora, some men joined in opposition against the god and his priest, bringing civil action against the latter that he feared would result in corporal punishment or fines; as Sarapis promised in a dream, however, this did not prove to be the case.[44]

This process unfolded over the course of many years, even a few generations. What is remarkable about the inscription, among other features, is that the fate of Sarapis rested for so long in the hands of an individual priest of uncertain pedigree, who converted his temporary living space into a makeshift "temple" for an Egyptian god. Whether Apollonius had actually held the religious office in Memphis that he professed on Delos is impossible to know. Either way, his activities on the island seem

---

40. Porphyry, *Plot.* 10. Cf. Garth Fowden, *The Egyptian Hermes: A Historical Approach to the Late Pagan Mind* (Princeton: Princeton University Press, 1993), 129–30; Dickie, *Magic and Magicians in the Greco-Roman World*, 230–31.

41. *IG* XI.4 1299. For translation and commentary, see Helmut Engelmann, *The Delian Aretalogy of Sarapis*, EPRO 44 (Leiden: Brill, 1975); Ian S. Moyer, "Notes on Re-Reading the Delian Aretology of Sarapis (*IG* XI.4 1299)," *ZPE* 166 (2008): 101–7. Moyer argues for a late-third- or early-second-century BCE date for the inscription on the basis of paleographic features. See also Hanges, *Paul, Founder of Churches*, 139–247.

42. Lines 1–5, 39.

43. Lines 13–18.

44. Line 24.

to qualify as freelance expertise until the "cult" had acquired more institutional characteristics, in this case a dedicated temple. At the very least, the inscription encourages us to examine the force of titles or offices that occur in our sources for Egyptian and other examples of foreign religion, which may, but do not always, imply the institutional structures such language typically connoted.

As I suggested in the last chapter, certain circumstances in Roman Egypt may have contributed to the basic plausibility of freelance experts in Egyptian religion, if not also their numbers. As Elizabeth Rawson observes, while intellectuals—and presumably some intellectualizing religious experts—traveled from Alexandria to Rome with ease once Egypt became a province, the requirement for Romans to obtain imperial permission to visit Egypt meant that few were able to seek out Alexandria's renowned cultural offerings and had to rely instead on portable versions thereof.[45] Furthermore, Roman administrative interventions in Egypt's civic temples and priesthoods may have upset traditional configurations of religious authority, displacing a number of temple priests and scribes.[46] In the wake of these reforms, many have argued, the Egyptian landscape filled with independent actors who might have some relationship with temples but were not necessarily regular members of their priesthoods.[47]

While there are numerous references to freelance Egyptian experts in our literary sources, the best witnesses to these transformations may be the many Roman-period religious texts and artifacts that seem to point to this sort of activity. Jonathan Z. Smith has proposed that the practices prescribed in the "magical" papyri recovered from Egypt constituted a compressed or miniaturized version of the activities and equipment of temples, an adaptation of "official traditions" for private purposes.[48] Whether the authors and consumers of these texts were actual priests is less important than the observation that religious services once restricted to temple contexts appear to have become more diffuse in late Ptolemaic and

---

45. Rawson, *Intellectual Life in the Late Roman Republic*, 318.

46. Frankfurter, *Religion in Roman Egypt*, 198–203; Gordon, "Memory and Authority in the Magical Papyri," 155.

47. A notable exception is Livia Capponi, who argues that Egyptian priests were not divested of their privileges to the extent that is commonly thought: "Priests in Augustan Egypt," 511–12.

48. Jonathan Z. Smith, "Trading Places," in *Ancient Magic and Ritual Power*, ed. Marvin Meyer and Paul Mirecki, RGRW 141 (Leiden: Brill, 1995), 13–27; cf. Gordon, "Memory and Authority in the Magical Papyri," 155.

Roman Egypt. Noting a tandem diversification and proliferation of divination procedures, oracular texts, and semiprecious amulets in the first and second centuries, Richard L. Gordon explains, "Techniques of miniaturization (of rituals, of ritual paraphernalia), of do-it-yourself, and individual action by the practitioner, become typical. The implication of this evidence is that the practitioner is imagined as having only a loose connection with an institution." Nevertheless, the detailed, fairly technical requirements of the rituals that they prescribe lead him to conclude, "A training in temple-magic is thus taken for granted."[49]

Gordon's remarks recall Juvenal's description of similar dynamics at Rome, where a concentration of self-authorized specialists promoted competition and innovation and also, if the right equipment was available, the pursuit of specialty secondarily, as clients or followers acquired religious skills in their own right.[50] This is not to suggest that all freelance experts in Egyptian religion were wholly inventive about the nature of their authority. To the contrary, some might have been current or former members of civic priesthoods who nevertheless employed their expertise, David Frankfurter submits, "either as a covert side-business, *or* as a way of maintaining authoritative tradition after religious institutions were in decline, *or* as a perfectly legitimate and traditional extension of official ritual practices."[51] Yet it is just as conceivable that someone who had never held priestly office would be all more ambitious in claiming institutional religious titles and forms of expertise in light of the aforementioned changes, especially outside Egypt where there was less risk of such pretensions being debunked.[52]

Similar possibilities might also have arisen after the destruction of the Jerusalem temple, insofar as the destabilization of the priesthood

---

49. Gordon, "Memory and Authority in the Greek Magical Papyri," 155.

50. By equipment I mean collections of spells, horoscopes, or oracles, ritual objects or materials, and so forth of the sort to which Juvenal refers.

51. David Frankfurter, "The Great, the Little, and the Authoritative Tradition in Magic of the Ancient World," *ARG* 16 (2014): 11–30, at 12; idem, *Religion in Roman Egypt*, 211. See also, Alan H. Gardiner, "Professional Magicians in Ancient Egypt," *PBSA* 39 (1917): 31–43. For an example of the instruction to assume the guise of an Egyptian priest in order to enhance one's divinatory abilities, see *PGM* IV.930–1114; Ian S. Moyer, "The Initiation of the Magician: Transition and Power in Graeco-Egyptian Ritual," in *Initiation in Ancient Greek Rituals and Narratives: New Critical Perspectives*, ed. David B. Dodd and Christopher A. Faraone (New York: Routledge, 2003), 219–38, esp. 224.

52. Dickie makes a similar point about priests and magicians not being mutually exclusive by necessity, though I disagree with the ontological distinction he draws between the religion and magic of the two, respectively (*Magic and Magicians in the Greco-Roman World*, 230).

introduced an element of confusion into expectations, at least among non-Judean audiences, about where, or with whom, its former authority now resided.[53] Whatever constraints on claims of priestly status (e.g., genealogies, political appointment) had been in place while the temple was standing were less clear once this civic priesthood no longer existed as an institutionally regulated entity. One wonders, then, whether this event did not to some extent embolden pretensions to Judean religious expertise.[54] Of course there were certainly nonpriestly groups of specialists involved in the temple's administration while it was still in operation, but it stands to reason that the plausibility of claims to possess skills or knowledge traditionally associated with either the priesthood or the Sadducees and Pharisees expanded considerably in its absence.

Owing to anachronistic expectations about the nature of Judean religion in the Roman world—that is, that Judaism was *a religion* more like modern religions, and therefore quasi-exceptional in its ancient context— the possibility of some Judeans participating in the religion of freelance experts is even more complicated than for other foreign specialists.[55] Here too the evidence is not lacking or unknown. Nevertheless, scholars have either been reluctant to take it at face value or sought to reconcile

---

53. Indeed, the narrative of Luke–Acts, whose author wastes no opportunity to connect Jesus and the apostles to the Jerusalem temple long after its destruction, seems to capitalize on this uncertainty to the benefit of second-century Christians by implying that this authority lay with Jesus and then his followers, and now resides with them.

54. For priestly and other genealogical records, see, e.g., Cohen, *The Beginnings of Jewishness*, 50 nn. 97–100. For a compatible suggestion regarding pretensions to priestly status in the absence of the temple, see Jörg Rüpke, "Starting Sacrifice in the Beyond: Flavian Innovations in the Concept of the Priesthood and Their Repercussions in the Treatise 'To the Hebrews,'" *RHR* 229 (2012): 5–30, esp. 10.

55. "Judean" has gained traction in recent years insofar as it foregrounds geographic and ethnic connotations of this language in contexts where such connotations eclipse the religious valences "Judean" might otherwise carry. Some of these insights arise from Steve Mason's important article, "Jews, Judaeans, Judaizing, Judaism: Problems of Categorization in Ancient History," *JSJ* 38 (2007): 457–512, in which Mason draws attention to the pronounced ethnographic dimension of "Judean" in many writings of the Greco-Roman period, particularly ones written by or for non-Judeans. I am persuaded by Mason's suggestion that using "Judean" in certain instances promotes a more precise understanding of how ancient peoples organized their knowledge of the world, although, for reasons stated in the introduction, I do not share his view that the term "religion" is inapplicable to antiquity (481–82). Indeed, I find "Judean" useful precisely because *Iudaeus*/Ἰουδαῖος evoked a suite of specific cultural practices associated with Judea, of which the Jerusalem temple and sacred or oracular writings were a central part. "Judean" thus points to Judea in a way that Jewish does not, at a time when geography was foundational to how Romans *imagined* the religious practices, institutions, and paraphernalia that they understood to emanate from particular regions, regardless of where the latter were actually encountered. My preference for "Judean religion" instead of Judaism thus reflects, on the one hand, a desire to avoid concepts of *religions* that

references to Judeans acting in this capacity with a model of proselytism and conversion that is exclusive to Judaism. Neither interpretation makes adequate sense of the sources, many of which, without special emphasis or ulterior motive, place Judeans among other purveyors of foreign religious offerings.[56]

As we saw earlier, Juvenal includes a Judean high priestess and interpreter of the laws of Jerusalem among other experts of this sort and notes that Judeans are known for inexpensive dream interpretation. Lucian, to the contrary, knows of a Syrian exorcist from Palestine who cured countless people afflicted by *daimones*, albeit for huge fees.[57] In another text he quips that one man purges himself with sacred medicine, while another is mocked by the incantations of imposters, and another still falls for the spells of a Judean.[58] Josephus admits and even takes pride in Judea's reputation for exorcism, recalling with approval the exorcisms and healings that he witnessed a Judean named Eleazar perform before the Flavians and their armies, aided by the wisdom of Solomon.[59] Indeed, it is because God taught Solomon "the art concerning *daimones*" (τὴν κατὰ τῶν δαιμόνων τέχνην) that Judeans have such effective techniques.[60] Acts mentions itinerant Judean exorcists who begin to adjure *daimones* in the name of the Jesus proclaimed by Paul, while Justin boasts that throughout the whole world—"even in your own city!"—Christians have exorcised

---

are anachronistic for this period, and, on the other, an interest in redescribing Judaism in terms that not only reflect this perspective, but also align with how Romans imagined and represented the assorted religious institutions, actors, and groups of other ethnic or provincial peoples. See also Wendt, "A Rereading of Judean Expulsions from Rome," 98–99. For a critical discussion of Mason's arguments see Cynthia Baker, "A 'Jew' by Any Other Name?" *JAJ* 2 (2011): 152–80; Seth Schwartz, "How Many Judaisms Were There? A Critique of Neusner and Smith on Definition and Mason and Boyarin on Categorization," *JAJ* 2 (2011): 208–38; Michael L. Satlow, "Jew or Judean?" in *The One Who Sows Bountifully: Essays in Honor of Stanley K. Stowers,* ed. Caroline Johnson Hodge et al., Brown Judaic Studies 356 (Atlanta, GA: SBL Press, 2013), 165–75.

56. See Wendt, "A Rereading of Judean Expulsions from Rome," 98–105, 122–26.

57. Lucian, *Philops.* 16. For the complexity and frequent conflation of "Judean" and "Syrian" at this time, see Andrade, *Syrian Identity in the Greco-Roman World,* 113–21.

58. Lucian, *Trag.* 171–73: ἄλλος ἐπαιδαῖς ἐπιθετῶν ἐμπαίζεται, Ἰουδαῖος ἕτερον μωρὸν ἐξάδει λαβών.

59. On Judean exorcism in the Second Temple period, see Gideon Bohak, *Ancient Jewish Magic* (New York: Cambridge University Press, 2008), 105–12; Frankfurter, "The Great, the Little, and the Authoritative Tradition," 20–21.

60. Josephus, *AJ* 8.44–49.

many who were possessed by *daimones* in the name of Jesus Christ.[61] "And they healed them," he insists, "though they had not been healed by all the others: exorcists and enchanters and healers."[62]

Josephus's writings contain a surplus of references to "false prophets" (ψευδοπροφῆται) and "charlatans" or "imposters" (γόητες). In addition to the Judean who posed as an expert in Mosaic wisdom in order to steal from Fulvia in the reign of Tiberius, he acknowledges several who drew popular followings in Judea on the basis of fraudulent claims and unrealized promises: John, son of Levi, who was always ready to indulge great expectations and incited the inhabitants of a small Galilean town to rebel during the Judean War; Theudas, who, styling himself a prophet, rallied thousands to the banks of the Jordan River where he intended to part its waters; and an unnamed Egyptian who led thirty thousand to the Mount of Olives where he revealed plans to force entry into Jerusalem—in the *Antiquities* Josephus adds that the city walls were to fall at his command—where he would assume power for himself.[63] These named figures join the anonymous ones who feature in most of the uprisings or calamitous events that Josephus chronicles, especially as the events of the war escalated. He pins the deaths of women and children taking refuge in the Jerusalem temple at the time of its siege on some "false prophet" who had urged them to go up to the court to receive signs of their salvation (τὰ σημεῖα τῆς σωτηρίας).[64] He was but one, Josephus reiterates, of the many "rogues and pretenders of God who beguiled [the people] at this time." [65]

Despite how they are portrayed and to what ends, it is apparent that some of these actors were well-received in Judea, as was the Samaritan

---

61. Acts 19:13. Not to mention Jesus's own talent at exorcism, which he passes on to his disciples. One wonders whether the gospels do not themselves reflect awareness of the particular skills for which Judeans were renowned. See Tony Costa, "The Exorcisms and Healings of Jesus Within Classical Culture," in *Christian Origins and Greco-Roman Culture: Social and Literary Contexts for the New Testament*, ed. Stanley E. Porter and Andrew W. Pitts (Leiden: Brill, 2013), 113–44.

62. Justin, *2 Apol.* 5.6: ὑπὸ τῶν ἄλλων πάντων ἐπορκιστῶν καὶ ἐπαστῶν καὶ φαρμακευτῶν μὴ ἰαθέντας, ἰάσθαντο (trans. Minns and Parvis).

63. Josephus, *AJ* 18.65–84; *BJ* 4.84–85; *AJ* 20.97–99; *BJ* 2.261–62, cf. *AJ* 20.169–71.

64. Josephus, *BJ* 6.285–86.

65. Josephus, *BJ* 6.288: οἱ μὲν ἀπατεῶνες καὶ καταψευδόμενοι τοῦ θεοῦ τηνικαῦτα παρέπειθον. Cf. *BJ* 2.264. For a brief discussion of some of these references, see David E. Aune, "The Use of ΠΡΟΦΗΤΗΣ in Josephus," *JBL* 101 (1982): 419–21.

"false prophet" who, vowing to reveal sacred vessels that Moses had deposited there led a crowd of his people to Mount Gerazim.[66] What many have in common, moreover, is the investment of their abilities and practices with legacies drawn from the holy Judean writings, or at least traditions they contained.[67] Eleazar traces his skills explicitly to the wisdom of Solomon. Theudas evokes Moses, Joshua, or Elisha more subtly with his promise to part the waters of the Jordan, as does the Egyptian, whose promises recall Joshua at the battle of Jericho, if the details that Josephus adds are trustworthy.[68] While the eventual biblical context of Abraham, Joseph, and Moses obscures their functional equivalence to counterparts from Greek, Persian, or Egyptian myth, for some Judean experts the patriarchs and prophets were akin to Orpheus, the Sibyl, Zoroaster, and Hermes, all of whom lent imprimaturs to texts, wisdom, miracles, and other religious talents.[69]

---

66. Josephus, AJ 18.85–87.

67. "Judean writings" does not correspond to a particular body of literature and could, without qualification, refer to anything written in Judea (the Dead Sea Scrolls, the Babatha archive, and so forth) while excluding most writings that would eventually become part of the biblical canon. While most of the texts I have in mind are, in fact, those of the Hebrew Bible, I prefer "Judean writings" to "biblical literature," "scripture," or "LXX" for several reasons. One is simply a desire to avoid anachronism for a period in which we do not know of what, exactly, Greek collections of these writings consisted. More importantly, I wish to include within my category any writings that a given Judean expert held to be sacred or authoritative, not only ones that would become canonical, or even non-canonical texts that are nevertheless well-known (e.g., Enochic literature), but also ones about which we know nothing, but which were of no lesser religious value to those who enlisted them (e.g., "the books of Solomon," whence Eleazar the exorcist derives his wisdom about *daimones*). It is also the case that my terminology resembles the language that such writers as Josephus, Philo, and Paul use to refer to the texts they found to be holy, oracular, or otherwise authoritative (e.g., "the oracles of God," "the holy books," or "the priestly writings of the Judeans"). The task of locating such Judeans as Eleazar and Paul within a wider field of religious experts requires that we reconcile the writings they utilized, and the manners in which they used them, with the kinds of writings and textual practices that are attested for non-Judeans in this context. Thus, "Judean writings" aligns more closely with literary corpora—*Sibylline Oracles, Chaldean Oracles*, Orphica, Hermetica, the books of Hystaspes, and so forth—enlisted by other freelance experts for any number of purposes: divination, prophecy, myth-making, incantations, and so forth. While "Judean writings" may be somewhat imprecise it is no more so than these other terms, which encompass a broad range of texts and textual applications. I revisit this matter extensively in chapter 3.

68. Cf. Ex 14:21; 2 Kgs 2:9–15; Jos 3:14–17, 6:1–20.

69. What Frankfurter characterizes as an "invented Great Tradition" in the sense that freelance experts who drew on Judean figures in this way were ultimately linking their authority and offerings to the institution of the Jerusalem temple and the literary traditions it represented ("The Great, the Little, and the Authoritative Tradition," 25).

The same cast of legendary Judeans appears frequently alongside these others in genealogies of wisdom and practices that were prolific in the imperial period. Vettius Valens praises the "most wonderful Abramos" for transmitting valuable astrological insights in his books, as well as for inventing and testing other things.[70] This link between Judeans and Chaldean astrology is common and can be found even in Josephus's adapted Genesis narrative.[71] Elsewhere Diodoros Siculus reports that Moses received his laws from the god who is invoked as Iao, and Varro notes that the Judean god is called by this name in the Chaldaean mysteries.[72] According to Pompeius Trogus, Moses inherited wisdom from his father Joseph, who was eminently skilled in prodigies, possessed full knowledge of divine law, and also established the science of dream interpretation.[73] For Strabo, Moses was a former Egyptian priest who invented aniconic worship to protest divine representation in the form of beasts or humans.[74] Non-Judean writers are not always so flattering. Regarding the authority of Moses, Apollonius Molon depicts the lawgiver as a *goēs*, while Alexander Polyhistor credits a Hebrew woman named *Mōso* with composing the laws.[75]

As in cases where the purported authorship of Orpheus, Zoroaster, Hystaspes, and Pythagoras legitimated religious practices, secret books, and wisdom traditions, these claims about figures from the Israelite past were not merely fanciful attributions but might offer resources for

---

70. Vettius Valens, 2.28.

71. E.g., Josephus, *AJ* 1.154–68; cf. Philo, *Abr.* 70. See Annette Yoshiko Reed, "Abraham as Chaldean Scientist and Father of the Jews: Josephus, *Ant.* 1.154–68, and the Greco-Roman Discourse About Astronomy/Astrology," *JSJ* 35 (2004): 119–58; Jeffrey Siker, "Abraham in Greco-Roman Paganism," *JSJ* 18 (1987): 188–208.

72. Diodorus Siculus, 1.94.1–2; Varro apud August. *De Cons. Ev.* 1.27.42. The gloss about the Phoenician meaning of Iao occurs in Herennius Philo's reference to Varro's identification of the Judean god (apud Lydus, *De Mens.* 4.53). Elsewhere in Varro's writings, however, he is equivalent to Jupiter.

73. Pompeius Trogas apud Justin, *Hist. Phil.* 36.2.11. See John G. Gager, *Moses in Greco-Roman Paganism*, SBLMS 16 (New York: Abingdon Press, 1972). This reputation for dream interpretation occurs in numerous sources; Porphyry admits that even Pythagoras leaned the exact science of dreams from the Hebrews (*Vit. Pyth.* 11).

74. Strabo, *Geogr.* 16.2.35–37. Abraham is also said to have debated with Egyptian priests. See Josephus, *AJ* 1.161; Reed, "Abraham as Chaldean Scientist and Father of the Jews," 130–32.

75. Apollonius Molon apud Josephus, *C. Ap.* 2.145–48; *Suda* s.v. Ἀλέξανδρος ὁ Μιλήσιος.

self-authorized specialists.[76] Some *Greek Magical Papyri* attribute to Moses assorted apocryphal books and charms, while Eleazar brought Solomon's famed wisdom to bear on matters of exorcism and healing.[77] Using a ring under whose seal was a root that Solomon prescribed, the exorcist would draw out the *daimōn* through the nose of the person whom it afflicted and then banish it by speaking Solomon's name and reciting ancient incantations he had composed. If one did not know that it was Josephus who attributed such traditions Solomon, one might infer that the writer in question possessed faulty knowledge of biblical literature. The passage is thus a useful reminder of how freely practices might be interpolated into stories rooted in Judean myth so as to create ancient precedents for contemporary religious skills and activities.

With the exception of John "the baptizer" and possibly, depending on the integrity of this controversial passage, also of Jesus "the anointed," Josephus's positive assessment of Eleazar is somewhat exceptional among his typically critical stories about Judean religious experts who are not priests or of priestly lineage.[78] To his mind, most put a fine point on the lesson that "innovation and reform in ancestral traditions weigh heavily in the scale that leads to the destruction of followers."[79] Philo also warns, "If anyone cloaking himself under the name and guise of a prophet and claiming to be possessed by inspiration lead us on to the worship of the gods recognized in the different cities, we ought not to listen to him and

---

76. Graf and Iles Johnston, *Ritual Texts for the Afterlife*, 165–84; Edmonds, *Redefining Ancient Orphism*, 24, 211. Morton Smith makes the interesting observation that the *Greek Magical Papyri* contain many spells that use the names of Jesus, Adam, Abraham, Isaac, Jacob, Moses, and Solomon as those of gods or god-like beings, whereas names of historical persons from Greek, Egyptian, or Persian tradition are not used in this capacity, although many such persons are named as authors of spells or magical books. On this basis, Smith posits, "magical deification may have been unusually prominent in Jewish tradition (as exorcism seems to have been)" (*Jesus the Magician*, 114). For the use of curses from Deuteronomy in these practical contexts, see Cohen, *The Beginnings of Jewishness*, 142; M. Louis Robert, "Malédictions funéraires grecques," *Comptes rendus de l'Académie des inscriptions et belles-lettres* 122 (1978): 241–89, at 244–55; Paul Trebilco, *Jewish Communities in Asia Minor*, SNTSMS 69 (Cambridge: Cambridge University Press), 60–69.

77. Josephus, *AJ* 8.44–49. For Moses in the papyri, see Gager, *Moses in Greco-Roman Paganism*, 134–61.

78. Josephus, *AJ* 18.116–17; *AJ* 18.63–64. On the so-called Flavian testimony I am persuaded by the analysis of Steve Mason and others, who for philological and stylistic reasons argue that some lines of the passage are original, while its more exuberant and messianic details are later scribal interpolations (*Josephus and the New Testament*, 225–36). Another exception to Josephus's typically negative view of such actors occurs in his narrative about the embrace of Judean religion by the royal family of Adiabene, which I discuss later.

79. Josephus, *AJ* 18.9.

be deceived by the name of a prophet. For such a one is no prophet, but a *goēs*, since his oracles and pronouncements are falsehoods invented by himself."[80] Although we should exercise caution about placing too much trust in the depictions of Josephus and Philo—or, for that matter, those of Juvenal or Lucian—these accounts share too many points of overlap with one another, and with other sources for freelance experts, to be written off entirely.

Furthermore, while we would not expect a writer such as Josephus to depict Judean specialists otherwise, it is important to recognize that his denunciations of would-be prophets and exegetes ultimately function as foils to his own prophetic and intellectual talents. Explaining that Judean rebels had been provoked to war in part by interpreting an ambiguous oracle in their holy writings (χρησμὸς ἀμφίβολος ἐν τοῖς ἱεροῖς εὑρημένος γράμμασιν) to mean that one from their country was about to become the king of the world, Josephus remarks that many wise men were led astray concerning its interpretation (πολλοὶ τῶν σοφῶν ἐπλανήθησαν περὶ τὴν κρίσιν), since the oracle referred not to a Judean but to Vespasian, as he correctly ascertained.[81] Tacitus and Suetonius reproduce the tradition about the oracle without mentioning Josephus by name, though Dio and Appian both acknowledge him directly.[82] Never reticent about his abilities, the man himself sums things up nicely: "Thus Josephus won his freedom as the reward for his predictions (τῶν προειρημένων) and his power of insight into the future was no longer discredited."[83] In sum, regardless of any one author's angle on freelance experts, on freelance experts in Judean religion, or on Judeans as a people, the evidence just considered indicates that many were either aware that Judeans participated in this sort of religious activity or found it plausible that they would do so. While freelance experts in Judean religion may appear less often in our sources than other kinds of foreign experts, they are not infrequent, and any theorization of

---

80. Philo, *Spec. Leg.* 1.315 (trans. F. H. Colson, LCL).

81. Josephus, *BJ* 6.310–13.

82. Tacitus, *Hist.* 5.13; Suetonius, *Vesp.* 4.5–6; Cassius Dio, 66.1.1–4; Appian apud Zonaras, 11.16. The latter two authors disagree, however, about the type of prophecy: the former states that Josephus ascertained these events through dream interpretation, the latter, by discovering an oracle in the sacred Judean writings.

83. Josephus, *BJ* 4.629.

this class of religious activity would be incomplete without accounting for their notable presence therein.

Moreover, like other purveyors of ethnically coded wisdom, skills, or practices, Judean experts were tied to particular ethnically coded forms of expertise.[84] A perusal of the sources collected in Menahem Stern's volumes of *Greek and Latin Authors on Jews and Judaism* yields a fairly regular assortment of such ideas about Judean religion, conveying a sense of the special religious skills for which Judeans were renowned: dream interpretation, prophecy, revelation, interpretation of oracles, revelations linked with literary prophecies, law instruction, exorcism, and also baptism, which is depicted variously as a purifying practice or even as an initiation rite that enacts essence change.[85] This assortment is not only internally consistent in sources penned by non-Judeans but also for a Judean author such as Josephus.[86]

Befitting the great number and variety of diviners that occur in our evidence for specialist activity, many of the capabilities ascribed to Judeans were divinatory in nature and often enlisted their holy writings. It is no accident that so many appealed to the authority of these texts, regardless of whether they utilized them directly within their respective offerings or only alleged knowledge of their contents in order to lend credibility to another religious practice or forms of expertise. Josephus links his own revelations with literary prophecy, inasmuch as he was enabled to understand the meaning of inspired dreams and ambiguously uttered prophetic statements by virtue of the fact that he was "not ignorant of the prophecies in the sacred books."[87] Likewise, the Essenes profess extraordinary powers

---

84. Since there are indications of Judeans assuming different specialist guises—from instructors of ethics to exorcists—my general criterion for delineating Judean *religious specialists* is that they directly enlisted their god (here, in the singular) and other non-obvious beings in their programs and services.

85. Menahem Stern, *Greek and Latin Authors on Jews and Judaism: Edited with Introductions, Translations, and Commentary I–III* (Jerusalem: Israel Academy of Sciences and Humanities, 1974). For the latter sense of baptism I have in mind the transformative effects that Paul ascribes to this rite, for which see chapter 4.

86. Notably, most of these skills and practices are attested in the authentic Pauline Epistles. See chapter 4.

87. Josephus, *BJ* 3.352. As Mason notes, for Josephus, a Judean of priestly descent, textual knowledge is inseparable from priestly authority, which is ultimately the source of his own wisdom and mysterious power, as it is for others of priestly lineage who also possess prophetic abilities (*Josephus and the New Testament*, 49; cf. *BJ* 3.356). Of course recourse to

of prognostication due to being well versed in the holy books, and seldom, he confirms, do they err in their predictions.[88]

That these texts were thought to contain information pertinent to first-century affairs is clear: Josephus claims several times that they foretell the entirety of world history, including the rise and fall of nations, while both Philo and Paul affirm their oracular profile.[89] Other scholars have demonstrated their literary influence on famous Latin poets of the early principate, which suggests a fairly broad awareness of Judean writings at least among the producers and consumers of other texts.[90] Regarding the question of which books were being read for prophetic content, rather than for tenets about the proper conduct of human life, Josephus appears to impute prophetic authorship or predictive potential to at least eighteen of the twenty-two texts he considers to be authoritative, if not the entirety of this implicit "canon."[91] And although he attests to a multiplicity of interests that the Judean writings address—prophecy, the proper conduct of human life, effective governance, among other applications—there is no obvious correlation between how he labels them and how they are read. Rather, the Judean "laws" (νόμοι), "oracles" (λόγιοι), "holy books" (ἱερὰ βιβλία), and "prophecies in the holy writings" (χρησμοὶ ἐν τοῖς ἱεροῖς γράμμασιν) seem to be largely interchangeable when he refers to this corpus collectively.

---

intellectual forms of divination makes sense for someone of Josephus's station; dreams concerning Judean affairs did not always depend on textual knowledge, however. In a discussion of dreams that cannot be solved until the events predicted occur, Artemidorus (*Oneirocrit.* 4.24) gives the example of a *praefectus castrorum* who in a dream saw written upon his sword ι κ θ. Only after a Judaic revolt in Cyrene did he come to understand that by the ι were meant the Judeans, by the κ the Kyrenaeans, by the θ Thanatos.

88. Josephus, *BJ* 2.159; cf. *AJ* 13.331. He also recalls how Simon the Essene correctly interpreted a dream of Archelaus in the time of Augustus when none of the seers (μάντεις) or Chaldeans whom he summoned were able to do so (*BJ* 2.112–13).

89. E.g., Josephus, *AJ* 10.266–81; *AJ* 11.1–3; *AJ* 11.331–39. See Heidi Wendt, "Galatians 3:1 as an Allusion to Textual Prophecy," *JBL* 135 (2016): 369–89.

90. See Nicholas Horsefall, "Virgil and the Jews," *Vergilius* 58 (2012): 67–80; Jan N. Bremmer, "Post Scriptum: Virgil and Jewish Literature," *Vergilius* 59 (2013): 157–64.

91. See, e.g., Josephus, *C. Ap.* 1.37–40. For Josephus's assertions about the authority of these texts, see Michael L. Satlow, *How the Bible Became Holy* (New Haven: Yale University Press, 2014), 244–47. Satlow further proposes that Josephus's knowledge of these texts was honed at Rome, insofar as the *Antiquities* reveals a "much sharper awareness of the 'holy writings'" than is the case for previous works, in which he treats the texts primarily as a collection of oracles. Moreover, Josephus relates that Titus had given him a gift of "holy books" after the

I have argued elsewhere that, for their prophetic value, Judean writings were on a par with the *Sibylline Oracles* and other oracular texts the Romans held in their state collection, which was rumored to include the *libri* of the Etruscan seer Vegoia and perhaps also texts of the *disciplina Etrusca*, the oracles of Marcius, and those of Albunea of Tibur.[92] Aelian seems to presume as much when he includes a Judean Sibyl among those of Erythraea, Samos, Egypt, Sardinia, and Cumae, while Pausanias too posits a Judean Sibyl: "There grew up among the Hebrews above Palestine a woman who gave oracles and was named Sabbe. They say that the father of Sabbe was Berosus, and her mother Erymanthe. But some call her a Babylonian Sibyl, others an Egyptian."[93] Seeking to disprove the evidence for Jesus that Christians draw out of these texts, Celsus equates "the predictions, whether they were actually spoken or not, made by the people of Judea after their usual manner, as even now is customary," with "the predictions of the Pythian priestess or of the priestesses of Dodona or of the Clarian Apollo or at Branchidae or at the shrine of Zeus Ammon, and of countless other prophets."[94]

Although it cannot be proven, I have also raised the possibility that the triumphal introduction of Judean writings to Rome resulted in their incorporation into the collection of prophetic corpora curated within the temple of Apollo Palatinus.[95] Josephus reports that after featuring a copy of the law in the Flavian triumph, Vespasian ordered that it, along with the purple veil of the Jerusalem temple, be deposited and kept in the imperial complex (ἐν τοῖς βασιλείοις).[96] Whereas the phrase is usually taken to mean the imperial residence—and therefore the emperor's removal of the law to his own home as evidence that he regarded it as merely an item of war booty—the use of the plural suggests rather the complex of houses, porticos, and other structures atop the Palatine, which included the temple where the *Sibylline Oracles* were kept. The proposal fits well

---

fall of the Jerusalem temple, which, Satlow suggests, may have been the first time that he actually possessed a copy of them (Josephus, *Vita* 418; *How the Bible Became Holy*, 247).

92. The references are scattered and include Livy, 25.23; Servius, *Aen.* 6.72; Lactantius, *Div. instit.* 1.6.12.

93. Aelian, *Var. hist.* 12.35; Pausanias, *Descr.* 10.12.9 (trans. W. H. S. Jones, LCL).

94. Origen, *C. Cels.* 7.3 (trans. Henry Chadwick, *Stern GLAJJ* 2:375).

95. Wendt, "The Fate of the Judean Writings in Flavian Rome," 107.

96. Josephus, *BJ* 7.150.

with the Romans' tendency to amass prophetic corpora, at least some of which seem to have found their way to the Palatine, whether they were placed in the temple or in its adjacent library.[97] That the copy of the law would have met with such a fate is all the more conceivable since the Judean writings were widely recognized for having predicted Rome's new dynastic arrangement.[98]

The importance of Egyptian religion in legitimating the Flavians' reign has received ample treatment. As Albert Henrichs argued, Vespasian's stop en route to Rome at the Serapeion of Alexandria, where he performed miraculous healings, underscored the security of his new position. The god's approval of the general-turned-emperor was signaled not only by the enablement of these abilities but also by the affirmation of the Egyptian priest Basilides. Of the event, Mary Beard writes, "Someone must have taken care to disseminate 'news' of Vespasian's Egyptian miracles, with all their allure of divinity that would have gone down well in some quarters."[99] The same scholars who thus characterize the role of Egyptian religion, however, view the ideological significance of Judea and Judean religion exclusively through the lens of military conquest. Martin Goodman concludes that the Flavians' war "waged on Judaism" was a permanent feature of their propaganda, while Beard has made a compelling case for viewing the subsequent triumph as an inaugural moment that

---

97. For the sacredness of certain libraries, including those of the temple of Apollo and the Templum Pacis, see Richard Neudecker, "Archives, Books, and Sacred Space in Rome," in König, Oikonomopoulou, and Woolf, *Ancient Libraries*, 312–31, at 320–99. For libraries in Flavian Rome more generally, see Pier Luigi Tucci, "Flavian Libraries in the City of Rome," in König, Oikonomopoulou, and Woolf, *Ancient Libraries*, 277–309, esp. 291–300.

98. It is not inconceivable that the temple veil, which, according to Josephus, was embroidered with complex astrological symbols (*BJ* 5.212–13), was considered a valuable divinatory instrument or object of study in its own right. In a piece about Rabbi Aqiba's visit to Rome, David Noy notes a reference to Rabbi Eleazar ben Jose visiting Rome, presumably sometime in the mid-second century, where he saw the veil (with bloodstains from sacrificial offerings) on public display: "Rabbi Aqiba Comes to Rome: A Jewish Pilgrimage in Reverse?" in *Pilgrimage in Greco-Roman and Early Christian Antiquity: Seeing the Gods*, ed. Jaś Elsner and Ian Rutherford (New York: Oxford University Press, 2005), 373–85, at 382. Where Eleazar encountered the veil (if he did at all) is unclear to Noy, although he finds it highly improbable that a Jewish sightseer would have been allowed into the imperial palace and speculates that it was taken to the Templum Pacis sometime after the Flavian triumph.

99. Beard, "The Triumph of Flavius Josephus," in *Flavian Rome: Culture, Image, Text*, ed. A.J. Boyle and W. J. Dominik (Leiden: Brill, 2003), 541–58, at 557.

transformed Vespasian and his sons from usurpers into an established imperial dynasty.[100]

The dichotomy of religious versus military legitimacy is misleading and rooted, I suspect, in the assumption that Judaism could not, like Egyptian religion or astrology, lend credibility to a "pagan" emperor. Furthermore, whatever positive attitude toward Judean religion might be gleaned from the Flavians' actions is overshadowed, understandably, by their role in the destruction and decommissioning of the temples at Jerusalem and Leontopolis, respectively. In the absence of a differentiated picture of Judean religion it is inevitable that efforts to dismantle these institutions, especially the former temple, are equivalent to a dismantling of Judaism as a whole.[101] The matter stands to be enriched by consideration of a more complex landscape of Judean religion, one that includes the activities of freelance experts as well as the widespread recognition of Judean texts as sources of religious wisdom and prophecies. While the Flavians might have struck strategic blows against a particular form of Judean religion—civic and other temple institutions in or associated with Judea—this did not stop them from simultaneously enlisting the prophecy of Josephus, a Judean of priestly ancestry, as well as oracles in Judean writings, among other divine signs that universally corroborated Vespasian's acclamation. Judea lent as much if not more religious legitimacy to the new dynasty as Egypt, even if the exact mechanisms of legitimation were à propos of each ethnic idiom: dream interpretation, literary divination, and the pronouncements of Josephus on the one hand, and signs issued at an oracular healing sanctuary and interpreted by Basilides on the other.[102]

Roman familiarity with Judeans and Judean religion is, of course, attested much earlier than the Flavian period. An embassy of Judeans had visited Rome during the Maccabean Revolt, while Pompey's conquest of Jerusalem in 63 BCE, the inclusion of captive Hasmonean royals and other spoils in his triple-triumph two years later, and subsequent battles on Judean soil all drew attention to the region and precipitated an influx of

---

100. Goodman, *Rome and Jerusalem*, 432; Beard, "The Triumph of Flavius Josephus," 552–53.

101. See James B. Rives, "Flavian Religious Policy and the Destruction of the Jerusalem Temple," in Edmondson, Mason, and Rives, *Flavius Josephus and Flavian Rome*, 145–66, esp. 151–66.

102. Wendt, "The Fate of the Judean Writings in Flavian Rome," 103–4.

Judean slaves to Rome.[103] Granting that he wrote about the period at some remove, Porphyry nevertheless asserts that the law of the Judeans, which had once flourished in only a small region of Syria, gradually extended to Italy, although not before the reign of Gaius Caesar.[104] It is in this vein that I inferred from Justin's remark about the punishment attached to reading "the prophets" that confiscations of privately circulating prophetic books during the reigns of Augustus and Tiberius might have even included Judean texts.

Regardless of the history of these writings at Rome, the reputation of their oracular character and potency must have been bolstered considerably by the role they were said to have played in both the events of the Judean War and the dynastic transformation that occurred in its wake. As further fodder, Josephus affirms several times that the Judean god was instrumental in the Romans' victory and also credits Titus with recognizing and honoring his assistance.[105] His claim that God had already departed from the temple prior to its destruction has even prompted speculation about whether some Romans understood the removal of Jerusalem cult paraphernalia to Rome as a sort of *evocatio*.[106] It may be impossible to know if anyone, let alone a significant number of people, actually thought that the Judean god had been incorporated into the Roman pantheon and now received cult there. At the very least, Josephus supplies ample evidence in his own person for the kinds of claims a professed expert in Judean religious *might* make for the benefit of Roman audiences. Regardless, one can imagine how a renewed focus on Judea, and Judean divination, in the mid- to late-first century CE fomented interest in *iudaica* that had already existed at Rome for some time.

---

103. Philo, *Leg.* 155; cf. Josephus, *BJ* 1.154, 180; *AJ* 14.71, 79, 97, 120, 275, 304, 313, 321; *AJ* 20.244; John M. G. Barclay, *Jews in the Mediterranean Diaspora: From Alexander to Trajan (323 BCE–117 CE)* (London: T&T Clark, 1996), esp. 290–91; Erich S. Gruen, *Diaspora: Jews Among Greeks and Romans* (Cambridge: Harvard University Press, 2002), 3, 20–23; Beard, *The Roman Triumph*, 7–41.

104. Porphyry, *Adv. Christ.* apud Augustine, *Ep.* 102.8.

105. On God foreordaining and bringing about both the Roman Empire and the Flavian dynasty, see Josephus, *BJ* 2.390–91; 3.351; 4.623; 5.367, 412; 6.109, 300–2, 312–13, 411–12. On Titus's acknowledgement of the Judean god, see Josephus, *BJ* 5.519.

106. Josephus, *BJ* 6.299–300. See John S. Kloppenborg, "*Evocatio Deorum* and the Date of Mark," *JBL* 124 (2005): 419–50, esp. 442–47.

Additionally, although Egyptianizing monuments and images enjoyed their greatest vogue under the Julio-Claudians, the Flavians evoked both Egypt and Judea vividly in the capital's cityscape.[107] Beyond the Colosseum, with the Judea inscription it bore, two monuments in particular—the Arch of Titus, (in)famous for its inner-relief depicting the triumphal procession of the temple's despoiled offering table and golden candelabrum, and the Templum Pacis, where these instruments were later installed—underscored the centrality of the Jerusalem cult to the new dynasty.[108] While allusions to this province are less obvious than the Egyptian-themed material attested so amply in Roman Italy, the impact of Judean monuments, objects, and images ought not be discounted for subtlety. The public displays of the Flavian triumph, made permanent in spaces designed to proclaim the era of Flavian rule, were visible reminders of Judean culture. On the basis of comparable dynamics with respect to other examples of foreign religion I propose that these features would have stimulated interest in certain forms of Judean religion—namely, ones purveyed by specialized exegetes and predicated on oracular texts—and, with this interest, a demand for expertise therein.

Foreign Royals and Courtly Experts

Another important consideration in accounting for the widespread recognition and appeal of Judean religion in the first century is the social status of some people said to have engaged in Judaic practices to varying degrees: members of the imperial family and other royal houses, provincial governors, and other social elites. Regarding *aegyptiaca* in the late republic, Diana E. E. Kleiner has argued that Italian fascination with Egypt quickened with the increasingly intimate relationship between Rome and Alexandria, as well as Julius Caesar and Cleopatra. Caesar's favorable impression of Alexandria during his Nilotic travels encouraged him to reorient his own city along the Tiber, while the Ptolemaic queen's high-profile

---

107. C. Brian Rose, "The Egyptianizing of Rome in the Wake of Actium," in *Festschrift for Prof. Orhan Bingöl* (Ankara: Bilgin Kültür Sanat Yayınları, 2013), 543–58; Fergus Millar, "Last Year in Jerusalem: Monuments of the Jewish War in Rome," in Edmondson, Mason, and Rives, *Flavius Josephus and Flavian Rome*, 101–28.

108. Géza Alföldy, "Eine Bauinschrift aus dem Colosseum," *ZPE* 109 (1995): 195–226; Carlos F. Noreña, "Medium and Message in Vespasian's Templum Pacis," *MAAR* 48 (2003): 25–43.

sojourn at his Roman villa had a palpable influence on everything, Kleiner argues, from Roman women's hairstyles to the popularity of Egyptian motifs in Roman art. Roger Beck posits similar effects with respect to the arrival of the former royal *familia* of Commagene—whose members took up residence at the capital following the deposition of Antiochus IV in 72 CE—and the emergence of the mysteries of Mithras shortly thereafter.[109] That these mysteries were conveyed through the adapted medium of astrology also suggests to Beck that their authorship lay in intellectual circles, maybe even the immediate circle of Ti. Claudius Balbillus—thought to be the son of Thrasyllus—whose daughter married a Commagenean prince.[110] Regardless of whether one is persuaded by this exact theory of Mithraic origins, at the very least it could shed light on why Persian-themed forms of religion, which had apparently been present at Rome in one form or another for some time, became more popular toward the end of the first century and began to coalesce around a particular divine figure affiliated with this eastern kingdom.

What has received less attention is the possibility that a similar pattern holds for another prominent royal family, the Herodians, whose members also resided at Rome for much of the first century and whose presence correlates with and might reasonably have contributed to an increase in enthusiasm for Judaic practices.[111] Josephus reports frequent and favorable dealings between the Herodian and Julio-Claudian royals and, on occasion, between the latter and Jerusalem priests. During the reign of Nero, for instance, Ishmael, the current high priest of the Jerusalem temple, accompanied by Helcias, the keeper of its treasury, traveled to Rome to entreat Nero regarding a controversial wall built in the temple precinct.[112] Their success owed much to the emperor's current

---

109. As Josephus writes, "And there they remained, treated with every respect" (*BJ* 7.243). See Roger Beck, "The Mysteries of Mithras: A New Account of Their Genesis," *JRS* 88 (1998): 115–28, esp. 37–38. As Richard L. Gordon has argued, it is specifically among Roman aristocrats and their dependents that interest in Mithras is first attested: "Mithraism and Roman Society," *Religion* 2 (1972): 92–121.

110. Beck, "The Mysteries of Mithras," 42–43 and n. 60; idem, "Whose Astrology? The Imprint of Ti. Claudius Balbillus on the Mithraic Mysteries," in *Beck on Mithraism: Collected Works with New Essays* (Burlington, VT: Ashgate, 2004), 323–29.

111. See Daniel R. Schwartz, "Herodians and *Ioudaioi* in Flavian Rome," in Edmonson, Mason, and Rives, *Flavius Josephus and Flavian Rome*, 63–78.

112. Josephus, *AJ* 20.195.

wife (and former mistress), Poppaea Sabina, who revered the Judean god
(θεοσεβὴς γὰρ ἦν), apparently in addition to her other dealings with foreign religion.[113] Insofar as the habits of Roman elites, especially members of the imperial family, tended to rouse popular interest and imitation, already in the Julio-Claudian period there are examples of imperial
and other elite women planting such seeds with respect to some form(s)
of Judean religion. Following Kleiner's analysis of the captivating effects
of Cleopatra's time at Rome, it stands to reason that Berenice, Herodian
queen and companion of Titus, stimulated popular imagination much
as Caesar's consort had over a century earlier.[114] While the relationship
between elite and popular trends at Rome was often dialectic, interest in
Judean religion among notable Romans corresponded, as either a catalyst or a reflection, to the habits of wider audiences.

Trivial though some of these details may seem, they contribute to a
fuller case for the heightened status of Judea and Judean religion in Rome
in the first century. Again, the Flavian period did not engender but accen-
tuated or amplified a trend apparent in earlier historical sources. Josephus
is eager in his refutation of Apion to cite gentile appreciation for Judean
religion throughout the whole world and, though typically ambivalent
about the wholesale embrace of Judaic customs, supplies in the last book
of the *Antiquities* extensive details about the house of Adiabene's adoption of such a life.[115] The story's implications for proselytism and conversion to Judaism have been written about at length and are of lesser interest for the moment than, first, the means by which Helena of Adiabene
and her son Izates became interested in Judean teachings and, second,
how their actions square with other instances of elite participation in

---

113. See E. Mary Smallwood, "The Alleged Jewish Tendencies of Poppaea Sabina," *JTS* 10
(1959): 329–35.

114. See Kleiner, *Cleopatra and Rome*; Ross Shepard Kraemer, "Typical and Atypical Jewish
Family Dynamics: The Cases of Babatha and Berenice," in *Early Christian Families in
Context*, ed. David Balch and Carolyn Osiek (Grand Rapids, MI: Eerdmans), 114–39; Glen
W. Bowersock, "Foreign Elites at Rome," in Edmondson, Mason, and Rives, *Flavius Josephus
and Flavian Rome*, 53–62. See also Cassius Dio, 67.14.1–3.

115. Josephus, *AJ* 20.17–96, esp. 34–53. For discussion of this episode as a matter of con-
version to Judaism, see Lawrence H. Schiffman, "The Conversion of the Royal House of
Adiabene in Josephus and Rabbinic Sources," in *Josephus, Judaism, and Christianity*, ed.
Louis H. Feldman and Gohei Hata (Detroit, MI: Wayne State University Press, 1987), 293–
312; Gary Gilbert, "The Making of a Jew: 'God-fearer' or Convert in the Story of Izates,"
USQR 44 (1991): 299–313.

foreign religion.[116] Regarding the first matter, it is immediately striking that Josephus's narrative prominently features not one but three figures who might be described as freelance experts in Judean religion: Ananias, a Judean merchant (Ἰουδαῖός τις ἔμπορος) who visited the king's wives at the port city of Charax Spasinou and taught them to worship God in the manner customary for Judeans (ἐδίδασκεν αὐτὰς τὸν θεὸν σέβειν, ὡς Ἰουδαίοις πάτριον ἦν) and, then, with their cooperation, persuaded Izates as well; the unnamed Judean who in Adiabene had already instructed Izates's mother Helena and brought her over to their laws (συνεβεβήκει δὲ καὶ τὴν Ἑλένην ὁμοίως ὑφ' ἑτέρου τινὸς Ἰουδαίου διδαχθεῖσαν εἰς τοὺς ἐκείνων μετακεκομίσθαι νόμους); and finally, Eleazar, another "Judean" but from the Galilee, who, after having found Izates reading the law of Moses, insisted that it was impious for the king to do so without first being circumcised.[117]

That Ananias was a merchant does not exclude him from acting as a religious expert for the benefit of the royal family. Many self-authorized specialists supported themselves, or at least alleged to do so, in order to deflect the problematic connotations of interest and profit that were intrinsic to this sort of religious activity—all the more so since he seems to have secured a permanent position at court henceforth.[118] Nor would Ananias be the first to wear these two hats: Marcion of Pontus was said to have captained many ships before settling at Rome to dedicate himself fully to his proprietary program of Christian teachings.[119] Whereas many theories of cult migration posit pious merchants as the passive agents behind the diffusion of foreign religion through major seaports such as Puteoli, Corinth, Delos, and Alexandria, cities rich in trade also attracted scores of freelance

---

116. For discussion and bibliography, see Shaye J.D. Cohen, "Respect for Judaism by Gentiles According to Josephus," *HTR* 80 (1987): 409–30, esp. 424–28.

117. Josephus, *AJ* 20.34–35; 20.43–44; cf. *BJ* 2.560, where Josephus describes the gentile wives of Damascus, also, as having gone over to Judean religion. For the language of being "drawn" or "brought over to" Judean practices, see Cohen, *The Beginnings of Jewishness*, 170–71.

118. Notably, Ananias's opposition to the desire of Izates to be circumcised stems from a fear of being punished should it become known that he had instructed the king in unseemly practices (Josephus, *AJ* 20.41).

119. For the sources, see Heikki Räisänen, "Marcion," in *A Companion to Second-Century "Heretics,"* ed. Antti Marjanen and Petri Luomanen, Suppl. to Vigiliae Christianae 76 (Leiden: Brill, 2005), 100–24, esp. 102–4.

experts who sought them out proactively.[120] As both Petronius and Acts make clear—not to mention the thrice-shipwrecked apostle Paul—these actors frequently traveled aboard merchant ships, which may partially explain why many "cults" seem to have spread along maritime routes.[121] Indeed, Apollonius—certainly no merchant—transported Sarapis's ancient cult objects from Memphis to sea-girt Delos aboard a well-banded ship.[122] The inscription is often read, not incorrectly, as a canonical account of cult migration, yet it signals the need for a subtler parsing of what social processes are being imagined in these scenarios. In this case, the migration of Sarapis's "cult" was the act of a solitary religious expert, a reminder that individuals and individual agency were often the primary engines of such processes.[123]

The all-consuming discussion about whether the story of the house of Adiabene qualifies as an instance of conversion to Judaism has distracted from the highly specific nature of the family's encounters with Judean religion, not to mention the strangeness of these three unrelated Judeans—none of whom Josephus aligns with a recognized type of religious authority (i.e., priestly ancestry or affiliation with one of the "Judean philosophies")—managing to secure positions within the royal household of a distant land.[124] Moreover, two of the figures in question, Ananias and Eleazar, differ sharply on the issue of circumcision, with

---

120. E.g., Ascough, "Networks of people, goods, and ideas in the circum-Mediterranean were web-like, spreading out in multiple directions, with persons travelling not only back and forth along one path, but diverting through other paths as well. ... In our imagined scenario the 'network' for transference of information would take place when one merchant speaks with a supplier, or another merchant, or ship captain, or perhaps through friends and social contacts, including those forged through membership in associations. As noted, physical networks on the land and sea facilitated such contacts" ("Redescribing the Thessalonians' 'Mission,'" 79).

121. Petronius, *Sat.* 100–14; Acts 20–21, 27–28; 2 Cor 11:25.

122. Lines 35–38.

123. E.g., Walter Burkert, *Ancient Mystery Cults* (Cambridge: Harvard University Press, 1989), 38; Hanges, *Paul, Founder of Churches*, 139–65. In most other respects my theorization of freelance expertise is compatible with theories of cult migration.

124. Admittedly, Eleazar is the only one of the three Judeans whose native region (the Galilee) is given; Ananias and Helena's unnamed instructor might have lived outside of Judea, even within the Kingdom of Adiabene. See, e.g., James P. Ware, who decides against viewing these three Judeans as "missionaries" because they were not, on his reading, actively seeking converts to Judaism: *Paul and the Mission of the Church: Philippians in Ancient Jewish Context* (Grand Rapids, MI: Baker Academic, 2011), 47–55.

the former resolutely forbidding Izates to be circumcised on the threat that he will leave the land should the king do so but with the latter, "who had a reputation for being extremely strict when it came to the ancestral customs (τὰ πάτρια)," insisting that it was impious to read the law without doing everything that it commanded.[125]

One problem with applying the paradigm of conversion to this narrative, then, is that the Judeans in question are made to act on behalf of a larger religious entity when Josephus provides no indication that this was the case. Closer parallels for their actions can be found, I would argue, among the courtly experts in (typically intellectualizing) foreign wisdom whom we have already encountered. One such figure appears in Josephus's story about a Judean from Cyprus named Atomos whom the Roman procurator Felix employed to pose as a *magos* in order to persuade Drusilla to leave her husband for him.[126] It is unclear whether Josephus is using *magos* pejoratively or simply to mean that Atomos encouraged Drusilla by performing some form of divination. There is a curious correspondence, however, between this figure and Bar-Jesus or Elymas, who appears in Acts alongside the Roman proconsul of Cyprus, Sergius Paulus, an intelligent man, according to the author, despite his dealings with a "magician" and "false prophet" (μάγος, ψευδοπροφήτης).[127] As a rival of the apostles, Elymas might earn this umbrage, but in view of the aforementioned Roman aristocratic habits, it is more likely that one in his role would have been an authority on some intellectualizing form of Judean religion.

To return to the house of Adiabene, it is also worth noting that when Helena visits Jerusalem to worship and offer sacrifices at the temple,

---

125. Josephus, *AJ* 20.43–5. À propos of the last chapter, Josephus says that Ananias objected to the rite in part because he feared that if it became known that the king had been circumcised then he, as the one who had instructed him in Judean religion, would be held responsible for encouraging unseemly practices and punished accordingly (20.41). The disagreement about the requirement of circumcision has unmistakable overtones of the conflict between Paul and the Jerusalem apostles (esp. Gal 2:7–14, 5:3–6:13). See J. Albert Harrill, *Paul the Apostle: His Life and Legacy in their Roman Context* (Cambridge: Cambridge University Press, 2012), 56–58; Mark D. Nanos, "The Question of Conceptualization: Qualifying Paul's Position on Circumcision in Dialogue with Josephus's Advisors to King Izates," in *Paul Within Judaism: Restoring the First-Century Context to the Apostle*, ed. Mark D. Nanos and Magnus Zetterholm (Minneapolis: Fortress, 2015), 105–52.

126. Josephus, *AJ* 20.142. See Cohen, *The Beginnings of Jewishness*, 79.

127. Acts 13:6–12. The coincidence of Judean *magoi*, Roman proconsuls, and Cyprus might stem from a literary relationship between Acts and the *Antiquities*. See Mason, *Josephus and the New Testament*, 251–93.

"which was," Josephus reminds his readers, "famous throughout the world," her actions are consistent with those of the many social elites who traveled to famed sanctuaries in the Roman period to undergo initiations, consult oracles, or bestow patronage. Undoubtedly, the degree of devotion to the Judean god that Helena and Izates exhibited was impressive and entailed specific requirements befitting his preferred manner of worship. Outside of Jerusalem, however, none of their actions, which included offering financial resources to the city's inhabitants during a harsh famine and commissioning pyramid tombs for the royal family in the temple's vicinity, would be construed as evidence for religious conversion. To the contrary, they are more or less in keeping with a pattern of elite involvement with foreign sanctuaries that, as we saw in chapter 1, became increasingly common in the Roman period.

As Shaye J. D. Cohen observes, Adiabene poses something of a conundrum for Josephus, who is usually more circumspect in his discussions of gentiles adopting Judean practices, possibly due to the gravid political implications that allegiance to Judean laws might hold for his Roman readers.[128] On the one hand, Helena and Izates's thoroughgoing embrace of Judean religion and subsequent patronage of Jerusalem are points of pride for an author with his apologetic interests.[129] On the other, any acknowledgement of their adoption of Judean religion—particularly the requirement of circumcision—requires explanation of how they came to be such fervent devotees of the Judean god in the first place, namely, though the efforts of freelance experts of the sort to whom Josephus frequently objects. One wonders whether his occasional ambivalence about the matter of non-Judeans taking up Judean practices might have much to do with the reality that self-authorized specialists were so regularly involved in such scenarios.[130]

And yet, whatever the drawbacks, it is also the case that the complicity of self-authorized experts in the story of the royal family of Adiabene is entirely in keeping with Josephus's aspiration to serve as an—if not

---

128. Cohen, "Respect for Judaism by Gentiles According to Josephus," 424–25.

129. Cf. Schiffman, "The Conversion of the House of Adiabene," 307–8.

130. This is clearly the case with the Mosaic wisdom instructors, whose actions at Rome occasioned an expulsion, and one that, whatever its scope, affected at least some of the city's Judean population. See Wendt, "A Rereading of Judean Expulsions from Rome," 112–14, 120–21.

the—authority on Judean religion and religious texts for the benefit of the Flavian emperors and other aristocratic or intellectual audiences at Rome.[131] Everything about the narrative, including its convenient placement toward the end of the *Antiquities*, serves to legitimate his new role. Taken together with his numerous references to the reverence Titus displayed for the Judean god upon recognizing his hand in bringing about a favorable (for the Romans) outcome of the war, one might infer a parallel between the Adiabene royals' relationship to Judean religion and the Flavians' own, with Josephus acting as their specialized, even priestly instructor. Goodman has proposed that his attempts to ingratiate himself to the Flavians may betray sights set on securing an appointment to the high priesthood should they decide to rebuild the Jerusalem temple.[132] While Goodman may be correct, the essence of his suggestion does not require so exact an ambition on Josephus's part; the foreign religious experts who ran in such circles, whatever their proximity to the imperial family, tended to fare quite well at Rome without holding any formal office. While Josephus is more akin to Thrasyllus, Chaeremon, Balbillus, Ptolemy Seleucus—an exact contemporary at Flavian court—and other foreign experts found within elite retinues than to Juvenal's priestess or dream interpreters, the difference is a ultimately a matter of factors such as his demonstrable intellectual abilities, his native social status, and the status of the patrons whom he wished to attract.[133] As was the case for the religious legislation examined in chapter 1, the contrast between "authorized" and "unauthorized" specialists was not self-evident or strict but involved different sources of legitimacy, levels of skill, and status. It may be in accordance with this logic that so many experts who, like Josephus, introduced their native gods, religious practices, and institutions to Roman audiences had a vested interest in producing normative accounts of their native religion that might then be used to discredit rivals working within the same idiom.

---

131. For Josephus's intended audiences, see Steve Mason, "Flavius Josephus in Flavian Rome: Reading Between the Lines," in Boyle and Dominik, *Flavian Rome: Culture, Image, Text,* 559–89; idem, "Of Audience and Meaning: Reading Josephus's *Bellum Iudaicum* in the Context of a Flavian Audience," in *Josephus and Jewish History in Flavian Rome and Beyond,* ed. Joseph Sievers and Gaia Lembi (Leiden: Brill, 2005), 71–100; Hannah M. Cotton and Werner Eck, "Josephus' Roman Audience: Josephus and the Roman Elites," in Edmondson, Mason, and Rives, *Flavius Josephus and Flavian Rome,* 37–52.

132. Goodman, *Rome and Jerusalem,* 447–48.

133. For a more extensive discussion of Josephus's position and activities in Flavian Rome, see Tessa Rajak, *Josephus: The Historian and His Society* (London: Duckworth, 1983);

Contestations Among Foreign Writer-Intellectuals

In the preceding pages I have cast a wide net in attempting to explain the recognition and appeal of foreign religious experts in the Roman period. While there is much insight to be gained from looking beyond literary sources for evidence that enhances our understanding of these dynamics, it is undoubtedly the case that writings were deeply and directly implicated in promoting them. In some cases, texts offered opportunities for nuanced differentiation: Josephus and Philo lay out for their readers normative schemes of Judean religion and philosophy while also decrying the misappropriations of other Judeans claiming expertise in such matters. Josephus had a stake in controlling the normative view of Judean religion at the expense of other would-be experts, and even Heliodorus's fictional Egyptian prophet delineates the unsavory purveyors of "popular" Egyptian wisdom who wallow among corpses, are ministrant to images, and rely on incantations from those who, like him, possess true wisdom because, as priests from a prophetic line, they are trained from youth to be companions of the gods and experts in the heavens.[134]

The same crop of authors who translated their respective cultural legacies into terms relatable and appealing to Roman readers also took pains to distance these legacies from those of other foreign cultures with which theirs might be amalgamated from an unnuanced perspective.[135] That Judeans and Egyptians were often pitted against one another in literature seems to have much to do with the number of characteristics their respective religious traditions were thought to share: great antiquity, authoritative writings and textual practices, and exotic writing

---

Joseph Sievers and Gaia Lembi, eds., *Josephus and Jewish History in Flavian Rome and Beyond* (Leiden: Brill, 2005); William den Hollander, *Josephus, the Emperors, and the City of Rome*, Judaism and Early Christianity 86 (Leiden: Brill, 2014). My remarks are not meant to imply, however, that Josephus was "a member of the lower entourage, in the same category as doctors and magicians, philosophers and buffoons." For this characterization of such actors, see Zvi Yavetz, "Reflections on Titus and Josephus," *GRBS* 16 (1975): 411–32, at 431–32.

134. Heliodorus, *Aeth.* 3.16.3–4; Gordon, "Memory and Authority in the Magical Papyri," 160–61.

135. It was not uncommon for Judeans to be grouped together with Syrians and Samaritans, which underscores some imprecision or fluidity in Roman ideas about foreign peoples.

systems, not to mention an intertwined epic history.[136] In the first centuries of the empire, the antipathies between them welled up from even deeper sources, namely, episodic interethnic tensions in Alexandria, which had a large Judean population.[137] That these events had repercussions at Rome is evident, for instance, in Philo's sustained criticism of Helicon, a learned imperial slave from Alexandria whose apparent knowledge of astrology, Judean teachings, and other specialized pursuits had attracted the notice of Caligula.[138] Philo details how, having gained the emperor's ear, Helicon wasted no opportunity to malign Judean laws and customs.[139] Further tainting Caligula's impression of Judeans was his advisor Apelles, a native of Ascalon, who spewed his poison, Philo explains, because there is perpetual animosity between the people of Ascalon and the Judeans, despite their common border.[140]

Josephus, of course, devotes an entire work to refuting Manetho, Chaeremon, and Apion, "Egyptians" who have libeled Judeans in ink. Naturally, he posits the superiority of Judean religion over Egyptian as one of the many reasons for their hostility.[141] Offering his own caricature of Egyptian religion, he writes, "[O]ur piety (εὐσέβεια) differs from that which is customary among those people, as much as the nature of God resides in irrational beasts. For it is an ancestral custom for them to esteem animals as gods, and this custom is universal, although there are local differences in the honors paid to them. These frivolous and altogether senseless people, accustomed from the beginning to erroneous ideas about the gods, were not capable of imitating the solemnity of our theology (θεολογία), and the sight of our numerous admirers filled them with envy."[142] Ultimately, however, he labors to dismantle, anecdote by anecdote, their inverse arguments for the prestige of Egyptian customs over and against those of the Judeans. Tellingly, a fragment ascribed to Chaeremon casts the habits

---

136. See also Christopher P. Jones, "Josephus and Greek Literature in Flavian Rome," in Edmondson, Mason, and Rives, *Flavius Josephus and Flavian Rome*, 201–8.

137. See esp. Barclay, *Jews in the Mediterranean Diaspora*, 48–81; Gruen, *Diaspora*, 54–83.

138. Philo, *Leg.* 26–27.

139. Philo, *Leg.* 27.171.

140. Philo, *Leg.* 27.203–6.

141. Josephus, *C. Ap.* 223.

142. Josephus, *C. Ap.* 224.4–226.1 (trans. Thackeray, LCL).

of Egyptian priests in a favorable and superior light: they pursue ascetic personal habits; they maintain a frugal diet, a state of ritual purity, and a distinctive bodily comportment; they are masters of philosophy; and they wield extraordinary ritual knowledge, among other qualities.[143]

The mutually antagonistic positions of these authors were at once strategies for disentangling the seemingly overlapping histories and cultures of Judea and Egypt and also arguments for the prestige of one set of cultural and religious practices over the other. It is no coincidence that many of the authors who wrote in such a capacity were, or had been, social elites within their native contexts and targeted opponents of comparable social location, skills, and audiences. Literary production thus offered one arena for asserting, refining, or contesting constructions of ethnicity and one that often overlapped with serving as a teacher or authority on exotic wisdom traditions, texts, rites, and other practices.

Conclusions

In this chapter I have drawn attention to the significant presence of foreign religious experts in the Roman Empire and attempted to show how attention to their activities both introduces greater nuance into our scholarly categories and also undermines impressions of difference between freelance experts operating within different ethnic, geographic, or cultural frameworks. While these methodological suggestions pertain to a number of scholarly categories for the evidence I have considered, their implications are most significant for the diverse actors, institutions, and phenomena that I have referred to collectively as "Judean religion." In particular, anachronistic assumptions about ancient Judaism have obscured the participation of some Judeans in the religion of freelance experts.[144] Indeed, many scholars have discounted the examples considered in this

---

143. Porphyry, *Abst.* 4.6–8; Chaeremon, frag. 10; Swetnam-Burland, "'Egyptian' Priests in Roman Italy," 337. On affinities between Chaeremon's characterization of Egyptian priests and Philo's of the Therapeutae, see Joan E. Taylor, *Jewish Women Philosophers of First-Century Alexandria: Philo's "Therapeutae" Reconsidered* (New York: Oxford University Press, 2003), 44–46. Plutarch also harmonizes strains of Egyptian myth in order to explicate the profound philosophical significance of familiar rites performed for Isis and Osiris (*De Is. et Os.* 352b).

144. The oversight is understandable, especially in light of the many proscriptions against some of these actors and forms of expertise that occur in authoritative Judean texts (e.g., Deut 19:10, Lev 20:27). Yet the same literature provides as many examples of acceptable

chapter on the grounds that there is insufficient support for mass conversions to Judaism in the Roman period. It is, however, the model of gentile attraction and conversion to Judaism—a basic premise of which is that such activities were approved by and undertaken on behalf of a larger religious entity—that hinders an accurate understanding of the evidence, even when the sources disclose numerous examples of freelance experts claiming specialty in texts, teachings, and other practices associated with Judea and for the benefit of non-Judean audiences.

To take the sources on their own terms counteracts the tendency to render Judeans religiously unique by locating some within a phenomenon that is well attested for other foreign specialists. Contributing another dimension to the existing body of work that argues for continuity between the Jerusalem temple and synagogues, and other temples and voluntary associations in the Greco-Roman world,[145] the presence of freelance experts reveals "Judean religion" to be both more varied and more comparable in its variety to Greek, Egyptian, or Persian religion, none of which are considered *religions* in the sense that Christianity and Judaism would eventually become.

Restoring Judean religious specialists to this picture also makes better sense of first- and second-century commentaries on the popularity of Judean practices among non-Judeans.[146] Seneca complains that Judean customs are received ubiquitously in his day, so much so that the conquered have given laws to their conquerors.[147] At least Judeans actually know the rationale for their observances, he concedes, unlike the majority of people, who imitate them out of ignorance. Tacitus explains the origins

---

forms of religious expertise—e.g., dream interpretation, prophecy, and healing—as injunctions against particular skills. One question we might consider, then, is whether Judeans who presented themselves as prophets or dream interpreters, or who divined from the Judean writings, were aware of textual prohibitions attached to certain forms of expertise and therefore developed certain skills and not others. That question, in turn, raises complicated questions about whether such things, if they were known at all, reflect awareness of actual texts or simply of norms about Judean religious practice that might have a textual basis.

145. See, e.g., Rajak and Noy, "*Archisynagogoi*," 75–93; Steve Mason, "*Philosophiai*: Greco-Roman, Judean and Christian," in Kloppenborg and Wilson, *Voluntary Association in Greco-Roman World*, 31–58.

146. See also Cohen, "Respect for Judaism by Gentiles According to Josephus," 428–29; idem, *The Beginnings of Jewishness*, 149–50; Barclay, *Mediterranean Diaspora*, 296; Wendt, "A Rereading of Judean Expulsions from Rome," 122–24.

147. Seneca apud Augustine *De civ. D.* 6.11.

of abstention from pork and leavened breads, fasting, sabbath, circumcision, distinctive burial customs, and aniconic cult, then laments that these *novi ritus* have gained traction among Romans.[148] He also mentions—much to his chagrin—that many non-Judeans are in the habit of contributing to the temple in Jerusalem: "The worst sort of people are the ones who, rejecting their ancestral religious practices, sent tribute and heaps of gifts [to Jerusalem], thereupon enriching the Judeans."[149] Juvenal warns that a father who gives up every seventh day to idleness will raise a son even more receptive to Judean customs, worshipping nothing but the divinity of the heavens, abhorring pork, taking to circumcision, and exchanging Roman law for Mosaic.[150]

Together these sources point to a wider phenomenon of non-Judeans taking up some Judean practices that might occur in any number of forms: special eating habits, festival observance, aniconic worship, consulting prophets or diviners, divining from Judean texts or studying them as intellectual resources, and traveling to or otherwise bestowing patronage on the Jerusalem temple. In many cases "Judean" and "Judaic" were employed loosely or imprecisely to capture anyone involved in any form of Judean religion. Dio, for instance, considers "Judean" all people who take up practices associated with Judeans. The former exist even among the Romans and, he adds, have increased to a great extent despite efforts made to curtail their enthusiasm.[151] Notably, he does not insist upon exact criteria for what it means to affect Judean customs, leaving us to imagine different kinds and degrees of engagement with ethnically coded practices, whose diverse practitioners might all be considered Judeans from certain perspectives. In this respect, Judean was in certain contexts akin to Chaldean, Babylonian, or Egyptian, language that evoked highly specific skills and practices and could be used without further qualification to denote foreign experts, as well as their followers.[152]

---

148. Tacitus, *Hist.* 5.5.

149. Tacitus, *Hist.* 5.5.1: *nam pessimus quisque spretis religionibus patriis tributa et stipes illuc congerebant, unde auctae Iudaeorum res.*

150. Juvenal, *Sat.* 14.96–106

151. Cassius Dio, 37.17.1. See also Cohen, *The Beginnings of Jewishness*, esp. 96–104.

152. Another instance where Judean seems to stand in for practitioners of Judaica occurs in Dio's account of certain people condemned under Domitian for having drifted into Judean

This way of thinking about ethnicity, that is, in terms of representations and coding, is in keeping with the growing body of scholarship that understands ancient ethnicities or ethnic identities to be constructed, fluid, and performative rather than natural, static, and assumed.[153] As Michael L. Satlow notes, ethnic language was inherently ambiguous, often but not always implying the religious practices of the region or people to which or whom it referred.[154] In the context of freelance expertise, however, the religious connotations of this language seem to have been pronounced and the incentives to identify selectively with ethnic representations especially compelling. Trappings of foreignness were not limited to human actors but extended equally to practices and artifacts, including texts. As Gordon argues with respect to astrological and ritual papyri from Egypt that were, despite their ostensible ethnic basis, written in Greek for Greek-speaking audiences interested in "traditional" Egyptian religious wisdom, there were multiple incentives attached in this period to playing up the exotic character of one's knowledge and artifacts, or even oneself.[155] It is to the relationship between ethnic coding and intellectual practices to which I now turn.

customs, a statement that is often read with Suetonius's recollection from the same period of an old man being forced to undress in order to determine whether he was circumcised (Cassius Dio, 67.14.1–3; Suetonius, *Dom.* 12.2). Central to both episodes is Domitian's rigorous application of the *fiscus iudaicus,* the tax base that he expanded as liberally as possible in order to maximize its extraction. See E. Mary Smallwood, "Domitian's Attitude toward the Jews and Judaism," *CP* 51 (1956): 1–13; Fergus Millar, "The *Fiscus Iudaicus* in the First Two Centuries," *JRS* 53 (1963): 29–42; Martin Goodman, "The *Fiscus Judaicus* and Jewish Identity," *JRS* 79 (1989): 40–44; Margaret Williams, "Domitian, the Jews and the 'Judaizers': A Simple Matter of Cupiditas and Maiestas?" *ZAG* 39 (1990): 196–211; Marius Heemstra, *The Fiscus Judaicus and the Parting of the Ways,* WUNT 2 277 (Tübingen: Mohr Siebeck, 2011).

153. On constructions of ethnic identity and acts of ethnic identification more generally, see Rogers Brubaker, *Ethnicity Without Groups* (Cambridge: Harvard University Press, 2006).

154. Satlow, "Jew or Judean?" 167.

155. Gordon, "Memory and Authority in the Magical Papyri," 155–58.

3

Rethinking "Magic," "Religion,"
and "Philosophy"

IF JUVENAL'S SIXTH satire was a convenient starting point for a discussion of ethnically coded experts and practices, it is his third that captures the stiff competition within particular subsets of freelance expertise, particularly among different kinds of writer-intellectuals. Framed as a chance encounter between Juvenal and a friend, Umbricius, who is departing Rome for Cumae, the latter complains that there is no longer room in the city for respectable skills and no reward for work. "What can I do at Rome?" he asks. "I don't know how to tell lies. I can't praise a bad book if it's bad and ask for a copy. I'm ignorant of the movement of the stars. I won't and can't predict someone's father's death. I've never examined the entrails of frogs."[1] Umbricius then vents frustration that customs from the Greek East are so in vogue among wealthy Romans that self-styled experts from its regions have procured posts in all of the great houses. "Say what you want him to be. In his own person he has brought anyone you like: *grammaticus, rhetor, geometres, pictor, aliptes, augur, schoenobates, medicus, magus*—your *Graeculus* has every talent. Tell him to go to heaven and he will."[2]

Umbricius's screed provides a tantalizing glimpse of the options and obstacles that confronted would-be specialists, as well as the robust profiles of those who were successful. As I noted in the introduction, for Juvenal and similar authors, versatility is not something to be championed but

---

1. Juvenal, *Sat.* 3.40–44 (trans. Susannah Morton Braund, LCL).

2. Juvenal, *Sat.* 3.75–80; cf. 2 Cor 12:2–4.

a sign that one is capable of affecting different guises without possessing any real expertise. The combinations of skills and knowledge that are for him an object of ridicule are equally attested, however, in sources less critical of these actors, including firsthand witnesses to their offerings. Each of the practices that Umbricius mentions—interpreting the movements of the stars, exchanging writings, divining, and even ascending to heaven to receive divine revelation—has either arisen or will arise in this study, as have many of the titles—*augur, medicus, magus*—he lists. In point of fact, the qualities he lampoons might as well apply to the apostle Paul, who also interacted with households and alleged or exhibited expertise in many of the aforementioned skills. The coincidence suggests that such offerings were to a point the norm in the period; it also serves as a reminder that there were always elements of subjectivity and normativity in the choice of labels that were applied to their purveyors.

Although I have characterized these figures as freelance experts in religion, others have treated them as practitioners of "magic" whose relationship to religion is complex.[3] The justification for drawing this distinction depends in part on the autonomy and self-authorization of the actors in question and in part on the seemingly insolent or benighted "eclecticism" of their practices. And yet, the notion that discrete disciplines or areas of expertise existed at this time for "magicians" or "hack philosophers" to appropriate owes much to contemporaneous writers embroiled in discursive efforts to codify particular entities self-advantageously. For many, it was precisely by ridiculing the "undisciplined" maelstrom of another's skills and practices that one was able to present and defend the integrity and coherence of one's own. Concepts such as magic and eclecticism inversely reflect these conditions because they imply that freelance experts in religion and philosophy were derivative of prior, more integral institutions, disciplines, or traditions.

In this chapter I argue the opposite, that disciplinary specialization and normative sensibilities about practices that should not be combined were a product of competition between freelance experts, especially writer-intellectuals, and not the other way around. First, using the formation of Roman discourses about magic as an example, I argue that this category took shape in response to the increasing diversification of religious experts

---

3. See, e.g., Dickie, who treats the same lines from Juvenal as evidence for the popularity of magic at Rome (*Magic and Magicians in the Greco-Roman World*, 194).

whose offerings ran the gamut from esoteric, intellectual teachings that drew heavily on philosophy to the sort of practices that more commonly fall under the scholarly rubric "magic" (curses, incantations, potions, etc.). Insofar as *magus* first denoted a Persian religious specialist in Latin literature, through this figure we can trace the transformation of an ethnically coded and typically intellectual form of expertise into a generic category for any and all practices associated with the religion of freelance experts.[4] That is, the discursive category "magic" that coalesced over the course of the imperial period developed in response to the growth and influence of this phenomenon. Therefore, I propose that the evidence for magic in the Roman period, and earlier, represents a significant part of the evidence for the religion of freelance experts.

Having made the case for treating this evidence as religion rather than magic, I then shift the focus to experts whose offerings enlisted intellectual practices and texts to a significant degree. Despite the reductive effect of Roman discourses about "magicians" and their ilk, many targets of such discourses were, in fact, literate specialists deeply enmeshed in the intellectual currents of their day. Since religious experts with intellectualizing tendencies resemble or overlap with similarly self-authorized actors I would not consider religious (e.g., philosophers, doctors), greater attention to these specialists improves the precision and nuance of my category. "Magic" is a particularly useful site for observing the convergence of practices—initiations, purifications, divination, textual exegesis, mythmaking, and so forth—that bear continuities with other religious and intellectual activities but are best classified as subsets of freelance *religious* expertise.

From Magus *to "Magician"*

Throughout his *Natural History,* Pliny offers an extensive treatment of the "deceptions of the *magi*" (*magicae vanitates*), his contempt for which seems to derive from the fact that their learned traditions are predicated on an epistemology more religious, in my sense, than forms of inquiry rooted in naturalistic explanation.[5] To elucidate the distinction he explains that the

---

4. For the figure of the *magos* and his eventual conflation with other kinds of self-authorized religious experts in earlier Greek literature, see, e.g., Dickie, *Magic and Magicians in the Greco-Roman World,* 41–43, 59–60.

5. Pliny, *Nat.* 30.1.1.

first men in this part of the world to learn the potential of "magical" herbs were Pythagoras and Democritus, who regarded the arcane use of plants, animal parts, and stones as an extension of the barbarian philosophical tradition that these Greek philosophers acquired from *magi*. While admitting that contemporary "doctors" and *magi* harness the special properties of the same substances for medicinal purposes of which he approves, Pliny paints the latter's *ars* as the dark side of *medicina*—frivolous, fraudulent, and insidious.[6] Their wisdom, he explains, has roots in "medicine" but was infused with the powers of *religio* (*vires religionis*) to acquire a superior and holier appearance. Since everyone is eager to learn the future, over time the *magi* also appropriated elements of "astrology" with the result that the *ars magica* became even more mottled.[7] Pliny concludes with a genealogy of "magic" that originates in Persia with Zoroaster but passes through Orpheus, Pythagoras, Plato, Democritus, Moses, Thessalian witches, and the druids to arrive at a global category that encompasses practices found throughout the Roman world.[8] Hence these practices are, he shows, ethnically particular in origins but universal in their evolution and present scope.

The genealogy is striking for a number of reasons, not the least of which is that it runs through figures to whom many freelance experts hitched their bailiwicks. I am more interested, however, in Pliny's apparent interest in disentangling and systematizing a convoluted set of ideas about the cultural particularity and interactions of "traditions" that seem anything but distinct at the time he writes. His literary treatment of the *magi* offers yet another example of how concepts about foreign religion or religious wisdom often amounted to basic scaffolding that might be fleshed out in various ways depending on the skills, aptitude, and ambitions of a given expert. In a context wherein rivalries between them were acute and many alleged multiple skills, a breakdown in ethnic coding might even be seen as a foreseeable consequence of competition within and across particular

---

6. Rives, "*Magus* and its Cognates in Classical Latin," 62–63.

7. For the relationship between the *magi's* wisdom and medicine, see Patricia Gaillard-Seux, "Magical Formulas in Pliny's *Natural History*: Origins, Sources, Parallels," in *"Greek" and "Roman" in Latin Medical Texts: Studies in Cultural Change and Exchange in Ancient Medicine*, ed. Brigitte Maire, Studies in Ancient Medicine 42 (Leiden: Brill, 2014), 201–23.

8. Pliny, *Nat.* 30.1.2, 30.2.3–4.14. Cf. Diogenes Laertius, who cites Clearchus of Soli on the point that both the Gymnosophists and the Judeans trace their origins to the *magoi* (*Vit. Phil.* 1.9).

subsets of freelance expertise whose edges were never especially sharp. As the characteristics that informed such concepts or titles became either less ethnically specific (e.g., hallmarks of Persian expertise came to be associated also with other kinds of specialists) or more complex (e.g., Persian experts became known for a more diverse array of skills and practices), one can imagine them being used less precisely to describe broader sets of actors united by qualities other than a shared ethnic idiom.

That the sense of *magus* thus expanded over the first century of the empire had much to do, I suspect, with the growth and diversification of the religion of freelance experts within the same window. Propelled by dynamics central to this sort of religious activity—competition, innovation, and the pursuit of niche forms of prestige—the various titles, specialty, and ethnic qualifications associated with freelance expertise compounded in such a way that it seems to have grown increasingly difficult to pin down the purview of any one figure, even for legislative purposes. The encroachment of the generic category "magic" on legislation issued within our window supports this reading. Although there was no law forbidding the practice of magic per se, many scholars have observed that the fairly limited scope of the *lex Cornelia de sicariis et veneficis* of 81 BCE expanded to address "a more general concern with religious deviance" as a strong view of this category developed.[9] Examples of those tried under the *lex Cornelia*, either as "magicians" or for having consulted them join the ad hoc decrees and edicts issued, as I argued in chapter 1, to address the regulatory challenges posed by freelance expertise.[10] In lieu of a specific legal category for the actors and practices in question, the consistency with which these measures targeted freelance experts suggests that they constituted an implicit category, and one that was inflected by antinormative discourses about "magic" that were developing concurrently and dialectically. On my reading, however, the issue underlying these actions was less a matter of religious deviance—although this was a contingent concern about certain actors—than of the general popularity and unwieldiness of specialists.

---

9. See James B. Rives, "Magic in Roman Law: The Reconstruction of a Crime," *CA* 22 (2003): 313–39, at 327. For the formation of a social discourse about magic in ancient Greece, see Dickie, *Magic and Magicians in the Ancient World*, 18–22; Kimberly B. Stratton, *Naming the Witch: Magic, Ideology, and Stereotype in the Ancient World* (New York: Columbia University Press, 2007), 39–46.

10. Richard L. Gordon and Francisco Marco Simón, "Introduction," in Gordon and Simón, *Magical Practice in the Latin West*, 1–49, esp. 10–11.

As to the question of why the *magus*, and not another figure or category of practice, came to stand in for freelance religious expertise more generally, I would suggest that its suitability had to do with the broad assortment of skills, including philosophy, for which *magi*, especially, were known. In the earliest Latin occurrences, *magus* denoted expertise in a finite set of skills that included esoteric wisdom and divination; even as the term outgrew its technical meaning, the philosophical character of the *magi's* wisdom remained salient for Roman-period writers, many of whom, like Pliny, relate stories about Pythagoras having studied with them.[11] As we saw in chapter 1, Nero was said to have been a patron of *magi* and underwent initiation into their mysteries after having been instructed in their wisdom at Rome by the *magus* Tiridates.[12] Pliny frequently links *magi* with barbarian and Greek philosophy, while Apuleius, in response to the charge that he used "magic" to woo a wealthy widow who had vowed not to remarry, proffers a textured definition of a *magus* as a Persian priest in the tradition of Zoroaster, who possesses profound knowledge about rites and other matters concerning the gods.[13] Although his accusers clearly understand *magus* as a general designation for a person who is able to achieve any desired object or outcome by means of occult methods, he insists that whatever negative connotations the term has acquired are erroneous. Moreover, such accusations have been employed just as inappropriately against philosophers and natural scientists through the errors of the ignorant.[14]

Pythagoras and the Problem of Religion, Magic, or Philosophy

This juncture of philosophy, usually that of Pythagoras, and the wisdom of the *magi* crops up time and again in Roman-period literature. P. Nigidius

---

11. Rives, "*Magus* and its Cognates in Classical Latin," 61.

12. Pliny, *Nat.* 30.14–17; Suetonius, *Ner.* 34.4; Smith, *Jesus the Magician*, 71–73; Francis, *Subversive Virtue*, 96. Oddly, Philostratus (*Vita Apoll.* 4.35) seems to contradict that report when he claims that Nero was antagonistic to philosophy because he suspected its devotees of being addicted to divination (μαντική) and of being diviners in disguise (ὡς μαντικῆς σχῆμα).

13. Apuleius, *Apol.* 26.

14. Apuleius, *Apol.* 25. For a fuller treatment of the text, see James B. Rives, "Legal Strategy and Learned Display in Apuleius' *Apology*," in *Paideia at Play: Learning and Wit in Apuleius*, ed. Werner Riess (Groningen: Barkhuis & Groningen University Library, 2008), 17–49.

Figulus, whom later sources, again, describe as a *Pythagoricus et magus*, apparently held the *magi* in high regard and wrote extensively about their cosmology and teachings.[15] He was not the only republican intellectual with Pythagorean leanings. Pliny reports that Varro was buried in a clay coffin with leaves of myrtle, olive, and black poplar "in the Pythagorean manner" (*Pythagorio modo*), while the *Aemilii*, one of Rome's most es-teemed and ancient patrician families, claimed the philosopher as their direct ancestor by way of his son Mamercus.[16]

For his Italian history, the appeal of Pythagoras for Romans was in one sense inevitable.[17] The association did not always carry favorable implica-tions, however. In a scathing speech against P. Vatinius, Cicero accuses him of putting forth the name of that most learned man to mask savage and barbarian habits: performing unheard of and impious sacrifices, evok-ing the spirits of the shades below, and making offerings of the entrails of murdered boys to the divine shades of the underworld (*Dii Manes*).[18] In this and other cases, being a "Pythagorean" is redolent of possessing the nega-tive qualities typically imputed to *magi*. An ancient commentator on the text attributes Cicero's comments to spite, shared by certain detractors for the unsavory people who had gathered around Nigidius, although they wished to think of themselves as followers of Pythagoras (*Pythagorae sectatores*).[19] Cicero also alleges that Ap. Claudius Pulcher, in whose writings he detects Pythagorean influence, was in the habit of consulting necromancers.[20]

Nevertheless, intellectual insights, wisdom traditions, practices, and texts that were either directly attributed to Pythagoras or coded as Pythagorean flourished in the first centuries BCE and CE. A man named Quintus Sextius formed a philosophical school at Rome that was ostensi-bly dedicated to the philosopher's teachings, though our only evidence for the group survives in the writings of Seneca, whose own teacher, Sotion, had been a member. The doctrines of the so-called Sextians overlapped

---

15. Rawson, *Intellectual Life in the Late Roman Republic*, 182, 292, 311.

16. Pliny, Nat. 35.160; Plutarch, *Vit. Aem.* 2.1–2.

17. So reckons Diogenes Laertius, *Vit. Phil.* 8.1.1.

18. Cicerco, *Vat.* 6.14; Rawson, *Intellectual Life in the Late Roman Republic*, 310 n. 62.

19. *Schol. Bob. in Vat.* 14.

20. Cicero, *Div.* 1.132–35, 1.140; Rawson, *Intellectual Life in the Late Roman Republic*, 292; Ripat, "Astrologers at Rome," 123–24. For these criticisms, Cicero writes more favorably of Pythagoras and visited the house where he allegedly died on a visit to Metapontum (*Fin.* 5.2).

substantially with those of the Stoics, but they adopted at least two practices with distinctively Pythagorean associations: strict adherence to a vegetarian diet and daily self-examinations of their moral progress. As Seneca describes the latter, a Sextian would ask himself, "What bad habit have you cured today?" "What temptation have you resisted?" "In what respects are you better?"[21] Cicero also mentions the habit of self-evaluation, which he calls a custom of the Pythagoreans (*Pythagoreorum mos*) and regards as a mnemonic exercise.[22]

A Pythagorean element characterizes many of the Middle Platonists, some of whom even referred to themselves as Pythagoreans.[23] Later philosophers who claimed Pythagoras's influence and attributed mathematical theories to him were occasionally referred to as *mathēmatikoi* (μαθηματικοί), as opposed to *akousmatikoi* (ἀκουσματικοί), the term for people who alleged to preserve his oral teachings.[24] *Mathēmatikos* was also a term for a rank of Pythagorean initiate or student, and although it is usually presumed that *mathematicus* is a straightforward synonym for *Chaldaeus* and *astrologus*, one wonders whether it instead denoted diviners whose techniques drew on Pythagorean theories or numerology. The first occurrence of the word in Latin appears at the same time as *magus* and coincides with a spike of interest in Pythagorean teachings and practices among Roman elites.[25] Not that there was always a distinct division

---

21. Seneca, *Ira* 3.36: *Quod hodie malum tuum senasti? Cui vitio obstitisti? Qua parte melior es?*. For a succinct overview of this reference and other sources for Pythagoras in the Roman period, see Charles H. Kahn, *Pythagoras and the Pythagoreans: A Brief History* (Indianapolis: Hackett, 2001), at 91. See also Constantinos Macris, "Pythagoras," in *The History of Western Philosophy of Religion, Vol. 1: Ancient Philosophy of Religion*, ed. Graham Oppy and Nick Trakakis (Durham, NC: Acumen, 2009), 23–39; Stefan Schorn, "Pythagoras in the Historical Tradition: From Herodotus to Diodorus Siculus," in Huffman, *A History of Pythagoreanism*, 296–314.

22. Cicero, *Sen.* 38.

23. For example, a number of philosophers who were prominent within and whose doctrines were continuous with their contemporary Platonism—e.g., Moderatus, Nicomachus, Numenius—nevertheless referred to themselves as Pythagoreans. See John M. Dillon, *The Middle Platonists: 80 B.C. to A.D. 220* (Ithaca, NY: Cornell University Press, 1996), 38, 341–83. Dillon also points to Pythagorean elements in the writings of Philo (140–50). See also Michael Trapp, "Neopythagoreans," in *Greek and Roman Philosophy 100 BC–200 AD, Vol. 2*, ed. Robert W. Sharples and Richard Sorabji (London: Institute of Classical Studies, 2007), 347–63.

24. Walter Burkert, *Lore and Science in Ancient Pythagoreanism*, trans. Edwin L. Minar Jr. (Cambridge: Harvard University Press, 1972), 192–208; Macris, "Pythagoras," 26.

25. The Latin word first appears in the writings of Cicero, e.g., *De or.* 1.10.1, 1.44.2; *Luc.* 82.3, 106.4, 118.22 (together with *Pythagorei*); *Fin.* 5.7.16, 5.9.10; *Tusc.* 1.5.2, 1.40.4, 5.18.4, 5.66.10; *Nat. d.* 2.51.10, 2.103.1, 3.27.7; *Div.* 2.10.9, 2.91.10.

between these different divinatory methods. While Thrasyllus is remembered foremost as an astrologer, Diogenes Laertius and Porphyry each describe him as a philosopher committed to the principles of Pythagoras and Plato, which he set out in writing.[26]

The projection of contemporary doctrines and practices onto the figure of Pythagoras was common already in the Platonic Academy, but a surge in Pythagorean pseudepigrapha, especially in Alexandria and Rome, beginning around the first century BCE suggest that this tendency was pronounced in our period.[27] Juba II of Mauretania, an avid student of Pythagoras's teachings, traveled to Rome with the express purpose of acquiring more writings attributed to the philosopher, which, along with other philosophical pseudepigrapha, were copious there.[28] An obvious Roman precedent for these writings is found in the tradition about the discovery during the republic of a stone chest at the foot of the Janiculum that contained the books of Numa Pompilius, seven in Latin that dealt with pontifical law and seven in Greek that contained ancient wisdom.[29] Citing Valerius Antias as his authority, Livy explains that the latter books were Pythagorean, thus confirming a common belief that Numa had been the philosopher's student.[30] After allegedly circulating for a time and

---

26. Porphyry, *Vit. Plot.* 20; Dillon, *The Middle Platonists*, 184–85.

27. For the "Pythagorism" of the Platonic Academy—that is, "a more than objective interest in the thought and personality of Pythagoras, and a tendency to try to reconstruct his teachings, fathering the theories of later men, including even one's own, on him in the process"— see Dillon, *The Middle Platonists*, 37–38; idem, "Pythagoreanism in the Academic Tradition: the Early Academy to Numenius," in *A History of Pythagoreanism*, ed. Carl A. Huffman (Cambridge: Cambridge University Press, 2014), 250–73. This tendency, Dillon notes, begins in Platonism with Speusippus, if not with Plato himself, and is observable in most later Platonists to a greater or lesser degree. For a detailed discussion of what the Academy's embrace of Pythagoras entailed, see Burkert, *Lore and Science in Ancient Pythagoreanism*, 83–96. For the profusion of pseudepigraphic writings in the Hellenistic and Roman periods, see Bruno Centrone, "The Pseudo-Pythagorean Writings," in Hoffman, *A History of Pythagoreanism*, 315–40, esp. 316–9; Jaap-Jan Flinterman, "Pythagoreans in Rome and Asia Minor Around the Turn of the Common Era," in Hoffman, *A History of Pythagoreanism*, 341–59, esp. 341–42.

28. Rawson, *Intellectual Life in the Late Republic*, 41–51, 291–94; Duane W. Roller, *The World of Juba II and Kleopatra Selene: Royal Scholarship on Rome's African Frontier* (New York: Routledge, 2003), 158–59; Kahn, *Pythagoras and the Pythagoreans*, 90.

29. Livy, 40.29.3–14.

30. On the connection between Numa and Pythagoras, see Erich S. Gruen, *Studies in Greek Culture and Roman Policy*, Cincinnati Classical Studies 6 (Leiden: Brill, 1990), 159–60. Numerous ancient writers disputed this claim for its anachronism, even if they are

generating considerable interest, the *praetor urbanus* burned them publicly for the potential they held to undermine Roman *religio*.[31]

Practical considerations preclude a discussion of the uncertainty surrounding the content of Pythagoras's philosophy or the controversial matter of the relationship between early Pythagoreans and those of the Roman period. However, as was the case for conceptions of foreign religion, a handful of Pythagorean characteristics appear often enough in our Roman sources to infer that they were fairly basic and widespread. As was the case in the previous chapter, I am less interested in the extent to which these concepts reflect an accurate understanding of Pythagorean philosophy than in how shared ideas about Pythagoras influenced the first-century figures and social formations that took up some aspect of his persona, wisdom, skills, or specific teachings.

Many writers report, for instance, that the Pythagoreans had a special interest in classifying the divine beings—heroes, souls of the dead, and *daimones*—who were instrumental in mediating between gods and humans.[32] Witnessing an even fuller set of characteristics, a letter attributed to Apollonius of Tyana claims that one receives edification in the following areas from keeping company with a "true" Pythagorean: "statesmanship, geometry, astronomy, arithmetic, harmonics, music, medicine, complete and god-given prophecy, and also the higher rewards—greatness of mind, of soul, and of manner, steadiness, piety, knowledge of the gods and not just supposition, familiarity with blessed spirits, self-sufficiency, persistence, frugality, reduction of essential needs,

---

sympathetic to the logic (e.g., Cicero, *Tusc.* 4.1.2–3; *Rep.* 2.28–29; Dionysius of Halicarnassus, *Ant. rom.* 2.59.1–22; Livy, 1.18.1–3; Ovid, *Fast.* 3.151–54). As Rawson notes, "It [took] probably until the end of the second century [CE] to kill the notion that King Numa had been a pupil of Pythagoras, who lived long after the date ascribed to the Roman king" (*Intellectual Life in the Late Roman Republic*, 245–46). As a case in point, Plutarch affirms the relationship in his biography of Numa (*Num.* 8.2–8, 22.34).

31. See Andreas Willi, "Numa's Dangerous Books: The Exegetical History of a Roman Forgery," *Mus Helv* 55 (1998): 139–72. For an excellent discussion of the incident and the place of books and writing in Roman religion more generally, see Duncan MacRae, *Legible Religion: Books, Gods, and Rituals in Roman Culture* (Cambridge: Harvard University Press, 2016).

32. Macris, "Pythagoras," 32–33. In *Against the Mathematici*, Sextus Empiricus claims that the followers of Pythagoras and Empedocles also held a doctrine of *pneuma* in which it was conceived as a single breath pervading the entire universe, uniting humans with gods, with one another, and even with irrational animals, an interesting *comparandum* for Paul's concept of *pneuma* in the next chapter (*Math.* 9.127).

ease of perception, of movement, and of breath, good color, health, cheerfulness, and immortality."[33] In addition to a number of advantages pertaining to character and health, the author promises that Pythagoras imparts divinatory expertise and true knowledge about and interaction with gods and *daimones*. Regarding this last point, it is noteworthy that Artemidorus includes *Pythagoristai* among the assorted diviners whose knowledge and techniques his manual will supplant.[34]

As is well known, Pythagoras was also linked with doctrines about the immortality of souls, including their postmortem transmigration and reincarnation.[35] While he was not the only ancient philosopher credited with such ideas, many viewed him as their original source.[36] The practical utility of these philosophical insights is manifest in references to freelance experts who claimed to be reincarnations of the famous philosopher. A man named Anaxilaus of Larissa, also a *Pythagoricus et magus*, was expelled from Rome in 28 BCE after alleging to possess the soul of Pythagoras and performing conjuring feats at elite banquets.[37] The same man either authored or lent his name to a text that Irenaeus cites when he accuses Marcus, a student of Valentinus who went on to form his own eponymous group, of consulting the *Paignia* of Anaxilaus for tricks to impress his followers.[38]

---

33. *Ep. Apoll.* 52 (trans. Christopher P. Jones, LCL). The dating and authorship of the letters is controversial. For an overview, see Robert J. Penella's introduction to *The Letters of Apollonius of Tyana: A Critical Text with Prolegomena, Translation and Commentary,* Mnemosyne Suppl. 56 (Leiden: Brill, 1979).

34. Artemidorus, *Oneirocrit.* 2.69. As Jaap-Jan Flinterman observes, "In quantity, this is a very modest testimony. . . . In quality, however, it is excellent evidence. Artemidorus was engaged in a polemic against real rivals, whose activities are amply attested. That such figures were not averse to diversify into activities such as healing and that they earned a reputation for miracle-working along the way seems plausible" ("Pythagoreans in Rome and Asia Minor around the Turn of the Common Era," 359). See also Jovan Bilbija and Jaap-Jan Flinterman, "Die markt voor mantiek: droomverklaring en andere divinatorische praktijken in de Oneirocritica van Artemidoros," *Lampas* 39 (2006): 246–66, esp. 259–64.

35. Here I follow Edmonds in using "reincarnation" rather than μετεμψύχωσις because, he explains, "of certain ancient Platonists, who argued that metempsychosis should imply a body having a series of souls rather than a soul having a series of bodies, the term for which would be *metensomatosis*" (*Redefining Ancient Orphism*, 283 n. 123).

36. E.g., Porphyry, *Vit. Pyth.* 19.8–14. Plato and the Academy incorporated and developed all of these elements.

37. Eusebius, *Chron. ad Olymp.* 188.

38. Irenaeus, *Haer.* 1.7.12. Irenaeus may have concocted the detail to strengthen his accusation of heresy, but it is no less valuable as a witness to the existence of such writings; Pliny

We cannot know how regularly freelance experts enlisted "Pythagorean" doctrines of the immortal soul and its cyclical reincarnation as tactics of legitimation, but Lucian's Alexander girds his thigh in gilded leather to imitate the philosopher.[39] In response to a question about whether the golden thigh confirms that he has the soul of Pythagoras, Alexander responds cryptically, "Pythagoras's soul now wanes and other times waxes; his, with prophecy gifted, from Zeus's mind takes its issue, sent by the father to aid good men in the stress of the conflict; then it to Zeus will return, by Zeus's own thunderbolt smitten."[40]

The golden thigh ruse serves for Lucian to punctuate Alexander's absurdity, all the more so since his prediction about being struck by lightning is falsified when he dies instead from an infection caused by the same contraption. Taken with the detail about Anaxilaus, however, the pretension of Pythagorean reincarnation is less suspicious. A comparable tradition also crops up in relation to two experts of the Antonine era: Julian, listed in the Suda as a Chaldean and philosopher, and his son of the same name, who is distinguished from his father as "the Julian called a theurgist" (τοῦ κληθέντος θεουργοῦ Ἰουλιανοῦ).[41] Either the elder Julian or his son was also the putative author of the *Chaldean Oracles*, a collection of prophetic verses written in Greek dactylic hexameter that enjoyed wide circulation and exegetical interest in the Roman period.[42] Few of the texts survive, and the fragments that do are preserved largely in the writings of later

---

also mentions books about Anaxilaus's conjuring methods, confirming that texts attributed to him had been circulating at Rome for some time (e.g., *Nat.* 19.4.23–25, 28.49.177–79). In addition to these references, Pliny cites Anaxilaus as an authority throughout Book 32.

39. The detail about the golden thigh stems from a popular story about Pythagoras revealing his own golden thigh to Abaris the Hyperborean to prove that he was the Hyperborean Apollo whom Abaris served (Porphyrt, *Vit. Pyth.* 28).

40. Lucian, *Alex.* 40.

41. *Suda* 433 and 434. For an overview of the evidence and its reliability, see Polymnia Athanassiadi, "Julian the Theurgist: Man or Myth?" in *Die Chaldaeischen Orakel: Kontext, Interpretation, Rezeption*, ed. Helmut Seng and Michel Tardieu (Heidelberg: University of Heidelberg Press, 2011), 193–208; Iles Johnston, *Ancient Greek Divination*, 160–1. See also E. R. Dodds, "Theurgy and its Relationship to Neoplatonism," *JRS* 37 (1947): 55–69, 56 n. 20; MacMullen, *Enemies of the Roman Order*, 106.

42. For the texts, see Ruth Dorothy Majercik, *The Chaldean Oracles: Text, Translation, and Commentary* (Leiden: Brill, 1989). On the Chaldean Oracles, see Ilinca Tanaseanu-Döbler, "Weise oder Scharlatane? Chaldaeerbilder der griechisch-römischen Kaiserzeit und die Chaldaeischen Orakel," in Seng and Tardieu, *Die Chaldaeischen Orakel: Kontext, Interpretation, Rezeption*, 19–42. See also Sarah Iles Johnston, *Hekate Soteira: A Study of Hekate's Roles in*

Christian critics.[43] These commentators on the oracles relate a tradition about how the elder Julian imbued his son with the deified soul of Plato so that he could function as a medium for verse *logia*, which his father then recorded and explicated in prose.[44] Scholars have rightly questioned the integrity of such stories for the authorship and unity they lent to the Chaldean corpus, not to mention a legitimate pedigree for its Platonic influences. Regardless of whether the two Julians actually composed the oracles or were merely attached retroactively to a composite collection of writings, the claim had a plausible pretext in the activities of other experts from the same period. In these examples it would appear that either self-authorized experts themselves or those who followed or wrote about them attributed the source of their power to reincarnation; they were not merely inspired by Pythagoras or Plato but might actually be one of these famous ancient philosophers.[45]

Pythagorean trappings are particularly poignant in Philostratus's biography of Apollonius of Tyana, who was active for much of the first century until his death sometime during or shortly after the reign of Nerva.[46] Like other freelance experts, Apollonius is shown to have possessed wisdom that spanned philosophy, divine mysteries, astrology, and other forms of divination, while his skills included healing, resurrection, exorcism, glossolalia, and the ability—also a Pythagorean legacy—to disappear and reappear at will.[47] Having studied with Babylonian *magoi*, Indian Brahmans, Hyrcanians, the *gymnoi* (γυμνοί) of Egypt, and priests of famous Greek sanctuaries, Apollonius embodies the sort of universal religious expertise

---

the Chaldean Oracles and Related Literature, American Classical Studies 21 (Atlanta: Scholars Press, 1990).

43. Namely, the fifth-century Neoplatonist philosopher Proclus, Proclus's own biographer, Marinus, and Michael Psellus. See Dodds, "Theurgy and its Relationship to Neoplatonism," 56; L. G. Westerink, "Proclus, Procopius, Psellus," *Mnemosyne* 10 (1942): 275–80, at 276.

44. Henri-Dominique Saffrey, "Les Néoplatoniciens et les Oracles Chaldaïques," *REA* 26 (1981): 209–25, at 225; See also Philip Merlan, "Religion and Philosophy from Plato's *Phaedo* to the Chaldean Oracles," *JHP* 1 (1963): 163–76.

45. Diogenes Laertius elaborates that Pythagoras had the gift of retaining memories in his soul so that any who inherited it could recall not only Pythagoras's own experiences but also those of his many reincarnations (*Vit. Phil.* 8.4–5).

46. See Philostratus, *Vit. Apoll.* 8.27; Francis, *Subversive Virtue*, 83–129.

47. Philostratus, *Vit. Apoll.* 1.9; 4.10; 4.45; 5.27; 1.19; 4.10, 8.5–10. He is also said to have written four books *On the Prophecies of the Stars* (*Vit. Apoll.* 3.41).

that Pliny disdains.[48] Hence Philostratus refutes the appearance—and even the charge—that Apollonius was a *magos*, placing him instead in the tradition of eminent philosophers, including Pythagoras, who gained inspiration from *magoi* without being seduced by their art.[49] As with other references we have considered, the *Vita* lacks specific Pythagorean teachings in favor of showing how Apollonius emulated the philosopher's example through his choice of clothing, grooming habits, and asceticism.[50] Once again, the intellectual heritage of Pythagoras may have been less important to an expert wishing to take up his mantle than the mantle itself.

While its late date and hagiographic inclination call into question the historicity of Philostratus's account, nothing in his basic depiction of Apollonius of Tyana is at odds with the evidence for other first-century specialists.[51] To the contrary, everything from Apollonius's Pythagorean affiliation to the accusation of "sorcery" (γοητεία) for which he is brought to trial before Domitian aligns with what we have seen of other participants in this sort of religious activity. Also in keeping with this evidence is the rich literary record that Apollonius's fame seems to have generated: various pseudepigrapha that circulated in his name, as well as conflicting biographies about his authenticity.[52] To some he was a *goēs* or a skillful *magos* who managed to persuade even distinguished philosophers of his "magic."[53]

---

48. See Parker, *The Making of Roman India*, 251–307; Abraham, "The Geography of Culture in Philostratus' *Life of Apollonius of Tyana*," esp. 466–69.

49. Philostratus, *Vit. Apoll.* 1.2; 5.12.3; 5.25.1; cf. 8.7.2, 8.7.9. Apollonius is initiated into the Eleusinian mysteries at Athens as well as at Epidaurus and makes a habit of introducing religious reform into the great sanctuaries of Greece and Egypt. On the disavowal of "magic" Francis writes, "*Goētes* . . . say that they alter fate by resorting to torturing the spirits of the dead, or by barbaric sacrifices, or by certain charms and ointments . . . while Apollonius obeyed the decrees of the Fates and foretold only those things that were destined to happen; and he foreknew these things not by *goēteia*, but from what the gods revealed" (*Subversive Virtue*, 97).

50. Philostratus, *Vit. Apoll.* 1.32.4; 5.37.3; Francis, *Subversive Virtue*, 105–7.

51. For the historiographic problems, see Francis, *Subversive Virtue*, 89. Previous scholarship has characterized Apollonius of Tyana as a θεῖος ἀνήρ, a category that I find problematic for reasons noted in the introduction. For the application of this approach, see Erkki Koskenniemi, "Apollonius of Tyana: A Typical θεῖος ἀνήρ?" *JBL* 117 (1998): 455–67; Christopher P. Jones, "Apollonius of Tyana, Hero and Holy Man," in *Philostratus's Heroikos: Religion and Cultural Identity in the Third Century C.E.*, ed. Ellen Bradshaw Aitken and Jennifer K. Berenson Maclean (Leiden: Brill, 2004), 75–84.

52. Philostratus, *Vit. Apoll.* 7.35.

53. Origen, *C. Cels.* 6.41; Cassius Dio, 77.18.14.

To others he was a true philosopher and prolific writer.[54] Reinscribing once again the relationship between magic and Pythagorean philosophy, in one of the letters attributed to him "Apollonius" writes to a Stoic rival, Euphrates: "You think that you should call philosophers who follow Pythagoras *magoi*, and similarly, no doubt, those who follow Orpheus. But I think that even those who follow Zeus should be called *magoi*, if they plan to be godly and just."[55] To the same person he explains, "The Persians call godly men *magoi*, so that one who worships the gods or one who has a godly nature is a *magos*."[56] Authentic or not, these remarks complicate the boundary between magic and philosophy, for what are *magi* but kinds of philosophers whose offerings prominently feature gods or figures with whom forms of religion with a distinctly philosophical character were regularly linked?

These stories reveal less about the historical Pythagoras and his doctrines than they do about how his persona, and for that matter Plato's, might be coopted by freelance experts who viewed their wisdom and practices to be continuous with those of esteemed philosophers on whom they drew.[57] Indeed, it may have been the very dearth of reliable information about Pythagoras that made him an apt mannequin upon which to drape the myriad practices and ideas for which he was apparently known.[58] The

---

54. Philostratus, *Vit. Apoll.* 4.19. For competing biographical traditions and other negative assessments of Apollonius, see D. H. Raynor, "Moeragenes and Philostratus. Two Views of Apollonius of Tyana," *CQ* 34 (1984): 222–26; Francis, *Subversive Virtue*, 90 n. 23. Francis notes one letter in which "Apollonius" writes, "But if two different stories are being told about me, as they will be in the future too, what is surprising about that? It is inevitable, whenever someone is thought outstanding in any respect, that he becomes the subject of contradictory stories. Take for example Pythagoras, Orpheus, Plato, Socrates: contradictory accounts were given of them not only in speech but in writing. Why discordant accounts are given of God himself" (*Epp. Apoll.* 48.2). The pedestrian content of the letter has suggested its authenticity to some. See Penella, *The Letters of Apollonius of Tyana*, 115; Francis, *Subversive Virtue*, 96.

55. *Epp. Apoll.* 16.

56. *Epp. Apoll.* 17. This statement seems to trade on both the tradition of *magoi* as esteemed and philosophically inclined religious experts from Persia, and also the more generic and derisive connotations of a *magos* as a "sorcerer."

57. Cf. MacMullen, *Enemies of the Roman Order*, 100.

58. It was widely known that Pythagoras himself never committed any of his teachings to writing, nor did any direct disciple record his teachings or pen his biography. Diogenes Laertius admits that there are some who insist that Pythagoras left no writings whatsoever but finds the assertion absurd and attributes to him three books (*Vit. Phil.* 8.5–6). See Macris, "Pythagoras," 27; Francis, *Subversive Virtue*, 106.

same considerations of vacancy and renown made him an important genealogical link for the plethora of wisdom traditions, texts, and religious skills that suffused the empire.[59] In view of the arguments of chapter 2, we should recall that not only Pythagoras and Plato but also Orpheus, Moses, and Zoraoaster were enlisted as precedents for the authority and specific practices of contemporary freelance experts.[60] While any famous figures might be credited with assorted skills, the fact that most were upheld as the authors or original architects of divinely inspired writings, laws, and teachings made them suitable to such roles, especially for intellectualizing experts and forms of religion.

Specialized Textual Practices in the Context of Religious Activity

The past decade has witnessed a surge of interest in specialized intellectual practices employed in the context of religious activity, foremost in the work of Peter T. Struck.[61] In his masterful history of the literary symbol, Struck traces its origins to the dual meaning of a *symbolon* as a kind of omen and as a secret piece of wisdom possessed by members of esoteric groups.[62] On this basis he theorizes a dynamic and coextensive relationship in the parallel developments of allegorical reading and divination.[63] While all acts of allegorical interpretation were forms of literary criticism and proceeded from an expectation that certain writings contained "some

---

59. Porphyry, *Vit. Pyth.* 6, 11. Porphyry also depicts Pythagoras as a philosopher whose audiences included not only men but also a number of women, a point that he makes on more than one occasion (*Vit. Pyth.* 18–9).

60. Graf and Iles Johnston, *Ritual Texts for the Afterlife*, 165–84; Smith, *Jesus the Magician*, 114.

61. Indeed, insofar as some ancient writers held prophetic style to be enigmatic by its very nature, the Judean writings, rich as they are in prophets and prophecy, were especially well suited to such an approach. On a related matter, see Struck, *Birth of the Symbol*, 166.

62. E.g., Struck, *Birth of the Symbol*, 178–79.

63. Struck, *Birth of the Symbol*, esp. 187–92. Cf. David Konstan, who suggests in his introduction to Heraclitus the Allegorist (c. late first or early second century CE): "The connection between religious cult and allegory is noteworthy, and shows that the interpretive strategy was put to wider use than that of redeeming Homer and the traditional poets. Indeed, it is possible that some of the impetus to the allegorization of the Homeric gods was derived from just such cultic contexts, which lent an immediate religious urgency to the enterprise" ("Introduction," *xviii*).

truer resonance, [a] subtle and profound knowledge that arrives in a concealed form and is waiting for a skilled reader to liberate it from its code," interpreters might differ considerably with respect to their motivations for applying allegorical methods to a text.[64] Some used the analytic tools of allegory to discern from the writings of Hesiod and Homer the deep structure of the cosmos or corroboration for later philosophical doctrines. Others, such as the author of the Derveni papyrus or the experts who produced the Orphic *lamellae*, drew on these skills and methods to develop and authorize seemingly proprietary religious teachings.[65]

The latter textual interpreters pursued allegorical reading methods in the context of what I would consider to be a religious activity, insofar as they imagined that god(s), *daimones*, angels, or divine *pneuma* participated directly in those methods. This sort of specialized exegesis was predicated on a shared attitude toward particular writings, namely, that they were divinely inspired and harbored concealed knowledge or mysteries that could be elucidated through specialized interpretation. Exegesis of these writings thus had grander consequences than other forms of literary criticism: the secrets and knowledge that they encoded pertained to divine beings, and their decipherment was a form of divination. Religious experts might apply the same interpretive tools to narrative texts, dreams, and oracles without any conceptual difficulty or distinction.[66] And while not everyone possessed the background and skills to divine from literature, the basic principles of this practice shared a common logic with forms of divination that lacked so elaborate an intellectual apparatus.[67]

---

64. Struck, *Birth of the Symbol*, 1.

65. For the texts of the *lamellae*, see Radcliffe G. Edmonds III, ed., *The "Orphic" Gold Tablets and Greek Religion: Further Along the Path* (Cambridge: Cambridge University Press, 2011), 15–67; Graf and Iles Johnston, *Ritual Texts for the Afterlife*, 1–49.

66. Struck, *Birth of the Symbol*, 32,

67. In a study of divination in the Derveni papyrus, Sarah Iles Johnston defines the general practice "as the acquisition of knowledge humans would not otherwise have, through a variety of methods." She thus understands the text's author as "an independent ritual practitioner who could operate as a diviner, an initiator, and perhaps other things as well," and his objective in the papyrus as, among other things, an attempt "to clarify for his audience the significance of some of the rituals that he offered" ("Divination in the Derveni Papyrus," in *Poetry As Initiation: The Center for Hellenic Studies Symposium on the Derveni Papyrus*, ed. Ionna Papadopoulou and Leonard Muellner [Cambridge: Harvard University Press, 2014], 89–105, at 89).

We inherit many examples from antiquity of writer-intellectuals who employed allegorical interpretation and other specialized reading methods to substantiate innovative religious teachings and other practices. A text such as the Derveni papyrus, which conveys a rare, firsthand perspective of someone actively engaged in this sort of activity, reveals how the exegesis of mythic literature might inform religious practice while simultaneously bolstering the authority and teaching of the self-authorized exegete.[68] Despite its fragmentary state, the "priest" who composed the text offers his proprietary interpretation of a theogonic poem that he characterizes "as a repository of great (and even sacred) hidden truths, which are conveyed in riddles ... in a manner that resembles the semantically dense language of oracular speech, esoteric philosophy, and cultic practice."[69] Much of the exegesis pertains to some imminent punishment of wicked people, escape from which entails both initiation into and the receipt of further instruction about his mysteries.[70]

Even these measures prove insufficient, however, if someone who has undergone initiation and instruction fails to truly understand what he or she has seen and heard. Thus the text is concerned above all else with reinforcing the deeper meanings of initiation, meanings that are conveyed specifically through the medium of Orphic literature.[71] The author is clear

---

68. For the text and interpretation, see Gábor Betegh, *The Derveni Papyrus: Cosmology, Theology, and Interpretation* (Cambridge: Cambridge University Press, 2004); Theokritos Kouremenos, George M. Parássoglou, and Kyriakos Tsantsanoglou, eds., *The Derveni Papyrus, Edited with Introduction and Commentary* (Florence: Casa Editrice Leo S. Olschki, 2006). For a succinct and general introduction to the text and relevant scholarship, see John T. Fitzgerald, "Myth, Allegory, and the Derveni Papyrus," in *Myth and Scripture: Contemporary Perspectives on Religion, Language, and Imagination*, ed. Dexter E. Callender Jr. (Atlanta: Society of Biblical Literature, 2014), 229–44. For its possible contribution to theorizations of earliest Christianity, see idem, "The Derveni Papyrus and Its Relevance for Biblical and Patristic Studies," *EC* 6 (2015): 1–22. For the Derveni author as a kind of religious expert, see Edmonds, "Extra-Ordinary People," passim; idem, *Redefining Ancient Orphism*, esp. 95–138.

69. Esp. cols. I–VI; cf., Rom 2:5–16. See Struck, *Birth of the Symbol*, 38.

70. The reconstruction of the first columns is debated. See Richard Janko, "Reconstructing (Again) the Opening of the Derveni Papyrus," *ZPE* 166 (2008): 37–52; Fitzgerald, "The Derveni Papyrus and Its Relevance for Biblical and Patristic Studies," 14 n. 79.

71. See Fitzgerald, "The Derveni Papyrus and Its Relevance for Biblical and Patristic Studies," 19. By "Orphic literature" I mean any writings that were attributed or otherwise connected to Orpheus for the purpose of freelance religious expertise. As Edmonds explains, "Orphic texts were not regarded in an essentially different way than other texts that made claims to insights into the nature of the gods and the cosmos. Nor are the Orphic texts characterized

that literal readings of this poem fail to disclose its true message; only those who have correctly deciphered the difficult riddles found in the texts of Orpheus achieve the sort of understanding he advocates.[72] These are not general remarks but ones aimed at rival specialists, with particular opprobrium reserved for the sort of Orphic initiators who, with a "hubbub of books," went door-to-door persuading households to undergo special purifications and initiations in order to escape the terrors of Hades.[73] In other words, the author is concerned foremost with distinguishing his learned religious expertise from that of other freelance experts alleging Orphic specialty, especially ones who enlisted texts, and presumably therefore intellectual practices, in their offerings. He is not, Radcliff G. Edmonds III concludes, "preaching sacred scripture to members of a secret sect, but displaying his expert knowledge and understanding through explication of a difficult poetic text. This understanding does not consist of some secret doctrine that provides the key to salvation; rather, it is his skill at exegesis itself that demonstrates his religious competence. . . . The ultimate justification for his disparagement of rivals is his superior understanding of Orpheus, the ideal extra-ordinary religious authority."[74]

Edmonds usefully points out that self-aggrandizing articulations of particular forms of expertise—in this text, "correct" Orphic exegesis and the accompanying initiation—are precisely what give rise to the impression that these forms constituted coherent categories of religious practice in the ancient Mediterranean world.[75] Yet the salient

---

by special Orphic myths, exclusive to the Orphica, that have special doctrinal significance to the initiate. On the contrary, the Orphic texts make use of the same mythological material, available to all the *bricoleurs* working in the Greek mythological tradition, and the meanings of those myths shift from version to version . . . without preserving some core of Orphic doctrine that identified the myths as Orphic" (*Redefining Ancient Orphism*, 95).

72. Col. VI, VII.4–5. As Fitzgerald notes, the author expresses regret about people who have wasted money on initiation and private instruction that they cannot appreciate (XX.3–12), then alleges "to [rectify] the problem by imparting to readers the knowledge that they ought to have received at the time of initiation but did not" ("The Derveni Papyrus and Its Relevance for Biblical and Patristic Studies," 21). See also Edmonds, *Redefining Ancient Orphism*, 133–35.

73. Plato, *Resp.* 364b–365a; Fitzgerald, "Myth, Allegory, and the Derveni Papyrus," 234; Edmonds, *Redefining Ancient Orphism*, 98–102.

74. Edmonds, "Extra-Ordinary People," 33; cf. Stowers, "The Religion of Plant and Animal Offerings," 48.

75. Edmonds, "Extra-Ordinary People," 34. In other words, the assumption that "Orphism," "Thergy," and other categories of religious practice were discrete in their respective ancient

issue for the Derveni author is his relationship not to a defined religious entity, but to rivals offering similar services whom he seeks to supplant through intellectual demonstrations that underscore the superiority of his skills.[76] "The Derveni papyrus," Edmonds explains, "is thus part of Plato's hubbub of books, competing for clientele in the marketplace of the fifth century amid the swirling controversies of the sophists of all types. The Derveni author is advertising his skill at a craft, that of a religious specialist, the type parodied by Aristophanes, denounced as charlatans by the Hippocratics, and scorned by Plato."[77] And although this author and his competitors are earlier than most figures considered in this study, both the subset of religious activity in which they engaged and also the tactics they employed are amply attested for our period, most notably in certain Hermetic, Orphic, and Pythagorean literature, and also, I argue in the next chapters, the Pauline Epistles and the second-century writings of rival Christian experts. Not unlike the Derveni author, Paul alleges to discern secret and hidden wisdom from the holy writings of the Judeans or "the oracles of God" by means of the divine *pneuma* through which God has revealed the mysteries of his eschatological plans.[78] Whereas ordinary readers of these texts are unable to comprehend the more profound meanings concealed within them, those who have received a portion of Christ's own *pneuma* through a purifying initiation rite are equipped to discern them and to appreciate their eschatological significance with unveiled minds.[79]

Importantly, the extraordinary meanings that these intellectualizing experts adduced from their respective literary corpora were not instances of theological speculation. Rather, they are better understood as

---

contexts owes much to the claims of the ancient writer-intellectuals who produced such discourses to construct and defend their own superior skills and knowledge.

76. Edmonds, "Extra-Ordinary People," 32.

77. Edmonds, *Redefining Ancient Orphism*, 129.

78. Rom 3:2; 1 Cor 2:7–10; Rom 16:25. For this quality of *pneuma*, see Stanley K. Stowers, "What Is 'Pauline Participation in Christ'?" in *Redefining First-Century Jewish and Christian Identities: Essays in Honor of Ed Parish Sanders,* ed. Fabian Udoh et al., CJAS (Notre Dame: University of Notre Dame Press, 2008), 352–71, esp. 361–64; Wendt, "Galatians 3:1 As an Allusion to Textual Prophecy," 383–85. See also Laura Salah Nasrallah, *An Ecstasy of Folly: Prophecy and Authority in Early Christianity* (Cambridge: Harvard University Press, 2004), 71.

79. 2 Cor 3:13–16, 4:3. I expand on this characterization of Paul and his literary exegesis in the next chapter.

myth-making undertaken in order to explain, justify, and even necessitate other practices comprising their offerings. As Sarah Iles Johnston characterizes the Derveni author's extensive discussion about the exact effects of his afterlife-related initiation rites in columns V and VI of the text, "The final result, here as elsewhere in the Derveni Papyrus, is an idiosyncratic, cerebral religious system that can justify the individual planks of its doctrines with reference to existing beliefs and practices, but which, as a whole, undoubtedly would have struck someone of average religious disposition as counterintuitive."[80] That is, its rich eschatological tapestry is not only purposive, in the sense that it lends significance to the author's scheme as a whole but also deliberately enmeshed in cultivating its own obscurity, exclusivity, and rarified mystique. All of these qualities, I suggest in the next chapter, are equally apparent in the writings of Paul.

The constellation of literate intellectual practices evident in these texts—myth-making through textual exegesis, the employment of philosophical discourses and techniques, the composition of new writings, and the ascription of special meanings to ordinary religious activities—amount to what Stanley K. Stowers has characterized as "the religion of the literate cultural producer." "These people were specialists," he explains, "by virtue of the skills, prestige, and legitimacy derived from their belonging to the perhaps 2 percent or less of people who were literate enough to produce and authoritatively interpret complex, written texts. Although small in number in any one location, they formed a large network ... united by a set of common literate practices that allowed skills, ideas, motifs, and so on to cross ethnic, linguistic, and status boundaries."[81] He further delineates literate specialists such as Thrasyllus and Josephus, who received patronage from the imperial family and other social elites, from more entrepreneurial versions thereof, including philosophers of various sorts. The latter experts were considerably freer than their more institutionally embedded or otherwise constrained counterparts to combine and apply intellectual practices in innovative ways, especially in the medium of writing. Remarking on how this innovation has been characterized in earlier scholarship, Stowers concludes elsewhere, "Such uses are probably misdescribed as eclecticism and syncretism because the thinkers well

---

80. Iles Johnston, "Divination in the Derveni Papyrus," 103–4.

81. Stowers, "The Religion of Plant and Animal Offerings," 41.

understood the doctrines that they adapted and endeavored to integrate these into their larger intellectual and practical projects."[82]

Although competitive dynamics between literate specialists crossed different social registers and niches of expertise, rivalries were sharpest among experts of comparable ability operating in similar areas, however these might be defined: rites or wisdom attributed to the same mythical founder, offerings framed within a common ethnic or cultural framework, or divine wisdom extracted through literary divination from the same texts. Contestations among Orphic initiators are pronounced in the Derveni papyrus, but the author is equally keen to distance the practices of initiators or *mystai* from those of *magoi*.[83] So too do many Hermetic writings contrast Hermes the "philosopher" with Zoroaster the "magician" and the "way of Hermes" with other initiation schemes that result in the divinization of the intiate.[84] Paul, whose own soteriological scheme closely resembles, *mutatis mutandis*, those of the Derveni author and some Hermetic writings with respect to both mechanism and supporting representations, consciously elevates himself above other kinds of intellectualizing specialists, including (other) Judean teachers, philosophers, and sophists.[85]

Since intellectualizing practices and texts transected ethnic or geographic specificity, it is unsurprising that rivalries among writer-intellectuals with similar skills and interests crossed putative

---

82. See Stanley K. Stowers, "The Dilemma of Paul's Physics: Features Stoic-Platonist or Platonist-Stoic?" in *From Stoicism to Platonism: The Development of Philosophy 100 BCE–100 CE*, ed. Troels Engberg-Pedersen (Cambridge: Cambridge University Press, forthcoming), 1–23, at 17. Cf. Fowden, who writes of the philosophical Hermeticists that they apparently saw nothing inconsistent in combining various figures from Greek and Egyptian myth, along with various intellectual elements, "that philosophical Hermeticism is not just a haphazard accumulation of separate elements, but a self-validating structure with its own conventions" (*The Egyptian Hermes*, 33).

83. Col. VI.8.9. See also Amir Ahmadi, "The *Magoi* and *Daimones* in Column VI of the Derveni Papyrus," *Numen* 61 (2014): 484–508.

84. See Fowden, *The Egyptian Hermes*, 109–11. For the texts, see Brian P. Copenhaven, *Hermetica: The Greek Corpus Hermeticum and the Latin Asclepius in a New English Translation with Notes and Introduction* (Cambridge: Cambridge University Press, 1992).

85. Such denunciations hardly flowed in only one direction: Epictetus criticizes, in addition to "false" Cynics and wonder-workers, those who, though having undergone baptism, are only acting the part of Judeans by priding themselves on principles that, in reality, they do not profess (*Diatr.* 2.9). Likewise, in the introduction I noted writer-intellectuals such as Galen, whose conception of medicine deliberately excluded healers with a religious epistemology,

ethnic or geographic boundaries.[86] And while particular wisdom traditions or corpora might be ethnically coded in the manner examined earlier, recent scholarship has emphasized how many books and traditions
of the Roman period that were presented as Persian, Egyptian, Judean,
or Chaldean reflected a common intellectual milieu characterized by an
expansiveness and flexibility of thought.[87] The writings of Plato and teachings of Pythagoras—not to mention their personae—were central to this
milieu. Platonic emphasis on "the broadly shared *telos* of likeness to God
and a broad interest in ancient texts" was expressly suitable to elaboration
within intellectualizing religious offerings, although other philosophical
concepts, notably ones drawn from Stoicism, were also germane to the
task. [88]

Since my theorization of the wider field of freelance expertise includes
many philosophers, these indications of shared discourses and other
affinities between philosophers and intellectualizing religious experts
make sense within this social context, all the more so since, again, the
disciplinary boundaries around "philosophy" and particular philosophical
schools of thought were being drawn or redrawn within the same timeframe.[89] For this reason it is backward to evaluate these points of overlap
from the top down, as though religious experts were misappropriating—
or appropriating at all—stable intellectual schemes; all freelance actors
were participating in a shared intellectual milieu that might crystallize in
different ways.

---

insofar as the valence of their diagnoses and treatments involved divine beings, even if their
practices resembled those of a "doctor" in other respects.

86. Here and elsewhere, by "traditions" I am referring to how certain forms of knowledge
were presented, rather than to their actual history and integrity.

87. Stowers, "The Dilemma of Paul's Physics," 16. For Judean elements in the Hermetica,
e.g., see Fowden, *The Egyptian Hermes*, 36 n. 139.

88. Stowers, "The Dilemma of Paul's Physics," 18. As Fowden notes, Chaeremon's portrayal of the priests of Egyptian gods depicted them not only as "philosophers" but also
as covert Pythagoreans (*The Egyptian Hermes*, 56 n. 34, 112). For a similar intellectual
milieu in ancient Greece, see, e.g., James Redfield, "The Philosophers and the Many," *HR*
50 (2010): 43–53; Francesc Casadesús, "The Transformation of the Initiation Language of
Mystery Religions into Philosophical Terminology," in *Greek Philosophy and Mystery Cults*,
ed. María José Martín-Velasco and María José García Blanco (Cambridge: Cambridge
Scholars, 2016), 1–26.

89. See, e.g., Harold Tarrant, "Platonist Educators in a Growing Market: Gaius; Abinus;
Taurus; Alcinous," in Sharples and Sorabji, *Greek and Roman Philosophy 100 BC–200 AD, Vol. 2*,
449–65.

What is remarkable is the sheer number of texts with these character-istics that flourished in the Roman period. I have already mentioned the Hermetica, the generally accepted dates of which span the late Ptolemaic period through the second century CE, as well as Pythagorean pseudepig-rapha, which enjoyed renewed interest in the first centuries BCE and CE.[90] The *Orphic Rhapsodies*, an assortment of texts linked with Orpheus, seem to have been compiled and systematized as a coherent collection within roughly the same timeframe.[91] Similar qualities to the ones described above—even if they occur at a lower register—are also found in the *Greek Magical Papyri*.[92] The conscious evocation of Egyptian temple institutions and priestly office in some texts ought not disallow their relevance to the phenomenon of freelance expertise, whether their authors were actual priests acting in a freelance capacity or entirely self-authorized special-ists merely claiming priestly titles.[93] And although much of the evidence for and exegetical interest in the *Chaldean Oracles* is late antique, again, the traditions about these texts place their origins in the Antonine period. These parallel developments may flesh out and help to explain why, as we saw earlier, the first and second centuries of the empire were rife with leg-islative incidents involving confiscations of privately circulating *Sibylline Oracles* and other prophetic writings, including those attributed to the Persian sage Hystaspes and the Judean prophets.

Within any of these literary groupings are texts that attest a breadth of skill, facility with intellectual practices, and application, but they all share common tactics of authorization, basic philosophical terminology, and alleged sources for the wisdom they contain. The degree of similarity is strongest among experts of comparable ability, irrespective of whether they trace their knowledge and practices to Pythagoras, Hermes Trismegistus, Hekate, Zoroaster, Orpheus, Moses, or Christ. If the constraints of exist-ing scholarly categories are set aside, such coincidences of emphases on

---

90. For the dating of the Hermetic literature, see Fowden, *The Egyptian Hermes*, 1–11.

91. See Edmonds, *Redefining Ancient Orphism*, 44–47, 148–59. Edmonds's analogy between the formation of the *Orphic Rhapsodies* and the compilation of the extant *Sibylline Oracles* as a distinct literary corpus is particularly germane to my point.

92. See Hans Dieter Betz, ed., *The Greek Magical Papyri in Translation, Including the Demotic Spells, Vol. 1: The Texts with an Updated Bibliography*, 2nd ed. (Chicago: University of Chicago Press, 1992).

93. See Gordon, "Memory and Authority in the Magical Papyri," 145–80; Moyer, "The Initiation of the Magician," 219–38.

the prophetic or esoteric value of certain writings, on revelations and mysteries, and on special initiations resulting in transformation and immortality suggests particularly high degrees of similarity among specialists of comparable skills and interests. It would not be otherwise, since the ability to commit a religious program to writing allowed for considerably more ambitiousness, more elaboration, and an exchange of ideas among the relatively few specialists capable of producing such writings in the first place. With the literary evidence thus redescribed, noted affinities between theurgists, Hermeticists, certain Judeans, and Christians of later centuries might have less to do with dynamic interactions between bounded traditions than with the common class of religious activity whence many of these forms of religion arose.

Intellectualizing Forms of Religion in the Roman Imperial Period

Late Classical and Hellenistic sources confirm that the employment of intellectual discourses and skills in the context of religious activity was not a unique product of the imperial period. Nevertheless, there are reasons to think that imperial conditions fostered intellectualizing forms of religion to an unprecedented degree. Clifford Ando has highlighted the symbolic power of literacy and writings in the ideology and bureaucratic administration of the empire, while other scholars have written at length about the collateral growth of public libraries, private book collections, the book industry, and a general culture of reading.[94] Since the religion of literate specialists "could not exist without writings, high literacy, networks of literate exchange, and various textually oriented interpretive practices,"[95] the promotion of writing, even symbolically, under the empire sheds light on the concomitant rise in popularity of religious offerings predicated on texts and literate knowledge. Edmonds argues for a comparable situation in fifth-century Athens, when the technological innovation of the book came to signify a claim to expertise for avant-garde intellectuals of any

---

94. Clifford Ando, *Imperial Ideology and Provincial Loyalty* (Berkeley: University of California Press, 2000), esp. 73–130. On the relationship between religion and writing in this period, see, e.g., Richard L. Gordon, "From Republic to Principate: Priesthood, Religion and Ideology," in Beard and North, *Pagan Priests*, 179–98; Beard, "Writing and Religion: Ancient Literacy and the Function of the Written Word in Roman Religion."

95. Stowers, "The Religion of Plant and Animal Offerings," 41.

type. That is, in this period, books became the medium through which would-be experts communicated their knowledge and abilities, and to the limited audiences who valued the skills that textual specialty implied.[96]

Other factors of note include the tendency for those with sufficient resources to do so to seek out *paideia* and support intellectual coteries, although we must imagine a spectrum of expertise that catered to a range of social locations and economic circumstances. Satirists have much to say about the ambitions of would-be specialists who sought to capitalize on such enthusiasms by aspiring to posts in wealthy households.[97] Regarding their motives, Lucian lists escape from poverty (a state that, in his view, most experts exaggerate), the pursuit of pleasure, and the prestige that accrues from associating with people of noble birth and high position.[98] As to the motives of would-be patrons, Lucian has a rather skeptical outlook: they surround themselves with learned experts not to acquire actual knowledge but because for the sake of appearances it is proper for men of a certain station to have in their escort people with a markedly intellectual appearance.[99] Women are also keen to keep such figures in their employ, since it adds to their other accomplishments if they seem cultured and interested in philosophy.[100]

Despite the specious motivations of patrons, aspiring experts bribe servants and jostle with rivals to secure such opportunities.[101] "You would put up with it if you had to act the part of a *magos* or a *mantis* or one of those fellows who promise legacies amounting to many thousands, governorships, and tremendous riches," Lucian rebukes them. "Many who have entered households, to make up for not knowing anything else that was useful, have professed to supply predictions, philters, love-charms, and incantations against enemies; yet they assert they are educated, wrap themselves in a philosopher's mantle, and wear beards that cannot be lightly sneered at."[102] His criticisms echo those of Umbricius: any hope of real specialty has succumbed to a demand for "magic," and usually of an exotic variety.

---

96. Edmonds, *Redefining Ancient Orphism*, 112–13, 115–16.

97. In addition to texts already mentioned, Lucian, *Ind., Ver. hist.,* and *Vit. auct.*

98. Lucian, *De merc.* 5, 7, 9.

99. Lucian, *De merc.* 25.16–31.

100. Lucian, *De merc.* 36.

101. Lucian, *De merc.* 11.

102. Lucian, *De merc.* 27.14–21, 40.12–23 (trans. A. M. Harmon, LCL).

As with all of satirical writings, these depictions must be taken with a grain of salt. But they illustrate a common manifestation of freelance expertise that occurred not in marketplaces or at the circus but in the domestic sphere. Whether specialists visited their clientele or followers episodically or enjoyed permanent positions among them, the household was one type of social formation with which these actors regularly overlapped. Moreover, one's role within that context might have an intellectual premise, but being a sort of teacher was not mutually exclusive with practices such as divination, forecasting, healing, and summoning divine beings.[103]

Within the broader trend of interest in intellectualizing forms of religion there was a particular appetite for exotic and esoteric forms of *paideia,* most notably among freedpersons and freeborn women. There is no single explanation for why this was the case, but earlier discussions have adumbrated several possibilities. On the one hand, demographic changes that occurred under Hellenistic and Roman rule created new audiences for certain religious specialty and services. Regarding the evidence for a diversification of practice in late Ptolemaic and Roman Egypt, Richard L. Gordon posits that a wealthy and increasingly hellenized population stimulated demand not only for expertise in Egyptian religion but also for texts and other *instrumentum*—technical amulets, astrology manuals, alchemical ingredients—that enabled the independent acquisition thereof.[104] Such developments are observable within and outside the temple, but they catered, he argues, to the interests of a relatively affluent, Greek-speaking potential clientele.[105] That the majority of "Egyptian" ritual, astrological, and other divinatory texts of the Roman period were written in Greek lends force to Gordon's proposition that they were intended foremost for hellenized consumers, although this act of translation "impelled a search for new ways of registering [their] Egyptian authenticity."[106] The previous chapter supplied several examples of how exoticism might be coded or affected to this end.

---

103. As Dickie surmises, wonder-working specialists were something of a commonplace in cities such as Rome, but "what [gave] them their entrée to the salons of the rich [was] their education" (*Magic and Magicians in the Greco-Roman World,* 198).

104. Gordon, "Memory and Authority in the Magical Papyri," 154–59.

105. Gordon also extends financial considerations to "the hierarchy of knowledge and prowess" in the *Greek Magical Papyri,* the intellectual caliber of whose texts depended on "how much the client was prepared to pay for a given service, and thus the effort worth investing in the contract" ("Memory and Authority in the Magical Papyri," 160).

106. Gordon, "Memory and Authority in the Magical Papyri," 162–63.

On the other hand, imperial conditions precipitated population displacement on a massive scale, with slavery as one of the most significant sources of upheaval. As I suggested in chapter 1, participation in the religion of freelance experts was generally high among former slaves, and intellectualizing subsets of this phenomenon are no exception. Their interest "may have had a basis," Stowers proposes, "in their minority or mixed ethnic statuses or other status inconsistencies that both alienated them from the dominant legitimate *paideia* [that is, Greek] and attracted them to an alternative."[107] The same explanation is also of relevance for understanding the attraction of freeborn women of all social orders to foreign offerings in which texts and intellectual practices were conspicuous. While the actual motivations that women had for seeking out expertise were surely more complex than an author such as Lucian allows, there is no shortage of corroboration for the relationships on which he is commenting. On women's involvement with intellectualizing specialists, we might recall Josephus's account of the instructors in Mosaic wisdom, but even more reliable is the ample evidence in the Pauline Epistles and second-century Christian sources that they were avid consumers of teachings and practices involving Christ.[108]

Magic or Freelance Religious Expertise?

In this chapter I have moved from the initial ethnic dimension of *magi* and its disintegration, to the formation of "magic" as an emic category that developed in response to the growth and diversification of the religion of freelance experts, to the association of Pythagoras and other philosophical wisdom with magic, to a subset of intellectualizing experts within the wider phenomenon of freelance religious expertise. My purpose in drawing these considerations together has been twofold: First, I propose that there is no evidence for magic apart from the religion of freelance experts and, therefore, that any theorization of religion in the ancient world is incomplete without sufficient attention to the actors and practices that are often dealt with in a separate intellectual context, one that is implicitly or explicitly set in opposition to religion. Second, I have attempted to draw attention to how the category

---

107. Stowers, "Kinds of Myth, Meals, and Power," 116.

108. I return to this matter in chapters 4 and 5.

of magic, as it is employed in much contemporary scholarship, collapses a vast range of skills, aptitude, and practices into a diminutive caricature of the magician that Lucian would whole-heartedly endorse. Yet what "magic" masks is that many of the actors included within this modern category were comparable to and in competition with more esteemed intellectualizing religious experts of the same period, some of whom were responsible for generating the particular forms of religion—intellectually focused, text-based, meaningful, universalizing—that would become integral to later concepts of "religion."[109]

Few would likely disagree with my characterization of magic as a form of religious activity, provided that the marginal, subversive, or illicit aspects of the magician's religion are acknowledged. As I noted in the introduction, however, such expectations often stem from an understanding of religion as a mechanism for promoting cohesion, inculcating shared norms and values, and reinforcing or naturalizing deeper social structures. For their own undisguised interests, as well as those of people who consulted them, freelance religious experts (or "magicians") are seen to clash with whatever optimal social functions religion is thought to accomplish. There is no shortage of ancient sources that support antinormative assessments of these actors, but this is precisely the problem: to reify "magic" as an analytical category is to take for granted the normative sense of "religion" that the same texts advocate.

Bernd-Christian Otto has argued persuasively that there is no consistent scholarly definition of "magic" whose criteria are not at least partially reliant on aspects of such interested portrayals. Whether the category is understood to correspond to an ambiguous or illegitimate sphere of rituals, to practices that somehow pervert or invert religion, or to exotic rites and techniques that supplement established traditions and specialists, the underlying premise remains that "magical" and "religious" actors and phenomena differ enough to warrant distinct labels and approaches. Even when these phenomena are arranged on a continuum, religion and magic are imagined as opposing poles whose examples are more or less of one or the other. "[W]hen opposed to 'religion,'" Otto writes, "'magic' was merely regarded as a refuse-heap for the elements which are not sufficiently

---

109. See Stowers, "The Religion of Plant and Animal Offerings," 50–51.

'valuable' to get a place within 'religion.' "[110] In the case of freelance expertise, the antinormative shade that most sources cast on the actors and practices in question renders their apparent popularity and appeal inexplicable. The conflation of this particular form of religious activity with discourses about charlatanry and magic has thus predisposed us to view the evidence through a distortive lens.

With the retention of emic categories such as "magic," then, we inherit subjective judgments about a form of religious activity whose appreciable expansion and influence were precisely what piqued strong antinormative discourses about it in the first place. The asymmetric inclusion of women in ancient discourses about magic is telling in this regard. There are many indications that women participated appreciably in the religion of freelance experts, as both purveyors and clients, and regularly, so it would seem, to pursue intellectual interests. Yet, in most sources these activities are held up as examples par excellence of deviant religious practice. Kimberly B. Stratton has shown that Greek and Roman authors are disproportionately critical of female experts; more often than not they are depicted as grotesque, predatory, libidinous, and sexually depraved and their agendas as frivolous but disquieting.[111] In one sense it is to be expected that ancient commentators on freelance expertise were emphatically negative about women who acted in this capacity. At the same time, the intensification of such stereotypes where women are concerned might have a basis in the fact that this form of religious activity afforded them greater opportunities for participation than other venues.

To be sure, there is great value in studying the development of discourses about magic in order to understand their scope and force in particular historical contexts, especially since, as Rives has shown, such discourses had a demonstrable impact on the criminalization of certain

---

110. Bernd-Christian Otto, "Towards Historicizing 'Magic' in Antiquity," *Numen* 60 (2013): 308–47, at 317. See also Otto's monograph on the topic, *Magie: Rezeptions- und diskursgeschichteliche Analysen von der Antike bis zur Neuzeit*, Religionsgeschichtliche Versuche und Vorarbeiten 57 (Berlin: de Gruyter, 2011). For a succinct overview of the intellectual history of the debates about the category of "magic," see Stratton, "Magic Discourse in the Ancient World," 243–46.

111. Stratton, *Naming the Witch*, esp. 79–96; idem, "Interrogating the Magic–Gender Connection" and "Magic, Abjection, and Gender in Roman Literature," in Stratton and Kalleres, *Daughters of Hekate*, 1–37 and 152–80.

actions under Roman law.[112] But there is equal value in disentangling them, as Stratton does with respect to discourses about women and magic, from the underlying religious actors and practices they seek to marginalize.[113] While she proffers a nuanced definition of "magic" that grants its cultural specificity and the ideological work the category accomplishes, in my view, the religion of freelance experts constitutes a more ontologically exact middle ground between recognizing "magic" as a social discourse with a particular history, and trying to understand the complex ways this discourse affected and molded the activities of the actual figures and phenomena to which is was applied.[114] "Freelance religious expertise" is less encumbered by the polemical valences of "magic," and thus less prone to the sort of uncritical blurring of discourse and analytical category that Stratton rightly critiques.

Conclusions

As we have seen in this chapter, the practices associated with *magi*, and then the discursive category "magic," cover the full spectrum from highly intellectualizing forms of religion that have much in common with the evidence for earliest Christianity to the sort of practices that scholars typically have in mind when they talk about "magicians" in the Greco-Roman world: divination, conjuring, spells, and so forth, which had less sophisticated intellectual valences or else lacked them entirely. Even within a body of literature attributed to a common figure—for instance, the writings of Orpheus, Pythagoras, or Hermes Trismegistus—one finds everything from texts dealing with the practicalities of initiations, the casting of horoscopes, and spells to more sophisticated philosophical articulations of Orphic or Hermetic wisdom brought to bear on religious rites.[115] While I am not

---

112. Rives, "Magic in Roman Law," 316; cf. Stratton, "Magic Discourse in the Ancient World," 246–47. See also Edmonds's discussion of emic versus etic definitions with respect to ancient discourses about "Orphism" (*Redefining Ancient Orphism*, 76–77).

113. Cf. Otto, who calls "on the one hand, for the abandonment of an abstract category of 'magic' and, on the other hand, for a systematic historicization of the ancient term, that is, for the reconstruction of its ancient semantics, functions, and contexts" ("Towards Historicizing 'Magic' in Antiquity," 339). See also John G. Gager, *Curse Tablets and Binding Spells from the Ancient World* (New York: Oxford University Press, 1992), 3–40, esp. 25.

114. See Stratton, "Magic Discourse in the Ancient World," 245–46.

115. See Fowden, *The Egyptian Hermes*, 116–17.

denying that the religion of freelance experts included many participants whose practices did not depend on formal learning, writings, or high degrees of literacy—quite the opposite, such actors probably represent the majority of specialists—the most enduring effects of this sort of religious activity stem from a subset of intellectualizing specialists seeking to differentiate themselves from one another, and often with other kinds of writer-intellectuals in view. It is to one such expert that I now turn, the apostle Paul, whose letters, once situated in this context, constitute a rare form of evidence for its internal dynamics matched only by sources such as the Derveni papyrus that offer intimate glimpses of how freelance religious experts operated in actual practice.

4

Paul, A Rare Witness to the Religion of Freelance Experts

IN THE PRECEDING pages I have argued for the salience of the religion of freelance experts in the Roman Empire, with each chapter yielding insights into its defining characteristics. As to the dynamics of this class of religious activity, I have identified such currents as self-authorization and legitimation, recognition and misrecognition, attraction, and competition. Regarding how freelance experts navigated these dynamics, I have isolated such tactics as claims of divine revelation or inspiration, often with verification through signs; appeals to having endured suffering and punishment on account of one's expertise; displays of specialized skills, particularly ones with intellectual valences; myth-making, often undertaken in conjunction with writings; and the creative fusion of elements found elsewhere in more discrete or doctrinaire arrangements. Ethnic coding could collude with these tactics in additional ways, multiplying the possibilities for how experts might represent their specialty or be labeled by others.

With a few notable exceptions, the evidence informing our picture so far is dominated by perspectives that are external to this phenomenon and thus pose considerable interpretive challenges to reconstructing how specialists attracted and sustained followers. In this chapter I argue for the apostle Paul's participation in the religion of freelance experts and the value of his letters as a sight line into its inner workings. Due to the theological motivations that have long influenced the study of these texts, Paul has been cast time and again in scholarship as a figure ultimately lacking in exact, or any, social and religious *comparanda*.[1] Even in publications that otherwise demonstrate his affinities with certain contemporaneous figures, some premise of Paul's own uniqueness, as well as that of his *ekklēsiai*, remains a default conclusion.[2] In my view, such comparisons tend to stop short of the thoroughgoing redescription they invite, perhaps for lack of a specific context that accommodates the full range of actors with whom Paul has been shown to bear similarities.[3]

Situating the apostle in a broader field of freelance expertise offers new comparative possibilities for understanding him as a first-century religious actor and also for explaining why he was recognizable and appealing to gentile audiences. Indications that his practices were contiguous with those of other self-authorized specialists appear throughout the letters he is thought to have authored. Proceeding slightly out of order from the preceding chapters, I consider how the conspicuously Judean framework

---

1. For example, in a recent article Brent Nongbri calls attention to how uncritical concepts of religion have had a distortive effect on Pauline scholarship. While I raise other problematic assumptions and categories—e.g., the scholarly retention of such theological or emic language as the Pauline "mission" and "apostle"—that pose obstacles to a normalized account of Paul as a Greco-Roman religious actor, I agree with Nongbri's critique and see continuities between my approach and the possible redescriptive directions he outlines. See Brent Nongbri, "The Concept of Religion and the Study of the Apostle Paul," *JJMJS* 2 (2015): 1–26, esp. 21–26. For a brief overview of what he calls these "theological modernist" readings of the Pauline Epistles, see Stowers, "Kinds of Myth, Meals, and Power," 106–9.

2. E.g. Hanges, who concludes, "[C]omparison with Hellenistic parallels and our explanation of certain early Christian patterns and phenomena in terms of Hellenistic precedents does not, in itself, *deny a certain uniqueness to Christianity*" (*Paul, Founder of Churches*, 399, emphasis added). In a similar fashion, Timothy Luckritz Marquis *likens* Paul to other wandering priests and prophets and calls attention to suspicions he would have faced due to this resemblance to them without considering seriously that Paul *may have been* one of these actors (*Transient Apostle*, passim). This is not to undermine the valuable contributions of these and other comparative studies, the insights of which have contributed immeasurably to my own work on Paul. I am especially indebted to recent scholarship on different aspects of Paul's thought, and, to my mind, the present analytical context could amplify or indicate new avenues of elaboration for future studies.

3. See, e.g., Dieter Georgi, *The Opponents of Paul in Second Corinthians* (Philadelphia: Fortress, 1986), 83–174. Surveying evidence for "missionary activity" in the first century, Georgi introduces many figures whom I have included in this study: the Judean deceivers at Rome, the Judean priestess and law interpreter, Eleazar, Alexander, Pergrinus, Apollonius of Tyana and other Neo-Pythagoreans, priests of Sarapis and Dionysus, and various figures in Acts. Although he usefully situates Judeans and Christians within this landscape, his model of rival missionaries competing for converts to their respective groups or religions reinscribes the distinctness of the latter entities. So too is Paul cast in essentially different terms from the θεῖος ἀνήρ concept that Georgi applies to many of Paul's opponents in order to explain their traction among his own followers.

of Paul's religious program and the role(s) of Judean writings therein, his enlistment of philosophy and other intellectualizing elements, his admissions to having endured punishments for the sake of his gospel, his travel itinerary, and his economic practices together justify placing him in this context. Touching on all of these topics are the various rivals, real and potential, from whom Paul sought to distinguish himself throughout his correspondence.

The preceding chapters have prepared us to theorize Paul as one freelance expert in Judean religion among others, and, more generally, as a purveyor of foreign religious wisdom or rites with a distinctly textual-intellectual bent. This characterization does not preclude considering him simultaneously as a mystery initiator, a self-styled priest, or any other role suggested by his claims and practices. As we have seen, few specialists boasted only one skill or were beholden to putative disciplinary boundaries. Against such a backdrop, then, Paul's apparent contradictions or oscillations between scholarly categories—Judaism and Hellenism, religion and philosophy, among others—are not only unproblematic but might be seen as predictable effects of the religious milieu in which he operated.[4] Therefore, it is my hope that the methodology I propose will also contribute to ongoing efforts to disentangle some of the most intricate knots in Pauline scholarship: Paul's relationship to Judaism, his relationship to philosophy, the identity of his opponents, and the reason(s) why he was punished, among other longstanding problems. While my focus falls on the broader task of redescribing Paul as a freelance expert, whenever possible I suggest how viewing their author in this context may hold new interpretive possibilities for the content of his epistles.

"What Advantage Has the Judean?"

Pauline scholarship has long been dominated by a central question or problem: What was Paul's relationship to Judaism? The proposed solutions to

---

4. To be clear, I do not see these as actual contradictions or oscillations. Rather, as I have noted in the preceding chapters, such perceived problems arise from the application of overly rigid and anachronistic categories to the ancient evidence, in this case Paul's thought and practices. For relevant discussion and a sense of the analytical challenges, see Troels Engberg-Pedersen, ed., *Paul Beyond the Judaism-Hellenism Dualism* (Louisville, KY: Westminster John Knox, 2001), esp. Dale B. Martin, "Paul and the Judaism/Hellenism Dichotomy: Toward a Social History of the Question," 29–62. For Paul's relationship to philosophers and other

the Paul–Judaism conundrum have grown more varied and nuanced in the past few decades, acceding a number of considerations now regarded by many as cruxes of Pauline interpretation.[5] Second to none is the insight that Paul's intended audiences were comprised primarily of gentiles and, with this insight, that his seemingly contradictory—and at times critical—statements about the law and Israel need to be read with them in mind.[6] The intended effects and reception of his rhetoric are, moreover, inscrutable without sufficient attention to cultural codes that he and his readers took for granted but that were not shared, or shared to the same extent, by later Pauline interpreters.[7] An important consequence of these methodological advances is that many scholars now situate Paul within Judaism rather than outside it, as working out of some branch of Jewish tradition, loosely conceived, while innovating upon it in ways that were not dissimilar to those of some of his Jewish contemporaries.[8]

While I am sympathetic to such readings of the epistles, I see a great advantage in localizing this question to the context of freelance expertise,

---

contemporary cultural specialists, see, e.g., Edwin A. Judge, "Paul's Boasting in Relation to Contemporary Professional Practice," *ABR* 16 (1968): 37–50; Abraham J. Malherbe, *Paul and the Popular Philosophers* (Minneapolis: Fortress, 1989); Troels Engberg-Pedersen, ed., *Paul in His Hellenistic Context* (Minneapolis: Fortress, 1995).

5. I have in mind such classic works as E. P. Sanders, *Paul and Palestinian Judaism: A Comparison of Patterns of Religion* (Minneapolis: Fortress, 1977) and Lloyd Gaston, *Paul and the Torah* (Vancouver: University of British Columbia Press, 1987). For a succinct overview of the New Perspective and the so-called Radical New Perspective on Paul, see Magnus Zetterholm, *Approaches to Paul: A Student's Guide to Recent Scholarship* (Minneapolis: Fortress, 2009), 95–126, 127–64. For a critique of the concepts of religion that undergird earlier New Perspective scholarship, see Nongbri, "The Concept of Religion and the Study of the Apostle Paul," 7–12. For the limitations of the approach with a focus on the essentialism of the categories Judaism and Christianity, see Pamela Eisenbaum, "Paul, Polemics, and the Problem of Essentialism," *BibInt* 13 (2005): 224–38.

6. E.g., Stanley K. Stowers, *A Rereading of Romans: Justice, Jews, and Gentiles* (New Haven: Yale University Press, 1998); John G. Gager, *Reinventing Paul* (New York: Oxford University Press, 2000).

7. See Stowers, *A Rereading of Romans*, esp. 16–33, 285–322; Ryan S. Schellenberg, *Rethinking Paul's Rhetorical Education: Comparative Rhetoric and 2 Corinthians 10–13*, ECL 10 (Atlanta: SBL Press, 2013).

8. See esp. the recent essays in Mark D. Nanos and Magnus Zetterholm, eds., *Paul Within Judaism: Restoring the First-Century Context to the Apostle* (Minneapolis: Fortress, 2015). See also Stowers, *A Rereading of Romans*, esp. 227–50; Paula Fredrickson, "Judaizing the Nations: The Ritual Demands of Paul's Gospel," *NTS* 56 (2010): 232–52, esp. 250; Matthew V. Novenson, *Christ Among the Messiahs: Christ Language in Paul and Messiah Language in Ancient Judaism* (New York: Oxford University Press, 2012).

with attention to the forms of Judean religion represented therein and those who purveyed them.[9] Instead of asking "What was Paul's relationship to Judaism?" we might ask, "What was Paul's relationship to self-authorized experts in Judean religion, and to non-Judean experts with whose skills, interests, and potential audiences his own overlapped?" The reframing may seem slight but holds significant implications for imagining the motivations behind the positions he took on matters of Judean religion. His statements about the law, Israelites, and Judaizing, for example, sound very different when we picture Paul competing with individual specialists for gentile followers rather than negotiating a complex relationship to Judaism or reconciling two *religions* or religious systems.[10]

Like other freelance experts, the self-proclaimed apostle to the gentiles did not inherit legitimacy by virtue of his social status or relationship to an existing religious institution. Given an admittedly tenuous history with the "assembly of God" (ἐκκλησία τοῦ θεοῦ), his situation was quite the opposite.[11] Hence Paul's challenge was to locate himself intelligibly but also advantageously in a competitive field of specialized offerings, a twofold prerogative that he pursued by demonstrating facility with multiple skills and practices for which first-century specialists were known. In particular, Paul presents himself to his audiences and seems to be recognized by them as a credible authority on religious practices associated with Judeans, as well as certain kinds of intellectual practices that were not mutually exclusive with Judean expertise but gestured beyond that frame of reference. At the same time, he labors to differentiate his own authority and religious program from those of similar actors, even those who are not religious but whose benefits resemble the ones that Paul promises to his audiences.[12]

---

9. This is not to suggest that there was any typical or "orthodox" arrangement of Judean (or any other type of) practices among freelance experts. To the contrary, the evidence in chapter 2 suggests that fulfilling general expectations about foreign religion left an expert free to introduce other elements into his or her program at will. Cf. Edmonds, *Redefining Ancient Orphism*, 211: "Orphic is not a precise term . . . with a fixed content defined by doctrines, practices, or even deities, but rather a label whose use was intended to have a particular effect—in this evidence, primarily an effect of increasing the authority, antiquity, and holiness of the rituals so described."

10. Cf. Edmonds, *Redefining Ancient Orphism*, 131: "The Derveni author should be seen . . . as trying to recruit a clientele rather than to destroy the whole edifice of traditional [Greek] religion."

11. E.g., Gal 1:13, 22.

12. For example, philosophers and their techniques for self-mastery and moral progress.

With respect to the first concern, gaining recognition, Paul adopts tactics consonant with what we have seen of other Judean experts. He speaks authoritatively about such notable Judean practices as law observance, dietary restrictions, and circumcision; he alleges to have undergone dedicated training in ancestral teachings, even aligning himself with a specific interpretive group by claiming to be a Pharisee in matters of the law; he cites or references prophecies from Judean writings that he interprets in light of his teachings about Christ; he offers allegorical exegesis of episodes from Israelite or Judean myth; and he alleges the ability to perform any sign or wonder even if he is reluctant to do so. Also in keeping with a trend that we have seen are Paul's persistent efforts to forge a connection with illustrious figures from Judean tradition, especially Moses.[13] Not unlike Eleazar and Theudas—or, for that matter, Greek specialists who claimed Orpheus as the architect of their religious offerings—Paul traces his skills to a religious figure of unequalled stature within his ethnic idiom. As M. David Litwa explains, "His statements, despite their polemical character, indicate the pervasive importance of Moses for Paul."[14] Beyond the verses in which Moses is mentioned by name, Litwa detects additional allusions to him in Paul's claim to have performed "signs and wonders," a phrase typically used in reference to the former's miracles.[15] And while the apostle might elevate his own status and teachings above the service of Moses , he nevertheless assumes and affirms the prophet's authority.[16]

Paul does more than harness Mosaic authority, however; he also projects back onto the famous Israelite prophet the central mechanism of his own religious program. In 1 Cor 10:2–4, he informs the Corinthians that their new ancestors the Israelites "were all under the cloud, and all passed through the sea, and all were baptized by Moses in the cloud and the sea. They also ate the *same* pneumatic food and drank the *same* pneumatic drink, for they drank from the pneumatic rock that followed them, and the rock was Christ." The language of sameness in these verses is telling

---

13. For Paul's cultivated self-presentation as a figure akin to Moses, see M. David Litwa, "Paul's Mosaic Ascent: An Interpretation of 2 Corinthians 12.7–9," *NTS* (2011): 238–57; idem, "Transformation Through a Mirror: Moses in 2 Cor. 3.18," *JSNT* 34 (2012): 286–97; Luckritz Marquis, *Transient Apostle*, 95–97, 103–11.

14. Litwa, "Paul's Mosaic Ascent," 239.

15. 2 Cor 12:12, cf. Deut 34:11. See also Jennifer T. Eyl, "By the Power of Signs and Wonders: Paul, Divinatory Practices, and Symbolic Capital" (PhD diss., Brown University), 2012.

16. E.g., 2 Cor 3:6–13.

for, presumably, Paul means that the food and drink consumed by the Israelites had the same quality and effect as the ritual meal he will go on to prescribe anew in 11:23–26. As did the Derveni author or (other) Orphic *bricoleurs*, who combined elements from the fluid repertoire of Greek myth to scaffold their respective initiation rites, Paul finds in Judean myth support for his own.[17] This version of the story about the Israelites' time in the wilderness forges a mythic precedent that anticipates his teachings about initiation through baptism, as well as the receipt and cultivation of *pneuma* from Christ through meaningful meal practices.[18]

Even if they differ at the level of particulars, these elements of Paul's religious program trade on familiar and widespread expectations about Judean religion, foremost of which was intimate familiarity with the inspired writings. As we saw earlier, most Judean experts mentioned in literature of the imperial period seem to have based their religious authority on familiarity with these texts, whether they enlisted them directly or only indirectly, to lend credence to a nonliterary skill such as dream interpretation. In this regard, Paul is no different. In Rom 3:1–2 he affirms the oracular character of Judean writings and also characterizes the Judeans as inherently propitious or skillful due to their possession of them. "What advantage has the Judean?" he asks. "Much, in every way. For in the first place they were entrusted with the oracles of God."[19] Although he goes on to reveal the mystery that a "hardening" (πώρωσις) has come upon the Judeans that prevents them from interpreting these oracles to the same ends as he while he is delivering God's message for gentiles, Paul grants that they, and he, were chosen by God to be the principal stewards and exegetes of his prophecies.[20]

---

17. Graf and Iles Johnston, *Ritual Texts for the Afterlife*, 94–136; Iles Johnston, "Divination in the Derveni Papyrus," 103–4. For Paul as a sort of *bricoleur*, see William Arnal, "Bringing Paul and the Corinthians Together? A Rejoinder and Some Proposals on Redescription and Theory," in Cameron and Miller, *Redescribing Paul and the Corinthians*, 75–104, esp. 80–82.

18. See Stowers, "Kinds of Myth, Meals, and Power," 127–41. Cavan W. Concannon evaluates the passage in terms of its genealogical significance and the historical connections being forged between ancient Israelites and the Corinthians, but without attention to the *ex post facto* precedent that Paul seems to be constructing for his own religious practices: *"When You Were Gentiles": Specters of Ethnicity in Roman Corinth and Paul's Corinthian Correspondence*, Synkrisis (New Haven: Yale University Press, 2014), 100–5.

19. Τί οὖν τὸ περισσὸν τοῦ Ἰουδαίου . . . ; πολὺ κατὰ πάντα τρόπον. μὲν γὰρ ὅτι ἐπιστεύθησαν τὰ λόγια τοῦ θεοῦ.

20. Rom 11:25. For the interpretation and significance of this verse, see Stowers, *A Rereading of Romans*, 217–18. Regarding exegesis undertaken among rival specialists laying claim to

In light of the considerable interest Judean writings engendered in the first century, it is fitting that Paul appeals on dozens of occasions to "what is written" (καθὼς γέγραπται) or to the authority of "the law and the prophets" (ὑπὸ τοῦ νόμου καὶ τῶν προφητῶν) and things foretold "through the prophets in the holy writings" (διὰ τῶν προφητῶν ἐν γραφαῖς ἁγίαις).[21] Tellingly, the preponderance of these phrases occurs in his letter to the Romans, where he also makes the most explicit claims about having identified and expounded oracles hidden in these texts.[22] Some—for instance, his citation of Hab 2:4 in Rom 1:17—seem to be ciphers for his religious program writ large, keys that he has extrapolated and imbued with special meanings that explain his present activities.[23] In general, the majority of verses that Paul cites and the episodes from which he adduces novel interpretations either arise from a text authored by a prophet or are extrapolated from a story rich in miracles and prophecies: the Abraham cycle or the wilderness period. That he favors texts whose oracular potential is pronounced suggests continuity with a broader trend in their divinatory application.[24]

The indispensability of Judean writings—or at least the traditions they contained—for communicating the significance of his practices is underscored by Paul's highly specific and purposive exegeses of myths about well-known Judean figures (Adam, Abraham, and Moses), which, in turn, explicate fundamental elements of his salvation scheme (reversing human

---

common literary corpora, defined broadly, Edmonds writes, "Each interpreter sees an important meaning in the text he is explaining, however bizarre the twists of reasoning may seem to other observers" (*Redefining Ancient Orphism*, 124). Rather, the display of wisdom and expertise achieved through these exegetical acts is precisely the point, however novel the interpretations might have appeared to others familiar with the texts or general traditions in question.

21. E.g., Rom 3:21; Rom 1:2; cf. 16:22. As Harrill notes, "Paul drew heavily on the Jewish scriptures, citing them more than ninety times in his letters and showing an impressive facility with memorized texts" (*Paul the Apostle*, 25).

22. Sixteen occurrences, compared to eleven in the combined Corinthian epistles and only four in Galatians.

23. Cf. Rom 15:20–21, where Paul, invoking Isa 51:15, makes it his ambition "to proclaim the *evangelion* not where Christ has already been named so that he does not build upon someone else's foundation. For a similar relationship between prophetic injunction and religious practice, see the interpretation of Isa 40:3 in 1QS 8:11–6 as a command to retreat to the wilderness for eschatological preparation.

24. For further discussion, see Wendt, "Galatians 3:1 as an Allusion to Textual Prophecy," 385–86.

mortality, acquiring Judean ancestry, and the ontological consequences of baptism, respectively).[25] While the content and application of his interpretations might have been somewhat idiosyncratic, he was hardly unique among first-century Judeans in adducing literary mysteries, prophecies, and eschatological narratives from Judean writings, nor, for that matter, in receiving messages from God through revelations, dreams, or other methods of divination.[26]

As Stanley K. Stowers has shown, Paul also resembles Judeans such as Philo and Josephus who conceived of the Judean law as a constitution for the Judean way of life with a focus on religion and ethics.[27] This understanding of the texts was not irreconcilable with their oracular character, as Josephus makes abundantly clear. In addition to finding in them prophecies of contemporary relevance, then, a number of first-century writers allied the law and law observance with Greco-Roman philosophical teachings about self-mastery in order to present Judeans as a uniquely self-mastered people and their writings as a program for controlling the passions and desires. Their law, moreover, was superior to the laws of other peoples, which not only nourished the passions but also promoted vice.[28] This is not to suggest that all Judeans held such a view about their law or had any concept of *the law*, for that matter. To the contrary, there is reason to think that the presentation of Judean texts as such was largely the project of writer-intellectuals—albeit ones operating in different social locations, with different interests—who were free to assign proprietary values to the term.[29] Just as philosophical groups shared a general curriculum of

---

25. For Paul's myth-making, see Caroline Johnson Hodge, *If Sons, Then Heirs: A Study of Kinship and Ethnicity in the Letters of Paul* (New York: Oxford University Press, 2007), 67–91; Ryan S. Schellenberg, "Does Paul Call Adam a 'Type' of Christ? An Exegetical Note on Romans 5:14," *ZNW* 105 (2014): 54–63; Litwa, "Transformation Through a Mirror," 253–54; Stowers, "Kinds of Myth, Meals, and Power," passim.

26. See esp. David E. Aune, *Prophecy in Early Christianity and the Ancient Mediterranean World* (Grand Rapids, MI: Eerdmans, 1983).

27. Stowers, *A Rereading of Romans*, 35–36.

28. Stowers, *A Rereading of Romans*, 58–59. The argument about the laws of other peoples promoting and multiplying passions and vices is in this instance Philo's (*Sacr. Abel* 15). So widespread was this concept, Stowers writes, that "when gentiles heard Jews talk about the advantages of and virtues produced by the law of Moses, they were hearing a familiar topic" (63).

29. This characterization of the law as a concept is compatible with Novenson's conclusions about χριστός, a fairly polysemous term that did not entail a highly particular set of criteria

physics, logic, and ethics yet developed their own doctrines within each of these areas, we might imagine a comparable variety in how some Judeans articulated the law's character and prescripts.[30] Josephus conveys such an impression in his descriptions of Pharisees, Sadducees, and Essenes and the number of possible position-takings on the law multiplies when one considers how any specialist or social formation might claim those appellations without adhering to strict criteria or being subject to oversight.[31]

Not only does Paul's characterization of the law as a rigorous ethical program fit a conception shared by first-century Judean intellectuals, he also avows a long history of excelling in its specialized interpretation. In Gal 1:13–14, he speaks of an earlier time ἐν Ἰουδαϊσμῷ using language that is highly suggestive of textual study and an intensification of Judean ancestral customs.[32] He refers to those activities as a particular "mode of life" (ἀναστροφή) and uses προκόπειν, a verb associated with philosophical progress, to describe his advancement to a specific grade or rank within whatever social formation supported them (συνηλικιώστης ἐν τῷ γένει μου).[33] I am inclined to interpret the description as an admission of

---

but might be elaborated creatively, with only a few constraints, by those who employed it (*Christ Among the Messiahs,* esp. 137–73, 178).

30. Just as one could use the term *logos* and its cognates in a general sense to encapsulate any and all of the teachings of a particular philosophical group, I wonder whether *nomos* had a comparably elastic meaning that could encompass any and all teachings and practices associated with Judeans.

31. That is, there was nothing to stop someone from taking up the title of Pharisee, regardless of whether others who identified as such would recognize the former in kind. Such a scenario would not be unlike self-authorized philosophers, *augures,* or *haruspices* aligning themselves with a recognized school or religious institution even if their relationship to that institution, its teachings or practices, and other self-authorized experts is unclear. Matthew's claim that scribes and Pharisees will traverse sea and land to make a single proselyte seems suggestive of something in this vein (23:15). For the diffuseness of Essene groups, see John J. Collins, *Beyond the Qumran Community: The Sectarian Movement of the Dead Sea Scrolls* (Grand Rapids, MI: Eerdmans, 2010), esp. 1–11.

32. The meaning of this language has been the subject of much debate. See Mason, "Problems of Categorization in Ancient History," esp. 69–70; Matthew V. Novenson, "Paul's Former Occupation in *Ioudaismos,*" in *Galatians and Christian Theology: Justification, Gospel, and Ethics in Paul's Letter,* ed. Mark W. Elliott et al. (Grand Rapids, MI: Baker, 2014), 24–39. I am not entirely persuaded that Paul's reference need, as Novenson concludes, connote "a sectarian political program" but am content to see the context implied as one of specialized Judean religious activity that may have been political.

33. See Hans Dieter Betz, *Galatians,* Hermeneia (Minneapolis: Fortress, 1989), 68 n. 114; Gustav Stählin, "προκοπή," *TDNT* 6:703–19. The *hapax legomenon* συνηλικιώστης is usually taken literally to mean people of the same age as Paul but would be a puzzling choice of

involvement in a group dedicated to the specialized interpretation of writings, one that identified as Pharisaic, although whether other Pharisees would have acknowledged the claim is a different matter.[34]

We need not look too far afield for a roughly contemporary Judean religious group whose organization and activities lend credence to this interpretation. The Community attested in the Dead Sea Scrolls exhibits these characteristics; its members also partook in rites and held representations similar to the ones that Paul imparts to his followers.[35] The *Rule of the Community* (1QS) speaks to internal differentiation among group members according to rank and also to a correspondence between ranks and degrees of knowledge.[36] The same text is explicit about the prominent role of intellectual practices, literary divination especially, in the religious activities of its members.[37] Numerous references promote study of the

---

words for articulating a simple age relationship. Paul enlists age metaphors elsewhere to discuss the pneumatic progress of the people in his own groups—for instance, when he reminds the Corinthians of a time when he could not speak to them as pneumatic people (ὡς πνευματικοῖς) but rather as fleshly people (ὡς σαρκίνοις), as infants in Christ (1 Cor 3:1)—it is plausible that *sunēlikiōstēs* carries the sense not of people of the same age as Paul but of people who were of the same grade or rank *en ioudaismō*. For other examples of philosophical progress in the epistles, see Laura B. Dingeldein, "'ὅτι πνευματικῶς ἀνακρίνεται': Examining Translations of 1 Corinthians 2:14," *NT* 55 (2013): 31–44.

34. That is, while Paul's claim to be a Pharisee in matters of law might mean that he was a recognized member of the body that Josephus portrays—a political-religious interest group, some of whose members wielded influence over Judean aristocrats and civic practices—it is equally plausible that he participated in another type of social formation that yoked itself to the authority and recognition of that group, yet whose own teachings may or may not have matched those attributed to the Pharisees by others. For this characterization of the Pharisees see Stowers, *A Rereading of Romans*, 77.

35. For an overview of these affinities, albeit one that employs some of the theological language and categories I consciously avoid, see Joseph A. Fitzmeyer, S.J., *The Dead Sea Scrolls and Christian Origins* (Grand Rapids, MI: Eerdmans, 2000), 28–35. For a more extensive and nuanced comparison of the eschatological schemes and initiations of the Dead Sea Scrolls Community and Paul, see Aaron Glaim, "Reciprocity, Sacrifice, and Salvation in Judean Religion" (PhD diss., Brown University, 2013), 210–43. For comparison of the Community with voluntary associations of the Greco-Roman world, see Moshe Weinfield, *The Organizational Pattern and the Penal Code of the Qumran Sect: A Comparison with Guilds and Associations of the Hellenistic-Roman Period*, NTOA 2 (Fribourg: Editions Universitaires, 1986).

36. E.g., 1QS 6.8–11, 14–23. For a compatible discussion regarding the initiation grades of the mysteries of Mithras, see Richard L. Gordon, "Ritual and Hierarchy in the Mysteries of Mithras," in North and Price, *The Religious History of the Roman Empire*, 325–65.

37. While this exegetical practice is more commonly referred to using the Hebrew and Aramaic term *pesher* (*pesharim* in the plural form), I have deliberately retained the language used in preceding chapters to highlight basic continuities in epistemological orientation—a particular text or body of texts is divinely inspired and replete with concealed mysteries that

instruction (תורה) and refer to teachings revealed from these writings that exhort members to ethical conduct.[38] Where there are ten members there must not be lacking one who studies the texts in this manner day and night, continually, with one member relieving the other.[39] As this and other scrolls make clear, Judean writings contained eschatological secrets that were to be revealed through the interpretations of individual exegetes and then shared with the rest of the group.[40] So too did the Community subscribe to the imminent eschatology disclosed by these methods, engage in Judean myth-making, conduct purifying initiations involving the spirit of God, examine the spirits of their members, consume special group meals involving ordinary items, practice nonliterary forms of divination such as physiognomy and astrology, and anticipate eternal life.

To be clear, the Community is not the only Judean social formation that might fit the general characteristics that I have isolated for comparison with Paul's earlier practices.[41] Nor am I claiming that Paul was a member

---

the skilled exegete might unlock—and interpretive methods between the different writer-intellectuals I consider in this study. For more traditional treatments of the topic that nevertheless align with this characterization, see, e.g., Lawrence H. Schiffman, *Reclaiming the Dead Sea Scrolls: The History of Judaism, the Background of Christianity, the Lost Library of Qumran* (Philadelphia: Jewish Publication Society, 1994), esp. 225–26; R. Glenn Wooden, "Guided by God: Divine Aid in Interpretation in the Dead Sea Scrolls and the New Testament," in *Christian Beginnings and the Dead Sea Scrolls*, ed. John J. Collins and Craig A. Evans (Grand Rapids, MI: Baker Academic, 2006), 101–20, esp. 104–6.

38. E.g., 1QS 1.9, 8.1.

39. 1QS 6.6–8.

40. For the eschatological dimensions of the scrolls, see John J. Collins, *Apocalypticism in the Dead Sea Scrolls* (New York: Routledge, 1997); idem, *The Scepter and the Star: Messianism in Light of the Dead Sea Scrolls*, 2nd ed. (Grand Rapids, MI: Eerdmans, 2010).

41. Many early studies of the scrolls sought problematically to find in them evidence of continuity with early Christianity, if not for Jesus himself in references to the Teacher of Righteousness. For critical engagement with this literature, see, e.g., John J. Collins, "A Messiah before Jesus?" and "An Essene Messiah? Comments on Israel Knohl, *The Messiah Before Jesus*," in Collins and Evans, *Christian Beginnings and the Dead Sea Scrolls*, 15–35 and 37–62. For the problems that arose with respect to Pauline comparisons, specifically, see Timothy H. Lim, "Studying the Qumran Scrolls and Paul in their Historical Context," in *The Dead Sea Scrolls as Background to Postbiblical Judaism and Early Christianity*, ed. James R. Davila, Studies on the Texts of the Desert of Judah 46 (Leiden: Brill, 2003), 135–56. In drawing attention to these correlations in the thought and practices of Paul and the Dead Sea Scrolls Community I am not presuming a direct line of influence running between them. Rather, the scrolls offer a useful point of comparison for refining our interpretive options for Gal 1:13–14 in a manner that does not reinscribe uncritically the scenario of *literal* persecution that we inherit from Acts 8:3, 9:1–2.

of that group, only that it is one example of a Judean social formation whose practices are consistent in some ways with the sort of scenario that I am proposing. Of course there are also important differences between the instructions prescribed in the scrolls and what Paul advocated for members of his own groups. Notably absent from the epistles are explicit encouragements for those "in Christ" to study Judean texts, suggesting that Paul might have reserved for himself this particular form of expertise, even if he did not actively discourage such pursuits. His writings also lack the cultivated archaism and reclaimed scribal ambitions of the Dead Sea Scrolls authors. Most important, and quite unlike them, he addresses audiences of non-Judeans and exhibits no obvious signs of consternation or rivalry with the Jerusalem temple priesthood.[42] Thus while Paul himself might have belonged to a group with stronger points of comparison to the Community, the groups that he sought to form seem different from it in any number of important ways.

What can be said with a higher degree of certainty is that Paul alleges to be well-versed in two sets of intellectual practices with which Judeans were commonly linked: emphasizing the inspired character of these texts in order to adduce prophecies and mysteries from them and proffering a philosophically informed concept of the law as a rigorous ethical program.[43] For his many points of continuity with other Judean specialists, however, Paul is also emphatic about how he differs from such figures.

---

42. However, this is not necessarily the case for other New Testament writers. See Maxine Grossman, "Priesthood as Authority: Interpretive Competition in First-Century Judaism and Christianity," in Davila, *The Dead Sea Scrolls as Background to Postbiblical Judaism and Early Christianity*, 117–31.

43. In this scenario, Paul's statement about having "persecuted" the assembly of God may also have a different tenor, not of interreligious tension or the top-down suppression of a new religious movement but something more along the lines of intellectual and other forms of competition between similar specialists. As we have seen in the preceding chapters, rivalries between freelance experts could be strident, and all the more so between figures or groups with similar practices. One wonders, then, whether the sense of διώκειν—the translation of which as "to persecute" is reserved exclusively for New Testament occurrences—might be construed instead as "to prosecute," "to impeach," "to discredit," or "to accuse," which fits well with the image of Paul trying to thoroughly discredit the teachings or claims of a rival group of Judean specialists. The additional emphasis that he places on having tried to destroy or ruin (πορθέω) the assembly does not, in my opinion, undermine that reading and can be attributed without difficulty to his rhetorical aim in raising the matter. The DSS authors use comparable polemical language to denounce their perceived opponents (e.g., 1QS 9.16–18, instructions against quarrelling with "men of the pit") and also in the context of specialized textual interpretation pursued in the context of religious activity (e.g., 1QS 6.6–8, 8.10–16).

He alleges that during his time *en ioudaismō* he demonstrated greater aptitude and eagerness for the ancestral teachings than others in his cohort (περισσοτέρως ζηλωτὴς ὑπάρχων τῶν πατρικῶν μου παραδόσεων) and that he fulfilled perfectly all requirements of the law while under it.[44] And in contrast to most other readers of Judean texts, he has received certain mysteries from God that illuminate new dimensions of meaning within them. He alludes to at least two means by which he acquired this knowledge: through direct and periodic revelations of the resurrected Christ and through an event in which "someone he knows" saw and heard secret things after being swept up into a heavenly realm.[45] As the result of what he has gained from these encounters, Paul is able to extract esoteric, eschatological knowledge from Judean texts, "a mystery kept secret for long ages but now disclosed though the prophetic writings made known to all the gentiles."[46] While most Judeans continue to read the old covenant with a veil over their minds, the same veil with which Moses shielded his face to keep Israel from glimpsing God's glory, those who accept Christ gaze upon his glory with unveiled faces.[47]

The prominence of other Judeans in the religion of freelance experts also changes the tenor of Paul's emphatic professions of Judean ancestry. "If anyone else has reason to be confident in the flesh," Paul has more.[48] Whatever permutation of Judean ethnicity one might claim—Hebrew, Israelite, membership in an Israelite tribe, descent from Abraham—he can boast of that as well.[49] For the defensive contexts in which these statements appear—as rebuttals to rivals who seem to have hinged their expertise to such claims—they are understood rightly to be embroiled in competition over religious authority and legitimacy, Paul's own versus that of

---

44. Gal 1:14; Phil 3:6. For περισσός as extraordinary ability, curiosity, or education, see *LSJ*, s.v.

45. Rom 3:1–2; 1 Cor 15:8–9; Gal 1:12, 2:2; 2 Cor 12:2–4.

46. Rom 16:25; cf. 1 Cor 2:7.

47. 2 Cor 3:13–16.

48. Phil 3:4–6.

49. Cf. 2 Cor 11:21–22. Interestingly, while Paul does on occasion use the language of Judean inclusively (e.g., Gal 2.15: Ἡμεῖς φύσει Ἰουδαῖοι), he usually frames his ancestry using language and categories with a textual, and maybe more consciously antique, basis: he is an *Israelite*, a *Benjaminite*. That is, Paul might have thus articulated his ancestry in combination with his other exegetical interests. For the rhetorical context of Paul's boasting, see Schellenberg, *Rethinking Paul's Rhetorical Education*, 97–122.

"false" or "super" apostles.[50] Others have read them as symptomatic of his conflicted identity as a colonial subject, a religious convert, or some other identity category. While these hermeneutics are not without value, it is important to recognize how appeals to ethnicity served as confirmation that Paul possessed the requisite background—as such a criterion might have been understood by his gentile audiences—to claim expertise in Judean religion, even if the positions he took on circumcision or law observance clashed with those of others claiming the same specialty.[51]

For the sake of his own recognition, then, the apostle to the gentiles had a considerable stake in confirming the special status that Judeans enjoyed vis-à-vis their national deity, as well as the benefits that relationship conferred. As he writes in Romans, it is to them that belong God's glory, the law, the promises, and the forefathers, and from them that came the anointed one he now proclaims.[52] Since this god's preference for his people was widely known, Paul's assertions that he is a Judean or can boast any other ethnic designation tied to Judean religion represented statements of religious authority in and of themselves.[53] Although he devised a set of teachings that catered to non-Judeans and extended the ostensible ethnic particularity of Judean religion to them, a large measure of his expertise lay in maintaining, even exaggerating, his Judean-ness for the sake of being intelligible (and credible) to his audiences. Moreover, with the exception of certain practices he deemed irrelevant for gentiles, his religious program relied on any number of Judean elements: the Judean god (God), the authority of Judean writings, the ancestry of Abraham, and the death and divinization of a Judean man. Far from a complicated relic of his Jewish past, Paul's "kindred according to the flesh" were integral to his

---

50. See Georg Strecker, "Die Legitimität des paulinischen Apostolates nach 2 Korinther 10–13," *NTS* 38 (1992): 566–86; Litwa, "Paul's Mosaic Ascent."

51. The lens of identity, which typically presumes Paul's *de facto* marginality as a Jewish subject of the Roman Empire, is especially inattentive to the opportunities that arose for religious actors like Paul, who might identify selectively to meet and cultivate interest in foreign religion to their own advantage. For a critique of postcolonial readings of Paul, see J. Albert Harrill, "Paul and Empire: Studying Roman Identity after the Cultural Turn," *EC* 2 (2011): 281–311; Heidi Wendt, "James C. Hanges, *Paul, Founder* of Churches: A Study in Light of the Evidence for the Role of 'Founder-Figures' in the Hellenistic-Roman Period. A Review Essay," *R&T* 3–4 (2014): 292–302.

52. Rom 9:4–5; cf. Rom 11:1.

53. For compatible discussions of how ethnicity figures into Paul's thought, see Denise Kimber Buell, *Why This New Race? Ethnic Reasoning in Early Christianity*, Gender, Theory,

alleged expertise; the cachet of Judean ancestry was a prerequisite for his success.[54]

"Where Is the One Who Is Wise?"

At the same time as Paul positioned himself as a kind of expert in Judean religion, it is also evident from the markedly intellectualizing discourses he employed—both in his own teachings and also against rivals—that he occupied, or wished to occupy, a niche of religious expertise that contained other writer-intellectuals.[55] As noted earlier, writer-intellectual (or philosopher) and Judean were not mutually exclusive forms of religious expertise, but there are reasons to think that Paul's intellectual demonstrations were not only for the benefit of rival Judean experts or audiences interested narrowly in Judean religion. On numerous occasions, he adopts language and images that were commonly employed to distinguish "good" philosophers from "charlatans" or "hucksters." As Abraham J. Malherbe has shown, the claim to have become "all things to all people" is a variation on a well-known *topos* developed most fully by the Cynics, who viewed the ideal teacher as one capable of adapting his or her approach to the moral condition of each person or group.[56] In deploying this philosophical discourse of adaptability, then, Paul presents himself as the sort of teacher who is both willing and able to cater to the moral (or pneumatic progress) of any student. Such a distinction also lies in the background of Paul's use of speech-in-character (προσωποποιία)—a device common in diatribe that takes as its object

---

and Religion (New York: Columbia University Press, 2005); Johnson Hodge, *If Sons, Then Heirs*, 43–66; Concannon, *"When You Were Gentiles."*

54. Rom 9:3.

55. See Stanley K. Stowers, "Paul and the Terrain of Philosophy," *EC* 6 (2015): 141–56.

56. 1 Cor 9:20–22; Abraham J. Malherbe, "Antisthenes and Odysseus, and Paul at War," in *Paul and the Popular Philosophers*, 91–119, esp. 118. Cf. Clarence E. Glad, who argues that Paul's ethic of adaptability and other psychogogic directives have stronger affinities with Epicurean philosophy: *Paul and Philodemus: Adaptability in Epicurean and Early Christian Psychagogy*. NTSup 81 (Leiden: Brill, 1995), 215–16. A comparable statement occurs in 1 Thess 2:7, where Paul likens himself to a gentle nurse patiently committed to the individual progress of members of his group while among them, an image commonly employed by Cynics to characterize the ideal philosopher, as opposed to the overly harsh methods of ones who confused reviling (λοιδορία) with the practice of frank speech (παρρησία), or to the abusiveness of "charlatans," who made up for a lack of substance by railing at the crowd. See Abraham J. Malherbe, "'Gentle as a Nurse': The Cynic Background to 1 Thessalonians 2," in *Paul and the Popular Philosophers*, 35–48, esp. 40–41.

a pretentious teacher of philosophy—to redress his Judean interlocutor in Rom 2:17–29.[57] The effect of adopting this rhetorical mode, Stowers explains, is that certain readers would have heard this dialogue as "philosopher talk" familiar from settings where teachers publicly addressed students and contended with one another.

It is in the same vein that Dio Chrysostom complained of the drudge philosophers who clutter street corners, alleys, and temple gates, laboring to entice followers with hackneyed philosophical commonplaces.[58] Paul's awareness and application of these and other concepts or discourses drawn from philosophy and rhetoric locates him firmly within a realm of intellectual competition between specialists purporting to offer benefits (e.g., character improvement or progress in virtue) acquired through teachings and techniques that might be mistaken for his own. This is not to suggest that Chrysostom and Paul understood their characterizations of bad philosophers in exactly the same way, but both utilized a philosophical strategy to differentiate competitive landscapes of similar offerings. Unlike Chrysostom, whose interest appears to lie in defending his "authentic" formulation of the Cynic *ethos* against "debased" versions that diminish its intellectual esteem and value, Paul uses this tool to shore up his authority as a *religious* expert, whose *religious* program contains points of commonality with rival schemes but ultimately supplants them.[59] After all, beyond exhibiting all the traits of a good philosopher, he has the additional, if not primary, distinction of having received his teachings not from any human source but directly from God.

---

57. Stowers, *A Rereading of Romans*, 144–48. Stowers cites places in Plutarch and Epictetus where each chides the superficiality, improper motivations, and ambition of would-be teachers who might study philosophy but cannot apply it in practice. But this particular teacher is no ordinary philosopher; he is a teacher of Judaic wisdom and practices and one whose students are gentiles. I return to the passage's connotations of charlatanry.

58. Dio Chrysostom, *Or.* 32.9. Compare these sentiments with Paul's caution about any who would oppose the teachings that the Romans have learned, people who do not serve Christ but their own bellies, and who by smooth speech (χρηστολογία) and flattery (εὐλογία) beguile the hearts of the simple-minded (Rom 16:18). Note the subtle parody on Chrysostom's own epithet, which was not an uncommon appellation for Greek rhetoricians and philosophers, and Paul's accusation of smooth speech. On the accusation of serving the belly, see Karl Olav Sandnes, *Belly and Body in the Pauline Epistles* (Cambridge: Cambridge University Press, 2004).

59. Cf. Malherbe, who notes, "Paul adopts a manner of exhortation that most likely was familiar to his readers, and he uses popular philosophical traditions with which they can be expected to have been familiar, yet he does so in a way different from philosophical preachers of his day ("Exhortation in 1 Thessalonians," in *Paul and the Popular Philosophers*, 49–66,

Paul's facility with philosophical discursive practices is also evident in his story about the gentiles' estrangement from the Judean god, which has resulted in a condition that is not only irremediably flawed but also continues to worsen with time.[60] As many have shown, this narrative brims with technical philosophical language and ideas: divinity was once naturally apparent to people, their turn from God was the result of undisciplined minds, and the consequence was surrender to unbridled passions.[61] The outcome of Paul's narrative is that gentiles exist in a state of helpless enslavement to these passions, even if their minds will otherwise; their fleshly bodies are impure instruments of wickedness, prone to every vice.[62] Consequently, God has become so enraged by their sinfulness that he is plotting an impending day of judgment.

While elements of this myth bear some relationship to Judean stories about degeneracy, it is equally if not more evocative of other, non-Judean etiologies circulating in the first century. These details do not exclude a Judean frame of reference, but if Romans were read or heard without knowledge of Genesis, they would be reminiscent of narratives about the decline or degeneration of humanity that were central in the thought of different philosophical schools, even though the trajectories and remedies

---

esp. n. 50). I agree with Malherbe's distinction between Paul's grounding of the ethics that he espouses in religion but not fully with his conclusion that Paul is unconcerned with the use of reason or the nature of character development because he prefers the sanctified rather than the rational life (61). Rather, I understand Paul to be subordinating philosophical techniques for character improvement to the benefits conferred by *pneuma* from Christ, the receipt of which promotes ethical behavior.

60. Rom 1:18–2:16.

61. The relevant bibliography is extensive. See, e.g., Troels Engberg-Pederson, *Cosmology and Self in the Apostle Paul* (New York: Oxford University Press, 2010); Emma Wasserman, *The Death of the Soul in Romans 7: Sin, Death, and the Law in Light of Hellenistic Moral Psychology*, WUNT 2.56 (Tübingen: Mohr Siebeck, 2006); idem, "Paul Beyond the Judaism/Hellenism Divide? The Case of Pauline Anthropology in Romans 7 and 2 Corinthians 4–5," in Udoh, *Redefining First-Century Jewish and Christian Identities*, 259–79; Stanley K. Stowers, "Paul's Four Discourses About Sin," in *Celebrating Paul: Festschrift in Honor of Jerome Murphy O'Conner, O.P., and Joseph A. Fitzmeyer, S.J.*, ed. Peter Spitaler, CBQMS 48 (Washington, DC: Catholic Biblical Association of America, 2011), 100–27; idem, "Paul and the Terrain of Philosophy," passim; George H. van Kooten, *Paul's Anthropology in Context: The Image of God, Assimilation to God, and Tripartite Man in Ancient Judaism, Ancient Philosophy and Early Christianity*, WUNT 232 (Tübingen: Mohr Sieback, 2008); M. David Litwa, *We Are Being Transformed: Deification in Paul's Soteriology*, BZNW 187 (Berlin: de Gruyter, 2012); Laura B. Dingeldein, "Gaining Virtue, Gaining Christ: Paul and Moral Development in Early Christianity" (PhD diss., Brown University, 2014).

62. Rom 1:29–31, 7:7–25; Gal 5:19–21.

for the resulting defects varied across individual teachers and groups.[63] Likewise, as we saw in the last chapter, this particular combination of philosophical vice, divine anger, and eschatology was not uncommon in the myth-making of intellectualizing religious experts, who offered proprietary solutions to flawed conditions that they devised and diagnosed.[64]

As with these other experts, theorizing Paul's thought and practices as part of a wider phenomenon of freelance religious expertise invites consideration of what his salvation scheme accomplished for him in this setting. That is, how did his narrative about Christ's eschatological significance for gentiles create a need for the exact skills and benefits that he offered?[65] As Emma Wasserman has demonstrated, Paul's characterization of the gentile predicament evokes in Platonic terms the disempowerment of reason in circumstances of extreme wickedness; even if a gentile wishes to comply with the requirements of the law, the mind, held captive by passions and appetites roused by sin, is incapable of reason, reflection, and judgment.[66] The solution to "this specific moral psychological plight" lies in the receipt of Christ's—ultimately, God's—divine *pneuma,* which holds the power to remake these captive minds and rebellious fleshly bodies so that they might gain release from a state of sin and death.[67]

In recent years numerous scholars have made the case that, in keeping with most of his intellectual contemporaries, Paul understands *pneuma* to be an mobile and intelligent substance with varied applications: it has transformative properties, it is revelatory of divine things, it enables special abilities, and, more basically, it is constitutive of human beings and all matter.[68] Employing such a concept of *pneuma,* he explains that only

---

63. That Paul has such narratives in mind gains additional support from 1 Cor 1:19–22, where he alludes to the flawed gentile condition and associates familiar contemporary actors—the sophist, scribe, and debater—with mistaken pursuits of wisdom that led humans astray.

64. See, esp., Graf and Iles Johnston, *Ritual Texts for the Afterlife,* 94–136.

65. Cf. Arnal, "[Paul's] use of the Christ myth is opportunistic, offered to solve a very particular problem that is a function of Paul and his context" ("Bringing Paul and the Corinthians Together?" 83).

66. Rom 7:23–24; Wasserman, "The Death of the Soul in Romans 7," 812–14. For the speaker in Romans 7 as an immoral gentile, see Stowers, *A Rereading of Romans,* 269–72; Thomas H. Tobin, *Paul's Rhetoric in Its Contexts: The Argument of Romans* (Peabody, MA: Hendrickson, 2004), 237; Wasserman, "The Death of the Soul in Romans 7," 814–15.

67. Rom 8:1–11; Wasserman, "The Death of the Soul in Romans 7," 810, 815.

68. See, esp., Engberg-Pederson, *Cosmology and the Self in the Apostle Paul,* 18; Stowers, "What Is 'Pauline Participation in Christ'?" passim.

gentiles who have received a portion of God's own *pneuma*, made available to them by Christ, will be spared the consequences of harsh divine judgment.[69] The remedy that he provides for their helpless condition not only cures them of their proclivity to sinfulness but also begins a process that, with time and subsequent actions, will transform their bodies from the normal human condition of perishability and mortality into ones that are imperishable and immortal.[70]

Paul's depiction of the dire predicament of his audiences thus sets up the essentiality of his salvation scheme and the indispensable role that divine *pneuma* from Christ will play in purifying and refashioning these otherwise helpless minds and bodies.[71] Through the rite of "immersion" or baptism, gentiles can be initiated into the mysteries of Christ, their flesh dying to sin just as the fleshly body of Jesus was crucified to be reborn with a portion of the pneumatic body in which he was raised.[72] The death enacted by baptism is not, or not only, metaphorical but has immediate physiological implications when God pours divine *pneuma* directly into the heart of the one baptized.[73] Even though some were wrongdoers prior to baptism, through this rite they are washed and sanctified as befits the inheritors of God's kingdom.[74] And just as sin and death no longer have dominion over Jesus Christ, those "in Christ" hold the potential to escape, as he did, the inevitable cycle of human mortality.[75] These benefits can even be obtained for people already dead, who, Paul assures his audiences will, like Jesus, be raised with new bodies.[76]

---

69. Stowers, "Kinds of Myth, Meals, and Power," 115.

70. See Litwa, *We Are Being Transformed*, 161–71, 212–25.

71. The particular significance of *pneuma* within Paul's program is also instructive for parsing his relationship to philosophers and other intellectuals whom I would not include within the category of freelance *religious* expertise. Whereas philosophers might develop doctrines of *pneuma*, Paul writes of the direct, active transmission of *pneuma*, its refashioning of human bodies, the special skills and discernment that it enables, and so forth.

72. Rom 6:6–11, 12:1.

73. Gal 4:6; Rom 8:15–17. For the genealogical implications of this receipt of *pneuma*, see Johnson Hodge, *If Sons, Then Heirs*, 96–107.

74. E.g., 1 Cor 6:9–11.

75. 1 Cor 15:54–56.

76. 1 Thess 4:13–16; 1 Cor 15:29–55. The prominence of this theme in Paul's writing suggests that it was an attractive benefit for some of the people who were receptive to his program, even if the notion of resurrection was a point of resistance, skepticism, or confusion

Caroline Johnson Hodge has demonstrated that the same concept of *pneuma* was also a useful tool for working through the theological dilemma of how to forge an aggregative genealogical connection between Judeans and gentiles.[77] For Paul, she argues, faithfulness in Christ is not only a program of behavior modeled on the righteous conduct of Abraham: in his version of Abraham's story, faithfulness, righteousness, and the inheritance that God promised to his descendants are transmitted through his seed to his offspring Christ, and then to the gentiles who share in Christ's body. The physiological reception of *pneuma* is critical to this adoption process as the mechanism that transforms gentiles into genetic and ethically suitable heirs of God's promise.[78] More than just a genealogical myth, Paul's innovative exegesis of the Abraham story also supplies the terms for the relationship between faithfulness and eternal life that *pneuma* realizes. Emphasizing the decaying bodies of Abraham and Sarah—at the time that God promised them an heir, his was as good as dead (τὸ ἑαυτοῦ σῶμα ἤδη νενεκρωμένον), while her womb was necrotic (τὴν νέκρωσιν τῆς μήτρας Σάρρας)—he constructs a paradigm of faithfulness in God's ability to create life from death that equally characterizes the faith of Jesus, who trusted that God would raise him from the dead, as well of those "in Christ," whose confidence in the same principle will be rewarded with eternal bodies, even if they have already died by the time Christ returns.[79]

This requirement of salvation is not, I would argue, a predictable outgrowth of Judean or other forms of ancient Mediterranean religion. To the contrary, the epistles disclose that Paul's teachings, like those of the Derveni author, were contingent on a robust set of representations and justifications. In this case, gentiles have unwittingly committed an egregious offense against God; he is furious and punitive; they face imminent judgment and guaranteed punishment; and there is only one way, Paul's way, to circumvent this otherwise inevitable course of events. Having laid

---

(e.g., 1 Cor 15:12–17). See Jonathan Z. Smith, "Re: Corinthians," in Cameron and Miller, *Redescribing Paul and the Corinthians* (Atlanta: SBL Press, 2011), 17–34.

77. Johnson Hodge, *If Sons, Then Heirs,* 67. See also Stanley K. Stowers, "ἐκ πίστεως and διὰ τῆς πίστεως in Romans 3:30," *JBL* 108 (1989): 665–74.

78. Johnson Hodge, *If Sons, Then Heirs,* 73.

79. Rom 4:19–24, 6:4–9, 8:11, 10:9; 1 Cor 6:14, 15:4, 15:12–56; 2 Cor 2:19, 5:15; Gal 1:1; 1 Thess 1:10.

out an elegant myth in which God will spare gentiles who share Christ's faithfulness and a portion of his pneumatic body, it falls to Paul and "legitimate" representatives of his teachings to prepare gentiles for this eschatological climax. He alone possesses the mysteries and textual expertise to reveal hidden clues about how it will unfold and what gentiles must do to withstand judgment. Paul's religious program is thus both exclusive and also direly imminent.[80]

The complexity of these teachings depends much on Paul's ability to communicate, elaborate, and reinforce them through letters exchanged with his followers. The same practice provided opportunities to safeguard his own religious authority by introducing and recommending people working on his behalf or by defending his character and claims remotely against the charges and incursions of rivals.[81] Competitive interests are further evident in the precautions that Paul takes to maintain his relevance to those who have undergone initiation into Christ's mysteries. He warns, for instance, that the transformative effects of baptism do not occur all at once but must be cultivated gradually, in accordance with his instructions, since they will only be realized fully upon Christ's return.[82] Some of these instructions involve the special meal that those in Christ should consume together to reinforce their collective participation in his body.[83] Though an ordinary meal, Paul ascribes special significance to the modest items that comprise it and insists that deeper understandings must be inferred when they are consumed. Indeed, if the meal is consumed with the incorrect disposition there may be grave consequences: many have become weak and ill, while some have already died.[84] As we saw earlier, to strengthen the warning he draws an explicit analogy between these meal practices and

---

80. Cf. Paul A. Holloway, "*Commendatio aliqua sui*: Reading Romans with Pierre Bourdieu," *EC* 2 (2011): 356–83, esp. 363, 377.

81. E.g., 1 Cor 16:1; 2 Cor 3:1; Rom 16:1; Phlm. For epistolary introductions and the metaphorical significance that Paul attaches to his letter-writing, see Luckritz Marquis, *Transient Apostle*, 90–94, 88–89.

82. E.g., 1 Cor 15:51–55; 2 Cor 1:22.

83. Stowers, "Kinds of Myth, Meals, and Power," 127–39.

84. 1 Cor 11:30. Stowers notes, "The person who does not distinguish the body, that is, perform an action with a certain social and ideological disposition, will bring down the judgment of the God who is present in that ritualized eating environment. Paul explains that many have been weak and sick and some have even died *because they ate the bread and drank the cup without this disposition* ("Kinds of Myth, Meals, and Power," 134, emphasis added).

those of the Israelites, who were likewise baptized by Moses and sustained in their wanderings by pneumatic food and drink before they succumbed to idolatry.[85] To avoid this risk, Paul's initiates should abide by his precepts, both ritually and ethically.

By demonstrating skills and knowledge in multiple areas of expertise Paul comes across as a legitimate distributer of offerings that are at once comparable to and demarcated from the teachings and services of other kinds of specialists.[86] And while the authentic epistles are replete with philosophical discursive practices, all of the moving parts in Paul's religious program are, again, enabled by the power of *pneuma*, understood as a form of divine agency that acts directly on people "in Christ." It is, moreover, only by virtue of receiving and continuing to cultivate Christ's *pneuma* that gentiles might be purified of past sinfulness and allotted bodies better equipped to exercise self-control and other desirable behavior that was typically conditioned in philosophical settings. For his familiarity with philosophy and rhetoric, it is at such a nexus that Paul's status as a religious expert—and not a philosopher, rhetorician, or other type of similarly self-authorized but nonreligious actor—is clearest. Though he makes ample use of intellectual skills, the immediate and ongoing involvement of God, Christ, and *pneuma* in his practices is vital to his form of expertise.

Redescribing Paul's Religious Activities

All of these considerations contribute to our understanding of how Paul gained recognition as an expert in religion, Judean religion specifically, while also differentiating himself from a diverse and overlapping field of rivals by insisting on the priority of his own scheme. The difference between Paul and a Judean writer such as Philo, whose metaphors of sin also employ Platonic moral psychology and other concepts drawn from philosophy, is that Paul harnesses his to the religious services he is offering, while Philo's project seems more theoretical, if not entirely evident to modern interpreters.[87] In using philosophical discursive practices in this

---

85. 1 Cor 10:6–12.

86. See Stowers, "Kinds of Myth, Meals, and Power," 141–42.

87. For a discussion of shared concepts in the writings of Philo and Paul, see Wasserman, "The Death of the Soul in Romans 7," 807–9. For a characterization of Philo's literary activities in terms consonant with the practices of other Alexandrian writer-intellectuals engaged

way, Paul is not beholden to a clear set of rules or a systematic philosophical program but is free to sample and elaborate concepts at will that are germane to his agenda. [88] His strong affinities with other experts in Judean religion, with intellectualizing religious experts working within other foreign idioms, and with philosophers participating in the wider field of freelance expertise make perfect sense in this context, as do his dissimilarities and idiosyncrasies.

It may be impossible to know to what extent other Judean specialists claimed to transmit the *pneuma* of God or Christ. Paul himself warns of people who proclaim another Jesus than the one whom he proclaimed, or transmit a different *pneuma* from the one his followers received, or teach a gospel different from the one they accepted.[89] At the very least, there are indications that other Judean experts demonstrated their religious authority along similar lines. From Paul's adamant avowals that he too is a descendent of Abraham, we might infer that some Judean experts claimed the same ancestry; it is not impossible that some even crafted genealogical myths involving Abraham, as he did.[90] Likewise, "The abundance of references—implicit and explicit—to Moses in the Corinthian correspondence" suggests to Litwa that Moses was also an important figure for Paul's opponents. "Although we cannot," he cautions, "determine the precise role of Moses for Paul's enemies, we can at least surmise that they appealed to him as a figure of impressive authority. . . . One of the keys to Paul's defense, then, is to show how he fits—and better fills—the Mosaic pattern of authority."[91] If this reading of Paul's appeals to Mosaic authority

---

in the sort of exegesis described by Struck, though not undertaken in the context of religious activity, see Maren R. Niehoff, *Jewish Exegesis and Homeric Scholarship in Alexandria* (Cambridge: Cambridge University Press, 2011), esp. 77–94, 133–85; Satlow, *How the Bible Became Holy*, 153–70.

88. Nor does this mean that Paul lacks proper understanding of Platonic philosophy, or any of the other intellectual influences present in his writings. He also has considerable flexibility to develop and hone connections between aspects of his program without condensing these into coherent theories. See Dingeldein, "Paul and Moral Development in Early Christianity," passim. Echoing this point, Edmonds writes, "The Derveni author is not trying to convey religious doctrine, eschatological or cosmological; he is showing off his abilities as an interpreter of enigmatic texts, as a thinker conversant with advanced philosophical cosmologies, and as a religious specialist who can provide a meaningful account of his religious activities" (*Redefining Ancient Orphism*, 138).

89. 2 Cor 11:4.

90. E.g., 2 Cor 11:22.

91. Litwa, "Paul's Mosaic Ascent," 239–40.

is correct, maybe Moses was integral also to the self-representation and teachings of some of his rivals at Corinth.

There are numerous *comparanda* for specialists—philosophers and doctors but also the so-called theurgists and the authors of Hermetic texts—who held concepts of *pneuma* as a transformative, divine substance, while Judeans were known, to Josephus and Epictetus alike, for combining baptism with purification and ethical behavior.[92] It is conceivable that some of the latter may have enlisted *pneuma* as the mechanism of their initiations or purifications, even if it was Paul himself who joined the concept with *the* Christ in precisely his way.[93] And while the language that he assigns to certain practices, benefits, and statuses (e.g., *charismata, pneumatikoi*) may be Pauline patois, redescribing the apostle's religious program in second-order terms allows us to compare and contrast his practices with the offerings of others like him.

Situating Paul in this social context also affects how we understand his preoccupation with the many "opponents" who crop up time again in his letters. Altogether, he admonishes "peddlers of God's word" (καπηλεύοντες τὸν λόγον τοῦ θεοῦ); "super-apostles" (ὑπερλίαν ἀπόστολοι); "false apostles" (ψευδαπόστολοι); "practitioners of deceit who disguise themselves as (or change their form into) apostles of Christ" (ἐργάται δόλιοι, μετασχηματιζόμενοι εἰς ἀποστολους Χριστοῦ); "arrogant people" (πεφυσιωμένοι); "dogs" (κύνες); "the mutilator of the flesh" (περιτομή); and, again, people claiming legitimacy as Hebrews, Israelites, and descendants of Abraham.[94] Some references to rival experts are straightforward, as when Paul tells the Corinthians that he will remain in Ephesus until Pentecost because a wide door for effective work has opened to him and

---

92. Josephus, *AJ* 18.116–19; Epictetus, *Diatr.* 2.9.

93. As Adela Yarbro Collins and John J. Collins have shown, Paul's depiction of Christ draws on ideas of divine kingship that appear in other Judean writings, including the Dead Sea Scrolls, though with a considerably different emphasis: *King and Messiah as Son of God: Divine, Human, and Angelic Messianic Figures in Biblical and Related Literature* (Grand Rapids: Eerdmans, 2008), 101–22. For further discussion of Paul's χριστός concept, see Novenson, *Christ Among the Messiahs*, 98–173.

94. 2 Cor 2:17; 2 Cor 11:5, 12:11; 2 Cor 11:13; 2 Cor 11:13, cf. κακοί εργάται in Phil 3:2; 1 Cor 4:19; Phil 3:2; 2 Cor 11:22. Interestingly, ἐργάτης was associated with Hermes and occasionally served as a substitute for his proper name. One wonders whether, in using this language, Paul is taking a subtle jab at Hermetic rivals, just as he seems to be doing with respect to Cynics.

there are many adversaries (ἀντικείμενοι πολλοί)."[95] Others, such as his remark about fighting with wild animals at Ephesus, are more allusive.[96] On some occasions he offers insight into the bases for these contestations, as when he reprimands the Galatians for straying from his teachings by adopting Judaic practices at the behest of other "Judaizing" experts.[97] In general, however, Paul discloses little if anything about the content of any false teachings that these rivals purveyed; rather, he rebuffs them with insinuations of false motives, desire for profit, and other improper actions.[98]

On the reasonable assumption that their quantity and character inform reconstructions of the "early Church," Paul's opponents have been taken up in assorted publications, often with a view to identifying them and the particular heresies they introduced into his gospel.[99] The candidates are remarkably assorted: proponents of Petrine Christianity, whose Jacobean legalism clashed with the Hellenistic libertine thrust of Pauline Christianity; the Jerusalem apostles; Judaizers; Gnostics influenced by the Essenes and mystery religions; Pneumatics; divine men; syncretists; traveling preachers; non-Christian teachers; Cybele-Attis cult eunuchs; Platonists; Pythagoreans; ascetics; and practitioners of magic.[100] While

---

95. 1 Cor 16:8–9.

96. 1 Cor 15:32. As Malherbe has shown, in this period fighting and killing wild beasts was a popular metaphor for characterizing a philosophical or religious opponent ("The Beasts at Ephesus," in *Paul and the Popular Philosophers*, 79–89). The charge carried an additional anti-Epicurean connotation for the school's reputation of living a "bestial life," and Malherbe points to other places in Paul's writings that indicate awareness of and deliberate engagement with this bias (84–88 and n. 72). The habit of describing rivals in terms resonant of Epicureans is not unknown in Judean and Christian literature; likewise the most vocal objectors to Alexander's oracle are Epicureans and Christians (*Alex.* 25, 38; cf. *Bis acc.* 20; *Fug.* 19). See Richard Jungkuntz, "Fathers, Heretics, and Epicureans," *JEH* 17 (1966): 3–10.

97. Gal 3:1–14.

98. See Stowers, "Kinds of Myth, Meals, and Power," 145.

99. See, e.g., Georgi, *The Opponents of Paul in Second Corinthians*. For an overview of scholarly interpretations of the opponents see E. Earle Ellis, "Paul and His Opponents: Trends in the Research," in *Christianity, Judaism, and Other Graeco-Roman Cults I*, ed. Jacob Neusner (Leiden: Brill, 1975), 264–73; Jerry L. Sumney, *Identifying Paul's Opponents: The Question of Method in 2 Corinthians*, JSOT 40 (Sheffield: JSOT, 1990); idem, "Studying Paul's Opponents: Advances and Challenges," in *Paul and His Opponents*, ed. Stanley E. Porter, Pauline Studies 2 (Leiden: Brill, 2005), 7–58.

100. Some scholars also propose specific and stable referents for certain terms that Paul uses to denounce rivals, suggesting, for example, that "super apostle" corresponds to the

many scholars have moved away from the presupposition that there was only one sort of opposition to Paul, most maintain that "the Church" was a manifest presence in such encounters.[101] Furthermore, despite heightened caution about reconstructing exact historical adversaries from his polemical language, there is still considerable speculation about the "belief systems" of these rivals.

The epistles disclose no such normative institutional backdrop—a highly coordinated "movement" or "Church"—for Paul's activities. To the contrary, Paul himself gives the impression that his rivals offered competing versions of pliable concepts and practices that had yet to stabilize into any form with clear priority at the time he wrote. I also find it unproductive to describe his rivalries in terms of conflicting doctrines, which presumes anachronistic concepts of orthodoxy and heresy insofar as, for contradicting Paul, his opponents are understood to have corrupted or innovated upon a tradition extending back to Jesus and his immediate followers.[102] Yet while Paul clearly interacted with people who knew Jesus, he never admits unequivocally to having received any tradition, teachings, or eschatological mysteries from them.[103] Instead he is adamant that his gospel is not of human origin: neither was it taught to him nor did he receive it from a human source; rather, it came to him in a revelation of Jesus Christ.[104] Then, after Christ was revealed to him, he conferred with no one, not even those in Jerusalem who were already apostles before him. When he did eventually meet with those people, they contributed nothing to him.[105]

Jerusalem apostles while "false apostle" refers to his opponents in Corinth. For a discussion of and the corresponding bibliography for each of these propositions see N. H. Taylor, "Apostolic Identity and the Conflicts in Corinth and Galatia," in Porter, *Paul and His Opponents*, 99–123, esp. 118 n. 90. See also Stowers, "Kinds of Myths, Meals, and Power," 107–8.

101. E.g., Sumney, "Studying Paul's Opponents," 47.

102. As Stowers argues, "If Paul and the apostles preached the gospel and that led to conversion and the formation of communities, then deviation from the unity of belief and sentiment implied in the concept of community must be like heresy. It was departure from an original state of purity in thought and action" ("The Concept of 'Community' and the History of Early Christianity," *MTSR* 23 [2011]: 238–56, at 243).

103. The possible exception is 1 Cor 15:1–3. While some take Paul's language of teaching a gospel that he, in turn, received to mean he acquired its contents from the people whose revelations of Christ he proceeds to list, in my view, the implicit subject from whom Paul received this knowledge is the resurrected Christ.

104. Gal 1:11–12.

105. Gal 1:16, 2:6.

The religion of freelance experts, which has been absent from these valuable discussions, offers a plausible social setting for competition between self-authorized and largely independent actors, who nevertheless communicated in any number of ways with one another and with other groups and institutions. Thus framed, Paul's rivalries do not require hypotheses about certain figures, circumstances, or points of disagreement, the details of which are largely conjectural and quickly supplanted by new proposals. The advantage of this approach is that it does not require an exact definition of what constitutes opposition or opponents, because complex competitive dynamics were fundamental to and predictable effects of this class of activity.[106] Whether we train our lens on the wider phenomenon of specialized offerings or focus it more narrowly on varieties of Judean experts, writer-intellectuals, mystery initiators, or authorities on Christ, evidence of rivalries in the epistles only strengthens the case for Paul's inclusion among other freelance experts who shared his competitive interests.

"With Far More Imprisonments, and Often Near Death"

So far we have seen that Paul resembles other freelance religious experts on at least three fronts: the conspicuously ethnicizing elements of his practices; his different applications of Judean writings; and his enlistment of other intellectual skills and discourses, particularly ones drawn from the realm of philosophy. These considerations point to his participation in this class of religious activity as I have mapped it, but others remain to be explored. I turn now to three other topics adumbrated in earlier chapters: the punishments that Paul alleges to have received, along with the possibilities and challenges these presented; his travel itinerary; and his basic economic practices, including the methods he employed to downplay their problematic connotations.

Earlier I argued that the first century of the imperial period transformed the profile of the religion of freelance experts, posing in turn a number of regulatory challenges for Roman and local administrators. Amassing evidence for the punishment of different varieties of specialists, I traced

---

106. A concern raised by Stanley E. Porter in "Did Paul Have Opponents in Rome and What Were They Opposing?" in Porter, *Paul and His Opponents*, 149–68.

an unofficial pattern of responses that escalated in frequency and severity within this timeframe. The legislative consequences of freelance expertise shed light on Paul's repeated references to having endured punishments and other hardships.[107] He complains to the Thessalonians of having suffered and been shamefully mistreated at Philippi and also of having been driven out of Judea; to the Corinthians he speaks of experiencing such affliction in Asia that he felt he had received a death sentence, and, in a previous letter, of fighting with beasts at Ephesus.[108] The last remark has been taken literally to mean that he faced wild animals in the arena and figuratively as a battle with the opponents he mentions later in the letter.[109] When Lucian uses the same phrase, however, it is for Roman administrators of Galatia to whom Alexander helped deliver the servants of a man who wrongly (thanks to Alexander) suspected their involvement in his son's murder.[110] No stranger to such dealings, Paul writes of having to be lowered in a basket down the wall of Damascus before the ethnarch under King Aretas could seize him.[111]

In each of these examples Paul invokes hardships that he has endured as proof of his apostolic legitimacy, over and against the illegitimacy of others engaging in similar activities. In 2 Cor 11:23–25, he asks of would-be rivals: "Are they attendants of Christ? ... I am a better one: with far more troubles, far more imprisonments, with countless floggings, and many times near death. Five times I have received from the Judeans the forty lashes minus one. Three times I was beaten with rods. Once I received a stoning."[112] John T. Fitzgerald has highlighted continuities between Paul's sufferings and the hardship or *peristasis* catalogues of first-century philosophers such as Epictetus and Seneca, who invoked the endurance of adverse circumstances as confirmation of one's philosophical virtue and

---

107. See also Wendt, "Christian Martyrdom and the Religion of Freelance Experts," 189–93.

108. 1 Thess 2:2, 15; 2 Cor 1:8–9; 1 Cor 15:32.

109. See Malherbe, "The Beasts at Ephesus," 84–88.

110. Lucian, *Alex.* 44.

111. 2 Cor 11:32–33. For the possible chronological significance of the reference, see Douglas A. Campbell, "An Anchor for Pauline Chronology: Paul's Flight from 'The Ethnarch of King Aretas' (2 Corinthians 11:32–33)," *JBL* 121 (2002): 279–302.

112. Διάκονοι Χριστοῦ εἰσιν ... ὑπὲρ ἐγώ· ἐν κόποις περισσοτέρως, ἐν φυλακαῖς περισσοτέρως, ἐν πληγαῖς ὑπερβαλλόντως, ἐν θανάτοις πολλάκις. ὑπὸ Ἰουδαίων πεντάκις τεσσεράκοντα παρὰ μίαν ἔλαβον, τρὶς ἐραβδίσθην, ἅπαξ ἐλιθάσθην, τρὶς ἐναυάγησα.

exemplary character.[113] According to Epictetus, the sage "suffers no harm even though he is soundly flogged, or imprisoned, or beheaded" but bears all of this with personal profit.[114] As to the intended effect of thus enumerating hardships, Fitzgerald argues that adversity occasioned the exhibition of virtue because it tested and revealed the recipient's true character, as well as, I would add, his authenticity and disinterest. "Serene endurance of the greatest possible calamities," he concludes, "is the definitive proof of . . . virtue and serves to distinguish the [person who is truly wise] from every charlatan who merely claims to be 'wise.' "[115]

As an intellectualizing religious expert versed in philosophical discourses, it makes sense that Paul would also be familiar with the function of *peristasis* catalogues and enlisted the punishments and other hardships he had endured as proof of his character. Beyond the rhetorical effect of having withstood suffering, however, there is a correlation in the particular hardships that appear on these lists and the legislation examined earlier: corporal punishments, imprisonment, expulsions or exile, and even the threat of death. This is fitting given that—beyond the basic fact that there were only so many ways to punish someone—many philosophers occupied one subset of the wider field of self-authorized specialists. Paul also seems aware of the potential benefits of being on the receiving end of punishments, especially in his letter to the Philippians, which he writes during a period of incarceration. Here he reports that imprisonment has actually furthered his agenda since the entire imperial guard knows he suffers for Christ, while those in Christ have been emboldened by his incarceration.[116] His notoriety has also spawned imitators, who, intending to increase Paul's suffering in prison, proclaim Christ from envy, rivalry, and selfish ambition. About such people he is unconcerned, since it matters not whether one's motives are false or true so long as Christ is proclaimed in every way.

These remarks provide a concrete example of how public censure might heighten the intrigue surrounding a recipient's teachings, improving his

---

113. Fitzgerald, *Cracks in an Earthen Vessel*, passim. See also Schellenberg, *Rethinking Paul's Rhetorical Education*, 123–40.

114. Epictetus, *Diatr.* 4.1.127; Fitzgerald, *Cracks in an Earthen Vessel*, 64.

115. Fitzgerald, *Cracks in an Earthen Vessel*, 115.

116. Phil 1:12–18. Cf. Phlm 1, 9–13 and Rom 16:7, where Paul also makes reference to imprisonment.

stature and fomenting his influence rather than undermining or suppress-
ing it. They also recall the rivalries that instigated or sustained the investigation of particular religious figures and groups, since Paul's language
implies that he attributes his imprisonment to conflicts with those trying
to increase his suffering.[117] In Galatians he mentions certain "false brothers" (ψευδαδέλφοι) secretly brought in to spy on a meeting in Jerusalem
with the intention of enslaving its participants.[118] He assures his readers
that he disclosed nothing of his gospel to them, but the concern is suggestive of informing on problematic activity that would otherwise be difficult
to identify.[119] In this vein, although the *rhetoric* of shared adversity—Paul's
own as well as that of Jesus, the Jerusalem assembly, and his groups—is
germane to his group-making interests, he is adamant that negative attention is not something to be courted. To the contrary, he urges followers
to respect and remain subject to governing authorities, to live quietly and
mind their own affairs, to continue working, and to pay taxes.[120] Since
legislation against the followers of freelance experts was often issued in
response to their perceived complicity in social disruption, these exhorta-
tions to civic responsibility guard against the potential consequences of
participating in religious activity thought, rightly or wrongly, to promote
such behavior.[121]

It is equally possible that Paul incurred suspicion merely for being a
traveling religious expert without obvious ties to the places he visited. As
Timothy Luckritz Marquis has argued, "insofar as he was one of a growing number of mercantile and spiritual wanderers taking advantage of
the increased mobility that attended Roman dominance" his transience

---

117. Harrill, *Paul the Apostle*, 67–68.

118. Gal 2:4–5.

119. This interpretation of the Galatians incident is largely shared by Mark D. Nanos, who
argues for the "thoroughly intra-Jewish nature of the social setting and polemic of Paul and
the other early believers in Christ of the period" ("Intruding 'Spies' and 'Pseudo-Brethren':
The Jewish Intra-Group Politics of Paul's Jerusalem Meeting [Gal 2:1–10]," in Porter, *Paul and
His Opponents*, 57–97, at 90). Nanos imagines a scenario in which members of rival Judean
groups such as the one Paul once belonged to intruded into the meeting of the assembly to
investigate and inform on its members.

120. 1 Thess 4:11–12; Rom 13:1–7.

121. Such considerations also push against reading these verses as examples of Paul's anti-
imperial agenda. Harrill demonstrates that on many occasions "Paul used language that
colluded with a particularly Roman discourse of authority," for instance, by using words that
correspond to specific civic duties ("Paul and Empire," 303; *Paul the Apostle*, 80, 93).

left him vulnerable to ambivalence about itinerant specialists.[122] At the same time, his movements around the Mediterranean world pivot strategically between cities or regions that were known for being especially conducive to freelance expertise. Rome's magnetism has been established, but Corinth too looms in the sources as a destination that specialists frequented. Agnotus the Pythagorean exorcised a ghost from a Corinthian house, while Diophanes the Chaldean set up shop there.[123] Cenchreae, the neighboring colony where Lucius underwent his first Isiac initiation, was also the home of Paul's patroness Phoebe. From Thessalonica—another bustling commercial port with a steady flow of traders—survives considerable evidence for foreign cults; it is reasonable to posit freelance experts as the progenitors of at least some.[124] Athens and its environs teemed with religious experts in this and earlier periods, while, as Guy MacLean Rogers has noted, the first and second centuries witnessed an expansion of the mysteries of Artemis of Ephesus along with a corresponding proliferation of all kinds of mysteries in the city's noncivic religious life.[125] One can imagine what opportunities the latter trend presented to a mystery-bearer such as Paul.[126] Another coincidence occurs in Galatia, where the apostle formed *ekklēsiai* and Alexander of Abonoteichus is said by Lucian to have roamed the countryside beguiling many receptive followers.[127] And even

---

122. Luckritz Marquis, *Transient Apostle*, 11.

123. Lucian, *Philops.* 33–36; Apuleius, *Metam.* 2.12–13. For Corinth as an emporium, see David K. Pettegrew, "The Diolkos and the Emporion: How a Land Bridge Framed the Commercial Economy of Roman Corinth," in *Corinth in Contrast: Studies in Inequality*, ed. Steven J. Friesen, Sarah A. James, and Daniel N. Schowalter (Leiden: Brill, 2014), 126–42. For the appeal of Paul's teachings to Corinth's sizeable freed population, in particular, see Laura Salah Nasrallah, " 'You Were Bought with a Price': Freedpersons and Things in 1 Corinthians," in Friesen, James, and Schowalter, *Corinth in Contrast*, 54–73. See also Concannon, who highlights both the cultural fabric of Corinth and calls attention to the significance of freedmen in its civic elite (*"When You Were Gentiles,"* 47–74).

124. Apuleius, *Metam.* 11.10–23; Rom 16:1. Ascough, "Redescribing the Thessalonians' 'Mission'," 61, 78. This was not the only Macedonian city that supported the growth of such phenomena: a famous inscription from Opus records the foundation of a household Sarapis association after its founder, Xenainetos, received instructions to do so from a political adversary who was visited by the god in a dream while sleeping in a shrine (*AGRW* 52; Ascough, "Redescribing the Thessalonians' 'Mission,' " 73).

125. For Athens, see Parker, *Polytheism and Society*, 116–35. For Ephesus, see MacLean Rogers, *The Mysteries of Artemis of Ephesos*, esp. 171–204.

126. 1 Cor 15:32, 16:8–9.

127. Lucian, *Alex.* 9, 18, 30, 44.

though Paul never claims to hail from Tarsus, the city drew many intellectual specialists, including Apollonius of Tyana, which may have influenced the decision to make it his home in Acts.[128]

Fictional though some of these figures or details may be, the settings of their activities are unlikely to have been purely fabricated. As I noted in chapter 2, many theories of cult migration posit merchants as the passive agents behind the spread of foreign religion, and yet cities rich in trade also attracted specialists such as Paul, who sought them out proactively for the opportunities they presented. Many of these places were also home to famous temples, games, or festivals, all of which beckoned wandering specialists. As Dio Chrysostom recalls of Corinth's Isthmian Games,

> [O]ne could hear crowds of wretched sophists around Poseidon's temple shouting and reviling one another, and their disciples, as they were called, fighting with one another, many writers reading aloud their stupid works, and many poets reciting their poems, while others applauded them, many wonder-workers showcasing their marvels (πολλῶν δὲ θαυματοποιῶν θαύματα ἐπιδεικνύντων), many diviners of signs issuing interpretations (πολλῶν δὲ τερατοσκόπων τέρατα κρινόντων), jurists innumerable perverting judgment, and peddlers (καπήλων) not a few peddling whatever they happened to have.[129]

Citing similar causes, Plutarch attributes the decline of the Delphic oracle to the begging priest (ἀγυρτικός) and market-dweller (ἀγοραῖος) who flock to ceremonies of the Great Mother and Sarapis where, with their deceptions and tricks, they prophesy from verse oracles either composed on the spot or taken from handbooks. It is on the account of cheats (ἀπατῶντες), sorcerers (γόητες) and lying prophets (ψευδομάντεις) such as these that, by his reckoning, the Pythia's poetry has been tarnished.[130] For the same

---

128. Acts 9:11, 21:39. Strabo writes that the people of Tarsus "have devoted themselves so eagerly not only to philosophy but also to the whole round of education in general, that they have surpassed Athens, Alexandria, or any other place that can be named where there have been schools and lectures of philosophers" (*Geogr.* 14.15.3; Harrill, *The Apostle Paul*, 24).

129. Dio Chrysostom, *Or.* 8.9 (trans. Cohoon, LCL with modifications). One thinks also of Peregrinus's spectacular suicide, performed at the Olympian Games for the crowds of sympathetic spectators the event drew (Lucian, *Peregr.* 38).

130. Plutarch, *De Pyth. orac.* 407c. For the Orphic connotations of this language, and of "the poets reciting their poems" in the preceding quotation, see Edmonds, *Redefining Ancient Orphism*, 202.

reason local magistrates in these cities or regions were experienced at handling such actors and with legislative precedents from Rome in view. Regardless of Paul's pretext for his itinerary, the places he visited were popular destinations for specialists and therefore predictable settings in which to run into the sort of problems outlined in chapter 2.

"Not that I Seek the Gift"

If the aforementioned considerations supply vague clues about how someone such as Paul might attract negative attention due to his religious activities, an even more probable source is the economic practices that feature prominently in his writings. Typically, Paul shies away from receiving compensation in exchange for the expertise and benefits he purveys; his integrity and the value of his message seem to require a disinterested countenance. In 1 Thess 2:3–5 he assures his audience, "Our appeal does not spring from deceit, or impure motives, or trickery, but just as we have been approved by God to be entrusted with the message of the gospel, even so we speak not to please mortals, but to please gods. . . . We never came with words of flattery or a pretext for greed." The opposition in 2 Cor 2:17 underscores this message poignantly: "Peddlers" (καπηλεύοντες) of religious teachings are motivated by self-interest, whereas Paul acts in the service of God, with no motivation beyond spreading his gospel. The "super apostles'" expectation of remuneration is the mark of professionals; Paul is an "amateur" (ἰδιώτης).[131] They prey upon and take advantage of the Corinthians; he was too weak for that.

On a few occasions Paul seems to respond to criticisms in kind leveled against him by rivals, for instance, when he insists, "We wronged no one (ἀδικεῖν), we entrapped (or seduced) no one (φθείρειν), we defrauded no one (πλεονεκτεῖν)."[132] Later in the same letter he uses imagery of weapons and fortification to refute the charge against him by "certain persons who reason that we are conducting ourselves according to the flesh (κατὰ σάρκα περιπατοῦντας)."[133] The accusation seems to be one of inconsistency,

---

131. 1 Cor 11:6, 20–21. See Luckritz Marquis for Paul's use of καπηλεύοντες (*Transient Apostle*, 135) and Eshleman's discussion of the force of ἰδιώτης among rival intellectuals (*The Social World of Intellectuals in the Roman Empire*, 68–77).

132. 2 Cor 7:2.

133. 2 Cor 10:2. For the meaning of the accusation, see Gerd Thiessen, *The Social Setting of Pauline Christianity: Essays on Corinth*, trans. and ed. John H. Schütz (Philadelphia:

either in teachings or in behavior, but it may also carry implications of financial dealings.[134] Although scholars have shied away from any appearance of interest or profit in Paul's activities, it is wholly unsurprising in the context of freelance expertise if rivals should denounce him in such terms, irrespective of whether there was any merit to their accusations. While his averred self-sufficiency, rejection of patronage, and vocal disinterest consciously distance him from such appearances, like other freelance experts Paul always hovered right at the edge of legitimacy, ever vulnerable to charges of impropriety, especially regarding the tricky matters of interest and compensation.[135]

It is also worth noting that despite his many statements about refusing support, Paul is clear that he is entitled to it. He asks the Corinthians, "If we have sown pneumatic resources (πνευματικά) in you, is it too much if we reap your worldly resources (σαρκικά)?" If others share your possessions should we not more?"[136] And, earlier, "Is it only Barnabas and I who have no right to refrain from working for a living? Who at the time pays the expenses for doing military service? Who plants a vineyard and does not eat any of its fruit? Or who tends a flock and does not get any of its milk?"[137] À propos of their preferred type of labor, Paul points out, "Those who are employed in the temple service get their food from the temple, and those who serve at the altar share in what is sacrificed at the altar. In the same way, the lord commanded that those who proclaim the gospel should get their living through the gospel."[138]

While Paul denies having made use of these entitlements, repeated reminders of his right to compensation underscore the transactional

---

Fortress Press, 1982), 64 n. 44; Malherbe, "Antisthenes and Odysseus, and Paul at War," 113–14.

134. Cf. 1 Cor 9:11–12; Rom 15:25–28.

135. For the preferred financial independence of philosophers and doctors, see Eshleman, *The Social World of Intellectuals in the Roman Empire*, 46, 77–88. While Paul's professions of disinterest are directed foremost against other Christ experts, they also distance him, as Luckritz Marquis notes, from other "charlatan" preachers of foreign gods, particularly Dionysus and Cybele (*Transient Apostle*, 71–72, 85). For him, however, it is foremost the problem of itinerancy against which Paul defended himself.

136. 1 Cor 9:11–12.

137. 1 Cor 9:6–7, 13–14.

138. For the Roman civic connotations of ἐξουσία as Paul uses it in this context, see Harrill, "Paul and Empire," 300.

dimension of freelance religious expertise. Nor is his refusal of support absolute.[139] In 2 Cor 11:8, the apostle recalls how he refrained from being a burden while in Corinth, even robbing other *ekklēsiai* by accepting their support in order to serve the group there. Likewise, he renews his gratitude to the Philippians for "help" (χρεία) that they sent more than once to Thessalonica.[140] "Not that I seek the gift," he assures them, "but I seek the fruit which increases to your credit. I have received full payment and more; I am filled, having received from Epaphroditus the gifts you sent, a fragrant offering, a sacrifice acceptable and pleasing to God. And my God will supply every need of yours according to his riches in glory in Jesus Christ."

Paul is more ambivalent about receiving patronage and other forms of support in exchange for the religious services that he provides than he is about other economic matters, namely, soliciting a service (διακονία) for the poor among the holy ones who are in Jerusalem (πτωχοί τῶν ἁγίων τῶν ἐν Ἰερουσαλήμ). References to his so-called collection appear frequently and less problematically in Paul's writings.[141] To the Corinthians he advises, "God loves a cheerful giver," a reminder that follows instructions for preparing a "blessing pledged previously" (προεπηγγελμένη εὐλογία) so that, when the brothers come, it is ready as a gift, not as an extortion (πλεονεξία).[142] For one who sows in blessings will reap in blessings, and they will be enriched in every way for their generosity. If Paul should arrive with Macedonian followers and find them unready, however, then he would be humiliated, to say nothing of them.

---

139. As Wayne A. Meeks notes, "In 1 Cor. 16:6 he tells of his plans to stay a time with them, perhaps over the winter, 'that you may send me on my way [*propempsēte*] wherever I may go.' The same expectation is voiced in 2 Cor. 1:16 for his journey to Judea, and he requests the same service in the meantime for Timothy (1 Cor. 16:11). . . . [In] such a context *propempein* generally 'means to equip him with all things necessary for the journey,' which would involve some financial outlay" (*The First Urban Christians: The Social World of the Apostle Paul*, 2nd ed. [New Haven: Yale University Press, 2003], 66). See also Abraham J. Malherbe, "The Inhospitality of Diotrephes," in *God's Christ and His People: Studies in Honour of Nils Alstrup Dahl*, ed. Jacob Jervell and Wayne A. Meeks (Oslo: Universitetsforlaget, 1977), 222–32 at 230 n. 11; Ronald F. Hock, *The Social Context of Paul's Ministry: Tentmaking and Apostleship* (Philadelphia: Fortress Press, 1980). *Pace* Luckritz Marquis, who takes Paul's refusal of support at face value (*Transient Apostle*, 44, 129).

140. Phil 4:15–19. Several ancient commentators read explicitly as "money for my needs."

141. E.g. 1 Cor 16:1–2; 2 Cor 9:1, 12; Rom 15:25, 31.

142. 2 Cor 9:4–7, 11.

I raise the matter of the collection not to impeach Paul but to demonstrate how, on this front too, his actions serve to highlight his social location. On the one hand, his economic practices seem to be more or less consistent with those of other specialists. Valerius Maximus tells of a proscribed aedile who escaped Rome undetected after donning the Isiac habit and passing through its streets under the pretense of taking a collection, while Juvenal laments the wastefulness of wives who, left to their own devices, are all too eager to squander their husbands' earnings on the roving priests of foreign gods.[143] We cannot know firsthand how other experts justified their collections, but, in the absence of evidence comparable to the epistles, we should imagine that their explanations were as compelling and seemingly disinterested as Paul's; it is by virtue of the evidence that his intentions and practices seem beyond reproach. On the other hand, it is clear that such collections were strongly and problematically associated with freelance expertise. Already in the late republic Cicero insisted that no one may have a collection (*stipem*) except the followers of the Idaean Mother—and they only on the permitted days—because collections fill the city with *superstitiones* and deplete households; hence they have been abolished at Rome.[144]

These examples confirm that collections undertaken on behalf of foreign gods were included in the broader set of legislative actions employed, I argued, to manage the presence and influence of freelance experts, especially in cities. For a closer analogy we might recall Josephus's story of the reprobate Judean who professed expertise in Mosaic wisdom in order to steal from an aristocratic woman by convincing her to send donations to the Jerusalem temple.[145] One wonders whether our differing impressions of the two Jerusalem collections—that one is theft, the other charity—is merely a matter of perspective. Whereas Josephus's account is colored by his normative bias against itinerant experts in Judean religion, Paul lays out a compelling rationale for his economic practices. It is also noteworthy that when Paul accuses the fictitious Judean teacher of hypocrisy, his

---

143. Valerius Maximus, 7.8.1–5; Juvenal, 6.560–64. Apuleius also links followers of the Syrian goddess with collections in his story of the Syrian priests whose divination racket compels Magna Mater to become a beggar (*mendicare compellunt, Metam.* 8.24). Connotations of begging and plunder recur throughout the vignette (e.g., *Metam.* 8.28–29, 9.8–9). Cf. Luckritz Marquis, *Transient Apostle*, 27.

144. Cicero, *Leg.* 2.22.9, 2.40.11.

145. Josephus, *AJ* 18.65–84.

denunciation accords item for item with the stock charges that Josephus levies against the Judean deceiver and his accomplices: theft, improper relations with married women, despoiling temples (ἱεροσυλεῖν)—or *the* Jerusalem temple—disregarding the law, and generally sullying God's reputation among non-Judeans through his actions.[146]

If Paul's ambivalence about the appearance of interest is predictable in view of the class of activity in which he participated, even more predictable are the efforts on the part of ancient Pauline pseudepigraphers and inter-preters to eliminate, minimize, or transform any hint of financial motiva-tion in his activities. Although references to the collection and material support appear in all but one of his epistles (Philemon), they are conspicu-ously absent from the letters of debated and pseudepigraphic authorship, as well as the narrative portrayal of his activities in Acts.[147] The for-profit connotation of religious professionals was a convenient vulnerability for critics such as Josephus and Lucian, cultural specialists who could afford to be disinterested, so to speak, and for whom the stereotype of the ex-ploitative "charlatan" was readily available and instantly discrediting. The revisionary inclinations of Pauline interpreters are easy to understand, all the more so by the second century, if not earlier, when these accusations had come to be applied to Christians.[148]

"In Every Way You Have Been Enriched"

Notwithstanding the aforementioned risks that might accompany having regular dealings with someone such as Paul, the preceding chap-ters speak to a broad range of religious and other interests that inhabit-ants of the Roman world pursued through participation in the religion of freelance experts: health, healing, afterlife concerns, care for the dead,

---

146. Rom 2:17–29. Cf. Lawrence Welborn, who argues that Paul occasionally mimics the boasting of the "quack holy man," a subset of the learned imposter, in order to parody the rivals against whom he inveighs: "The Runaway Paul," *HTR* 92 (1999): 115–63, at 150–51. Arnal views this as a general rhetorical address aimed at anyone of Israel who could ever behave unrighteously despite having the law ("Bringing Paul and the Corinthians Together?" 90).

147. See David J. Downs, *The Offering of the Gentiles: Paul's Collection for Jerusalem and Its Chronological, Cultural, and Cultic Contexts*, WUNT 2.248 (Tübingen: Mohr Siebeck, 2008), 1, 63–72.

148. For example, Celsus objects not to the cult of Cybele per se but to the itinerant priests and prophets, who, as do Christians with their god, earn a living in her name (Origen, *C.*

character improvement, social mobility, opportunities for patronage, group membership, conviviality, and so on. It is fitting that the epistles contain numerous references to women, freedpersons, and slaves—maybe even members of the Herodian *familia*—demographics that, again, seem to have engaged amply in this sort of religious activity.[149] Any number of the attractions that drew such people to other kinds of foreign religion might have been satisfied within a Pauline *ekklēsia,* and with additional benefits.

Not only does Paul himself wield several forms of religious expertise, he also promises that upon receiving divine *pneuma* those "in Christ" will acquire special abilities (χαρίσματα, or "favors," in his language) that were common coin in the offerings of first-century specialists: wisdom, knowledge, healing, miracle-working, prophecy, discerning spirits (πνεύματα), speaking in tongues, and interpreting tongues.[150] He assures his audiences that they have collectively accrued any and all specialty: "In every way you have been enriched in him [Christ] in speech and knowledge of every kind (ἐν παντὶ λόγῳ καὶ πάσῃ γνώσει) . . . so that you are not lacking in any divine favor (ἐν μηδενὶ χαρίσματι) as you await the revealing of our lord, Jesus Christ."[151] Hence, through participation in a Pauline group, one stood to acquire mysterious wisdom and knowledge rooted in ancient, oracular texts, religious skills, health or healing, and an escape from death with the prospect of immortality, even by means of resurrection for any who have already died or might die before Christ returns.[152]

Whether Paul's audiences were persuaded entirely by his full salvation scheme is a question we cannot answer, though there are several indications in his letters of resistance to certain elements (e.g., the resurrection)

Cels. 1.9). Origen takes umbrage at being likened to these actors, as well as to the followers of Mithras and Sabazius, who apparently had similar reputations.

149. See Stowers, *A Rereading of Romans,* 79; Nasrallah, "Freedpersons and Things in 1 Corinthians," 55.

150. 1 Cor 12:4–11; Rom 12:6–8.

151. 1 Cor 1:5–7.

152. Of course, not everyone "in Christ" would acquire all of the roles or abilities of which Paul speaks, maybe only one or a few. They are also ranked, as he explains in 1 Cor 12:28, with apostles first, then prophets, teachers, deeds of power, healing, and so on. Collectively, however, the acquisition of any of these "favors" would have been seen as an attractive prospect,

and also of benefits that people might have enjoyed without needing to accept his eschatology in its entirety. As some scholars have suggested, it is possible that literate followers were less interested in Paul's salvation narrative per se than they were in consuming foreign *paideia*, or even trying their own hands at revealing divine mysteries from esoteric writings.[153] As with other examples of his practices and modes of authorization—namely, the receipt of divine revelations and visions—there was no barrier to people with comparable skills putting their own intellectual abilities to similar forms of religious innovation.

For all of Paul's instructions, we should also entertain the likelihood of a considerable gap between what he wanted his correspondents to do and what they actually thought or did.[154] After all, many aspects of his program fit prior frames of reference and are not incomparable with known theological narratives or entrepreneurial offerings. It stands to reason that people employed local concepts to situate aspects of his mythological narratives and religious program and also as they made sense of his instructions. As Ron Cameron and Merrill P. Miller suggest about the Corinthians, "If we acknowledge the capacity for experimentation with multiple modes of religion, we should expect that one of the forms that Corinthian response to Paul would take would be their own experiments in myth-making and ritual related to their own differentiated social interests."[155] We have abundant evidence for inhabitants of the Roman world adjusting their religious practices creatively—reconciling novelty and innovation with entrenched social commitments and individual interests—and there is no reason to think that the same processes of resistance and negotiation did not obtain for these practitioners.

One persistent argument for Paul's uniqueness as a first-century religious actor is that he formed and maintained "communities" or "churches," whereas other freelance experts did not share this objective. We have already reviewed some of his methods for creating and reinforcing a sense

---

especially since Paul is adamant that all hold equal value within Christ's corporate body (1 Cor 12:4–27).

153. Stowers, "Kinds of Myth, Meals, and Power," 142; Ron Cameron and Merrill P. Miller, "Redescribing Paul and the Corinthians," in Cameron and Miller, *Redescribing Paul and the Corinthians*, 245–302, esp. 293.

154. Stowers, "Kinds of Myth, Meals, and Power," 112.

155. Cameron and Miller, "Redescribing Paul and the Corinthians," 257.

of groupness: depicting his audiences as members of a single body who are ontologically (or pneumatically) identical to one another but different from other people, appealing to their common experiences of suffering and obligation, reminding them of mysteries and an impending apocalyptic scenario that they alone understand, and using letters to iterate his particular teachings.[156] However, as Stowers has argued, it is the scholarly habit of imagining Pauline and other early Christian social formations as romanticized "communities" of believers that ultimately makes them incomparable with other first-century groups.[157] In his view, two things are clear from Paul's writings: "[First], Paul very much wanted the people to whom he wrote to be a community, and he held a theory saying that God had miraculously made them into a community 'in Christ'; second, [these people] never did sociologically form a community and only partly and differentially shared Paul's interests and formation."[158] Rather, Pauline *ekklēsia* were likely comparable to other social formations that arose from the religion of freelance experts and, as many have shown, they stand to benefit from being redescribed in terms that are consistent with the regular followings that coalesced around individuals who fit this mold.[159] Paul's epistles do bear witness to the considerable work that went into establishing and regularizing groups and to the range of tactics a specialist might employ in order to realize these ambitions.

"Not Peddlers of God's Word, Like So Many"

This reading of the Pauline Epistles does not amount to a comprehensive treatment of Paul's religious program, both because our record of it is incomplete and because it was probably never rigorously systematic in the

---

156. Meeks provides a thorough overview of words, phrases, and concepts that promote group boundaries and cohesion with a particular focus on apocalyptic narratives (*The First Urban Christians*, 85–92, 174–78). See also Stowers, "Kinds of Myth, Meals, and Power," 148.

157. Stowers, "The Concept of 'Community' and the History of Early Christianity," 238.

158. Stowers, "Kinds of Myth, Meals, and Power," 109.

159. See, e.g., John S. Kloppenborg, "Greco-Roman *Thiasoi*, the *Ekklēsia* at Corinth, and Conflict Management," in Cameron and Miller, *Redescribing Paul and the Corinthians*, 187–218; idem, "Membership Practices in Pauline Christ Groups," *EC* 4 (2013): 183–215; Stanley K. Stowers, "Does Pauline Christianity Resemble a Hellenistic Philosophy?" in Cameron and Miller, *Redescribing Paul and the Corinthians*, 219–43; Richard Last, *The Pauline Church and the Corinthian Ekklēsia: Greco-Roman Associations in Comparative Context*, SNTSMS 164 (Cambridge: Cambridge University Press, 2016).

first place.[160] Instead I have isolated a number of elements that are consonant with skills, practices, interests, dynamics, and competitive strategies that we have examined in the preceding chapters. Moreover, although doing so has required disaggregating Paul's thought and practices as a heuristic enterprise, this ought not distort the relative coherence of his program. To the contrary, as artifacts of freelance expertise the epistles reveal how seamlessly assorted skills, discourses, and other practices might be interwoven into a composite scheme that demonstrates a need for the specific services Paul offered: purification, character reform, essence change and divinization, the acquisition of specialized religious skills, care for ancestors, salvation or escape from eschatological judgment, and ultimately deification and immortality.

I also wish to preempt the possibility that some who read the arguments of this chapter might wonder whether the upshot is that Paul was a charlatan. There are at least two problems with this question, both of which limit the response to an either/or proposition: *either* we accept Paul's self-presentation as a sincere and disinterested servant of God, *or* we take it on the authority of his so-called opponents that he was a fraud. Many scholars have too readily embraced the characterizations of authors who stood to gain from depicting freelance experts in a negative light. At the same time, Paul's own claims—both those he makes about himself and his negative portrayals of rivals—have been taken largely at face value by modern interpreters when the same benefit of the doubt would not be given to similar first-century actors, most of whom, I imagine, were persuaded by and managed to persuade others of the value and efficacy of their offerings.

Part of the problem stems from the retention of anachronistic or theological language in Pauline scholarship. Most scholars take up the language of "apostle" uncritically, neglecting to reconcile it with the assorted titles that self-authorized experts adopted in order to lend an air of exceptionality to their respective roles and services. Therefore, that Paul and other figures mentioned in his epistles were *apostles*, and not magicians

---

160. As Edmonds writes, "The focus of the Derveni author throughout his treatise is not on doctrinal consistency or even systematic exposition of his cosmological or theological ideas; rather, he focuses again and again upon his own superior ability at exegesis and the importance of making use of his skills to arrive at a true understanding. His treatise is his exhibition of his technique, just as other sophists in the marketplace of ideas made use of the new technology of books to demonstrate and validate their expertise" (*Redefining Ancient Orphism*, 136).

or false prophets, exempts them from the comparative enterprise. The il-logic of this position is especially evident for the elusive Simon Magus, whose calculatedly dismissive epithet is often reproduced in scholarship, thus obscuring his apparent prominence among early experts on Christ. Regardless of whether the accounts of Justin and Irenaeus contain reliable kernels, both are under the impression, and grudgingly admit, that Simon gained such a following at Rome in the time of Claudius that a statue hon-oring him was erected on Tiber Island.[161] Irenaeus strengthens the case against him with fodder from the narrative of Acts, in which Simon at-tempts to purchase and is denied the power of divine *pneuma*.[162]

And yet these characterizations of Simon as a scheming and financially motivated "magician" exploit predictable tropes about freelance experts that were employed by a spectrum of authors, including other participants in the same activity. That Paul comes across as more defensible has much, if not everything, to do with the nature of our evidence: we have his own writings, in which he controls his self-representation and explains his ac-tions, as well as a rich and favorable historiographic tradition about him. Neither of these bodies of evidence supplies reliable criteria for adjudicat-ing self-understanding or sincerity, any more than the portrayals of free-lance religious expertise furnished by Josephus and Lucian.

My efforts to situate Paul among other freelance experts are thus not meant to cast suspicion upon him but rather to demonstrate his many af-finities with these actors. Tacking between the either/or paradigm, I have tried to establish an alternative course that does not require evaluating Paul's sincerity or, for that matter, deciding whether he consciously made choices that promoted his recognition and attraction, adopted different discursive modes, alleged more than one specialty, or designed a robust re-ligious program. The positions he took may have been deliberate choices, or they may have simply reflected his intuitive reasoning and background. Either way, they help us to understand how he would have been received by his audiences, regardless of whether the role they slotted him into was

---

161. Justin, 1 *Apol.* 26.1–2; Irenaeus, *Haer.* 1.23.1. The statue, which Justin says bore the in-scription "To Simon, the holy god" (*Simoni Deo Sancto*), was discovered in the sixteenth century and honors not Simon but the Sabine deity "Semo Sancus, the god of truth" (*Semoni Sanco Deo Fidio*).

162. Acts 8:18–20. For the scholarship on Simon, see Wayne A. Meeks, "Simon Magus in Recent Research," *RelSR* 3 (1977): 137–42; Stephen Haar, *Simon Magus: The First Gnostic?* BZNW 119 (Berlin: de Gruyter, 2003).

that of Judean prophet, ethical teacher, philosopher, diviner, mystery initiator, or some combination thereof. More than anything the epistles demand that we refrain from dogmatism in our depictions of any of these types. Paul was a kind of expert in Judean religion who had a demonstrable facility with practices and concepts generally associated with philosophers and other kinds of teachers, as well as with initiators in the mysteries of foreign gods. The elements of his religious program, which could be parceled into a number of categories—mystery cults, philosophy, Judaism, or Christianity—were mutually entailing.

5

Christian Rivals Within the Framework of Freelance Expertise

IN THE PRECEDING chapters I have established a framework for theorizing the religion of freelance experts that moves beyond distinctions drawn between its participants on the basis of particular skills, titles, ethnic coding, or the content of their programs. Thus far I have been more interested in the activities of individual experts operating outside existing religious institutions than in the range of more institutional social formations—private temples, voluntary associations, schools of instruction, and so forth—that might plausibly have arisen from the former. The purpose of this final chapter, then, is to begin to explore the connections between freelance expertise and groups or institutions that might owe their genesis to this class of religious activity. Indeed, there is a tantalizing coincidence in the growth and diversification of freelance religious expertise over the course of the first century and the emergence of new or more discernible religious phenomena sometime during the second. Within roughly the same time frame, for example, the record of religious practices involving Mithras and Christ becomes both more plentiful and richer, if not yet as regularized or commonplace as either will be toward the end of that century, into the third.[1] Given the abundance of Persian and

---

1. The earliest epigraphic evidence for Mithras is typically dated c. 80–120 CE. See Beck, "The Mysteries of Mithras," 117–19; Richard L. Gordon, "Mithraism and Roman Society," *Religion* 2 (1972): 92–121. For the late-second or third-century dating of Roman *mithraea*, see L. Michael White, "The Changing Face of Mithraism at Ostia: Archaeology, Art, and the Urban Landscape," in *Contested Spaces: Houses and Temples in Roman Antiquity and the New Testament*, ed. David L. Balch and Annette Weissenreider, WUNT 285 (Tübingen: Mohr Siebeck, 2012), 435–92.

Judean religious specialists attested in the first century, it is worthwhile to consider whether there is a relationship between these actors and later Persian- and Judean-themed forms of religion that are better understood as types of voluntary associations.

In this final chapter I propose that the context of freelance expertise offers a tenable social setting for investigating the "origins" of religious phenomena first attested in the first and second centuries but one that necessarily transforms how such quests for origins have been formulated. In my view, the explanatory potential of the evidence for freelance experts has been overlooked in at least two areas of scholarship. Neither have we fully appreciated their contributions to broader religious transformations that occurred during the Roman Empire, nor has the prominence of this class of activity in the first and second centuries been given sufficient consideration in scholarship on the emergence of specific religious groups or institutions more visible in later periods.

Building on my arguments for placing Paul and his fellow apostles within this framework, I offer preliminary suggestions of how it may enrich our understanding of competition among second-century "Christian" experts, including the widening chasm between Judeans and Christians—as a category of actors apart from Judean religion—that characterize this time. A number of recent publications have addressed these topics with great sophistication. Most, however, begin from some premise of groups and leadership, with less attention to the individuals responsible for assembling the composite religious programs attested in the sources, for designating the markers of "real" expertise within these areas, for diffusing proprietary religious teachings and discourses of difference, and for attracting regular followers. Using rival Christian teachers at Rome as my primary example, I reorient investigations into the origins and development of early Christianity into a more profitable methodological endeavor: a sort of origins account whose outcome is not an exact historical moment, figure, or genealogy but instead a delimited class of religious activity that is not specific to Christians yet accommodates and explains the dynamics apparent in Christian sources, defined broadly. In so doing I am not reducing the yields of this larger study to the problem of Christian origins; rather, as was the case with the Pauline Epistles, the value of turning now to these texts lies in the light they shed on freelance expertise more generally and how particular participants navigated its challenges and possibilities.

A Territory to Partition

It has become a scholarly commonplace that second-century sources point not only to tremendous variety among self-identifying Christians but also to complex negotiations between Christians and assorted opponents against whom they defined themselves, particularly Jews and philosophers. The problem of how to adequately represent such diversity is, as Karen L. King has observed, that the selective characteristics that inform our scholarly categories tend to give the impression of a well-bounded homogeneity within imagined groups, while also creating overly sharp external distinctions between them.[2] King observes further that the constructedness of these categories—for her, principally orthodoxy, heresy, and Gnosticism—is too easily forgotten, with the result that such bounded, distinct groups are read into the second-century evidence, when texts from this period might instead reflect efforts to form and maintain groups through discursive productions of difference.

Likewise attentive to how certain authors employed discourses to draw, reinscribe, and police the boundaries between Jews and Christians, Daniel Boyarin locates around the time of Justin Martyr the emergence, first, of Christianity, and, later, Judaism as distinct categories for religious practice.[3] Training her lens on second-century intellectuals, Kendra Eshleman aligns intra-Christian contestations about religious authority with debates among philosophers, teachers, and doctors engaged in parallel processes of self-definition and legitimation. "Christians, sophists, and philosophers," she explains, "faced a common problem: the need to demarcate the boundaries of a group in which membership was highly desirable (at least in some quarters), but poorly defined and institutionally fluid. In response . . . they brought to bear an illuminatingly similar repertoire of social strategies that start from the assumption that affiliations map affinities and can thus be used both to evaluate and to revise identity claims."[4]

---

2. Karen L. King, "Factions, Variety, Diversity, Multiplicity: Representing Early Christian Differences for the 21st Century," *MTSR* 23 (2011): 216–37, at 223. See also idem, *What Is Gnosticism?* (Cambridge: Harvard University Press, 2003), esp. 20–54; idem, "Which Early Christianity?" in *Oxford Handbook of Early Christianity*, ed. Susan Ashbrook Harvey and David G. Hunter (New York: Oxford University Press, 2008), 66–84, esp. 71–72; Michael Williams, *Rethinking Gnosticism: An Argument for Dismantling a Dubious Category* (Princeton: Princeton University Press, 1996).

3. See Boyarin, *Border Lines* with further elaboration in "Rethinking Jewish Christianity: An Argument for Dismantling a Dubious Category," *JQR* 99 (2009): 7–36.

4. Eshleman, *The Social World of Intellectuals in the Roman Empire*, 15.

The work of King, Boyarin, and Eshleman are but three examples, though most notable ones, of a growing body of scholarship that approaches literature of the second century with a view to how the discursive efforts of various kinds of writer-intellectuals gave rise henceforth to impressions of coherent and essentially distinct concepts of Christianity, Judaism, and Gnosticism, orthodoxy and heresy, and disciplines of philosophy, medicine, and law. I find these arguments compelling and would suggest that the context of freelance expertise supplies an even more exact sense of both the field in which such labors were undertaken and to what ends. That is, the important contributions of these scholars stand to be enriched by recognition, to employ a popular metaphor, of the precise "territory" whose borders were being drawn through the strategies they identify. Placing the discursive contestations of self-authorized experts within the particular social arena that I have delimited in this study allows us to model "diversity" first at the level of individual actors rather than the social formations they ostensibly, but do not necessarily, represent. For despite their focus on specific authors who illustrate these dynamics, the primary units of analysis for most studies of early Christianity remain groups—religious communities, churches (or *the* Church), schools, or voluntary associations—when much of the evidence points instead to intense rivalries between would-be experts whose rhetoric and interests, King reminds us, may or may not reflect such entities.

Christian Competition as the Religion of Freelance Experts

As I have argued throughout this study, religious experts of the early imperial period participated in a common form of religious activity that encompassed a range of skills and practices that could be purveyed in isolation or bundled together in more complex and ambitious configurations. Expertise in religion was but one dimension of a wider field of specialty that was characterized as a whole by common dynamics and interactivity among specialists of similar ability. Paul's was one such comprehensive religious program, the contents of which he elaborated through the exegesis of prophecies and mythic episodes from inspired writings, as well as various philosophical discourses: an applied theory of divine *pneuma*, narratives about moral decline, concepts of moral failure and progress, and techniques for self-mastery. His myth-making was inseparable from initiation into the mysteries of Christ through baptism, the effects of which would spare those now "in Christ" from a human condition and eschatology that he articulated. All of these claims were situated within a broader concept of Judean religion in which Paul alleged expertise, even as he discouraged certain elements for his *gentile* audiences. Judean religion, in this sense, was not an isolated specialty but was analogous to other foreign religious offerings or to intellectual programs rooted in foreign texts. Furthermore, someone such as Paul might also have more in common with experts claiming alternate "traditions"—Pythagorean, Orphic, Hermetic, Zoroastrian—or working within other cultural milieus—Greek, Egyptian, Persian, Chaldaean—than with Judean experts who lacked his abilities and interests.

The skills and strategies on which Paul relied to construct his religious authority continued to define the offerings of many second-century "Christian" experts, as did other qualities and practices typically associated with freelance expertise. Even prior to the second century, however, there are indications of contact between post-Pauline authorities on Christ and this wider phenomenon. In chapter 2 I argued that historical developments of the Flavian era accrued value to certain forms of Judean religion, namely, those purveyed by specialists and predicated on writings. It is no accident, I think, that our historical record of "Christian" writings— by which, following Radcliffe G. Edmonds III's definition of Orphica, I simply mean any texts that somehow feature Christ or contain themes commonly related to him—expands considerably in the last decades of the first century, into the second, as do independent witnesses to Christ devotees of the sort found in the writings of Pliny, Tacitus, and Suetonius. The sheer quantity of this literature compared to earlier in the first century is remarkable and, for most authors' particular uses of Judean prophecy, might be seen to confirm the effects that I postulated earlier.

Beyond the expansion of the Christian literary record within this window, the texts themselves yield a number of clues that help to locate their authors within the context of freelance religious expertise. The most obvious is the broad assortment of rivals who crop up in these texts and how the texts themselves are implicated in promoting and safeguarding their authors' own authority and teachings over and against those of any other. The Pastoral Epistles are preoccupied with myths and endless genealogies, with those who desire to be instructors of the law without understanding what they are saying or the matters about which they make assertions, and with any who pay attention to Judaic myths or to the commandments of people who reject the truth, among other complaints.[5] As the author of 1 Timothy assures the letter's eponymous recipient, whereas Timothy's actions accord with prophecies made about him, others among the faithful, Hymenaeus and Alexander, have been relinquished to Satan.[6] These are hardly the only early Christian texts to address such concerns. While detailing the beastly punishments that await him, Ignatius cautions the Smyrneans of wild beasts in human form, who have been convinced neither by the words of the prophets nor the law of Moses and who deny that Jesus Christ bore human flesh.[7] And while he *could* indict such people personally, Ignatius assures his readers, he sees no reason to even record their disbelieving names in writing.[8] To Polycarp he advises, "Do not allow those who appear trustworthy yet who deliver contrary teachings daze you," and later in the same letter, "Flee the evil arts; indeed, deliver a teaching about them."[9]

Many of these statements might be characterized as intramural contestations among diverse kinds of experts in Judean religion, insofar as their authors continue to appeal to the authority of Judean writings, even while taking contrary positions on notable Judean practices.[10] Tellingly, most indications of competition in this literature have to do with the integrity and interpretation of these texts, whether they were put to the task of prophecy,

---

5. 1 Tim 1:3–4, 7; Tit 1:13–14. From these, the author continues, come envy, wordy disputation, blasphemy, and useless "hidden senses" (ὑπόνοιαι πονηραί), the last item of which, interestingly, was a recognized technical term for allegorical reading methods. On ὑπόνοια see Struck, *Birth of the Symbol*, esp. 42–43, 145–58. See also Bart D. Ehrman, *Forgery and Counterforgery: The Use of Literary Deceit in Early Christian Polemics* (New York: Oxford University Press, 2013); Benjamin White, "How to Read a Book: Irenaeus and the Pastoral Epistles Reconsidered," *VC* 65 (2011): 125–49; Wendt, "Galatians 3:1 as an Allusion to Textual Prophecy," 387–88.

6. 1 Tim. 1:18–20.

7. Ignatius, *Smyrn.* 4.1.

8. Ignatius, *Smyrn.* 5.3.

9. Ignatius, *Poly.* 3.1, 5.1 (trans. Bart D. Ehrman, LCL).

10. For similar arguments regarding Jewish/Judean diversity and the relationship between texts and constructions of religious authority, see Charlotte Elisheva Fonrobert, "The *Didascalia Apostolorum:* A Mishnah for the Disciples of Jesus," *JECS* 9 (2001): 483–509. As Fonrobert writes, "That shared project [of Jewish and Christian writers] may be identified as laying claim to the inheritance of Scripture and the divine promise and will enshrined in it. ... That shared project is, therefore the construction of an *authoritative* and hence persuasive voice for the interpretation of those Scriptures and the meaning of the divine will. Neither the rabbis nor the author of the *Didascalia*, nor most Jewish or Christian authors of the formative centuries, simply *have* or own such authority which we attribute to them retrospectively" (486).

genealogical speculation, or myth-making.[11] The fervent insistence of a second-century writer such as Justin that Christ fulfilled all prophecies in the Judean writings might be seen to capitalize deliberately on their recognized oracular value.[12] Indeed, echoes of the Flavian prophecy are unmistakable when he attributes to Moses the prophecy that "a ruler shall not fail from Judah . . . and he shall be the expectation of the nations, binding his foal to the vine, washing his garment in the blood of the grape."[13] Only now it is Justin, not Josephus, who delivers the superior interpreter of the prophecy and Christ to whom it points. Naturally, previous interpreters "did not accurately understand the things they heard through the prophets, but imitated in erring fashion the things concerning our Christ."

In his *Dialogue with Trypho*, Justin is even starker in his claim that Christians have wrested from Judeans exegetical authority over the oracles contained in these writings. Considering such engagements with Judean ethnicity and ethnically coded practices in the context of this study allows us to see them even more clearly as a series of position-takings among rival specialists. These sources also raise interesting possibilities with respect to the sort of complex category negotiations whose effects are observable for other ethnic or geographic subsets of freelance expertise (e.g., Persian, Chaldean) but whose exact processes and stakes are not attested for lack of the same quality of evidence. That is, the discursive negotiations of Judean-ness about which Boyarin and others have written might represent a more general tendency for the strong ethnic or geographic connotations of certain practices to wane in inverse proportion to the number of specialists offering them, and in different configurations. In light of the complex and differential ways that freelance experts utilized ethnically coded

---

11. See Judith M. Lieu, *Christian Identity in the Jewish and Graeco-Roman World* (New York: Oxford University Press, 2004), esp. 38–40.

12. Esp. Justin, 1 *Apol.* 32.1–42.1. See, e.g., Oskar Skarsaune, *The Proof from Prophecy: A Study in Justin Martyr's Proof-Text Tradition: Text-Type, Provenance, Theological Profile* (Leiden: Brill, 1987). Justin is but one example among many writers and texts of the late first and second centuries to insist that Jesus fulfills all Judean prophecies. In addition to the gospels, especially Matthew with its distinctive fulfillment citations, the author of the *Epistle of Barnabas*, like Justin, advocates a departure from notable Judean customs and literal exegesis of the texts while insisting that all the prophets prophesied of Jesus. For an excellent discussion of this text and other contestations over scriptural authority and interpretation, see Maren R. Niehoff, "A Jewish Critique of Christianity from Second-Century Alexandria: Revisiting the Jew Mentioned in *Contra Celsum*," *JECS* 21 (2013): 151–75, esp. 171–75.

13. Justin, 1 *Apol.* 54.2–6 (trans. Minns and Parvis).

practices and writings, the assorted stances of Justin, Marcion, Ptolemy, and other second-century teachers vis-à-vis Judean practices and experts might mirror dynamics among other specialists claiming a common cultural idiom or specialty. Indeed, one wonders how different these exegetical rivalries really were from the ones found in the Derveni papyrus. Of course much had taken place in Judea in the decades that separated Paul from these writers who consciously identify as Christians. First and foremost, oracles in the Judean writings had apparently been enlisted once again, and in a very high-profile way, to legitimate a leader coming forth from Judea, this time Simon bar Kokhba.[14] Whether out of expediency or necessity, one can imagine how specialists in Judean religion, broadly construed, might have sought to distance themselves from the province, even as they retained Judean texts.[15]

Intramural and Extramural Contestations

By the middle decades of the second century, and maybe, as we would expect, given an intensified interest in Judean writings from the final decades of the first, it seems that the contours of "Judean religion" within the specific context of freelance expertise had broadened—or else narrowed,

---

14. For an overview of the Bar Kokhba Revolt, see Hanan Eshel, "The Bar Kokhba Revolt, 132–135," in *The Cambridge History of Judaism, Vol. 4: The Late Roman-Rabbinic Period,* ed. Steven T. Katz (New York: Cambridge University Press, 2006), 105–27. For scholarly debates regarding the revolt's causes, events, and consequences, see, e.g., Peter Schäfer, *Der Bar Kokhba-Aufstand* (Tübingen: Mohr Siebeck, 1981); idem, "Hadrian's Policy in Judea and the Bar Kokhba Revolt: A Reassessment," in *A Tribute to Geza Vermes: Essays on Jewish and Christian Literature and History,* ed. Philip R. Davies and Richard T. White, JSOT Suppl. 100 (Sheffield: Sheffield Academic Press, 1990), 281–303; Werner Eck, "The Bar Kokhba Revolt: The Roman Point of View," *JRS* (1999): 76–89; Peter Schäfer, ed., *The Bar Kokhba War Reconsidered: New Perspectives on the Second Jewish Revolt Against Rome* (Tübingen: Mohr Siebeck, 2003); Giovanni Battista Bazzana, "The Bar Kokhba Revolt and Hadrian's Religious Policy," in *Hadrian and the Christians,* ed. Marco Rizzi, Millenium–Studien 30 (Berlin: de Gruyter, 2010), 85–109. Even before the Bar Kokhba Revolt the Diaspora Revolts of 115–117 CE had exacerbated tensions between Judeans and local populations in Egypt, especially Alexandria. Many have argued that these events were points of rupture between Judeans and Christians in Alexandria. See, e.g., Miriam Pucci Ben Zeev, "The Uprisings in the Jewish Diaspora," in Katz, *The Cambridge History of Judaism,* 93–104; Birger A. Pearson, "Cracking a Conundrum: Christian Origins in Egypt," *ST* 57 (2003): 61–75.

15. For consideration of the effects of the Bar Kokhba Revolt on negotiations of Judean religious expertise, including self-identifying Christians as a subset thereof, see Heidi Wendt, "From Herodians to Hadrian: The Shifting Status of Judean Religion in Post-Flavian Rome," *Forum* (forthcoming 2017).

depending on how one looks at it—with contestations among would-be experts occurring primarily along the lines of literary exegesis and production. This is not the same degree of ethnic coding that one finds in the Pauline Epistles, where Judean ancestry is indispensable to the form of expertise Paul claims. Rather, exegesis of Judean writings seems to have become a thing unto itself, irrespective of the interpreter's own ethnic credentials, so to speak. In some cases, the texts themselves might be the only ethnicizing element of a specialist's offering.[16] It is at this time, I would suggest, that this study converges with the aforementioned scholarship on the discursive production of difference among intellectualizing experts, Judeans and Christians especially, through writing, literary interpretation, and other intellectual practices.

Yet for an understandable focus on relations between Judeans and self-identifying Christians, it is often overlooked how many Christian writings from this period vilify other kinds of specialists nearly as often as "heretics" and Judeans or "Judaizers." In addition to assorted examples from Acts, the Didache urges readers neither to practice divination, magic, or sorcery nor to use incantations, astrology, or rites of purification, nor even to wish to see or hear these things.[17] This author also supplies criteria for how an audience that is unequivocally receptive to iterant teachers, apostles, and prophets thus far unknown to them might discern those who come in the name of the lord from "charlatans."[18]

Justin alludes or refers explicitly to any number of experts whom I would include in my category of freelance expertise: philosophers, named and generic individuals, as well as schools of thought; Judean teachers or exegetes; non-Judean (and non-Christian) exegetes of Judean writings; and mystery initiators, in addition to Christian "heretics." While Trypho and the Judean specialists he represents are Justin's primary focus in the *Dialogue*, he implies that Judean texts are also read by other kinds of experts, in relation to divinities other than Christ. Explaining to Trypho that Jesus's birth in a cave in Bethlehem fulfilled an aforementioned prophecy

---

16. Cf. Bruce Chilton, "Justin and Israelite Prophecy," in *Justin Martyr and His Worlds*, ed. Sara Parvis and Paul Foster (Minneapolis: Fortress, 2007), 77–87; Tessa Rajak, "Talking at Trypho: Christian Apologetic as Anti-Judaism in Justin's *Dialogue with Trypho the Jew*," in *The Jewish Dialogue with Greece and Rome: Studies in Cultural and Social Interaction*, AGJU 48 (Leiden: Brill, 2001), 511–33.

17. Acts 16:6, 19:18–19; Didache 3.4.

18. Didache 11.2.

in Isaiah, he adds that by these same words those who transmit the mysteries of Mithras were urged by the Devil to declare that they were initiated by Mithras himself in a place they call a cave.[19]

What are we to make of Justin's remark about the appropriation of the Judean writings by literate specialists who read them in relation to Mithras? On the one hand, the claim is germane to Justin's oft-repeated refrain that Moses is older than all poets and philosophers and therefore that their myths, prophecies, and intellectual traditions are derivative of his books. Hence we might regard with suspicion the image of Mithras initiators finding in Isaiah further evidence for the cosmogony of their god and the rite to which this story lent meaning. On the other, interactions between Judean and Persian experts and texts are not inconceivable in the context of freelance expertise, where the exegesis of inspired writings was put to the task of contemporary myth-making quite liberally and at the discretion of individual exegetes.[20] Notably, Justin also mentions "Greek" and "Persian" texts—the books of the Sibyl and Hystaspes, respectively—when he notes the penalty of being caught with these or the Judean prophets in one's possession. Likewise, the earlier prophecy about Christ has been misconstrued by Greek poets (possibly Orphics). It is therefore tempting to entertain the possibility that specialists whose religious programs were oriented around different gods or semi-divine figures, and undergirded by different narratives of human defect and remedy, might seek corroboration for their teachings in a range of prophetic writings. Just as Justin himself finds Christ adumbrated by symbols scattered throughout the writings of Plato, what would preclude non-Christian literate specialists from discerning that their proprietary wisdom was foreshadowed in the famed Judean oracles?

An even more assorted crop of freelance experts appears in Justin's *Apologies,* where he argues that an emperor who is persuaded by those who conjure the dead (νεκρομαντεῖαι), *magoi* and their assistants (πάρεδροι),

---

19. Justin, *Dial.* 78.6.

20. To the contrary, the extant *Sibylline Oracles*, with their distinctive blends of Greek and Judean motifs, may offer concrete examples of this sort of scenario. See John J. Collins, "The Jewish Transformation of the Sibylline Oracles," in *Sibille e Linguaggi oracolari: Mito, storia, tradizione: Atti del convegno internazionale di studi Macerata-Norcia, 20–24 Settembre 1994,* ed. Ileana Chirassi Colombo and Tullio Seppilli (Rome: Istituti Editoriali e Poligrafici Internazionali, 1998), 369–87; J. L. Lightfoot, *The Sibylline Oracles: With Introduction, Translation, and Commentary on the First and Second Books,* 219–53; Wendt, "The Fate of the Judean Writings in Flavian Rome," 108–9.

dream-senders (ὀνειροπομποί), and philosophers should be willing to entertain Christian teachings.[21] Justin also concedes that certain philosophers have, at times, deservedly received punishment without compromising more esteemed philosophers or the schools with which the culprits claimed affiliation.[22] Hence he proposes criteria for discerning "true" Christians from those who might pose as such but who actually deserve the punishments being inflicted indiscriminately on anyone by that name.[23] Later he foretells his own demise at the hand of Crescens, "that lover of noise and empty praise, for it would not be right to call such man a lover of wisdom (sc. a philosopher) since, to gratify and please the erring multitude, he publicly testifies about things of which he knows nothing, namely that Christians are godless and irreligious."[24]

On the subject of punishment, Justin's story of the Christian teacher Ptolemy, who was investigated and put to death at the instigation of a man whose wife divorced him after receiving Christian instruction, bears an uncanny resemblance to Josephus's account of Egyptian and Judean religious experts who were similarly punished.[25] While Justin's narrative differs in perspective, the two share a number of structural affinities: a specialist in novel religious practices or teachings influences a woman, whose husband reports him to a Roman authority on charges of adultery or theft. Although one might assume that the prefect of Justin's story, if reliable, punished Christians due to their religious beliefs, I find it more plausible that he took "Christians" to be akin to *magi, mathematici*, Chaldeans, Judeans, and others of their ilk.[26] Since, as many scholars have proposed, this Ptolemy may be one and the same as the Valentinian teacher whose *Epistle to Flora* is preserved by Epiphanius, the story also serves as a reminder that normative conceptions of Christian teachings (and teachers) were perpetually in flux during the second century and liable to be formulated differently as a matter of perspective.[27] Both Ptolemies are attested at

---

21. Justin 1 *Apol.* 18.3–6.

22. Justin 1 *Apol.* 4.7–8.

23. Justin 1 *Apol.* 26.1–5.

24. Justin 2 *Apol.* 8.1–2.

25. Justin, 2 *Apol.* 2.1–20.

26. See Wendt, "Christian Martyrdom and the Religion of Freelance Experts," 197.

27. Ptolemy, *Letter to Flora* apud Epiphanius, *Panarion* 33.3.3–10. For arguments that the two teachers named Ptolemy are the same person, see Peter Lampe, *From Paul to*

Rome within the same period and instructed women of social standing on matters of marriage and divorce. If one entertains the possibility that they the same person, then Ptolemy's conflicting status for Justin—a known denouncer of "heretics" who nevertheless decries the teacher's unjust execution in the *Second Apology*—and for later heresiologists is revealing of how quickly and unpredictably these lines might be redrawn.[28]

These examples, which could be multiplied considerably, offer a preliminary sense of how many Christian sources from the late first and second centuries continue to betray dynamics of competition with a broad spectrum of specialists. Although it exceeds the chronological scope of this study, there are reasons to suspect that these dynamics persist well into the third. In a rather striking statement, Tertullian admits that even though Christians pose no problem to Roman authorities, there are certain people who may truly complain of suffering losses on their account: *venenarii, magi, haruspices, harioli,* and *mathematici.* "To be unprofitable to people such as these," he qualifies, "is in itself profitable."[29] Inasmuch as all varieties of freelance experts rivaled one another for clients interested in ostensibly novel or exotic wisdom, texts, divinatory methods, and other religious practices, Tertullian's remark divulges the place of Christians within a checkered lot of experts and skills, even at a time when certain Christian groups were acquiring a more institutional bearing.

Across the aisle, Christians make notable appearances in Lucian's biographies of Alexander and Peregrinus: the former tangles with them, along with Epicureans, in public settings and explicitly excludes both from his mysteries; the latter, as we saw, takes a turn as one of their leaders, interpreting their books and even composing new ones.[30] If Lucian's

---

Valentinus: Christians at Rome in the First Two Centuries, trans. Michael Steinhauser, ed. Marshall D. Johnson (Minneapolis: Fortress, 2003), 238–40; Ismo Dunderberg, "Valentinian Teachers at Rome," in *Christians as a Religious Minority in a Multicultural City: Modes of Interaction and Identity Formation in Early Imperial Rome,* ed. Jürgen Zangenberg and Michael Labin (London: T&T Clark, 2004), 157–74, at 163; idem, *Beyond Gnosticism: Myth, Lifestyle, and Society in the School of Valentinus* (New York: Columbia University Press, 2008), 90–92 and n. 97.

28. For Justin's denunciation of Valentinians, see *Dial.* 35; Dunderberg, "Valentinian Teachers in Rome," 159.

29. Tertullian, *Apol.* 43. Elsewhere Tertullian writes that the followers of Marcion are for the most part *mathematici* because they make their living from the stars of the demiurge (*Adv. Marc.* 1.18).

30. Lucian, *Alex.* 25, 38; *Pergr.* 11–13.

interlocutor Celsus, who wrote a book exposing the *magoi*, is also the
Celsus of a work denouncing Christians, then their inclusion among the
sort of actors whom these authors take pains to disparage is striking.[31]
Galen mentions Christians on a few occasions, once as a foil in their gull-
ibility to overly dogmatic doctors and philosophers and another time for
drawing their beliefs from parables and miracles, in contrast to philosophers of a more empirical inclination (though he is willing to concede
that Christians sometimes act the part of those who practice philosophy).[32]
Elsewhere he notes that certain doctors liken those who practice medicine
without scientific knowledge to Moses, who composed his laws by divine
inspiration, without offering "proof." And yet, as H. Gregory Snyder has
observed, Galen's insistence on proof and the proper use of texts is mir-
rored suspiciously by Justin's characterization of Judean literary prophecies as "proof" in support of Christian teachings.[33] Both, moreover,
enjoyed overlapping sojourns at Rome, where Galen regularly gave public
intellectual demonstrations, including in competitive textual exegesis.[34]

Rival Christian Intellectuals
in Second-Century Rome

Although specialists were hardly limited to Rome, any number of them,
and a striking number of would-be Christian ones, found their way there

---

31. For Celsus, see Michael Frede, "Celsus's Attack on the Christians," in *Philosophia Togata
II: Plato and Aristotle at Rome*, ed. Jonathan Barnes and Miriam T. Griffin (Oxford: Clarendon,
1997), 232–40; Robert Louis Wilken, *The Christians as the Romans Saw Them*, 2nd ed. (New
Haven: Yale University Press, 2003), 94–125. On Celsus's possible use in *The True Doctrine*
of an earlier Judean source, see Niehoff, "A Jewish Critique of Christianity from Second-
Century Alexandria," 154–59. If Niehoff is correct in affirming the existence of such a source,
this only strengthens the evidence that certain Christians participated in a broader network
of writer-intellectuals, regardless of whether the latter were acting as freelance religious
experts.

32. Galen, *Puls. diff.* 2.4, 3.3. For these passages and others that mention followers of Christ,
see Richard Walzer, *Galen on Jews and Christians* (Oxford: Oxford University Press, 1949),
10–16; Wilken, *The Christians as the Romans Saw Them*, 68–83.

33. H. Gregory Snyder, "The Classroom in the Text: Exegetical Practices in Justin and
Galen," in *Christian Origins and Greco-Roman Culture: Social and Literary Contexts for the New
Testament*, ed. Stanley E. Porter and Andrew W. Pitts (Leiden Brill, 2013), 663–85, esp. 664–
65. See also M. J. Edwards, "On the Platonic Schooling of Justin Martyr," *JTS* 42 (1991): 17–34.

34. Often while lecturing in front of the Templum Pacis, in the library of which Galen is
thought to have kept a number of books, including works in progress. See Galen, *Comp.
Med.* 1; *Libr. Propr.* 2; Neudecker, "Archives, Books, and Sacred Space in Rome," 328–29.

in the second century. I have argued that the capital was, punitive risks aside, highly conducive to this sort of religious activity, especially to intellectualizing offerings couched in the exotic.[35] Rome is thus an especially evocative setting in which to imagine the interactions between the many Christian experts who converged on the capital in the middle part of the second century.[36] The roster includes but is not limited to Marcion, Apelles, Syneros, Lucanus, Valentinus, Ptolemy, Marcus, Hegessipus, Justin, Tatian, and Irenaeus, not to mention the earlier "apostolic" bishops and presbyters chronicled by some of these writers.[37] This list builds on a not insignificant quantity of first-century specialists: Paul and his many named associates, apparently Simon (so-called *magus*), Menander, and maybe other apostles about whom later traditions would form. If the time frame is extended later then many others who spent time or were based permanently in Rome join the ranks of these earlier figures.

I suggest that this evidence for second-century Christian diversity at Rome maps neatly onto the terrain of freelance religious expertise as I have delimited it. One area of this class of activity would comprise

---

35. For the Roman Christian evidence, see Jürgen Zangenberg and Michael Labin, eds., *Christians as a Religious Minority in a Multicultural City: Modes of Interaction and Identity Formation in Early Imperial Rome*, (London: T&T Clark, 2004); Einar Thomassen, "Orthodoxy and Heresy in Second-Century Rome," *HTR* 97 (2004): 241–56.

36. As Lampe aptly remarks, "To work inductively on the level of local history means to move from the level of the empire down to the individual cities—*and* later to compile data from the individual cities, to compare them and thus to advance to more general statements. Rome as the capital city might be . . . more representative for the entire empire than other cities. For Tacitus the history of the empire is portrayed to a great extent as the history of the city of Rome. *How* representative the social history of Christianity in the city of Rome was for ancient Christianity as a whole, however, will first become apparent when more studies from other parts of the empire are produced" (*From Paul to Valentinus*, 409). For the value of local histories, see also King, "Representing Early Christian Differences for the 21st Century," 233.

37. For the chronology of Marcion's time in Rome, see Paul Foster, "Marcion: His Life, Works, Beliefs, and Impact," *ExpTim* 121 (2010): 269–80. For Valentinus and his students in Rome, see Dunderberg, "Valentinian Teachers in Rome," 159–60 and n. 15; Einar Thomassen, *The Spiritual Seed: The Church of the "Valentinians,"* Nag Hammadi and Manichaean Studies 60 (Leiden: Brill, 2006). For Justin in Rome, see H. Gregory Synder, "'Above the Bath of Myrtinus': Justin Martyr's 'School' in the City of Rome," *HTR* 100 (2007): 335–62. For Irenaeus's probable stay in the city in the middle part of the second century, en route to Lyons from Smyrna, see Jared Secord, "Irenaeus at Rome: The Greek Context of Christian Intellectual Life in the Second Century," in *Irénée entre Asie et Occident*, ed. Agnès Bastit-Kalinowska, Collection des Études Augustiniennes (Turnhout: Brepols, forthcoming). For all other figures, see Lampe, *From Paul to Valentinus*, and Antti Marjanen and Petri Luomanen, eds., *A Companion to Second-Century Christian "Heretics,"* Suppl. to Vigiliae Christianae 76 (Leiden: Brill, 2005).

writer-intellectuals such as Marcion, Justin, Valentinus, and Irenaeus, while other areas or subsets would comprise nontextual diviners, inspired prophets, exorcists, and Christian experts whose practices need not emphasize writings or at least not to the same degree.[38] Due to the nature and survival of the evidence, the former experts are attested more plentifully than the latter types, though we should be cautious about presuming on a priori grounds that the activities of intellectualizing experts were the dominant form of "Christian religion" in this period.[39] Nevertheless, the proximity and mutual awareness of rival Christian writer-intellectuals at Rome is remarkable, even though the capital was but one of many places where such figures might encounter one another or one another's followers.[40]

Although rival Christian experts denounced one another in harsh polemics, they were also mutually aware of and knowledgeable about one another's practices and writings. Insofar as Rome was thick with ancient libraries, book vendors, and other writer-intellectuals, it is reasonable to surmise that Christian writers were part of a broader literary network that involved the exchange of writings, even if only for the purpose of disparaging the work of a rival in favor of one's own.[41] "As co-members of a small and marginal movement," Snyder postulates, "their 'social distance' would be less than

38. For less specialized but still literate divinatory practices, see, e.g., AnneMarie Luijendijk, *Forbidden Oracles? The Gospel of the Lots of Mary*, Studien und Texte zu Antike und Christentum (Tübingen: Mohr Siebeck, 2014).

39. Writings are notably absent, for example, from Pliny's description of Christian practices as they were confessed to him by the Christians whom he interrogated in Pontus and Bythinia.

40. Cities such as Alexandria, Ephesus, and Smyrna were also prominent sites for freelance expertise and also seem to have drawn numerous Christian experts. See the discussion of Irenaeus's encounters with Valentian groups scattered throughout the empire in Dunderberg, "Valentinian teachers at Rome," 158. For awareness of Christian writings among other writer-intellectuals, see, again, Niehoff, "A Jewish Critique of Christianity from Second-Century Alexandria," 159–71.

41. Eshleman, *The Social World of Intellectuals in the Roman Empire*, esp. 149–76, 213–58. See also H. Gregory Snyder, *Teachers and Texts in the Ancient World: Philosophers, Jews, and Christians*, Religion in the First Christian Centuries (New York: Routledge, 2000); Bazzana, "Early Christian Missionaries as Physicians," passim; Daniel Ullucci, *The Christian Rejection of Sacrifice* (New York: Oxford University Press, 2011); Richard Last, "The Social Relationships of Gospel Writers: New Insights from Inscriptions Commending Greek Historiographers," *JSNT* 37 (2015): 223–52.

their 'as-the-crow-flies' distance."[42] In other words, our evidence of their conflicts only tells part of a story that seems to have entailed rich and regular interaction, not only among Christians but also between Christian and other participants in the wider phenomenon of freelance expertise. So too are the spaces in which Christian religious activities unfolded—primarily private homes but possibly also public venues where specialists were known to cluster and compete—continuous with the social contexts that we have encountered in preceding chapters.[43]

Ismo Dunderberg offers an excellent illustration of these overlapping social spheres in his study of the myth-making of Valentinus and his students. In particular, he shows how features of the general Valentinian cosmogony, as best as it can be reconstructed, projected into the mythic realm a philosophically nuanced narrative of the very source of human defect that Valentinian teachings then remedied through the therapy of emotions. "[I]t does not have to be assumed that Valentinus was taught by Stoic teachers of philosophy," he writes. Rather, "The idea of cosmic sympathy was common coin in antiquity, and also other Stoic cosmological views were embraced by many non-Stoic authors in the Roman era."[44] *Comparanda* for this particular combination of philosophical thought and religious activity are found in the *Corpus Hermeticum*, whose authors drew similarly upon elements of Stoic cosmology to elaborate a distinctly Egyptian-themed narrative that warranted the various religious practices connected to it. Dunderberg notes further correlations between the gradated levels of instruction available to Valentinian and Hermetic students, with more profound teachings revealed incrementally as one progressed along a path of wisdom.[45]

These affinities between Christian and non-Christian specialists went beyond mere resemblances in representations and discourses. In the

---

42. Snyder, "Justin Martyr's 'School' in the City of Rome," 361. Snyder puts forth the intriguing suggestion that Justin's school was located near the Porta Capena, nearby to where the Flavia Sophe inscription, as well as two others thought to be Christian epitaphs, were discovered along the Via Latina. For the epigraphic text and its interpretive implications, see H. Gregory Snyder, "The Discovery and Interpretation of the Flavia Sophe Inscription: New Results," *VC* 68 (2014): 1–59.

43. See, e.g., Eshleman, *The Social World of Intellectuals*, 25–26.

44. Dunderberg, *Beyond Gnosticism*, 161. For the philosophical dimension of Marcion's teachings, see John G. Gager, "Marcion and Philosophy," *VC* 26 (1972): 53–59.

45. Dunderberg, "Valentinian Teachers in Rome," 173–74; Fowden, *The Egyptian Hermes*, 103.

context of third-century Rome, Nicola Spanu has argued that, far from having been irremediably separate from his other students, the "gnostic" disciples whom Plotinus debates in *Ennead II* [33] were never considered by the philosopher to be a demarcated group within his school.[46] To the contrary, the main (and seemingly only) point of distinction conveyed in Plotinus's critique of them is subtle and epistemological: a particular inter- pretation of Platonic metaphysics has led to erroneous expectations about the efficacy of practices he deems "magical" and, with respect to exorcism, to an improper understanding of the cause and remedy of a "medical" condition.[47] The characterization of "gnostic" epistemology and practice in this text does, however, have ample corroboration in the *Greek Magical Papyri*, yet another reminder of how assumptions, skills, and techniques might be shared by text-oriented specialists of similar aptitude, whatever their degrees of intellectualism.[48]

Continuities between Christian experts and the wider phenomenon of freelance expertise are only strengthened if one considers the full range of practices evident in our Christian sources, even those that are critical of figures overly invested in philosophy, astrology, or numerology.[49] Here Irenaeus underscores the value of differentiating critical discourses or commentaries on such practices from the practices themselves. For his extensive treatment of Valentinian cosmology, Ireneaus ultimately objects less to the Valentinians' reliance on numerology in their teachings than to the significance that they derive from certain numbers to support their scheme of *aeons*. "This is inconsistent and entirely stupid," he protests, "because every number occurs in scriptures in a variety of ways."[50] To illustrate the problem he proceeds to demonstrate the significance that

---

46. Nicola Spanu, "The Magic of Plotinus' Gnostic Disciples in the Context of Plotinus' School of Philosophy," *JLARC* 7 (2013): 1–14. See also idem, *Plotinus, Ennead II 9 [33] "Against the Gnostics"—A Commentary*, Studia Patristica Suppl. 1 (Leiden: Peeters, 2012); Dylan M. Burns, *Apocalypse of the Alien God: Platonism and the Exile of Sethian Gnosticism*, Divinations (Philadelphia: University of Pennsylvania Press, 2014), 32–47.

47. Spanu, "The Magic of Plotinus' Gnostic Disciples," 5–6.

48. Spanu, "The Magic of Plotinus' Gnostic Disciples," 9–14.

49. Irenaeus connects Marcus with Anaxilaus of Larissa, known for having written books on divination, conjuring, and the special properties of plants (*Haer.* 1.13.1). Later he claims that Saturninus and Basilides are "just like the astrologers," whose theories they accept and then adapt to their purposes (*Haer.* 1.24.7).

50. Irenaeus, *Haer.* 2.24.3–4 (trans. Dominic J. Unger).

could be attached to the number five according to this logic: there are five letters in *sōtēr, patēr,* and *agapē,* among other words commonly found in the gospels. Jesus blessed five loaves of bread and fed five thousand men, and there are five fingers and toes and five appendages of the human body (the arms, the legs, and the head). In other words, any arbitrary cipher can yield some meaningless pattern when applied to authoritative texts.

Lest someone conclude from his dismissiveness that the details of the gospels are arbitrary and aimless, however, Irenaeus assures his readers, "On the contrary, all things have clearly been made by God harmonious and beautiful with great wisdom and care. . . . One must, however, not connect these things with the number thirty, but with *an existing system.* Nor should one make an inquiry into God by means of numbers and syllables and letters."[51] In other words, numerology is not the issue but the significance that the Valentinians attach to the *wrong* numbers (8, 12, and 30), when it is, by Irenaeus's reckoning, the number four that matters; indeed, it is on this basis that he justifies his selection of four gospels, before defending his particular choices by assuring his readers of the pristine authorship of these "legitimate" texts.[52] He then connects the fourfold gospel with the number, and number of faces, of the cherubim on which Christ is enthroned, and then back again to the four evangelists represented by the aspects of these faces.[53] To summarize: not eight, twelve, or thirty, but four.

Echoing a point made by scholars such as King and David Brakke, if we set aside or discard altogether concepts of "proto-orthodoxy" and "heresy" for this early period, then the practices of a writer-intellectual such as Irenaeus appear to have more in common than not with those of the "heretics" whom he disparages.[54] If we restore him and his rivals to the urban environment of second-century Rome, the commonalities across these writer-intellectuals come even more to life, as do their concerns about one another. It is clear the authors of the aforementioned texts presumed that their audiences had, or were likely to have, ongoing interactions with freelance experts who might cater to their interests.

51. Irenaeus, *Haer.* 2.25.1 (emphasis added).

52. Irenaeus, *Haer.* 3.11.8.

53. See Annette Yoshiko Reed, "ΕΥΑΓΓΕΛΙΟΝ: Orality, Textuality, and the Christian Truth in Irenaeus' *Adversus Haereses,*" *VC* 56 (2002): 11–46.

54. See David Brakke, *The Gnostics: Myth, Ritual, and Diversity in Early Christianity* (Cambridge: Harvard University Press, 2010), esp. 1–28.

Alternatively, certain practices in which these audiences were engaging might give rise to someone among them claiming religious knowledge and expertise in one's own right: by appealing to a new revelation, unlocking another textual mystery, elaborating a more complex and esoteric cosmogony, or tracing a different genealogy for Christ. Many extant Christian authors strongly discourage either possibility, while also depicting specialists as innovators upon an established tradition that resides with institutional groups already in existence.

It is methodologically dubious, however, to take for granted that those who complain about Christian innovators represent a different kind of religious activity. All the more so when the basis for this assumption is that some allege to be "office-holders" appointed in the apostolic tradition and charged with protecting the integrity of Christian communities from any who would corrupt the shared practices that unite them. On the one hand, and as many scholars have noted, the same modes of authorization were equally available to and enlisted by any number of rival Christian authorities. Ptolemy concludes his letter with the promise that Flora will receive further teachings and methods of self-examination, provided that she is deemed worthy of the apostolic tradition he has received by succession.[55] Clement of Alexandria reports that Basilides was the student of Glaukias, the interpreter of Peter, while Valentinus was in a line of Pauline authority stemming from his own teacher Theudas, an alleged companion of Paul.[56] On the other hand, appeals to tradition, apostolic authority, stable teachings, and continuous leadership structures are not necessarily evidence that such things were already in place but that particular authors wanted them to be and employed the same proactive rhetoric used by other specialists pursuing similar aims.[57]

---

55. Ptolemy, *Flor.* 7.8.

56. Clement, *Strom.* 7.108.1; Birger A. Pearson, "Basilides the Gnostic," in Marjanen and Luomanen, *A Companion to Second-Century Christian "Heretics,"* 1–31, at 4. Likewise, in the *Tripartite Tractate* and the *Testimony of Truth*, whose authors would be viewed as "heretics" by Irenaeus, we glimpse "heretics" acting as heresiologists. See Geoffrey S. Smith, *Guilt by Association: Heresy Catalogues in Early Christianity* (New York: Oxford University Press, 2015), 54.

57. Eshleman explores common struggles over category definition and who had the right to define "true" expertise therein, the participation of writings in processes of authorization and legitimation, and a general focus origins and pedigree, often in conjunction with genealogies of succession (*The Social World of Intellectuals in the Roman Empire*, passim).

Writings and Textual Practices Among Rival Christian Experts

The approach I have outlined in this study invites us to consider how these authors, acting as freelance experts in Christian teachings and practices, utilized literary production to promote their own authority, to distance themselves from the problematic connotations of this sort of religious activity, and to produce social formations that accorded with their particular interests and concerns. For a "bishop" such as Irenaeus, the ideal type of Christian social formation entailed regular leadership structures and few opportunities for the creativity that certain intellectual practices could engender. In light of these interests, it is unsurprising that he discourages curiosity, ongoing prophecy, and specialized textual interpretation, as well as other pursuits that might promote self-authorized expertise. Whether the groups he idealizes, let alone a network of such groups, actually existed is a different question, although I am in no way suggesting that Christian experts with these interests were entirely unsuccessful. It is important to recognize, however, that not all Christian experts of the second century seem to have shared Irenaeus's concerns about textual sleuthing, ongoing literary interpretation, revelations, and other practices that might give rise to a departure from earlier teachings. The circle of Valentinus seems both to have encouraged these practices and also to have produced any number of religious experts with proprietary religious programs and followings in their own right.[58] "Already," Irenaeus remonstrates, "many offshoots of many heretical sects have been made from the ones we have mentioned, because many of these people, in fact all, wish to be teachers and to forsake the heresy in which they had been. They insist on teaching in a *novel* manner, composing from one teaching another tenet, and then another from that. They declare themselves inventors of any opinion which they may have patched together."[59]

Despite the many reasons to be skeptical of Irenaeus's depictions of "heretics," the underlying issues that concern him pertained equally to any self-authorized specialty. Christian expertise was available to anyone able to gain recognition as such an expert, with the result that Christian forms of religion might proliferate and diversify with few, if any, constraints.

---

58. Cf. Dunderberg, "Valentinian Teachers in Rome," 157, 166.

59. Irenaeus, *Haer.* 1.28.1.

Equally predictable in this context are the specific tropes that Irenaeus uses to discredit rival Christian experts: they initiate people into the mysteries of Christ; they enlist a number of skills and practices to buttress their own expertise (numerology, astrology, divination, etc.); they "misread" authoritative texts in support of their own agendas; and they produce their own narratives, parables, and myths to lend additional credence to their teachings.[60] Moreover, and not unlike Alexander, Peregrinus, or Josephus's Mosaic wisdom instructors, the Valentinians also charge large sums of money for the proprietary wisdom they dispense.[61]

Earlier I argued that letters were indispensable tools in the service of Paul's ambitions *quo* religious expert.[62] For him, the ability to commit a religious program to writing seems to have invited and supported vastly greater possibilities with respect to intricate myth-making, sophisticated explanations about the need for and effects of particular practices, and the events or details of his eschatological scenario. Letters were also vital for defending his teachings and apostolic integrity against the mischaracterizations of rivals seeking to capitalize on his absence. It is along similar lines that Eshleman highlights commonalities between Second Sophistic writers laboring to define "legitimate" academic disciplines and the tactics of second-century Christian writers who sought to elevate their own religious programs—or ones to which they subscribed—above those of other would-be Christian leaders and their followings.[63] On the use of writings to draw boundaries around groups, disciplines, and categories of practices, we gain additional insight from critics of freelance expertise, who perpetuated stereotypes about the interested charlatan precisely in

---

60. For initiations pertaining to death, particularly among the followers of Valentinus's student Marcus, see Nicola Denzey Lewis, "*Apolytrosis* as Ritual and Sacrament: Determining a Ritual Context for Death in Second-Century Marcosian Valentinianism," *JECS* 17 (2009): 525–61. Denzey Lewis's reconstruction of this afterlife rite holds interesting comparative possibilities with the Orphic initiations outlined in the Derveni papyrus and inferred from Orphic *lamellae*, which are nearly always recovered from funerary contexts.

61. Irenaeus, *Haer.* 1.4.3.

62. Stowers, "The Concept of 'Community' and the History of Early Christianity," 242.

63. As I noted in the preceding chapter, some of these writers attempted to recuperate earlier apostolic figures such as Paul by removing, minimizing, or otherwise transforming problematic connotations of their activities; this is most notable in Pauline pseudepigrapha, which, again, lack any references to the collection. Philostratus similarly distances Apollonius of Tyana from any appearance of charlatanry when he informs his readers that he has undertaken writing the biography in part to correct the mistaken impression that his subject was a *goēs*.

order to distinguish their own knowledge and skills from that of their subjects. This is not to suggest that all of the authors in question were necessarily freelance experts but that discursive tactics for delineating degrees of cultural or religious authority were shared by writer-intellectuals of different social locations, who adopted them in the service of different interests.

Recognition of the myriad, active roles of text within this class of religious activity holds important implications for making sense both of the expansive and esoteric writings (cosmogonies, secret teachings, revelations) of certain experts and groups and of the literature more invested in inculcating norms (heresy catalogues, apologies, canon lists).[64] The production and interpretation of writings were deeply enmeshed in efforts to either enable or constrain the possibilities of self-authorized religious expertise in an ecology teeming with stimuli for innovation. Irenaeus captures these possibilities aptly in his complaint,

> [The Valentinians] claim the truth was not handed down by writings, but by a living voice, of which matter Paul said, "Yet among the mature we do impart wisdom—although it is not the wisdom of this world." And each one claims as this wisdom that which he discovers by himself, which is really a fiction, so that their truth may fittingly be in Valentinus at one time, at another in Marcion, at another in Cerinthus, finally in Basilides, or even in one who disputes against these and would not be able to say anything pertaining to salvation. For each one of them, being totally corrupt, is not ashamed to deprave the rule of truth and preach himself.[65]

While Irenaeus's classifications should always be taken with a grain of salt, there may be more truth than some scholars allow in his insistence that many "heretical" groups owed their genesis to an individual founder.

---

64. The yields of such a focus have been demonstrated especially in recent work on Marcion. See, e.g., Jason D. BeDuhn, *The First New Testament: Marcion's Scriptural Canon* (Salem, OR: Polebridge, 2013); Marcus Vinzent, *Marcion and the Dating of the Synoptic Gospels*, Studia Patristica Suppl. 2 (Leuven: Peeters, 2014). See also David Brakke, "Scriptural Practices in Early Christianity: Towards a New History of the New Testament Canon," in *Invention, Rewriting, Usurpation: Discursive Fights over Religious Traditions in Antiquity*, ed. Jörg Ulrich, Anders-Christian Jacobsen, and David Brakke, Early Christianity in the Context of Antiquity 11 (Frankfurt: Peter Lang, 2012), 263–80; John S. Kloppenborg, "Literate Media and Early Christian Groups: The Creation of a Christian Book Culture," *JECS* 22 (2014): 21–59.

65. Irenaeus, *Haer.* 3.2.1.

This is not to affirm the actual existence of all such groups. As Geoffrey S. Smith observes, "Heresy catalogues are ... designed to organize otherwise unaffiliated Christian teachers into coherent intellectual, social, and scholastic communities so that they might be discredited, demonized, and disenrolled en masse."[66] For the same reason, however, we should be equally, if not more, skeptical of the carefully cultivated impression of corporate unity that implicitly underpins Irenaeus's heresiological scheme.

Individuals Before Groups

The distortive tendencies of heresiological writers are well known, as is the baggage of "orthodoxy" and "heresy" and less fraught replacement terms that nevertheless preserve the same distinction between mainstream and deviant Christian groups.[67] Brakke has argued that Irenaeus's legacy has influenced historians of early Christianity in at least two distinct ways: "First, his view that Christianity started out as a single, fairly uniform religion and then became more diverse, whether for good or for ill, has remained influential. Scholars may not share Irenaeus's confidence that Jesus himself taught a true Christian doctrine that later bishops faithfully preserved, but they have at times reproduced his basic story in their own ways."[68] The second line of influence involves how scholars explain this trajectory of diversification in the first few centuries. "[H]istorians of today," Brakke writes, "depict the early Christians as needing to establish their identity by differentiating themselves from Greco-Roman paganism

---

66. Smith, *Guilt by Association*, 15. I am less persuaded by Smith's characterization of heresy catalogues as purely polemical blacklists. For further discussion of the various classificatory schemata devised in these texts, see Todd S. Berzon, *Classifying Christians: Ethnography, Heresiology, and the Limits of Knowledge in Late Antiquity* (Berkeley: University of California Press, 2016), esp. 58–97.

67. Regarding the problems with more neutral replacement terms for "orthodoxy" and "heresy," Dunderberg writes, "These designations may create the impression of greater neutrality and scholastic precision, but in fact they carry with themselves the same basic idea that makes the traditional discourse of orthodoxy and heresy problematic. 'Mainstream' in the new jargon means pretty much the same thing as 'orthodoxy' in the older one, that is, the form of Christianity that assumed a normative position in the Roman Empire at the beginning of the fourth century. ... In consequence, the distinction between 'mainstream' and 'sectarian' forms of early Christianity is none other than the old discourse of orthodoxy and heresy in a new guise" (*Beyond Gnosticism*, 19).

68. Brakke, *The Gnostics*, 3–4.

on the one hand and from Judaism on the other—and sometimes there is a third alternative, Gnosticism. Diversity resulted as Christians responded to these challenges in different ways. That there is a single thing called 'Christianity,' however diverse, is not really questioned."

Brakke's point is well taken, for despite many laudable efforts to dispense with this polemical scheme the specters of writers such as Irenaeus still linger faintly in the implicit retention of the entity on behalf of which he and other "proto-orthodox" authors presumably wrote. In my view, we have not done enough to dispense with the idea that *some* normative Christian group existed in Rome—whether the Church, a network of churches, or even several communities operating semiautonomously—with the result that scholars of early Christian diversity cannot help but calculate degrees of affinity with or deviation from that entity.[69] Such assumptions are evident, for example, in the oft-repeated claim that Marcion was expelled from the Christian community at Rome, or that Valentinus sought but failed to be elected its "bishop." The implication of such narratives is that before Marcion or Valentinus there was a coalition of like-minded Christians with sufficient institutional clout to meaningfully expel from their ranks or demote someone whose teachings clashed with theirs. Of course any social formation with basic membership practices might devise internal structures of office and choose to exclude or subordinate certain individuals. And yet the presumed force of these actions against known "heretics" seems much stronger, as though they are akin to acts of excommunication undertaken within a fairly developed institutional setting.[70] As John S. Kloppenborg reminds us, however, in none of the late-first- and early-second-century Christian evidence are there clear

---

69. For the a priori expectation of a Roman Christian community or church, see, e.g., Smith, who writes, "*The Christian community in Rome* was not only large in number and active in the circulation of Christian literature; it also attracted influential Christians from across the Roman Empire. Many enterprising teachers, such as Valentinus, Hermas, Marcion, even Justin himself traveled to the Empire's capital city to participate in its vibrant Christian culture by *offering their unique vision of the message of Jesus* and availing themselves to the abundant resources therein" (*Guilt by Association*, 77, emphasis added). Apparent in this excerpt is Smith's assumption that these second-century teachers were drawn to and wished to join a preexisting corporate entity in Rome, even if many would find this community unreceptive to their "unique" teachings.

70. For a useful discussion of the membership practices of voluntary associations in the Hellenistic and Roman periods, including possible references in New Testament literature to the departure or expulsion of members, see Kloppenborg, "Membership Practices in Pauline Christ Groups," 186–87.

indications of the duties, duration, or selection procedures for Christian offices of the sort that might lend credence to this picture.[71]

I raise this matter because calibrating rival Christian teachers in relation to some axiomatic Roman church or Christian community begs an important question about the nature of Christian forms of religion in this period and place. However much one stresses their variety, a semblance of the normative scheme will remain in *any* premise of initial and ongoing coherence among certain Christians (i.e., the "proto-orthodox").[72] To be clear, all of the freelance experts considered in this study might be said to have worked out of and innovated upon some tradition in the sense that they located themselves within and satisfied basic expectations about familiar specialty to gain recognition and give shape to their practices. Some of these specialists labored to form groups of followers and, in so doing, sought to delimit and naturalize the boundaries of their respective disciplines, schools, initiations, or philosophies. Within particular subsets of activity, one might also find coalitions of experts collaborating with one another, occasionally or in a more sustained manner, to enhance the perceived legitimacy of all. However, it is easier to recognize *these* as active, constructive labors undertaken by interested individuals than when we observe similar efforts on the part of Judeans or Christians.

The challenge of acknowledging the freelance dimension of Christian evidence is greater since most studies proceed from churches or religious communities as though they are *sui generis*. To begin from groups is to posit a platform of regularity with which all subsequent evidence of "diversity" must then be reconciled. The advantage of reframing these sources as evidence for the religion of freelance experts is that doing so restores all would-be Christian experts to an equal footing when what it meant to be such an expert was still largely, if not entirely up for grabs. Situated within the framework of this study, figures such as Justin, Marcion, Valentinus, Ptolemy, and Irenaeus are easier to imagine as individuals actively engaged

---

71. Kloppenborg adds, "The problems involved in drawing a picture of the early Christ-groups are exacerbated by the fact that our documents are written using insider language, theological explanations, and rhetorical flourishes that resist an easy translation into more empirical descriptions" ("Membership Practices in Pauline Christ Groups," 183).

72. Cf. King, "Representing Early Christian Differences for the 21st Century," 217. Even invoking such terms as "variety" and "varieties" or "diversity" and "diversities" implies departure from a condition of coherence or stability. Although I have made occasional use of this language, one wonders whether reframing the problem of "Christian diversity" within the context of freelance expertise might obviate the need for any of these descriptive terms.

in promoting their own authority within an explicitly "Christian" idiom. This is not to suggest that there were no Christian groups of which to speak in this period but rather that we should be cautious about presuming, as some ancient writers insist, that the boundaries and authority of the ones that did were necessarily acknowledged beyond their own membership. These authors are all the more valuable as windows into how *notions* of shared thought and practice, of corporate identity, might be cultivated and reinforced. Indeed, many devised ambitious geographic schemes in which unanimous *ekklēsiai* not only existed, but were also united in networks spanning large swaths of the Roman Empire. [73]

Conclusions

In this chapter I have sketched an illustration of how the religion of free-lance experts may offer a new methodology for explaining the emergence, development, and ongoing diversification of distinctly Christian forms of religion. While far more elaboration is needed, our earliest evidence for Christian experts maps onto a prior and more capacious class of religious activity that is not specific to Christians, or to Jews and Christians. Arranging our evidence in this way does not require talking about origins in any limited sense, aside from positing that "Christianity," in its full multiformity, first arose from this context and developed variously in ac-cordance with the particular skills and practices of individual Christian ex-perts. Nor does it require positing any common features of "Christianity" in the first two centuries, beyond the basic item that what unites this par-ticular form of religious expertise is the figure of Christ, not unlike com-parably diverse Orphic and Pythagorean phenomena that seem to have proliferated within the same class of religious activity.

Such a framework contributes to earlier and ongoing efforts to describe early Christian diversity without projecting onto the second century later concepts of orthodoxy and heresy. The advantage of drawing this evi-dence into the religion of freelance experts is that the seemingly intrac-table dichotomy of mainstream versus sectarian groups dissolves into a sea of individual agents. We can parse this class in different ways, facet-ing and filtering its participants to exhibit any number of productive but

---

73. For additional examples of this corporate rhetoric with discussion of its intended effect, see Berzon, *Classifying Christians*, 49–53, 58–97.

nonessential points of comparison between them. Within the subset of intellectualizing religious experts the possibilities are especially rich: interpreters of oracular or inspired writings (Judean, Persian, Sibylline, Orphic, or Chaldean); figures who enlisted philosophical discursive practices in the context of religious activity (Paul, Valentinus, Marcion, Justin, Pythagoreans, Orphics, Neoplatonists); or varieties of afterlife initiators (Pauline, Orphic, Marcosian, Hermetic). None of these possibilities are mutually exclusive. Instead we must imagine a kaleidoscope of potential relationships, with new patterns in the evidence crystallizing as we rotate the angles of our mirrors.

Conclusion

FREELANCE EXPERTS IN
THE RELIGIOUS MARKETPLACE?

IN THIS BOOK I have isolated a particular class or type of religious activity, the religion of freelance experts, within the religious landscape of the Roman Empire and argued for its impact on significant religious developments of the first two centuries. In considering the heterogeneity of many specialized offerings, as well as the assorted social formations that might arise from specialist activity, I have modeled a methodology that is not beholden to the boundaries of problematic scholarly categories. Rather, theorizing religion as a matter of practices that involve the imagined participation of gods and similar beings allows us to juxtapose and compare examples of such practices wherever they occur, and in whatever combinations. The religious actors on whom I have trained my focus were "freelance" with respect to the nature of their authority and their peripheral relationship to existing institutions and groups. At the same time, they bore complex, even mutually beneficial, relationships with other forms of religious activity, blending seamlessly into the different social ecologies of the Roman world.

The considerations of the preceding chapters yield a typology of freelance experts in religion, nested within a wider field of specialists whose practices were not, or were less religious. To the extent that these areas of expertise were porous and interlocking, a high degree of fluidity across their putative boundaries, such as they were, should not only be allowed but is to be expected. Degrees of similarity are especially apparent for the subset of religious experts whom I have called "writer-intellectuals" because their offerings either depended on literate forms of knowledge or made ample use of writings and textual practices. Whereas some experts had nothing to do with books and intellectual pursuits, others were fluent in the discourses of recognizable intellectual circles, especially ones inflected by philosophy.

In one sense, texts are not altogether different from other kinds of artifacts—astrological charts, horoscopes, divining paraphernalia, special items, or images—that were utilized in the context of freelance religious expertise. This aspect of writings is important, inasmuch as they tend to be regarded foremost as repositories of thought with insufficient attention to their materiality and the range of social practices that were encoded in their production, reading, and interpretation. However, specific sociocultural factors enabled the use of writings and also tied the experts who possessed the requisite skills to writers and readers operating in different social locations. This field of intellectuals transected the class of religious activity that I have theorized; it simultaneously included actors with similar abilities but who were not freelance experts on account of the nature of their legitimacy, their wealth or social standing, and dynamics of power.

Attention to the necessary preconditions for intellectualizing forms of religion should not, however, overshadow the prominence of freelance experts who lacked intellectual or philosophical pretensions. While writings supply or are themselves some of the richest evidence for specialist activity, I have tried to be mindful of the range of strategies available to experts who, though not writer-intellectuals, shouldered the same burdens of recognition and legitimacy as all self-authorized actors. Some modeled their offerings on the practices of famous religious institutions while others took advantage of new global horizons and tastes for the exotic in crafting their self-presentations. Those who were able to do so might even appeal to the notional prestige and perceived power of writing, regardless of whether the characters they inscribed made sense or whether they or their clients could read them. Others enlisted curiosity items, strange images, materials ascribed unusual properties, and so on.[1] Although making determinations about whether an object was employed in such ways is a tenuous

---

1. As Ripat remarks, "[For such actors,] expertise might not have been as important as the impression of expertise" ("Astrologers at Rome," 125). For a helpful discussion of the power of writing, which may or may not entail the degree of literacy implied in the preceding paragraph, see David Frankfurter, "The Magic of Writing and the Writing of Magic: The Power of the Word in Egyptian and Greek Tradition," *Helios* 21 (1994): 189–221.

enterprise, the possibility, at least, should always be kept in mind when evaluating small archaeological finds that could have held this potential.[2]

I would suggest that all of the *instrumentum* incorporated into specialized offerings can and should be theorized as part of a continuum that also includes writings. Occupying one end are religious texts that disclose their authors' facility with fairly specialized intellectual practices: esotericism, literary and other forms of divination (astrology, numerology), philosophical discourses and techniques, and so forth. While there is considerable room for classifying the literature produced within this subset of freelance expertise, framing it in this way encourages consideration of what work writings might accomplish for the relatively few specialists with the ability to produce or prominently feature them. On the same end of the spectrum fall collections of spells or sayings, more basic divinatory books, horoscopes, and so forth; even though the intellectual character of these writings may vary they can be evaluated productively in similar terms. Even further along lie inscribed objects and more instrumental texts—lots, *defixiones*, amulets, and so forth—, which should be included among other writings produced, interpreted, or consulted by specialists but organized, to the extent possible, on the basis of the differential skills required to produce them. On the opposite end of the spectrum belong those artifacts that were not associated with writings or intellectual practices in any way: amulets and gemstones that did not bear inscriptions, tokens of initiation, funerary objects intended to aid the deceased in the afterlife, divining apparatus, and images of the sort allegedly supplicated by Nero and certainly by Apuleius. Again, it may be methodologically dubious to make determinations about whether any such items should be interpreted within the framework of freelance expertise, yet we know from multiple literary accounts that specialists commonly dealt with them. The sources also offer glimpses of specialists conveying expertise in more ephemeral ways, through dress or bodily comportment, even nomenclature.

Given the relative freedom enjoyed by participants in this class of religious activity, the assorted practices and ethnicizing attributes that might

---

2. I have in mind, for example, the assortment of finds (curse tablets, effigies, vessels, and so forth) excavated from the *fons Annae Perennae* in Rome's Parioli neighborhood, as well as gemstones, amulets, and other items that might plausibly have been produced or conferred by freelance experts. See Marina Piranomonte, "Religion and Magic at Rome: The Fountain of Anna Perenna," in Gordon and Simón, *Magical Practice in the Latin West*, 191–213. Jürgen Blänsdorf, "The Texts from the *Fons Annae Perennae*," in Gordon and Simón, *Magical Practice in the Latin West*, 215–44.

comprise their programs were exponential and protean. The principal constraint on their creativity was whether their intended audiences would recognize them as experts and find their teachings and other practices credible and appealing. For these reasons, the logic or rationality of specialized offerings was determined not by any stable, objective metric but through complex and contingent equations whose operations reflected the field positions and relations of experts, the dispositions of audiences, current tastes, and other material conditions.[3] The pronounced competitive dimension of this class of religious activity, which percolated through the wider field of self-authorized specialists, only compounded its complexity and proclivity for innovation.

Having theorized the religion of freelance experts in terms of interests and competition, I want to clarify that my conceptualization of this class and its dynamics is not identical to the "religious marketplace" model that has become commonplace in many studies of religious change in the Roman Empire. A basic assumption of this model is that people pursued new religious options because they had grown dissatisfied with or lost confidence in traditional religion, that phenomena attested for the first time in the imperial period compensated for perceived deficiencies in institutions that were viewed increasingly as too outdated, ritualistic, or impersonal.[4] Implicit in this assumption is the existence of stable and universal religious needs that could be satisfied with varying degrees of success by competing religious "firms."[5] In the pluralistic religious economy of the empire, the most successful religions, then, were ones that maximized such needs while offering the most attractive benefits and compelling explanations for how they would be delivered.

Since many applications of the marketplace metaphor seek to account for the emergence and eventual success of Christianity in the Roman

---

3. Although some of this language is indebted to Bourdieu's theorization of the religious field, unlike him I do not envisage this or any other social field as a closed system whose structure was determined by hierocratic institutions. Rather, the terms of religious expertise were "continuously renegotiated through the exchange of ideas across social groups" (Verter, "Spiritual Capital," 157).

4. E.g., Rodney Stark, *The Rise of Christianity: A Sociologist Reconsiders History* (Princeton: Princeton University Press, 1996); idem, "Religious Competition and Roman Piety," *IJRR* 2 (2006): 1–30. For additional examples and critical engagement with the application of the metaphor to the ancient Mediterranean world, see David Engels and Peter Van Nuffelen, "Religion and Competition in Antiquity: An Introduction," in Engels and Van Nuffelen, *Religion and Competition in Antiquity*, 9–44.

5. Stark, *The Rise of Christianity*, 39.

world, it is no accident that the religious needs posited are often reverse-engineered from the very benefits that early Christians alleged to offer.[6] Rodney Stark, for example, argues that people had a natural inclination toward forms of religion that were rational, moral, and salvation-oriented; the central doctrines of Christianity thus "prompted and sustained attractive, liberating, and effective social relations and organizations."[7] Furthermore, its stability and universality cut like a beacon through the mayhem of a social arena in which people were thrown together helter-skelter, speaking many languages and worshipping all manner of gods.[8] The evidence considered in this study refutes the most basic elements of Stark's scheme. The sheer variety of would-be experts active in the first century contradicts his claim that religious "professionals" were "produced only within monotheism." But there are additional problems. One is that many freelance experts, not only Judeans and Christians, alleged to represent and have special relationships with a single god, often one credited with supreme or singular abilities, if not always to the exclusion of deities. So too did many present their proprietary divine wisdom as a revealed or ultimate truth. On the basis of what we now know about the competitive and innovative dynamics of this class of activity, I would argue that the promotion of one supreme deity might be a predictable *effect* of this sort of religious activity but not its prerequisite. In a context wherein specialists vied with one another by boasting multiple skills and specialty, totalizing claims about divinity might be viewed as yet another competitive strategy.

---

6. Cf. Leif E. Vaage, who writes, "While Christianity plainly emerged, developed, and spread throughout the Mediterranean basin, that is did so, within the confines of the Roman Empire, intentionally or self-consciously as a particular social (political; philosophical) project, with the recruitment of new members as a founding feature of its official purpose, is anything but clear. Again, I say this because it is precisely this sort of unargued assumption that, in turn, tends to make self-evident the highly questionable historical judgments about Christianity's predictable, inevitable, understandable, probable, reasonable subsequent success" ("Ancient Religious Rivalries and the Struggle for Success," 16).

7. Stark, *The Rise of Christianity*, 211. For an excellent overview and critique of Stark's historical theories, see Roger Beck, "The Religious Market of the Roman Empire: Rodney Stark and Christianity's Pagan Competition," in Vaage, *Religious Rivalries in the Early Roman Empire and the Rise of Christianity*, 233–52.

8. Stark, *The Rise of Christianity*, 213. Stark expands his argument about the moral superiority of Christianity in *Cities of God: The Real Story of How Christianity Became an Urban Movement and Conquered Rome* (New York: HarperOne, 2007), 30. For a sustained critique of the rational choice approach to the study of religious preference, see Verter, "Spiritual Capital," 164–69.

The most serious flaw in many applications of the marketplace model lies in the concept of certain religious needs that all inhabitants of the empire shared and they struggled to meet by navigating a bewildering mass of alternatives.[9] In so imaging this setting, Stark and others presume that the practices and emphases one finds in early Christian offerings—self-mastery, moral progress, relief from sin, salvation, and eternal life—were basic and that other forms of religious activity addressed them inadequately. Thus the gradual success of Christianity lay in a widespread realization of its ability to meet or fulfill those needs.[10] "When monotheism and polytheism collide," Stark concludes, "monotheism always wins. Easily. It does so because it offers far more, and does so with far greater credibility, making it the choice of philosophers as well as of the people."[11] It simply was not the case that the forms of religion Stark has in mind optimally realized preexisting and shared religious needs. To the contrary, sources such as the Derveni papyrus and the Pauline Epistles provide excellent evidence for how such needs were *created by* freelance experts who deliberately contrasted their specialized knowledge and the benefits they purveyed with more ordinary forms of religion. To presume that Paul's salvation scheme generated interest because it satisfied an inherent impetus for salvation, and more rationally than other religious options, ignores all of the work that Paul devoted to demonstrating why and for what purpose people required his form of salvation in the first place.

To be fair, other scholars to apply the marketplace model to the Roman Empire have done so with greater nuance and circumspection.[12] Nevertheless, most presume that it operated in the manner of an ideal

---

9. Stark, *Cities of God*, 33.

10. Moreover, he identifies a market trend preceding Christianity, since he claims that "oriental religions" attracted a following by virtue of placing a similar emphasis on morality and atonement (*Cities of God*, 88).

11. Stark, *Cities of God*, 208.

12. E.g., John A. North, who has argued that over the course of the imperial period people gradually shifted their religious allegiance away from civic religion in favor of group identity: "The Development of Religious Pluralism," in *The Jews among Pagans and Christians in the Roman Empire*, ed. Judith Lieu, John A. North, and Tessa Rajak (London: Oxford University Press, 1992), 174–93. See also Christoph Auffarth, "*Religio migrans*: Die Orientalischen Religionen' im Kontext antiker Religionen. Ein theoretisches Modell," in *Religioni in contatto nel mondo antico. Modalità di diffusione e processi di interferenza. Atti del 3 colloquiosu "le religioni orientali nel mondo greco e romano," Loveno di Menaggio (Como) 26–28 Maggio 2006*, ed. Corinne Bonnet, Sergio Ribichini, and Dirk Steuernagel, Mediterranea 4 (Rome: Fabrizio Serra Editore, 2008), 333–63; MacLean Rogers, *The Mysteries of Artemis of Ephesos*, 259–92.

free market, whose competitors began with equal advantages and enjoyed greater or lesser success depending on the demand for their products.[13] Yet neither was the value of freelance expertise fixed nor were the positions a specialist might take unhindered.[14] While aspects of the marketplace metaphor are useful—foremost of which are its emphases on competition and the individual agency of the clients, students, or followers who were the "consumers" of freelance expertise—like any metaphor it has its limits. All of the freelance experts we have considered had to establish and convince people of the value of their religious offerings, precisely because their potential audiences did not automatically value them as such or have an obvious need for them.[15] How a particular offering fared was ultimately a matter of historically contingent factors rather than universal consumer needs and behaviors.[16]

Throughout the book I have argued that studies of religion in the Roman Empire stand to benefit from moving beyond undifferentiated scholarly categories and corporate entities—cults, religious communities, groups, religions, or religious systems—to consider how individual actors contributed to broader dynamics of change. In my view, theorizing freelance expertise and its intersections with other forms of religious activity and social practice requires finer instruments and units of analysis than the marketplace metaphor imparts. Cults and communities do not adapt, compete, and innovate; rather, individual religious actors, or certain individuals within groups, are more often the engines of these processes. A focus on freelance experts thus makes it easier to imagine or even observe changes taking place, and rapidly so. And while these religious actors are a valuable object of study in their own right, I have argued that in this historical context they are integral to our understanding of the emergence and spread of what would become Christianity, although not before at least another century of negotiation, innovation, and diffusion had taken place.

---

13. In criticizing this assumption I am not suggesting the alternative, that the empire's "religious marketplace," such as it existed, was tightly regulated by the state.

14. Verter, "Spiritual Capital," 159.

15. Cf. Beck, "The Religious Market of the Roman Empire," 233; Rives, *Religion in the Roman Empire*, 168–69; Stowers, "Kinds of Myths, Meals, and Power," 108.

16. Cf. Verter, "Spiritual Capital," 163.

Bibliography

Abraham, Roshan. "The Geography of Culture in Philostratus' *Life of Apollonius of Tyana*." *CJ* 109 (2014): 465–80.

Ahmadi, Amir. "The *Magoi* and *Daimones* in Column VI of the Derveni Papyrus." *Numen* 61 (2014): 484–508.

Alföldy, Géza. "Eine Bauinschrift aus dem Colosseum." *ZPE* 109 (1995): 195–226.

Anderson, Graham. *Sage, Saint, and Sophist: Holy Men and Their Associates in the Early Roman Empire*. New York: Routledge, 1994.

Ando, Clifford. "The Ontology of Religious Institutions." *HR* 50 (2010): 54–79.

———. "Evidence and Orthopraxy: A Review Article of John Scheid, *Quand faire, c'est croire. Les rites sacrificiels des Romains*." *JRS* 99 (2009): 171–81.

———. *A Matter of the Gods: Religion and the Roman Empire*. Berkeley: University of California Press, 2008.

———. *Imperial Ideology and Provincial Loyalty in the Roman Empire*. Berkeley: University of California Press, 2000.

Andrade, Nathanael J. *Syrian Identity in the Greco-Roman World*. Cambridge: Cambridge University Press, 2013.

Arnal, William E. "Bringing Paul and the Corinthians Together? A Rejoinder and Some Proposals on Redescription and Theory." Pages 75–104 in *Redescribing Paul and the Corinthians*. Edited by Ron Cameron and Merrill P. Miller. ECL 5. Atlanta: Society of Biblical Literature, 2011.

Ascough, Richard A. "Redescribing the Thessalonians 'Mission' in Light of Greco-Roman Associations." *NTS* 60 (2014): 62–82.

Ascough, Richard A., Philip A. Harland, and John S. Kloppenborg, eds. *Associations in the Greco-Roman World: A Sourcebook*. Waco, TX: Baylor University Press, 2012.

Athanassiadi, Polymnia. "Julian the Theurgist: Man or Myth?." Pages 193–208 in *Die Chaldaeischen Orakel: Kontext, Interpretation, Rezeption*. Edited by Helmut Seng and Michel Tardieu. Heidelberg: University of Heidelberg Press, 2011.

Auffarth, Christoph. "*Religio migrans:* Die 'Orientalischen Religionen' im Kontext antiker Religionen. Ein theoretisches Modell." Pages 333–63 in *Religioni in contatto nel Mediterraneo antico: Modalità di diffusione e processi di interferenza. Atti del 3 colloquiosu "le religioni orientali nel mondo greco e romano," Loveno di Menaggio (Como) 26–28 Maggio 2006.* Edited by Corinne Bonnet, Sergio Ribichini, and Dirk Steuernagel. Mediterranea 4. Rome: Fabrizio Serra Editore, 2008.

Aune, David E. *Prophecy in Early Christianity and the Ancient Mediterranean World.* Grand Rapids, MI: Eerdmans, 1983.

———. "The Use of ΠΡΟΦΗΤΗΣ in Josephus." *JBL* 101 (1982): 419–21.

Baker, Cynthia. "A 'Jew' by Any Other Name." *JAJ* 2 (2011): 153–80.

Barclay, John M. G. *Jews in the Mediterranean Diaspora: From Alexander to Trajan (323 BCE–117 CE).* Edinburgh: T&T Clark, 1996.

Barton, Tamsyn. *Ancient Astrology.* London: Routledge, 1994.

Bauman, R. A. "The Suppression of the Bacchanals: Five Questions." *Historia* 39 (1990): 334–48.

Bazzana, Giovanni Battista. "The Bar Kokhba Revolt and Hadrian's Religious Policy." Pages 85–109 in *Hadrian and the Christians.* Edited by Marco Rizzi. Millenium–Studien 30. Berlin: de Gruyter, 2010.

———. "Early Christian Missionaries as Physicians: Healing and its Cultural Value in the Greco-Roman Context." *NT* 51 (2009): 232–51.

Beard, Mary. *The Roman Triumph.* Cambridge: Harvard University Press, 2007.

———. "The Triumph of Flavius Josephus." Pages 543–58 in *Flavian Rome: Culture, Image, Text.* Edited by A. J. Boyle and W. J. Dominik. Leiden: Brill, 2003.

———. "Writing and Religion: Ancient Literacy and the Function of the Written Word in Roman Religion." Pages 35–58 in *Literacy in the Roman World.* Edited by Mary Beard, Alan K. Bowman, and Mireille Corbier. JRS Suppl. 3. Ann Arbor: University of Michigan Press, 1991.

———. "Priesthood in the Roman Republic." Pages 19–48 in *Pagan Priests: Religion and Power in the Ancient World.* Edited by Mary Beard and John A. North. Ithaca, NY: Cornell University Press, 1990.

———. "Acca Larentia Gains a Son." Pages 41–61 in *Images of Authority: Papers Presented to Joyce Reynolds.* Edited by Mary Margaret Mackenzie and Charlotte Roueché, Cambridge Philological Society, Suppl. 16. Cambridge: Cambridge Philological Society, 1989.

Beard, Mary, and John A. North, eds. *Pagan Priests: Religion and Power in the Ancient World.* Ithaca, NY: Cornell University Press, 1990.

Beard, Mary, John A. North, and Simon R. F. Price. *Religions of Rome, Vol. 1: A History.* Cambridge: Cambridge University Press, 1998.

———. *Religions of Rome, Vol. 2: A Sourcebook.* Cambridge: Cambridge University Press, 1998.

Beck, Roger. *A Brief History of Ancient Astrology.* Malden, MA: Wiley-Blackwell, 2007.

————. "The Religious Market of the Roman Empire: Rodney Stark and Christianity's Pagan Competition." Pages 233–52 in *Religious Rivalries in the Early Roman Empire and the Rise of Christianity*. Edited by Leif E. Vaage. Waterloo: Wilfred Laurier University Press, 2006.

————. "Whose Astrology? The Imprint of Ti. Claudius Balbillus on the Mithraic Mysteries." Pages 323–29 in *Beck on Mithraism: Collected Works with New Essays*. Burlington, VT: Ashgate, 2004.

————. "The Mysteries of Mithras: A New Account of Their Genesis." *JRS* 88 (1998): 115–28.

BeDuhn, Jason B. "Mani and the Crystallization of the Concept 'Religion' in Third Century Iran." Pages 247–75 in *Mani at the Court of Persian Kings: Studies on the Chester Beatty Kephalaia Codex*. Edited by Iain Gardner, Jason BeDuhn, and Paul Dilley. Nag Hammadi and Manichaean Studies 87. Leiden: Brill, 2015.

————. *The First New Testament: Marcion's Scriptural Canon*. Salem, OR: Polebridge, 2013.

Ben Zeev, Miriam Pucci. "The Uprisings in the Jewish Diaspora." Pages 93–104 in *The Cambridge History of Judaism, Vol. 4: The Late Roman-Rabbinic Period*. Edited by Steven T. Katz. New York: Cambridge University Press, 2006.

Bendlin, Andreas. "On the Uses and Disadvantages of Divination: Oracles and Their Literary Representations in the Time of the Second Sophistic." Pages 175–250 in *The Religious History of the Roman Empire: Pagans, Jews, and Christians*. Edited by John A. North and Simon R. F. Price. Oxford: Oxford University Press, 2011.

Bergmann, Bettina. "The Art of Ancient Spectacle." Pages 9–36 in *The Art of Ancient Spectacle*. Edited by Bettina Bergmann and Christine Kondoleon. New Haven: Yale University Press.

Berzon, Todd S. *Classifying Christians: Ethnography, Heresiology, and the Limits of Knowledge in Late Antiquity*. Berkeley: University of California Press, 2016.

Betegh, Gábor. *The Derveni Papyrus: Cosmology, Theology, and Interpretation*. Cambridge: Cambridge University Press, 2004.

Betz, Hans Dieter. *The Greek Magical Papyri in Translation: Including the Demotic Spells, I: The Texts with an Updated Bibliography*. 2nd ed. Chicago: University of Chicago Press, 1992.

————. *Galatians: A Commentary on Paul's Letter to the Churches in Galatia*. Philadelphia: Fortress, 1979.

Bilbija, Jovan, and Jaap-Jan Flinterman. "Die markt voor mantiek: droomverklaring en andere divinatorische praktijken in de Oneirocritica van Artemidoros." *Lampas* 39 (2006): 246–66.

Blänsdorf, Jürgen. "The Text from the *Fons Annae Perennae*." Pages 215–44 in *Magical Practice in the Latin West: Papers from the International Conference Held at the University of Zaragoza 30 Sept.–1 Oct. 2005*. Edited by Richard L. Gordon and Francisco Marco Simón. RGRW 168. Leiden: Brill, 2010.

Bodel, John. "Cicero's Minerva, *Penates*, and the Mother of the *Lares*. An Outline of Roman Domestic Religion." Pages 248–275 in *Household and Family Religion in Antiquity: Contextual and Comparative Perspectives*. Edited by John Bodel and Saul M. Olyan. Malden, MA: Wiley-Blackwell, 2008.

Bodel, John, and Saul M. Olyan. *Household and Family Religion in Antiquity*. Malden, MA: Blackwell, 2008.

Bohak, Gideon. *Ancient Jewish Magic*. New York: Cambridge University Press, 2008.

Bourdieu, Pierre. *The Field of Cultural Production: Essays on Art and Literature*. New York: Columbia University Press, 1993.

———. *The Logic of Practice*. Translated by Richard Nice. Stanford, CA: Stanford University Press, 1990.

———. *Outline of a Theory of Practice*. Cambridge: Cambridge University Press, 1977.

Bowersock, Glen W. "Foreign Elites at Rome." Pages 53–62 in *Flavius Josephus and Flavian Rome*. Edited by Jonathan Edmondson, Steve Mason, and James B. Rives. Oxford: Oxford University Press, 2005.

Boyarin, Daniel. "Rethinking Jewish Christianity: An Argument for Dismantling a Dubious Category." *JQR* 99 (2009): 7–36.

———. *Borderlines: The Partition of Judeao-Christianity*. Divinations. Philadelphia: University of Pennsylvania Press, 2004.

Boys-Stone, G. R. *Post-Hellenic Philosophy: A Study of its Development from the Stoics to Origen*. Oxford: Oxford University Press, 2001.

Bradley, Keith R. *Slavery and Rebellion in the Roman World, 140 B.C–70 B.C.* Bloomington: Indiana University Press, 1989.

Brakke, David. "Scriptural Practices in Early Christianity: Towards a New History of the New Testament Canon." Pages 263–80 in *Invention, Rewriting, Usurpation: Discursive Fights over Religious Traditions in Antiquity*. Edited by Jörg Ulrich, Anders-Christian Jacobsen, and David Brakke, Early Christianity in the Context of Antiquity 11. Frankfurt: Peter Lang, 2012.

———. *The Gnostics: Myth, Ritual, and Diversity in Early Christianity*. Cambridge: Harvard University Press, 2010.

Bremmer, Jan N. "Post Scriptum: Virgil and Jewish Literature." *Vergilius* 59 (2013): 157–64.

———. "Peregrinus' Christian Career." Pages 729–47 in *Flores Florentino: Dead Sea Scrolls and Other Early Jewish Studies in Honor of Florentino Garcia Martinez*. Edited by Anthony Hillhorst, Emile Puech, and Eibert Tigchelaar. Leiden: Brill, 2007.

Brent, Frederick E. "Religion Under Trajan: Plutarch's Resurrection of Osiris." Pages 72–92 in *Sage and Emperor: Plutarch, Greek Intellectuals, and Roman Power in the Time of Trajan (98–117 A.D.)*. Edited by Philip A. Stadter and Luc Van der Stockt. Symbolae 29. Leuven: Leuven University Press, 2002.

Brown, Peter. "The Rise and Function of the Holy Man in Late Antiquity, 1971–1997." *JECS* 6 (1998): 353–76.

———. "The Rise and Function of the Holy Man in Late Antiquity." *JRS* 61 (1971): 80–101.

Brubaker, Rogers. *Ethnicity Without Groups*. Cambridge: Harvard University Press, 2004.

Buell, Denise Kimber. *Why This New Race? Ethnic Reasoning in Early Christianity*. Gender, Theory, and Religion. New York: Columbia University Press, 2005.

Burkert, Walter. *Ancient Mystery Cults*. Cambridge: Harvard University Press, 1987.

———. *Lore and Science in Ancient Pythagoreanism*. Translated by Edwin L. Minar Jr. Cambridge: Harvard University Press, 1972.

Burns, Dylan M. *Apocalypse of the Alien God: Platonism and the Exile of Sethian Gnosticism*. Divinations. Philadelphia: University of Pennsylvania Press, 2014.

Cameron, Ron, and Merrill P. Miller. "Redescribing Paul and the Corinthians." Pages 245–302 in *Redescribing Paul and the Corinthians*. Edited by Ron Cameron and Merrill P. Miller. ECL 5. Atlanta: Society of Biblical Literature, 2011.

Cancik, Hubert. "Die 'Repraesentation' von 'Provinz' (nationes, gentes) in Rom. Ein Beitrag zur Besinnung von 'Reichsreligion' vom 1. Jahrhundert v. Chr." Pages 129–43 in *Römische Reichsreligion und Provinzialreligion*. Edited by Hubert Cancik and Jörg Rüpke. Tübingen: Mohr Siebeck, 1997.

Cappelletti, Sylvia. *The Jewish Community of Rome: From the Second Century b.c. to the Third Century C.E.* Supplements to the Journal for the Study of Judaism. Leiden: Brill, 2006.

Capponi, Livia. "Priests in Augustan Egypt." Pages 501–28 in *Priests and State in the Roman World*. Edited by James H. Richardson and Federico Santangelo. PAWB 33. Stuttgart: Steiner, 2011.

Casadesús, Francesc. "The Transformation of the Initiation Language of Mystery Religions into Philosophical Terminology." Pages 1–26 in *Greek Philosophy and Mystery Cults*. Edited by María José Martín-Velasco and María José García Blanco. Cambridge: Cambridge Scholars, 2016.

Cassius Dio. *Roman History*. Translated by Earnest Cary and Herbert Baldwin Foster. LCL. 9 vols. Cambridge: Harvard University Press, 1914–27.

Centrone, Bruno, "The Pseudo-Pythagorean Writings." Pages 315–40 in *A History of Pythagoreanism*. Edited by Carl A. Huffman. Cambridge: Cambridge University Press, 2014.

Charlesworth, James H. *The Dead Sea Scrolls. Hebrew, Aramaic, and Greek Texts with English Translations, Vol. I: Rule of the Community and Related Documents*. Tübingen: Mohr Siebeck, 1994.

Chilton, Bruce. "Justin and Israelite Prophecy." Pages 77–87 in *Justin Martyr and His Worlds*. Edited by Sara Parvis and Paul Foster. Minneapolis: Fortress, 2007.

Clay, Diskin. "Lucian of Samosata: Four Philosophical Lives (Nigrinus, Demonax, Peregrinus, Alexander Pseudomantis)." *ANRW* II. 36.5 (1992): 3406–50.

Clinton, Kevin. "Stages of Initiation in the Eleusinian and Samothracian Mysteries." Pages 50–78 in *Greek Mysteries: The Archaeology of Ancient Greek Secret Cults*. Edited by Michael B. Cosmopoulos. London: Routledge, 2003.

———. "Eleusis and the Romans: Late Republic to Marcus Aurelius." Pages 161–82 in *The Romanization of Athens*. Edited by Michael C. Hoff and Susan I. Rotroff. Oxford: Oxbow, 1997.

———. "The Eleusinian Mysteries: Roman Initiates and Benefactors, Second Century B.C. to A.D. 267." *ANRW* II. 18.2 (1989): 1499–539.

Cohen, Shaye J. D. *The Beginnings of Jewishness: Boundaries, Varieties, Uncertainties*. Berkeley: University of California Press, 1999.

———. "Respect for Judaism by Gentiles According to Josephus." *HTR* 80 (1987): 409–30.

Cole, Susan Guettel. "The Mysteries of Samothrace During the Roman Period," *ANRW* II. 18.2 (1989): 1564–98.

Collar, Anna. *Religious Networks in the Roman Empire: The Spread of New Ideas*. Cambridge: Cambridge University Press, 2013.

Collins, Adela Yarbro, and John J. Collins. *King and Messiah as Son of God: Human and Angelic Messianic Figures in Biblical and Related Literature*. Grand Rapids, MI: Eerdmans, 2008.

Collins, John J. *Beyond the Qumran Community: The Sectarian Movement of the Dead Sea Scrolls*. Grand Rapids, MI: Eerdmans, 2010.

———. *The Scepter and the Star: Messianism in Light of the Dead Sea Scrolls*, 2nd ed. Grand Rapids, MI: Eerdmans, 2010.

———. "A Messiah before Jesus?" Pages 15–35 in *Christian Beginnings and the Dead Sea Scrolls*. Edited by John J. Collins and Craig A. Evans. Grand Rapids, MI: Baker Academic, 2006.

———. "An Essene Messiah? Comments on Israel Knohl, *The Messiah Before Jesus*." Pages 37–62 in *Christian Beginnings and the Dead Sea Scrolls*. Edited by John J. Collins and Craig A. Evans. Grand Rapids, MI: Baker Academic, 2006.

———. "The Jewish Transformation of the Sibylline Oracles." Pages 369–87 in *Sibille e Linguaggi oracolari: Mito, storia, tradizione. Atti del convegno internazionale di studi Macerata-Norcia, 20–24 Settembre 1994*. Edited by Ileana Chirassi Colombo and Tullio Seppilli. Rome: Istituti Editoriali e Poligrafici Internazionali, 1998.

———. *Apocalypticism in the Dead Sea Scrolls*. New York: Routledge, 1997.

Collins, John J., and Craig A. Evans, eds. *Christian Beginnings and the Dead Sea Scrolls*. Grand Rapids, MI: Baker Academic, 2006.

Connelly, Joan Breton. *Portrait of a Priestess: Women and Ritual in Ancient Greece*. Princeton: Princeton University Press, 2007.

Copenhaven, Brian P. *Hermetica: The Greek Corpus Hermeticum and the Latin Asclepius in a New English Translation with Notes and Introduction*. Cambridge: Cambridge University Press, 1992.

Costa, Tony. "The Exorcisms and Healings of Jesus within Classical Culture." Pages 113–44 in *Christian Origins and Greco-Roman Culture: Social and Literary Contexts for the New Testament*. Edited by Stanley E. Porter and Andrew W. Pitts. Leiden: Brill, 2013.

Cotton, Hannah M., and Werner Eck, "Josephus' Roman Audience: Josephus and the Roman Elites." Pages 37–52 in *Flavius Josephus and Flavian Rome*. Edited by Jonathan Edmondson, Steve Mason, and James B. Rives. Oxford: Oxford University Press, 2005.

Cramer, Frederick H. "Expulsion of Astrologers from Ancient Rome." *C&M* 12 (1951): 9–50.

Cuomo, Serafina. *Pappus of Alexandria and the Mathematics of Late Antiquity*. Cambridge: Cambridge University Press, 2000.

Damon, Cynthia. *Tacitus "Histories" Book I*. Cambridge Greek and Latin Classics. Cambridge: Cambridge University Press, 2003.

D'Arms, John. "Memory, Money, and Status at Micenum: Three New Inscriptions from the *Collegium* of the Augustales." *JRS* 90 (2000): 126–44.

Den Hollander, William. *Josephus, the Emperors, and the City of Rome*. Ancient Judaism and Early Christianity 86. Leiden: Brill, 2014.

Dickie, Matthew W. *Magic and Magicians in the Greco-Roman World*. New York: Routledge, 2001.

Dillon, John M. "Pythagoreanism in the Academic Tradition: The Early Academy to Numenius." Pages 250–73 in *A History of Pythagoreanism*. Edited by Carl A. Huffman. Cambridge: Cambridge University Press, 2014.

———. *The Middle Platonists: 80 B.C. to A.D. 220*. Ithaca, NY: Cornell University Press, 1996.

Dillon, John M., and A. A. Long, eds. *The Question of "Eclecticism": Studies in Later Greek Philosophy*. Hellenistic Culture and Society 3. Berkeley: University of California Press, 1988.

Dillon, Sheila, and Katherine E. Welch, eds. *Representations of War in Ancient Rome*. Cambridge: Cambridge University Press, 2006.

Dimitrova, Nora M. "*Theoroi* and Initiates in Samothrace." *Hesperia Suppl* 37 (2008): iii–xvi, 1–280.

Dingeldein, Laura B. "Paul and Moral Development in Early Christianity: Who Has the Mind of Christ?" PhD diss., Brown University, 2014.

———. "'ὅτι πνευματικῶς ἀνακρίνεται': Examining Translations of 1 Corinthians 2:14." *NT* 55 (2013): 31–44.

Dio Chrysostom. *Orations*. Translated by J. W. Cohoon and H. Lamar Crosby. 5 vols. LCL. Cambridge: Harvard University Press, 1932–51.

Dodds, E. R. *Pagan and Christian in an Age of Anxiety*. New York: Norton, 1970.

———. "Theurgy and its Relationship to Neoplatonism." *JRS* 37 (1947): 55–69.

Downs, David J. *The Offering of the Gentiles: Paul's Collection for Jerusalem and Its Chronological, Cultural, and Cultic Contexts*. WUNT 2.248. Tübingen: Mohr Siebeck, 2008.

Dunderberg, Ismo. *Beyond Gnosticism: Myth, Lifestyle, and Society in the School of Valentinus*. New York: Columbia University Press, 2008.

———. "Valentianian Teachers at Rome." Pages 157–74 in *Christians as a Religious Minority in a Multicultural City: Modes of Interaction and Identity Formation in Early Imperial Rome*. Edited by Jürgen Zangenberg and Michael Labin. London: T&T Clark, 2004.

Duthoy, Robert. "Les Augustales." *ANRW* II. 16.2 (1978): 1254–309.

Eck, Werner. "The Bar Kokhba Revolt: The Roman Point of View." *JRS* (1999): 76–89.

Edmonds, Radcliffe G. III. *Redefining Ancient Orphism: A Study in Greek Religion*. Cambridge: Cambridge University Press, 2013.

———. ed., *The "Orphic" Gold Tablets and Greek Religion: Further Along the Path*. Cambridge: Cambridge University Press, 2011.

———. "Extra-Ordinary People: *Mystai* and *Magoi*, Magicians and Orphics in the Derveni Papyrus," *CP* 103 (2008): 16–39.

Edwards, Catharine, and Greg Woolf. "Cosmopolis: Rome as World City." Pages 1–20 in *Rome the Cosmopolis*. Edited by Catharine Edwards and Greg Woolf. Cambridge: Cambridge University Press, 2006.

———, eds. *Rome the Cosmopolis*. Cambridge: Cambridge University Press, 2006.

Egelhaaf-Gaiser, Ulrike. "Fickle Coloured Religion: Charlatans and Exegetes in Apuleius' *Metamorphoses*." Pages 85–104 in *Holy Men and Charlatans in the Ancient Novel*. Edited by Stelios Panayotakis, Gareth Schmeling, and Michael Paschalis. ANS 19. Groningen: Barkhuis & Groningen University Library, 2015.

Edwards, M. J. "On the Platonic Schooling of Justin Martyr." *JTS* 42 (1991): 17–34.

Ehrman, Bart D. *Forgery and Counterforgery: The Use of Literary Deceit in Early Christian Polemics*. New York: Oxford University Press, 2013.

Eisenbaum, Pamela. "Paul, Polemics, and the Problem of Essentialism." *BibInt* 13 (2005): 224–38.

Ellis, E. Earle. "Paul and his Opponents: Trends in the Research." Pages 264–73 in *Christianity, Judaism, and other Graeco-Roman Cults I*. Edited by Jacob Neusner. Leiden: Brill, 1975.

Elsner, Jaś. "Classicism in Roman Art." Pages 270–97 in *Classical Pasts: The Classical Traditions of Greece and Rome*. Edited by James Porter. Princeton: Princeton University Press, 2006.

Engberg-Pederson, Troels. *Cosmology and the Self in the Apostle Paul: The Material Spirit*. Oxford: Oxford University Press, 2011.

———. ed., *Paul Beyond the Judaism-Hellenism Dualism*. Louisville, KY: Westminster John Knox, 2001.

Engelmann, Helmut. *The Delian Aretology of Sarapis*. EPRO 44. Leiden: Brill, 1975.

Engels, David, and Peter Van Nuffelen. "Religion and Competition in Antiquity: An Introduction." Pages 9–44 in *Religion and Competition in Antiquity*. Edited by David Engels and Peter Van Nuffelen. Collection Latomus 343. Brussels: Latomus, 2014.

Eshel, Hanan. "The Bar Kokhba Revolt, 132–135." Pages 105–27 in *The Cambridge History of Judaism, Vol. 4: The Late Roman-Rabbinic Period*. Edited by Steven T. Katz. New York: Cambridge University Press, 2006.

Eshleman, Kendra. *The Social World of Intellectuals in the Roman Empire*. Cambridge: Cambridge University Press, 2012.

Eyl, Jennifer T. "By the Power of Signs and Wonders: Paul, Divinatory Practices, and Symbolic Capital." PhD diss., Brown University, 2012.

Feeney, Dennis C. *Caesar's Calendar: Ancient Time and the Beginnings of History*. Berkeley: University of California, 2007.

Firenze, Paul. "Value and Economics of Religious Capital." PhD diss., Brown University, 2013.

Fitzgerald, John T. "The Derveni Papyrus and Its Relevance for Biblical and Patristic Studies." *EC* 6 (2015): 157–78.

———. "Myth, Allegory, and the Derveni Papyrus." Pages 229–42 in *Myth and Scripture: Contemporary Perspectives on Religion, Language, and Imagination*. Edited by Dexter E. Callender Jr. Atlanta: SBL Press, 2014.

———. *Cracks in an Earthen Vessel: An Examination of Catalogues of Hardships in the Corinthian Correspondence*. SBLDS 99. Atlanta: Scholars Press, 1988.

Fitzmeyer, Joseph A., S. J. *The Dead Sea Scrolls and Christian Origins*. Grand Rapids, MI: Eerdmans, 2000.

Fleming, Rebecca. *Medicine and the Making of Roman Women: Gender, Nature, and Authority from Celsus to Galen*. New York: Oxford University Press, 2000.

Flinterman, Jaap-Jan. "Pythagoreans in Roman and Asia Minor Around the Turn of the Common Era." Pages 341–59 in *A History of Pythagoreanism*. Edited by Carl A. Huffman. Cambridge: Cambridge University Press, 2014.

Fonrobert, Charlotte Elisheva. "The *Didascalia Apostolorum*: A Mishnah for the Disciples of Jesus." *JECS* 9 (2001): 483–509.

Foster, Paul. "Marcion: His Life, Works, Beliefs, and Impact." *ExpTim* 121 (2010): 269–80.

Fowden, Garth. *The Egyptian Hermes: A Historical Approach to the Late Pagan Mind*. Princeton: Princeton University Press, 1993.

———. "The Pagan Holy Man in Late Antique Society." *JHS* 102 (1982): 33–59.

Francis, James A. *Subversive Virtue: Asceticism and Authority in the Second-Century Pagan World*. University Park: Pennsylvania State University Press, 1995.

Frankfurter, David. "Review of *Before Religion: A History of a Modern Concept*, by Brent Nongbri." *JECS* 23 (2015): 632–34.

———. "The Great, the Little, and the Authoritative Tradition in Magic of the Ancient World." *ARG* 16 (2014): 11–30.

———. "Dynamics of Ritual Expertise in Antiquity and Beyond: Towards a New Taxonomy of 'Magicians.'" Pages 159–78 in *Magic and Ritual in the Ancient World*. Edited by Marvin Meyer and Paul Mirecki. RGRW 141. Leiden: Brill, 2002.

———. *Religion in Roman Egypt: Assimilation and Resistance.* Princeton: Princeton University Press, 1998.

———. "The Magic of Writing and the Writing of Magic: The Power of the Word in Egyptian and Greek Traditions." *Helios* 21 (1994): 189–221.

Frede, Michael. "Celsus's Attack on the Christians." Pages 232–40 in *Philosophia Togata II: Plato and Aristotle at Rome.* Edited by Jonathan Barnes and Miriam T. Griffin. Oxford: Clarendon, 1997.

Fredrickson, Paula. "Judaizing the Nations: The Ritual Demands of Paul's Gospel." *NTS* 56 (2010): 232–52

Frier, Bruce W. *The Rise of the Roman Jurist: Studies in Cicero's Pro Caecina.* Princeton: Princeton University Press, 1985.

Gaillard-Seux, Patricia. "Magical Formulas in Pliny's *Natural History:* Origins, Sources, Parallels." Pages 201–23 in *"Greek" and "Roman" in Latin Medical Texts: Studies in Cultural Change and Exchange in Ancient Medicine.* Edited by Brigitte Maire. Studies in Ancient Medicine 42. Leiden: Brill, 2014.

Gamble, Harry Y. "The Book Trade in the Roman Empire." Pages 23–36 in *The Early Text of the New Testament.* Edited by Charles E. Hill and Michael J. Kruger. Oxford: Oxford University Press, 2012.

Gager, John G. *Reinventing Paul.* New York: Oxford University Press, 2000.

———. *Curse Tablets and Binding Spells from the Ancient World.* New York: Oxford University Press, 1992.

———. "Marcion and Philosophy." *VC* 26 (1972): 53–59.

———. *Moses in Greco-Roman Paganism.* SBLMS 16. New York: Abingdon Press, 1972.

Galinsky, Karl. "Continuity and Change: Religion in the Augustan Semi-Century." Pages 71–82 in *A Companion to Roman Religion.* Edited by Jörg Rüpke. Malden, MA: Blackwell, 2007.

———, ed. *Cambridge Companion to the Age of Augustus.* New York: Cambridge University Press, 2005.

Gardiner, Alan H. "Professional Magicians in Ancient Egypt." *PBSA* 39 (1917): 31–43.

Gaston, Lloyd. *Paul and the Torah.* Vancouver: University of British Columbia Press, 1987.

Georgi, Dieter. *The Opponents of Paul in Second Corinthians.* Philadelphia: Fortress, 1986.

Gilbert, Gary. "The Making of a Jew: 'God-fearer' or Convert in the Story of Izates." *USQR* 44 (1991): 299–313.

Glad, Clarence E. *Paul and Philodemus: Adaptability in Epicurean and Early Christian Psychagogy.* Supplements to Novum Testamentum 81. Leiden: Brill, 1995.

Glaim, Aaron. "Reciprocity, Sacrifice, and Salvation in Judean Religion." PhD diss., Brown University, 2013.

Goodman, Martin. *Rome and Jerusalem: The Clash of Ancient Civilizations.* New York: Vintage Books, 2008.

———. "Jewish Proselytizing in the First-Century." Pages 91–116 in *Judaism in the Roman World: Collected Essays*. Ancient Judaism and Early Christianity 66. Leiden and Boston: Brill, 2007.

———. "Texts, Scribes, and Power in Roman Judea." Pages 79–90 in *Judaism in the Roman World: Collected Essays*. Ancient Judaism and Early Christianity 66. Leiden: Brill, 2007.

———. "The *Fiscus Judaicus* and Jewish Identity." *JRS* 79 (1989): 40–44.

Gordon, Richard L. "Individuality, Selfhood, and Power in the Second Century: The Mystagogue as a Mediator of Religious Options." Pages 146–72 in *Religious Dimensions of the Self in the Second Century CE*. Edited by Jörg Rüpke and Greg Woolf. Studien und Texte zu Antike und Christentum 76. Tübingen: Mohr Siebeck, 2013.

———. "Ritual and Hierarchy in the Mysteries of Mithras." Pages 325–65 in *The Religious History of the Roman Empire*. Edited by John A. North and Simon R.F. Price. New York: Oxford University Press, 2011.

———. "Memory and Authority in the Magical Papyri." Pages 145–80 in *Historical and Religious Memory in the Ancient World*. Edited by Beate Dignas and R. R. R. Smith. Oxford: Oxford University Press, 2002.

———. "From Republic to Principate: Priesthood, Religion, and Ideology." Pages 62–83 in *Pagan Priests: Religion and Power in the Ancient World*. Edited by Mary Beard and John A. North. Ithaca, NY: Cornell University Press, 1990.

———. "Mithraism and Roman Society." *Religion* 2 (1972): 92–121.

Gordon, Richard L., and Francisco Marco Simón. "Introduction." Pages 1–49 in *Magical Practice in the Latin West: Papers from the International Conference Held at the University of Zaragoza 30 Sept.–1 Oct. 2005*. Edited by Richard L. Gordon and Francisco Marco Simón. RGRW 168. Leiden: Brill, 2010.

Gordon, Richard L., and Francisco Marco Simón, eds. *Magical Practice in the Latin West: Papers from the International Conference Held at the University of Zaragoza 30 Sept.–1 Oct. 2005*. RGRW 168. Leiden: Brill, 2010.

Graf, Fritz, and Sarah Iles Johnston. *Ritual Texts for the Afterlife: Orpheus and the Bacchic Gold Tablets*. 2nd ed. New York: Routledge, 2013.

Griffin, Miriam T. "Philosophy, Politics, and Politicians at Rome." Pages 1–37 in *Philosophia Togata I: Essays on Philosophy in Roman Society*. Edited by Miriam T. Griffin and Jonathan Barnes. Oxford: Oxford University Press, 1989.

Grossman, Maxine. "Priesthood as Authority: Interpretive Competition in First-Century Judaism and Christianity." Pages 117–31 in *The Dead Sea Scrolls as Background to Postbiblical Judaism and Early Christianity*. Edited by James R. Davila. Studies on the Texts of the Desert of Judah 46. Leiden: Brill, 2003.

Gruen, Erich S. *Diaspora: Jews amidst Greeks and Romans*. Cambridge: Harvard University Press, 2002.

———. *Studies in Greek Culture and Roman Policy*. Cincinnati Classical Studies 7. Leiden: Brill, 1990.

Guittard, Charles. *Carmen et prophéties à Rome*. Turnhout, Belgium: Brepols, 2007.

Haack, Marie-Laurence. *Prosopographie des haruspices romains*. Rome: Istituti Editoriali Poligrafici Internazionali, 2006.

———. *Les haruspices dans le monde romain*. Scripta Antiqua 6. Pessac: Ausonius, 2003.

Haar, Stephen. *Simon Magus: The First Gnostic?* BZNW 119. Berlin: de Gruyter. 2003.

Hall, Jonathan M. *Hellenicity: Between Ethnicity and Culture*. Chicago: University of Chicago Press, 2002.

Hanges, James C. *Paul, Founder of Churches: A Study in Light of the Evidence for the Role of Founder-Figures in the Hellenistic-Roman Period*. WUNT 292. Tübingen: Mohr Siebeck, 2012.

Harland, Philip A. *Dynamics of Identity in the World of Early Christians: Associations, Judeans, and Cultural Minorities*. Edinburgh: T&T Clark, 2009.

———. "Familial Dimensions of Group Identity (II): 'Mothers' and 'Fathers' in Associations and Synagogues of the Greek World." *JSJ* 38 (2007): 57–79.

———. *Associations, Synagogues, and Congregations: Claiming a Place in Ancient Mediterranean Society*. Minneapolis: Fortress Press, 2003.

Harrill, J. Albert. *Paul the Apostle: His Life and Legacy in Their Roman Context*. Cambridge: Cambridge University Press, 2012.

Harris, William V. *Dreams and Experience in Classical Antiquity*. Cambridge: Harvard University Press, 2009.

Harris-McCoy, Daniel E., *Artemidorus' Oneirocritica: Text, Translation, and Commentary*. Oxford: Oxford University Press, 2012.

Harrison, Stephen, John Hilton, and Vincent Hununk. *Apuleius: Rhetorical Works*. Oxford: Oxford University Press, 2002.

Heemstra, Marius. *The Fiscus Judaicus and the Parting of the Ways*. WUNT 2.277. Tübingen: Mohr Siebeck, 2011.

Henrichs, Albert. "Vespasian's Visit to Alexandria." *ZPE* 3 (1968): 51–80.

Hock, Ronald F. *The Social Context of Paul's Ministry: Tentmaking and Apostleship*. Philadelphia: Fortress, 1980.

Hodge, Caroline Johnson. *If Sons, Then Heirs: A Study of Kinship and Ethnicity in the Letters of Paul*. New York: Oxford University Press, 2007.

Holloway, Paul A. "*Commendatio aliqua sui*: Reading Romans with Pierre Bourdieu." *EC* 2 (2011): 356–83.

Hölscher, Tonio. *The Language of Images in Roman Art*. Translated by Anthony Snodgrass and Annemarie Künzl-Snodgrass. New York: Cambridge University Press, 2004.

Horsefall, Nicholas. "Virgil and the Jews." *Vergilius* 58 (2012): 67–80.

Horster, Marietta. "Living on Religion: Professionals and Personnel." Pages 331–41 in *A Companion to Roman Religion*. Edited by Jörg Rüpke. Malden, MA: Blackwell, 2007.

Houston, George W. "Tiberius and the Libraries: Public Book Collections and Library Buildings in the Early Roman Empire." *Libr Cult Rec* 43 (2008): 247–69.

Humm, Michel. "Numa and Pythagoras: The Life and Death of a Myth." Pages 35–52 in *The Roman Historical Tradition: Regal and Republican Rome*. Edited by James H. Richardson and Federico Santangelo. PAWB 33. Oxford: Oxford University Press, 2014.

Irenaeus. *Against the Heresies*. Translated by Dominic J. Unger. 3 vols. Ancient Christian Writers. New York: Newman, 1992–2012.

Janiszewski, Paweł, Krystyna Stebnicka, and Elżbieta Szabat. *Prosopography of Greek Rhetors and Sophists of the Roman Empire*. Translated by Dorota Dzierzbicka. Oxford: Oxford University Press, 2015.

Janko, Richard. "Reconstructing (Again) the Opening of the Derveni Papyrus." *ZPE* 166 (2008): 37–52.

Johnston, Sarah Iles. "Divination in the Derveni Papyrus." Pages 89–105 in *Poetry as Initiation: The Center for Hellenic Studies Symposium on the Derveni Papyrus*. Edited by Ionna Papadopoulou and Leonard Muellner. Cambridge: Harvard University Press, 2014.

———. *Ancient Greek Divination*. Malden, MA: Wiley-Blackwell, 2008.

———. *Restless Dead: Encounters between the Living and the Dead in Ancient Greece*. Berkeley: University of California Press, 1999.

———. *Hekate Sotereia: A Study of Hekate's Roles in the Chaldean Oracles and Related Literature*. American Classical Studies 21. Atlanta: Scholars Press, 1990.

Jones, Christopher P. "Josephus and Greek Literature in Flavian Rome." Pages 201–8 in *Flavius Josephus and Flavian Rome*. Edited by Jonathan Edmondson, Steve Mason, and James B. Rives. Oxford: Oxford University Press, 2005.

———. "Apollonius of Tyana, Hero and Holy Man." Pages 75–84 in *Philostratus's Heroikos: Religion and Cultural Identity in the Third Century c.e.* Edited by Ellen Bradshaw Aitken and Jennifer K. Berenson Maclean. Leiden: Brill, 2004.

———. *Culture and Society in Lucian of Samosata*. Cambridge: Harvard University Press, 1986.

Josephus. Translated by Henry St. J. Thackeray et al. 10 vols. Loeb Classical Library. Cambridge: Harvard University Press, 1926–65.

Judge, Edwin A. "Paul's Boasting in Relation to Contemporary Professional Practice." *ABR* 16 (1968): 37–50.

Jungkuntz, Richard. "Fathers, Heretics, and Epicureans." *JEH* 17 (1966): 3–10.

Juvenal and Persius. Translated by Susanna Morton Braund. LCL. Cambridge: Harvard University Press, 2004.

Kahn, Charles H. *Pythagoras and the Pythagoreans: A Brief History*. Indianapolis: Hackett, 2001.

King, Karen L. "Factions, Variety, Diversity, Multiplicity: Representing Early Christian Differences for the 21st Century." *MTSR* 23 (2011): 216–37.

———. "Which Early Christianity?" Pages 66–84 in *Oxford Handbook of Early Christianity*. Edited by Susan Ashbrook Harvey and David G. Hunter. New York: Oxford University Press, 2008.

―――. *What Is Gnosticism?* Cambridge: Harvard University Press, 2003.

Kleiner, Diana E. E. *Cleopatra and Rome.* Cambridge: Harvard University Press, 2005.

Klingshirn, William E. "Investing the *sortilegus*: Lot Divination and Cultural Identity in Italy, Rome, and the Provinces." Pages 137–61 in *Religion in Republican Italy.* Edited by Celia E. Schultz and Paul B. Harvey Jr. Yale Classical Studies 33. New York: Cambridge University Press, 2006.

Kloppenborg, John S. "Literate Media and Early Christian Groups: The Creation of a Christian Book Culture." *JECS* 22 (2014): 21–59.

―――. "Membership Practices in Pauline Christ Groups." *EC* 4 (2013): 183–215.

―――. "Greco-Roman *Thiasoi*, the *Ekklēsia* at Corinth, and Conflict Management." Pages 187–218 in *Redescribing Paul and the Corinthians.* Edited by Ron Cameron and Merrill P. Miller. ECL 5. Atlanta: Society of Biblical Literature, 2011.

―――. "*Evocatio Deorum* and the Date of Mark." *JBL* 124 (2005): 419–50.

―――. "Collegia and *Thiasoi*: Issues in Function, Taxonomy, and Membership." Pages 16–30 in *Voluntary Associations in the Graeco-Roman World.* Edited by John S. Kloppenborg and Stephen G. Wilson. New York: Routledge, 1996.

Kloppenborg, John S., and Stephen G. Wilson, eds. *Voluntary Associations in the Graeco-Roman World.* New York: Routledge, 1996.

König, Jason. "Competitiveness and Non-Competitiveness in Philostratus' Lives of the Sophists." Pages 279–300 in *Competition in the Ancient World.* Edited by Nick Fisher and Hans van Wees. Swansea: Classical Press of Wales, 2011.

―――. "The Cynic and Christian Lives of Lucian's *Peregrinus*." Pages 227–54 in *The Limits of Ancient Biography.* Edited by Brian C. McGing and Judith Mossman. Swansea: Classical Press of Wales, 2006.

König, Jason, Katerina Oikonomopoulou, and Greg Woolf, eds. *Ancient Libraries.* Cambridge: Cambridge University Press, 2013.

Konstan, David. "Introduction." Pages xi–xxx in *Heraclitus: Homeric Problems.* Edited and translated by Donald A. Russell and David Konstan. SBLWGRW 14. Leiden: Brill, 2005.

Koskenniemi, Erkki. "Apollonius of Tyana: A Typical θεῖος ἀνήρ?" *JBL* 117 (1998): 455–67.

Kouremenos, Theocritos, George M. Parássoglou, and Kyriakos Tsantsanoglou, eds. *The Derveni Papyrus.* Studi e testi per il Corpus dei papyri filosofici greci e latini 13. Florence: L.S. Olschki, 2006.

Kraemer, Ross Shepard. "Giving Up the Godfearers." *JAJ* 5 (2014): 61–87.

―――. *Unreliable Witnesses: Religion, Gender, and History in the Greco-Roman Mediterranean.* New York: Oxford University Press, 2011.

―――. *Women's Religions in the Greco-Roman World: A Sourcebook.* New York: Oxford University Press, 2004.

―――. "Typical and Atypical Jewish Family Dynamics: The Cases of Babatha and Berenice." Pages 114–39 in *Early Christian Families in Context.* Edited by David Balch and Carolyn Osiek. Grand Rapids, MI: Eerdman's, 2003.

———. *Her Share of the Blessings: Women's Religions Among Pagans, Jews, and Christians in the Greco-Roman World*. New York: Oxford University Press, 1994.

Kuttner, Ann L. "Culture and History at Pompey's Museum." *TAPA* 129 (1999): 343–73.

Lampe, Peter. *From Paul to Valentinus: Christians at Rome in the First Two Centuries*. Translated by Michael Steinhauser. Edited by Marshall D. Johnson. Minneapolis: Fortress, 2003.

Last, Richard. *The Pauline Church and the Corinthian Ekklēsia: Greco-Roman Associations in Comparative Context*. SNTSMS 164. Cambridge: Cambridge University Press, 2016.

———. "The Social Relationships of Gospel Writers: New Insights from Inscriptions Commending Greek Historiographers." *JSNT* 37 (2015): 223–52.

Lewis, Nicola Denzey. "*Apolytrosis* as Ritual and Sacrament: Determining a Ritual Context for Death in Second-Century Marcosian Valentinianism." *JECS* 17 (2009): 525–61.

Lieu, Judith M. *Christian Identity in the Jewish and Graeco-Roman World*. New York: Oxford University Press, 2004.

Lightfoot, J. L. *The Sibylline Oracles: With Introduction, Translation, and Commentary on the First and Second Books*. Oxford: Oxford University Press, 2007.

Lim, Timothy H. "Studying the Qumran Scrolls and Paul in their Historical Context." Pages 135–56 in *The Dead Sea Scrolls as Background to Postbiblical Judaism and Early Christianity*. Edited by James R. Davila. Studies on the Texts of the Desert of Judah 46. Leiden: Brill, 2003.

Litwa, M. David. "Transformation through a Mirror: Moses in 2 Cor. 3.18." *JSNT* 34 (2012): 286–97.

———. *We Are Being Transformed: Deification in Paul's Soteriology*. BZNW 187. Berlin: de Gruyter, 2012.

———. "Paul's Mosaic Ascent: An Interpretation of 2 Corinthians 12.7–9." *NTS* (2011): 238–57.

Lott, J. Bert. "The Prince and the Cutting Prophet: A Commentary on Dio 55.31.2-3." Unpublished paper presented at "Religion in Pieces," an interdisciplinary conference sponsored by the Society for Ancient Mediterranean Religions and the Joukowsky Institute for Archaeology and the Ancient World. Brown University, Providence, RI. April 29, 2012.

Lucian. Translated by A. M. Harmon. 8 vols. LCL. Cambridge: Harvard University Press, 1913.

Luijendijk, AnneMarie. *Forbidden Oracles? The Gospel of the Lots of Mary*. Studien und Texte zu Antike und Christentum. Tübingen: Mohr Siebeck, 2014.

MacMullen, Ramsay. *Roman Social Relations: 50 B.C. to A.D. 284*. New Haven: Yale University Press, 1974.

———. *Enemies of the Roman Order: Treason, Unrest, and Alienation in the Roman Empire*. Cambridge: Harvard University Press, 1966.

MacRae, Duncan. *Legible Religion: Books, Gods, and Rituals in Roman Culture.* Cambridge: Harvard University Press, 2016.

Macris, Constantinos. "Pythagoras." Pages 23–39 in *The History of Western Philosophy of Religion, Vol. 1: Ancient Philosophy of Religion.* Edited by Graham Oppy and Nick Trakakis. Durham: Acumen, 2009.

Majercik, Ruth Dorothy. *The Chaldean Oracles: Text, Translation, and Commentary.* Leiden: Brill, 1989.

Malherbe, Abraham J. "Hellenistic Moralists and the New Testament." *ANRW* II. 26.1 (1992): 267–333.

———. "Antisthenes and Odysseus, and Paul at War." Pages 91–119 in *Paul and the Popular Philosophers.* Minneapolis: Fortress, 1989.

———. "Exhortation in 1 Thessalonians." Pages 49–66 in *Paul and the Popular Philosophers.* Minneapolis: Fortress, 1989.

———. "'Gentle as a Nurse': The Cynic Background to 1 Thessalonians 2." Pages 35–48 in *Paul and the Popular Philosophers.* Minneapolis: Fortress, 1989.

———. "*Mē Genoito* in the Diatribe and Paul." Pages 25–33 in *Paul and the Popular Philosophers.* Minneapolis: Fortress, 1989.

———. *Paul and the Popular Philosophers.* Minneapolis: Fortress, 1989.

———. *Paul in His Hellenistic Context.* Minneapolis: Fortress, 1989.

———. "The Beasts at Ephesus." Pages 79–89 in *Paul and the Popular Philosophers.* Minneapolis: Fortress, 1989.

———. "The Inhospitality of Diotrephes." Pages 222–32 in *God's Christ and His People: Studies in Honor of Nils Alstrup Dahl.* Edited by Jacob Jervell and Wayne A. Meeks. Oslo Bergen: Universitetsforlaget, 1977.

Marjanen, Antti, and Petri Luomanen, eds. *A Companion to Second-Century Christian "Heretics."* Suppl. to Vigiliae Christianae 76. Leiden: Brill, 2005.

Marquis, Timothy Luckritz. *Transient Apostle: Paul, Travel, and the Rhetoric of Empire.* Synkrisis. New Haven: Yale University Press, 2013.

Marshall, Anthony J. "Women on Trial Before the Roman Senate." *EchCl* 34 (1990): 333–66.

Martin, Dale B. *Inventing Superstition: From the Hippocratics to the Christians.* Cambridge: Harvard University Press, 2004.

———. "Paul and the Judaism/Hellenism Dichotomy: Toward a Social History of the Question." Pages 29–62 in *Paul Beyond the Judaism-Hellenism Dualism.* Edited by Troels Engberg-Pedersen. Louisville, KY: Westminster John Knox, 2001.

———. *The Corinthian Body.* New Haven: Yale University Press, 1995.

Mason, Steve. "Pharisees in the Narratives of Josephus." Pages 185–215 in *Josephus, Judea, and Christian Origins.* Peabody, MA: Hendrickson, 2009.

———. "Jews, Judeans, Judaizing, Judaism: Problems of Categorization in Ancient History." *JSJ* 38 (2007): 457–512.

———. "Flavius Josephus in Flavian Rome: Reading on and Between the Lines." Pages 559–89 in *Flavian Rome: Culture, Image, Text.* Edited by A. J. Boyle and W. J. Dominik. Leiden: Brill, 2003.

————. *Josephus and the New Testament*. 2nd ed. Peabody, MA: Hendrickson, 2003.

————. "*Philosophiae:* Greco-Roman, Judean, and Christian." Pages 31–58 in *Voluntary Associations in the Graeco-Roman World*. Edited by John S. Kloppenborg and Stephen G. Wilson. New York: Routledge, 1996.

McCutcheon, Russell T. *The Discipline of Religion: Structure, Meaning, Rhetoric.* London: Routledge, 2003.

Meeks, Wayne A. *The First Urban Christians: The Social World of the Apostle Paul.* 2nd ed. New Haven: Yale University Press, 2003.

————. "Simon Magus in Recent Research," *RelSR* 3 (1977): 137–42.

Merlin, Philip. "Religion and Philosophy from Plato's *Phaedo* to the Chaldean Oracles." *JHP* 1 (1963): 163–76.

Meyboom, Paul G. P. *The Nile Mosaic of Palestrina: Early Evidence of Egyptian Religion in Italy.* RGRW 121. Leiden: Brill, 1994.

Millar, Fergus. "Last Year in Jerusalem: Monuments of the Jewish War in Rome." Pages 101–28 in *Flavius Josephus and Flavian Rome*. Edited by Jonathan Edmondson, Steve Mason, and James B. Rives. Oxford: Oxford University Press, 2005.

————. "The *Fiscus Iudaicus* in the First Two Centuries." *JRS* 53 (1963): 29–42.

Minns, Denis, and Paul Parvis. *Justin, Philosopher and Martyr: Apologies.* Oxford Early Christian Texts. New York: Oxford University Press, 2009.

Moyer, Ian S. "Notes on Re-reading the Delian Aretology of Sarapis (*IG* XI.4 1299)." *ZPE* 166 (2008): 101–7.

————. "The Initiation of the Magician: Transition and Power in Graeco-Egyptian Ritual." Pages 219–38 in *Initiation in Ancient Greek Rituals and Narratives: New Critical Perspectives*, ed. David B. Dodd and Christopher A. Faraone. New York: Routledge, 2003.

Murphy, Trevor. *Pliny the Elder's Natural History: An Empire in the Encyclopedia.* New York: Oxford University Press, 2004.

Nanos, Mark D. "The Question of Conceptualization: Qualifying Paul's Position on Circumcision in Dialogue with Josephus's Advisors to King Izates." Pages 105–52 in *Paul Within Judaism: Restoring the First-Century Context to the Apostle*. Edited by Mark D. Nanos and Magnus Zetterholm. Minneapolis: Fortress, 2015.

————. "Intruding 'Spies' and 'Pseudo-Brethren': The Jewish Intra-Group Politics of Paul's Jerusalem Meeting." Pages 57–97 in *Paul and His Opponents*. Edited by Stanley E. Porter. Pauline Studies 2. Leiden: Brill, 2005.

Nanos, Mark D., and Magnus Zetterholm, eds. *Paul Within Judaism: Restoring the First-Century Context to the Apostle.* Minneapolis: Fortress, 2015.

Nasrallah, Laura Salah. "'You Were Bought with a Price': Freedpersons and Things in 1 Corinthians." Pages 54–73 in *Corinth in Contrast: Studies in Inequality*. Edited by Steven J. Friesen, Sarah A. James, and Daniel N. Schowalter. Leiden: Brill, 2014.

————. *An Ecstasy of Folly: Prophecy and Authority in Early Christianity.* Cambridge: Harvard University Press, 2004.

Neudecker, Richard. "Archives, Books, and Sacred Space in Rome." Pages 312–31 in *Ancient Libraries*. Edited by Jason König, Katerina Oikonomopoulou, and Greg Woolf. Cambridge: Cambridge University Press, 2013.

Niehoff, Maren R. "A Jewish Critique of Christianity from Second-Century Alexandria: Revisiting the Jew Mentioned in *Contra Celsum*." *JECS* 21 (2013): 151–75.

———. *Jewish Exegesis and Homeric Scholarship in Alexandria*. Cambridge: Cambridge University Press, 2011.

Nongbri, Brent. "The Concept of Religion and the Study of the Apostle Paul." *JJMJS* 2 (2015): 1–26.

———. *Before Religion: A History of a Modern Concept*. New Haven: Yale University Press, 2013.

———. "Dislodging 'Embedded' Religion: A Brief Note on a Scholarly Trope." *Numen* 55 (2008): 440–60.

Noreña, Carlos. "Medium and Message in Vespasian's Templum Pacis." *MAAR* 48 (2003): 25–43.

North, A. John. "Pagans, Polytheists, and the Pendulum." Pages 125–43 in *The Spread of Christianity in the First Four Centuries: Essays in Explanation*. Edited by William V. Harris. Columbia Studies in the Classical Tradition 27. Leiden: Brill, 2005.

———. "The Development of Religious Pluralism." Pages 174–93 in *The Jews among Pagans and Christians in the Roman Empire*. Edited by Judith Lieu, John A. North, and Tessa Rajak. London: Oxford University Press, 1992.

———. "Diviners and Divination at Rome." Pages 51–71 in *Pagan Priests: Religion and Power in the Ancient World*. Edited by Mary Beard and John A. North. Ithaca, NY: Cornell University Press, 1990.

Nousek, Debra L. "Echoes of Cicero in Livy's Bacchanalian Narrative (39.8–19)." *CQ* 60 (2010): 156–66.

Novenson, Matthew V. "Paul's Former Occupation in *Ioudaismos*." Pages 24–39 in *Galatians and Christian Theology: Justification, Gospel, and Ethics in Paul's Letter*. Edited by Mark W. Elliott, Scott J. Hafemann, N.T. Wright, and John Frederick. Grand Rapids, MI: Baker, 2014.

———. *Christ Among the Messiahs: Christ Language in Paul and Messiah Language in Ancient Judaism*. New York: Oxford University Press, 2012.

Noy, David. "Rabbi Aqiba Comes to Rome: A Jewish Pilgrimage in Reverse?" Pages 373–85 in *Pilgrimage in Greco-Roman and Early Christian Antiquity: Seeing the Gods*. Edited by Jaś Elsner and Ian Rutherford. New York: Oxford University Press, 2005.

———. *Foreigners at Rome: Citizens and Strangers*. London: Duckworth, 2000.

———. *Jewish Inscriptions of Western Europe II: The City of Rome*. Cambridge: Cambridge University Press, 1995.

Nutton, Vivian. "Healers in the Medical Market Place: Toward a Social History of Graeco-Roman Medicine." Pages 1–58 in *Medicine in Society. Historical Essays*. Edited by Andrew Wear. Cambridge: Cambridge University Press, 1991.

O'Conner, Jerome Murphy, and James H. Charlesworth, eds. *Paul and the Dead Sea Scrolls*. New York: Crossroad, 1990.

Orlin, Eric M. *Foreign Cults in Rome: Creating a Roman Empire*. New York: Oxford University Press, 2010

———. "Octavian and Egyptian Cults: Redrawing the Boundary of Romanness." *AJP* 129 (2008): 231–53.

———. "Foreign Cults in Republican Rome: Rethinking the Pomerial Rule." *MAAR* 47 (2002): 1–18.

———. *Temples, Religion, and Politics in the Roman Republic*. Leiden: Brill, 1997.

Östenberg, Ida. *Staging the World: Spoils, Captives, and Representation in the Triumphal Procession*. Oxford Studies in Ancient Culture and Representation. Oxford: Oxford University Press, 2003.

Ostrow, Steve E. "'Augustales' Along the Bay of Naples: A Case for Their Early Growth." *Historia* 34 (1985): 64–101.

Otto, Bernd-Christian. "Towards Historicizing 'Magic' in Antiquity." *Numen* 60 (2013): 308–47.

———. *Magie: Rezeptions- und diskursgeschichteliche Analysen von der Antike bis zur Neuzeit*. Religionsgeschichtliche Versuche und Vorarbeiten 57. Berlin: de Gruyter, 2011.

Panayotakis, Costas. "Encolpius and the Charlatans." Pages 31–46 in *Holy Men and Charlatans in the Ancient Novel*. Edited by Stelios Panayotakis, Gareth Schmeling, and Michael Paschalis. ANS 19. Groningen: Barkhuis & Groningen University Library, 2015.

Parke, Herbert W. *Sibyls and Sibylline Prophecy in Classical Antiquity*. Edited by Brian C. McGing. New York: Routledge, 1988.

Parker, Grant. *The Making of Roman India*. Cambridge: Cambridge University Press, 2008.

———. "Obelisks Still in Exile: Monuments Made to Measure?" Pages 209–22 in *Nile into Tiber: Egypt in the Roman World. Proceedings of the 3rd International Conference of Isis Studies, Faculty of Archaeology, Leiden University, May 11–14, 2005*. Edited by Laurent Bricault, Miguel John Versluys, and Paul G. P. Meyboom. RGRW 159. Leiden: Brill, 2007.

———. "Topographies of Taste: Indian Textiles and Mediterranean Contexts." *AO* 34 (2007): 19–37.

———. "*Ex oriente luxuria*: Indian Commodities and Roman Experience." *JESHO* 45 (2002): 40–95.

Parker, Holt. "Women and Medicine." Pages 107–24 in *A Companion to Women in the Ancient World*. Edited by Sharon L. James and Sheila Dillon. Malden, MA: Wiley-Blackwell, 2012.

Parker, Robert. *Polytheism and Society at Athens*. New York: Oxford University Press, 2005.

Patterson, John. *Landscapes and Cities: Rural Settlement and Civic Transformation in Early Imperial Italy*. Oxford: Oxford University Press, 2006.

Pausanias. *Description of Greece.* Translated by W. H. S. Jones. 5 vols. LCL. Cambridge: Harvard University Press, 1918–35.

Pearson, Birger A. "Basilides the Gnostic," Pages 1–31 in *A Companion to Second-Century Christian "Heretics."* Edited by Antti Marjanen and Petri Luomanen. Leiden: Brill, 2005.

———. "Cracking a Conundrum: Christian Origins in Egypt." *ST* 57 (2003): 61–75.

Penella, Robert J. *The Letters of Apollonius of Tyana: A Critical Text with Prolegomena, Translation, and Commentary.* Mnemosyne Suppl. 56. Leiden: Brill, 1979.

Penner, Hans H. "The Poverty of Functionalism." *HR* 11 (1971): 91–97.

Perry, Jonathan S. "Organized Societies: *Collegia.*" Pages 499–515 in *The Oxford Handbook of Social Relations in the Roman World.* Edited by Michael Peachin. Oxford: Oxford University Press, 2011.

Pettegrew, David K. "The Diolkos and the Emporion: How a Land Bridge Framed the Commercial Economy of Roman Corinth." Pages 126–42 in *Corinth in Contrast: Studies in Inequality.* Edited by Steven J. Friesen, Sarah A. James, and Daniel N. Schowalter. Leiden: Brill, 2014.

Philo. Translated by F. H. Colson, G. H. Whitaker, and R. Marcus. 12 vols. LCL. Cambridge: Harvard University Press, 1929–62.

Philostratus. *Apollonius of Tyana.* Translated by Christopher P. Jones. 3 vols. LCL. Cambridge: Harvard University Press, 2005–06.

Piranomonte, Marina. "Religion and Magic at Rome: The Fountain of Anna Perenna." Pages 191–213 in *Magical Practice in the Latin West: Papers from the International Conference Held at the University of Zaragoza 30 Sept.–1 Oct. 2005.* Edited by Richard L. Gordon and Francisco Marco Simón. RGRW 168. Leiden: Brill, 2010.

Pollard, Elizabeth Ann. "Magic Accusations Against Women in Tacitus's *Annals.*" Pages 183–218 in *Daughters of Hekate: Women and Magic in the Ancient World.* Edited by Kimberly B. Stratton and Dayna S. Kalleres. New York: Oxford University Press, 2014.

Pollitt, J. J. "The Impact of Greek Art on Rome." *TAPA* 108 (1978): 155–74.

Porter, Stanley E. "Did Paul have Opponents in Rome and What Were They Opposing?" Pages 149–68 in *Paul and His Opponents.* Edited by Stanley E. Porter. Pauline Studies 2. Leiden: Brill, 2005.

———. ed. *Paul and His Opponents,* Pauline Studies 2. Leiden: Brill, 2005.

Potter, David. *Prophets and Emperors: Human and Divine Authority from Augustus to Theodosius.* Cambridge: Harvard University Press, 1994.

Price, Simon R. F. "Religious Mobility in the Roman Empire." *JRS* 102 (2012): 1–19.

Räisänen, Heikki. "Marcion." Pages 100–24 in *A Companion to Second-Century "Heretics."* Edited by Antti Marjanen and Petri Luomanen. Suppl. to Vigiliae Christianae 76. Leiden: Brill, 2005.

Rajak, Tessa. "Talking at Trypho: Christian Apologetic as Anti-Judaism in Justin's *Dialogue with Trypho the Jew.*" Pages 511–33 in *The Jewish Dialogue with Greece and Rome: Studies in Cultural and Social Interaction.* AGJU 48. Leiden: Brill, 2001.

———. *Josephus: The Historian and His Society*. London: Duckworth, 1983.

Rajak, Tessa, and David Noy. "*Archisynagogoi*: Official, Title and Social Status in the Greco-Jewish Synagogue." *JRS* 83 (1993): 75–93.

Ramelli, Ilaria L. E. "Lucian's Peregrinus as Holy Man and Charlatan and the Construction of the Contrast between Holy Men and Charlatans in the *Acts of Mari*." Pages 105–20 in *Holy Men and Charlatans in the Ancient Novel*. Edited by Stelios Panayotakis, Gareth Schmeling, and Michael Paschalis. ANS 19. Groningen: Barkhuis & Groningen University Library, 2015.

Rawson, Elizabeth. *Intellectual Life in the Late Roman Republic*. Baltimore: Johns Hopkins University Press, 1985.

Raynor, D. H. "Moeragenes and Philostratus. Two Views of Apollonius of Tyana," *CQ* 34 (1984): 222–26.

Redfield, James. "The Philosophers and the Many." *HR* 50 (2010): 43–53.

Reed, Annette Yoshiko. "Abraham as Chaldean Scientist and Father of the Jews: Josephus, *Ant.* 1.154–168, and the Greco-Roman Discourse About Astronomy/Astrology." *JSJ* 35 (2004): 119–58.

———. "ΕΥΑΓΓΕΛΙΟΝ: Orality, Textuality, and the Christian Truth in Irenaeus' *Adversus Haereses*." *VC* 56 (2002): 11–46.

Richardson, James H., and Federico Santangelo, eds. *Priests and State in the Roman World*. PAWB 33. Stuttgart: Steiner, 2011.

Richter, Daniel S. *Cosmopolis: Imagining Community in Late Classical Athens and the Early Roman Empire*. New York: Oxford University Press, 2011.

Ripat, Pauline. "Expelling Misconceptions: Astrologers at Rome." *CP* 106 (2011): 114–54.

———. "The Language of Oracular Inquiry in Roman Egypt." *Phoenix* 60 (2006): 304–28.

Rives, James B. "Religion in the Roman Provinces." Pages 420–44 in *The Oxford Handbook of Roman Epigraphy*. Edited by Christer Bruun and Jonathan Edmondson. New York: Oxford University Press, 2014.

———. "Control of the Sacred in Roman Law." Pages 165–80 in *Law and Religion in the Roman Republic*. Edited by Olga Tellegen-Couperus. Mnemosyne Supplements 336. Leiden: Brill, 2012.

———. "*Magus* and its Cognates in Classical Latin." Pages 53–77 in *Magical Practice in the Latin West: Papers from the International Conference Held at the University of Zaragoza 30 Sept.–1 Oct. 2005*. Edited by Richard L. Gordon and Francisco Marco Simón. RGRW 168. Leiden: Brill, 2010.

———. "Legal Strategy and Learned Display in Apuleius' *Apology*." Pages 17–49 in *Paideia at Play: Learning and Wit in Apuleius*. Edited by Werner Riess. Groningen: Barkhuis & Groningen University Library, 2008.

———. *Religion in the Roman Empire*. Malden, MA: Wiley-Blackwell, 2007.

———. "Magic, Religion, and Law: The Case of the *Lex Cornelia de sicariis et veneficiis*." Pages 47–67 in *Religion and Law in Classical and Christian Rome*. Edited by

Clifford Ando and Jörg Rüpke. Potsdamer Altertumswissenschaftliche Beiträge 31. Stuttgart: Steiner, 2006.

———. "Flavian Religious Policy and the Destruction of the Jerusalem Temple." Pages 145–66 in *Flavius Josephus and Flavian Rome*. Edited by Jonathan Edmondson, Steve Mason, and James B. Rives. Oxford: Oxford University Press, 2005.

———. "Magic in Roman Law: The Reconstruction of a Crime." *CA* 22 (2003): 313–39.

Robert, M. Louis. "Malédictions funéraires grecques." *CRAIBL* 122 (1978): 241–89.

Rogers, Guy MacLean. *The Mysteries of Artemis of Ephesos: Cult, Polis, and Change in the Graeco-Roman World*. Synkrisis. New Haven: Yale University Press, 2013.

Roller, Duane W. *The World of Juba II and Kleopatra Selene: Royal Scholarship on Rome's African Frontier*. New York: Routledge, 2003.

Rose, Brian C. "The Egyptianizing of Rome in the Wake of Actium." Pages 543–58 in *Festschrift for Prof. Orhan Bingöl*. Edited by Orhan Bingöol. Ankara: Bilgin Kültür Sanat Yayınları, 2013.

———. "The Parthians in Augustan Rome." *AJA* 109 (2005): 21–75.

———. "'Princes' and Barbarians on the Ara Pacis." *JRA* 94 (1990): 453–67.

Rüpke, Jörg. *From Jupiter to Christ: On the History of Religion in the Roman Period*. Translated by David M. B. Richardson. Oxford: Oxford University Press, 2014.

———. "Starting Sacrifice in the Beyond: Flavian Innovations in the Concept of the Priesthood and Their Repercussions in the Treatise 'To the Hebrews.'" *RHR* 229 (2012): 5–30.

———. *The Roman Calendar from Numa to Constantine: Time, History, and the Fasti*. Translated by David M. B. Richardson. Malden, MA: Wiley-Blackwell, 2011.

———. *Fasti Sacerdotum: A Prosopography of Pagan, Jewish, and Christian Officials in the City of Rome*. Oxford: Oxford University Press, 2008.

———. *The Religion of the Romans*. Cambridge: Polity Press, 2007.

Rutgers, Leonard Victor. "Roman Policy Toward the Jews: Expulsions from the City of Rome During the First Century C.E." *CA* 13 (1994): 56–75.

———. *The Jews in Late Ancient Rome: Evidence of Cultural Interaction in the Roman Diaspora*. Leiden: Brill, 1994.

Saffrey, Henri-Dominique. "Les Néoplatoniciens et les Oracles Chaldaïques." *REA* 26 (1981): 209–25.

Salem, M. S. "Ennius and the 'Isiaci Coniectores.'" *JRS* 28 (1938): 56–59.

Samma, Evelyne. *Les médecins dans le monde grec: Sources épigraphiques sur la naissance d'un corps medical*. Droz: Génève, 2003.

Sanders, E. P. *Paul and Palestinian Judaism: A Comparison of Patterns of Religion*. Minneapolis: Fortress, 1977.

Sandnes, Karl Olav. *Belly and Body in the Pauline Epistles*. Cambridge: Cambridge University Press, 2004.

Santangelo, Federico. "Law and Divination in the Late Roman Republic." Pages 31–55 in *Law and Religion in the Roman Republic*. Edited by Olga Tellegen-Couperus. Mnemosyne Suppl. 336. Leiden: Brill, 2012.

————. *Sulla, the Elites, and the Empire: A Study of Roman Policies in Italy and the Greek East*. Impact of Empire 8. Leiden: Brill, 2007.

Satlow, Michael L. *How the Bible Became Holy*. New Haven: Yale University Press, 2014.

————. "Jew or Judean?" Pages 165–75 in *The One Who Sows Bountifully: Essays in Honor of Stanley K. Stowers*. Edited by Caroline Johnson Hodge, Saul M. Olyan, Daniel Ullucci, and Emma Wasserman. Brown Judaic Studies 356. Atlanta: SBL Press, 2013.

Schäfer, Peter. "Hadrian's Policy in Judea and the Bar Kokhba Revolt: A Reassessment." Pages 281–303 in *A Tribute to Geza Vermes: Essays on Jewish and Christian Literature and History*. Edited by Philip R. Davies and Richard T. White. JSOT Suppl. 100. Sheffield: Sheffield Academic Press, 1990.

————. *Der Bar Kokhba-Aufstand*. Tübingen: Mohr Siebeck, 1981.

————, ed. *The Bar Kokhba War Reconsidered: New Perspectives on the Second Jewish Revolt Against Rome*. Tübingen: Mohr Siebeck, 2003.

Schatzki, Theodore R. *The Site of the Social: A Philosophical Account of Social Life and Change*. University Park: Pennsylvania State University Press, 2002.

Scheid, John. "Greco-Roman Cultic Societies." Pages 535–47 in *The Oxford Handbook of Social Relations in the Roman World*. Edited by Michael Peachin. Oxford: Oxford University Press, 2011.

————. *Quand faire, c'est croire: les rites sacrificiels des Romains*. Paris: Aubier, 2011.

————. "Graeco Ritu: A Typically Roman Way of Honoring the Gods." *HSCP* 97 (1995): 15–31.

Schellenberg, Ryan S. "Does Paul Call Adam a 'Type' of Christ? An Exegetical Note on Romans 5:14." *ZNW* 105 (2014): 54–63.

————. *Rethinking Paul's Rhetorical Education: Comparative Rhetoric and 2 Corinthians 10–13*. ECL 10. Atlanta: SBL Press, 2013.

Schiffman, Lawrence H. *Reclaiming the Dead Sea Scrolls: The History of Judaism, the Background of Christianity, the Lost Library of Qumran*. Philadelphia: Jewish Publication Society, 1994.

————. "The Conversion of the Royal House of Adiabene in Josephus and Rabbinic Sources." Pages 293–312 in *Josephus, Judaism, and Christianity*. Edited by Louis H. Feldman and Gohei Hata. Detroit: Wayne State University Press, 1987.

Schilbrack, Kevin. "Religions: Are There Any?" *JAAR* 78 (2010): 1112–28.

Schmeling, Gareth. "The Small World of the Holy Man: A Small Beginning in the *Satyrica*." Pages 17–29 in *Holy Men and Charlatans in the Ancient Novel*. Edited by Stelios Panayotakis, Gareth Schmeling, and Michael Paschalis. ANS 19. Groningen: Barkhuis & Groningen University Library, 2015.

Schorn, Stefan. "Pythagoras in the Historical Tradition: From Herodotus to Diodorus Siculus." Pages 296–314 in *A History of Pythagoreanism*. Edited by Carl A. Huffman. Cambridge: Cambridge University Press, 2014.

Schultz, Celia E. *Women's Religious Activity in the Roman Republic*. Chapel Hill: University of North Carolina Press, 2006.

Schwartz, Daniel R. "Herodians and *Ioudaioi* in Flavian Rome." Pages 63–78 in *Flavius Josephus and Flavian Rome*. Edited by Jonathan Edmondson, Steve Mason, and James B. Rives. Oxford: Oxford University Press, 2005.

Schwartz, Seth. "How Many Judaisms Were There? A Critique of Neusner and Smith on Definition and Mason and Boyarin on Categorization." *JAJ* 2 (2011): 208–38.

Secord, Jared. "Irenaeus at Rome: The Greek Context of Christian Intellectual Life in the Second Century." Pages 1–20 (page numbers provisional) in *Irénée entre Asie et Occident*. Edited by Agnès Bastit-Kalinowska. Collection des Études Augustiniennes. Turnhout: Brepols, forthcoming.

Sedley, David. "The School, from Zeno to Arius Didymus." Pages 7–32 in *The Cambridge Companion to the Stoics*. Edited by Brad Inwood. Cambridge: Cambridge University Press, 2003.

Sievers, Joseph, and Gaia Lembi, eds. *Josephus and Jewish History in Flavian Rome and Beyond*. Leiden: Brill, 2005.

Siker, Jeffrey. "Abraham in Greco-Roman Paganism." *JSJ* 18 (1987): 188–208

Skarsaune, Oskar. *The Proof from Prophecy: A Study in Justin Martyr's Proof-Text Tradition: Text-Type, Provenance, Theological Profile*. Leiden: Brill, 1987.

Slingerland, H. Dixon. *Claudian Policymaking and the Early Imperial Repression of Judaism at Rome*. South Florida Studies in the History of Judaism 160. Atlanta: Scholars Press, 1997.

Smallwood, E. Mary. *The Jews Under Roman Rule: From Pompey to Diocletian*. Leiden: Brill, 1976.

———. "The Alleged Jewish Tendencies of Poppaea Sabina." *JTS* 10 (1959): 329–35.

———. "Domitian's Attitude toward the Jews and Judaism." *CP* 51 (1956): 1–13.

Smith, Geoffrey S. *Guilt by Association: Heresy Catalogues in Early Christianity*. New York: Oxford University Press, 2015.

Smith, Jonathan Z. "Re: Corinthians." Pages 17–34 in *Redescribing Paul and the Corinthians*. Edited by Ron Cameron and Merrill P. Miller. ECL 5. Atlanta: SBL Press, 2011.

———. "Religion, Religions, Religious." Pages 179–96 in *Relating Religion: Essays in the Study of Religion*. Chicago: University of Chicago Press, 2004.

———. "Trading Places." Pages 13–27 in *Ancient Magic and Ritual Power*. Edited by Marvin Meyer and Paul Mirecki. RGRW 141. Leiden: Brill, 1995.

Smith, Morton. *Jesus the Magician: Charlatan or Son of God?*. San Francisco: Harper & Row, 1978. Repr., *Jesus the Magician: A Renowned Historian Reveals How Jesus Was Viewed by the People of His Time*. San Francisco: Hampton Roads, 2014.

Snyder, H. Gregory. "The Discovery and Interpretation of the Flavia Sophe Inscription: New Results," *VC* 68 (2014): 1–59.

———. "The Classroom in the Text: Exegetical Practices in Justin and Galen." Pages 663–85 in *Christian Origins and Greco-Roman Culture: Social and Literary*

Contexts for the New Testament. Edited by Stanley E. Porter and Andrew W. Pitts. Leiden: Brill, 2013.

———. "'Above the Bath of Myrtinus': Justin Martyr's 'School' in the City of Rome," *HTR* 100 (2007): 335–62.

———. *Teachers and Texts in the Ancient World: Philosophers, Jews, and Christians.* Religion in the First Christian Centuries. New York: Routledge, 2000.

Spanu, Nicola. "The Magic of Plotinus' School of Gnostic Disciples in the Context of Plotinus' School of Philosophy." *JLARC* 7 (2013): 1–14.

———. *Plotinus, Ennead II 9 [33] "Against the Gnostics"—A Commentary.* Studia Patristica Suppl. 1. Leiden: Peeters, 2012.

Stählin, Gustav. "προκοπή." *TDNT* 6:703–19.

Stern, Menahem. *Greek and Latin Authors on Jews and Judaism. Edited, With Introductions, Translations, and Commentary I–III.* Jerusalem: Israel Academy of Sciences and Humanities, 1974.

Stowers, Stanley K. "The Dilemma of Paul's Physics: Features Stoic- Platonist or Platonist-Stoic?" Pages 1–23 (page numbers provisional) in *From Stoicism to Platonism: The Development of Philosophy 100 BCE–100 CE.* Edited by Troels Engberg-Pedersen. Cambridge: Cambridge University Press, 2016.

———. "Paul and the Terrain of Philosophy." *EC* 6 (2015): 141–56.

———. "Does Pauline Christianity Resemble a Hellenistic Philosophy?" Pages 219–44 in *Redescribing Paul and the Corinthians.* Edited by Ron Cameron and Merrill P. Miller. ECL 5. Atlanta: SBL Press, 2011.

———. "Kinds of Myths, Meals, and Power: Paul and the Corinthians." Pages 105–50 in *Redescribing Paul and the Corinthians.* Edited by Ron Cameron and Merrill P. Miller. ECL 5. Atlanta: Society of Biblical Literature, 2011.

———. "Paul's Four Discourses About Sin." Pages 100–27 in *Celebrating Paul: Festschrift in Honor of Jerome Murphy-O'Conner, O. P., and Joseph A. Fitzmeyer, S. J.* Edited by Peter Spitaler. CBQMS 48. Washington, DC: Catholic Biblical Association of America, 2011.

———. "The Concept of 'Community' and the History of Early Christianity." *MTSR* 23 (2011): 238–56.

———. "The Religion of Plant and Animal Offerings Versus the Religion of Meanings, Essences, and Textual Mysteries." Pages 35–56 in *Ancient Mediterranean Sacrifice.* Edited by Jennifer Wright Knust and Zsuzsanna Várhelyi. New York: Oxford University Press, 2011.

———. "The Ontology of Religion." Pages 434–49 in *Introducing Religion: Essays in Honor of Jonathan Z. Smith.* Edited by Willi Braun and Russell T. McCutcheon. New York: Equinox, 2008.

———. "Theorizing Religion of Ancient Households and Families." Pages 5–19 in *Household and Family Religion in Antiquity: Contextual and Comparative Perspectives.* Edited by John Bodel and Saul M. Olyan. Malden, MA: Wiley-Blackwell, 2008.

————. "What Is Pauline Participation in Christ?" Pages 352–71 in *Redefining First-Century Jewish and Christian Identities: Essays in Honor of Ed Parish Sanders*. Edited by Fabian E. Udoh, Susannah Heschel, Mark Chancey, and Gregory Tatum. CJAS. South Bend, IN: Notre Dame University Press, 2008.

————. *A Rereading of Romans: Justice, Jews, and Gentiles*. New Haven: Yale University Press, 1994.

————. "ἐκ πίστεως and διὰ τῆς πίστεως in Romans 3:30," *JBL* 108 (1989): 665–74.

Stark, Rodney. *Cities of God: The Real Story of How Christianity Became and Urban Movement and Conquered Rome*. New York: HarperOne, 2007.

————. "Religious Competition and Roman Piety." *IJRR* 2 (2006): 1–30.

————. *The Rise of Christianity: A Sociologist Reconsiders History*. Princeton: Princeton University Press, 1996.

Stratton, Kimberly B. "Interrogating the Magic–Gender Connection." Pages 1–37 in *Daughters of Hekate: Women and Magic in the Ancient World*. Edited by Kimberly B. Stratton and Dayna S. Kalleres. New York: Oxford University Press, 2014.

————. "Magic Discourse in the Ancient World." Pages 243–54 in *Defining Magic: A Reader*. Edited by Bernd-Christian Otto and Michael Stausberg, Critical Categories in the Study of Religion. New York: Routledge, 2014.

————. "Magic, Abjection, and Gender in Roman Literature." Pages 152–80 in *Daughters of Hekate: Women and Magic in the Ancient World*. Edited by Kimberly B. Stratton and Dayna S. Kalleres. New York: Oxford University Press, 2014.

————. *Naming the Witch: Magic, Ideology, and Stereotype in the Ancient World*. New York: Columbia University Press, 2007.

————. "The Rhetoric of 'Magic' in Early Christian Discourse: Gender, Power, and the Construction of 'Heresy.'" Pages 89–114 in *Mapping Gender in Ancient Religious Discourses*. Edited by Todd Penner and Caroline Vander Stichele. Biblical Interpretation 84. Leiden: Brill, 2006.

Stratton, Kimberly B., and Dayna S. Kalleres. *Daughters of Hekate: Women and Magic in the Ancient World*. New York: Oxford University Press, 2014.

Strecker, Georg. "Die Legitimität des paulinischen Apostolates nach 2 Korinther 10–13." *NTS* 38 (1992): 566–86.

Struck, Peter T. *The Birth of the Symbol: Ancient Readers at the Limits of Their Texts*. Princeton: Princeton University Press, 2004.

Suetonius. Translated by J. C. Rolfe. 3 vols. LCL. 2nd edition. Cambridge: Harvard University Press, 1998.

Sumney, Jerry L. "Studying Paul's Opponents: Advances and Challenges." Pages 7–58 in *Paul and His Opponents*. Edited by Stanley E. Porter. Pauline Studies 2. Leiden: Brill, 2005.

————. *Identifying Paul's Opponents: The Question of Method in 2 Corinthians*. JSOT 40. Sheffield: JSOT Press, 1990.

Swetnam-Burland, Molly. "'Egyptian' Priests in Roman Italy." Pages 336–53 in *Cultural Identity in the Ancient Mediterranean*. Edited by Erich S. Gruen. Los Angeles: Getty Research Institute, 2011.

———. "Egyptian Objects, Roman Contexts: A Taste for Aegyptiaca in Italy." Pages 113–36 in *Nile into Tiber: Egypt in the Roman World. Proceedings of the 3rd International Conference of Isis Studies, Faculty of Archaeology, Leiden University, May 11–14, 2005*. Edited by Laurent Bricault, Miguel John Versluys, and Paul G. P. Meyboom. RGRW 159. Leiden: Brill, 2007.

Tacitus. *The Histories and the Annals*. Translated by Clifford H. Moore and John Jackson. 4 vols. LCL. Cambridge: Harvard University Press, 1937.

Takács, Sarolta A. "Initiations and Mysteries in Apuleius' Metamorphoses." *ElectronAnt* 12 (2008): 73–87.

———. "Politics and Religion in the Bacchanalia Affair of 186 B.C.E." *HSCP* 100 (2000): 301–10.

———. "Alexandria in Rome." *HSCP* 97 (1995): 263–76.

———. *Isis and Sarapis in the Roman World*. RGRW 124. Leiden: Brill, 1995.

Tanaseanu-Döbler, Ilinca. "Weise oder Scharlatane? Chaldaeerbilder der griechisch-römischen Kaiserzeit und die *Chaldaeischen Orakel*." Pages 19–42 in *Die Chaldaeischen Orakel: Kontext, Interpretation, Rezeption*. Edited by Helmut Seng and Michel Tardieu. Heidelberg: University of Heidelberg Press, 2011.

Tarrant, Harold. "Platonist Educators in a Growing Market: Gaius; Abinus; Taurus; Alcinous." Pages 449–65 in *Greek and Roman Philosophy 100 BC–200 AD II*. Edited by Robert W. Sharples and Richard Sorabji. London: Institute of Classical Studies, 2007.

Taylor, Joan E. *Jewish Women Philosophers of First-Century Alexandria: Philo's "Therapeutae" Reconsidered*. New York: Oxford University Press, 2003.

Taylor, N. H. "Apostolic Identity and the Conflicts in Corinth and Galatia." Pages 99–123 in *Paul and His Opponents*. Edited by Stanley E. Porter. Pauline Studies 2. Leiden: Brill, 2005.

The Apostolic Fathers. Translated by Bart D. Ehrman. 2 vols. LCL. Cambridge: Harvard University Press, 2003.

Thiessen, Gerd. *The Social Setting of Pauline Christianity: Essays on Corinth*. Translated and edited by John H. Schütz. Philadelphia: Fortress Press, 1982.

Thomassen, Einar. *The Spiritual Seed: The Church of the "Valentinians."* Nag Hammadi and Manichaean Studies 60. Leiden: Brill, 2006.

———. "Orthodoxy and Heresy in Second-Century Rome." *HTR* 97 (2004): 241–56.

Tobin, Thomas H. *Paul's Rhetoric in Its Contexts: The Argument of Romans*. Peabody, MA: Hendrickson, 2004.

Trapp, Michael. "Neopythagoreans." Pages 347–63 in *Greek and Roman Philosophy 100 BC–200 ad II*. Edited by Robert W. Sharples and Richard Sorabji. London: Institute of Classical Studies, 2007.

Trebilco, Paul. *Jewish Communities in Asia Minor*. SNTSMS 69. Cambridge: Cambridge University Press.

Tucci, Pier Luigi. "Flavian Libraries in the City of Rome." Pages 277–309 in *Ancient Libraries*. Edited by Jason König, Katerina Oikonomopoulou, and Greg Woolf. Cambridge: Cambridge University Press, 2013.

Ullucci, Daniel. *The Christian Rejection of Sacrifice*. New York: Oxford University Press, 2011.

Vaage, Leif E. "Ancient Religious Rivalries and the Struggle for Success: Christians, Jews, and Others in the Early Roman Empire." Pages 3–19 in *Religious Rivalries in the Early Roman Empire and the Rise of Christianity*. Edited by Leif E. Vaage. Waterloo: Wilfred Laurier University Press, 2006.

Van den Kerchove, Anna. "Le mode de revelation dans les *Oracles Chaldaïques* et dans les traits hermétiques." Pages 145–62 in *Die Chaldaeischen Orakel: Kontext, Interpretation, Rezeption*. Edited by Helmut Seng and Michel Tardieu. Heidelberg: University of Heidelberg Press, 2011.

Van der Horst, Pieter Willem, trans. *Chaeremon: Egyptian Priest and Stoic Philosopher*. Leiden: Brill, 1984.

Van Kooten, George H. *Paul's Anthropology in Context: The Image of God, Assimilation to God, and Tripartite Man in Ancient Judaism, Ancient Philosophy, and Early Christianity*. WUNT 232. Tübingen: Mohr Siebeck, 2008.

Várhelyi, Zsuzsana. *The Religion of Senators in the Roman Empire: Power and the Beyond*. Cambridge: Cambridge University Press, 2010.

Versluys, Miguel John. "Aegyptiaca Romana: The Widening Debate." Pages 1–14 in *Nile into Tiber: Egypt in the Roman World. Proceedings of the 3rd International Conference of Isis Studies, Faculty of Archaeology, Leiden University, May 11–14, 2005*. Edited by Laurent Bricault, Miguel John Versluys, and Paul G. P. Meyboom. RGRW 159. Leiden: Brill, 2007.

———. *Aegyptiaca Romana: Nilotic Scenes and the Roman Views of Egypt*. RGRW 144. Leiden: Brill, 2002.

Versnel, Hank S. "Destruction, *Devotio*, and Despair in a Situation of Anomy: The Mourning for Germanicus in Triple Perspective." Pages 541–618 in *Perennitas: Studi in onore di Angelo Brelich: Promossi dalla Cattedra di Religioni del mondo classico dell'Università degli Studi di Roma*. Rome: dell'Ateneo, 1980.

Verter, Bradford. "Spiritual Capital: Theorizing Religion with Bourdieu Against Bourdieu." *Sociol Theor* 21 (2003): 150–74.

Vinzent, Marcus. *Marcion and the Dating of the Synoptic Gospels*. Studia Patristica Suppl. 2. Leuven: Peeters, 2014.

Wallace-Hadrill, Andrew. *Rome's Cultural Revolution*. New York: Cambridge University Press, 2008.

———. "'*Mutatas Formas*': The Augustan Transformation of Roman Knowledge." Pages 55–84 in *The Cambridge Companion to the Age of Augustus*. Edited by Karl Galinsky. New York: Cambridge University Press, 2007.

Walzer, Richard. *Galen on Jews and Christians*. Oxford: Oxford University Press, 1949.

Ware, James P. *Paul and the Mission of the Church: Philippians in Ancient Jewish Context*. Grand Rapids, MI: Baker Academic, 2011.

Wasserman, Emma. "Paul Beyond the Judaism/Hellenism Divide? The Case of Pauline Anthropology in Romans 7 and 2 Corinthians 4–5." Pages 259–79 in *Redefining First-Century Jewish and Christian Identities: Essays in Honor of Ed Parish Sanders*. Edited by Fabian E. Udoh et Susannah Heschel, Mark Chancey, and Gregory Tatum. CJAS. Notre Dame, IN: University of Notre Dame Press, 2008.

———. *The Death of the Soul in Romans 7: Sin, Death, and the Law in Light of Hellenistic Moral Psychology*. WUNT 2.56. Tübingen: Mohr Siebeck, 2008.

———. "The Death of the Soul in Romans 7: Revisiting Paul's Anthropology in Light of Hellenistic Moral Psychology." *JBL* 126 (2007): 793–816.

Weinfield, Moshe. *The Organizational Pattern and the Penal Code of the Qumran Sect: A Comparison with Guilds and Associations of the Hellenistic-Roman Period*. NTOA 2. Fribourg: Editions Universitaires, 1986.

Welborn, Lawrence. "The Runaway Paul." *HTR* 92 (1999): 115–63.

Wendt, Heidi. "From Herodians to Hadrian: The Shifting Status of Judean Religion in Post- Flavian Rome," *Forum* (2017): 1–30.

———. "Galatians 3:1 as an Allusion to Textual Prophecy." *JBL* 135 (2016): 369–89.

———. "*Ea Superstitione:* Christian Martyrdom and the Religion of Freelance Experts." *JRS* 105 (2015): 183–202.

———. "'Entrusted with the Oracles of God': The Fate of the Judean Writings in Flavian Rome." Pages 101–9 in *A Most Reliable Witness: Essays in Honor of Ross Shepard Kraemer*. Edited by Susan Ashbrook Harvey, Nathaniel DesRosiers, Shira L. Lander, Jacqueline Z. Pastis, and Daniel Ullucci. Brown Judaic Studies 358. Atlanta: Society of Biblical Literature, 2015.

———. "*Iudaica Romana:* A Rereading of Judean Expulsions from Rome." *JAJ* 6 (2015): 97–126.

———. "Paul, Founder of Churches: A Study in Light of the Evidence for the Role of 'Founder-Figures' in the Hellenistic-Roman Period. A Review Essay," *R&T* 3–4 (2014): 292–302.

Westerink, Leendert Gerrit. "Proclus, Procopius, Psellus." *Mnemosyne* 10 (1942): 275–80.

White, Benjamin. "How to Read a Book: Irenaeus and the Pastoral Epistles Reconsidered." *VC* 65 (2011): 125–49.

White, L. Michael. "The Changing Face of Mithraism at Ostia: Archaeology, Art, and the Urban Landscape." Pages 435–92 in *Contested Spaces: Houses and Temples in Roman Antiquity and the New Testament*. Edited by David L. Balch and Annette Weissenreider. WUNT 285. Tübingen: Mohr Siebeck, 2012.

Whitmarsh, Tim. *The Second Sophistic*. Greece & Rome 35. Oxford: Oxford University Press, 2005.

———. *Greek Literature in the Roman Empire: The Politics of Imitation*. Oxford: Oxford University Press, 2001.

Wilken, Robert Louis. *The Christians as the Romans Saw Them.* 2nd ed. New Haven: Yale University Press, 2003.

Willi, Andreas. "Numa's Dangerous Books: The Exegetical History of a Roman Forgery." *Mus Helv* 55 (1998): 139–72.

Williams, Margaret H. "Domitian, the Jews and the 'Judaizers': A Simple Matter of Cupiditas and Maiestas?" *ZAG* 39 (1990): 196–211.

———. "The Expulsion of the Jews from Rome in A.D. 19." *Latomus* 48 (1989): 765–84.

———. "θεοσεβὴς γαρ ἥν: The Jewish Tendencies of Poppaea Sabina." *JTS* 39 (1988): 97–111.

Williams, Michael. *Rethinking Gnosticism: An Argument for Dismantling a Dubious Category.* Princeton: Princeton University Press, 1996.

Wilson, Stephen G. "Voluntary Associations: An Overview." Pages 1–15 in *Voluntary Associations in the Graeco-Roman World.* Edited by John S. Kloppenborg and Stephen G. Wilson. New York: Routledge, 1996.

Wooden, Glenn R. "Guided by God: Divine Aid in Interpretation in the Dead Sea Scrolls and the New Testament." Pages 101–20 in *Christian Beginnings and the Dead Sea Scrolls.* Edited by John J. Collins and Craig A. Evans. Grand Rapids, MI: Baker Academic, 2006.

Woolf, Greg. "Female Mobility in the Roman West." Pages 351–68 in *Women and the Roman City in the Latin West.* Edited by Emily Hemelrijk and Greg Woolf. Leiden: Brill, 2013.

Yavetz, Zvi. "Reflections on Titus and Josephus." *GRBS* 16 (1975): 411–32.

Zangenberg, Jürgen, and Michael Labin, eds. *Christians as a Religious Minority in a Multicultural City: Modes of Interaction and Identity Formation in Early Imperial Rome.* London: T&T Clark, 2004.

Zanker, Paul. *The Power of Images in the Age of Augustus.* Ann Arbor: University of Michigan Press, 1988.

Index